Houghton Mifflin Reading

Teacher's Edition

Grade 6

Triumphs

Back to School

Theme 1 **Courage**
Focus on **Poetry**

Theme 2 **What Really Happened?**
Focus on **Plays**

Theme 3 **Growing Up**

▶ **Theme 4** **Discovering Ancient Cultures**
Focus on **Myths**

Theme 5 **Doers and Dreamers**
Focus on **Speeches**

Theme 6 **New Frontiers: Oceans and Space**

Senior Authors J. David Cooper, John J. Pikulski

Authors Kathryn H. Au, David J. Chard, Gilbert G. Garcia,
Claude N. Goldenberg, Phyllis C. Hunter, Marjorie Y. Lipson,
Shane Templeton, Sheila W. Valencia, MaryEllen Vogt

Consultants Linda H. Butler, Linnea C. Ehri, Carla B. Ford

HOUGHTON MIFFLIN   BOSTON

LITERATURE REVIEWERS

Consultants: Dr. Adela Artola Allen, Associate Dean, Graduate College, Associate Vice President for Inter-American Relations, University of Arizona, Tucson, AZ; **Dr. Manley Begay,** Co-director of the Harvard Project on American Indian Economic Development, Director of the National Executive Education Program for Native Americans, Harvard University, John F. Kennedy School of Government, Cambridge, MA; **Dr. Nicholas Kannellos,** Director, Arte Publico Press, Director, Recovering the U.S. Hispanic Literacy Heritage Project, University of Houston, TX; **Mildred Lee,** author and former head of Library Services for Sonoma County, Santa Rosa, CA; **Dr. Barbara Moy,** Director of the Office of Communication Arts, Detroit Public Schools, MI; **Norma Naranjo,** Clark County School District, Las Vegas, NV; **Dr. Arlette Ingram Willis,** Associate Professor, Department of Curriculum and Instruction, Division of Language and Literacy, University of Illinois at Urbana-Champaign, IL

Teachers: Sylvia Brown, Lawrence Middle School, Lawrence, NY; **Debbie Carr,** Comanche Middle School, Comanche, OK; **Nancy Chin,** Justice Thurgood Marshall Middle School, Marion, IN; **Daniel Lee,** Alisal Community School, Los Angeles, CA; **Patricia Olsen,** Memorial Middle School, Las Vegas, NM; **Ronald E. Owings,** Jones Middle School, Marion, IN

PROGRAM REVIEWERS

Linda Bayer, Jonesboro, GA; **Sheri Blair,** Warner Robins, GA; **Faye Blake,** Jacksonville, FL; **Suzi Boyett,** Sarasota, FL; **Carol Brockhouse,** Madison Schools, Wayne Westland Schools, MI; **Patti Brustad,** Sarasota, FL; **Jan Buckelew,** Venice, FL; **Maureen Carlton,** Barstow, CA; **Karen Cedar,** Gold River, CA; **Karen Ciraulo,** Folsom, CA; **Marcia M. Clark,** Griffin, GA; **Kim S. Coady,** Covington, GA; **Eva Jean Conway,** Valley View School District, IL; **Marilyn Crownover,** Tustin, CA; **Carol Daley,** Sioux Falls, SD; **Jennifer Davison,** West Palm Beach, FL; **Lynne M. DiNardo,** Covington, GA; **Kathy Dover,** Lake City, GA; **Cheryl Dultz,** Citrus Heights, CA; **Debbie Friedman,** Fort Lauderdale, FL; **Anne Gaitor,** Lakeland, GA; **Rebecca S. Gillette,** Saint Marys, GA; **Buffy C. Gray,** Peachtree City, GA; **Merry Guest,** Homestead, FL; **Jo Nan Holbrook,** Lakeland, GA; **Beth Holguin,** San Jose, CA; **Coleen Howard-Whals,** St. Petersburg, FL; **Beverly Hurst,** Jacksonville, FL; **Debra Jackson,** St. Petersburg, FL; **Vickie Jordan,** Centerville, GA; **Cheryl Kellogg,** Panama City, FL; **Karen Landers,** Talladega County, AL; **Barb LeFerrier,** Port Orchard, WA; **Sandi Maness,** Modesto, CA; **Ileana Masud,** Miami, FL; **David Miller,** Cooper City, FL; **Muriel Miller,** Simi Valley, CA; **Walsetta W. Miller,** Macon, GA; **Jean Nielson,** Simi Valley, CA; **Sue Patton,** Brea, CA; **Debbie Peale,** Miami, FL; **Loretta Piggee,** Gary, IN; **Jennifer Rader,** Huntington, CA; **April Raiford,** Columbus, GA; **Cheryl Remash,** Manchester, NH; **Francis Rivera,** Orlando, FL; **Marina Rodriguez,** Hialeah, FL; **Marilynn Rose,** MI; **Kathy Scholtz,** Amesbury, MA; **Kimberly Moulton Schorr,** Columbus, GA; **Linda Schrum,** Orlando, FL; **Sharon Searcy,** Mandarin, FL; **Melba Sims,** Orlando, FL; **Judy Smith,** Titusville, FL; **Bea Tamo,** Huntington, CA; **Dottie Thompson,** Jefferson County, AL; **Dana Vassar,** Winston-Salem, NC; **Beverly Wakefield,** Tarpon Springs, FL; **Joy Walls,** Winston-Salem, NC; **Elaine Warwick,** Williamson County, TN; **Audrey N. Watkins,** Atlanta, GA; **Marti Watson,** Sarasota, FL

Supervisors: Judy Artz, Butler County, OH; **James Bennett,** Elkhart, IN; **Kay Buckner-Seal,** Wayne County, MI; **Charlotte Carr,** Seattle, WA; **Sister Marion Christi,** Archdiocese of Philadelphia, PA; **Alvina Crouse,** Denver, CO; **Peggy DeLapp,** Minneapolis, MN; **Carol Erlandson,** Wayne Township Schools, IN; **Brenda Feeney,** North Kansas City School District, MO; **Winnie Huebsch,** Sheboygan, WI; **Brenda Mickey,** Winston-Salem, NC; **Audrey Miller,** Camden, NJ; **JoAnne Piccolo,** Westminster, CO; **Sarah Rentz,** Baton Rouge, LA; **Kathy Sullivan,** Omaha, NE; **Rosie Washington,** Gary, IN; **Theresa Wishart,** Knox County Public Schools, TN

English Language Learners Reviewers: Maria Arevalos, Pomona, CA; **Lucy Blood,** NV; **Manuel Brenes,** Kalamazoo, MI; **Delight Diehn,** AZ; **Susan Dunlap,** Richmond, CA; **Tim Fornier,** Grand Rapids, MI; **Connie Jimenez,** Los Angeles, CA; **Diane Bonilla Lether,** Pasadena, CA; **Anna Lugo,** Chicago, IL; **Marcos Martel,** Hayward, CA; **Carolyn Mason,** Yakima, WA; **Jackie Pinson,** Moorpark, CA; **Jenaro Rivas,** NJ; **Jerilyn Smith,** Salinas, CA; **Noemi Velazquez,** Jersey City, NJ; **JoAnna Veloz,** NJ; **Dr. Santiago Veve,** Las Vegas, NV

CREDITS

Cover

Cover Illustration Copyright © 2005 by Leo & Diane Dillon.

Photography

Theme Opener © Richard T. Nowitz/CORBIS. **358A** AP/Wide World Photos. **360** © Charles & Josette Lenars/CORBIS. **381** © AFP/CORBIS. **387S** © Konrad Wothe/Minden Pictures. **387T** © Richard Nowitz. **388** © John Wang/Getty Images. **407CC** Greek National Tourist Office. **407BB** © Getty Images. **407DD** © Corbis/Creatas. **408** © CORBIS. **414** Hemera Technologies, Inc. **429L** Kyle Krause/Index Stock Imagery.

Illustration

All kid art by Morgan-Cain & Associates.

ACKNOWLEDGMENTS

Grateful acknowledgment is made for permission to reprint copyrighted material as follows:

Theme 4

"Chinook Wind Wrestles Cold Wind," from *They Dance in the Sky: Native American Star Myths,* by Jean Guard Monroe and Ray A. Williamson. Copyright © 1987 by Jean Guard Monroe and Ray A. Williamson. Reprinted by permission of Houghton Mifflin Company.

"The Day of Disaster," by Michael Burgan from *National Geographic World* Magazine, December 1999 issue. Copyright © 1999 by the National Geographic Society. Reprinted by permission of the National Geographic Society.

"Our Gifts from the Greeks," by Ann Jordan adapted from *Appleseeds* Magazine, December 1999 issue: Children of Ancient Athens. Copyright © 1999 by Cobblestone Publishing, 30 Grove Street, Suite C, Peterborough, NH 03458. All rights reserved. Reprinted by permission of Carus Publishing Company.

"The Remarkable Voyages of Zheng He," by Amy Butler Greenfield from *Cricket* Magazine, April 2001 issue, Vol. 28, No. 8. Copyright © 2001 by Amy Butler Greenfield. Reprinted by permission of Cricket Magazine.

STUDENT WRITING MODEL FEATURE

Special thanks to the following teachers whose students' compositions appear as Student Writing Models: **Cindy Cheatwood,** Florida; **Diana Davis,** North Carolina; **Kathy Driscoll,** Massachusetts; **Linda Evers,** Florida; **Heidi Harrison,** Michigan; **Eileen Hoffman,** Massachusetts; **Julia Kraftsow,** Florida; **Bonnie Lewison,** Florida; **Kanetha McCord,** Michigan

Discovering Ancient Cultures

Theme 4

Reading Strategies evaluate; summarize; monitor/clarify; phonics/decoding

Comprehension author's viewpoint; bias and assumption; cause and effect; topic, main idea, and details

Decoding Longer Words suffixes *-ic, -al, -ure;* suffixes *-ion, -ation;* unstressed syllables; /sh/ and /zh/ sounds; different sounds for the letters *wh;* the /ə/ sounds

Vocabulary multiple-meaning words; synonyms; prefixes and suffixes

Spelling the /sh/ sound; adding *-ion* or *-ation;* unstressed syllables

Grammar adjectives; proper adjectives; comparing with adjectives; comparing with *good* and *bad;* adverbs that modify verbs and adjectives; comparing with adverbs

Writing explanation; information paragraph; compare/contrast paragraph; process writing: research report

Listening/Speaking/Viewing giving a speech; viewing for information and details; comparing forms of information

Information and Study Skills using multiple sources to locate information; note taking; comparing information in different forms

Theme 4

Discovering Ancient Cultures

CONTENTS

Selection 1

Nonfiction

Below Level

On Level

Above Level

Language Support

Writing Process ▶

Selection 2
The Great Wall

Nonfiction

Below Level   *On Level*   *Above Level*   *Language Support*

Selection 3
The Royal Kingdoms of Ghana, Mali, and Songhay
Life in Medieval Africa

Patricia and Fredrick McKissack

Nonfiction

Below Level   *On Level*   *Above Level*   *Language Support*

Legend

Nonfiction

MYManagement

Focus on Genre

MYTHS

Below Level   *On Level*   *Above Level*   *Language Support*

Leveled Theme Paperbacks

Leveled Bibliography

BOOKS FOR INDEPENDENT READING AND FLUENCY BUILDING

 To build vocabulary and fluency, choose books from this list for students to read outside of class. Suggest that students read for at least thirty minutes a day, either independently or with an adult who provides modeling and guidance.

Key

 Science

 Social Studies

 Multicultural

 Music

 Math

 Classic

 Art

 Career

Classroom Bookshelf

WELL BELOW LEVEL

Seeker of Knowledge
by James Rumford
Houghton 1999 (32p)
Jean-François Champollion deciphered Egypt's ancient hieroglyphs.

Mythological Monsters of Ancient Greece
by Sara Fanelli
Candlewick 2002 (27p)
Among the fourteen monster collages included here are Medusa, Argus, and Echidna.

 Sundiata: Lion King of Mali∗
by David Wisniewski
Clarion 1992 (32p)
Sundiata overcame physical handicaps to rule the empire of Mali.

Run with Me, Nike!
by Cassandra Case
Smithsonian 2000 (32p)
Tomás suddenly finds himself transported back to the Olympic Games in ancient Greece.

Hercules
by Robert Burleigh
Harcourt 1999 (32p)
Burleigh tells the story of Hercules and the last of his twelve labors.

BELOW LEVEL

 African Beginnings
by James Haskins
Lothrop 1998 (48p)
Eleven African kingdoms, from ancient Kush to 16th-century Kongo, are presented here.

 **The Ch'I-Lin Purse**
by Linda Fang
Farrar 1994 (127p)
The author retells ancient Chinese stories she heard in Shanghai.

The 5,000-Year-Old-Puzzle
by Claudia Logan
Farrar 2002 (48p)
A fictional young boy traveling with his parents takes the reader on a real archaeological dig in Egypt in 1924.

The Gods and Goddesses of Ancient China
by Leonard Everett Fisher
Holiday 2003 (36p)
The author describes seventeen of the gods and goddesses believed by the ancient Chinese to bring a person success or failure.

ON LEVEL

City of the Gods∗
by Caroline Arnold
Clarion 1994 (48p)
Arnold explores the history of Mexico's ancient city, Teotihuacán.

The Emperor's Silent Army: The Terra Cotta Warriors of Ancient China
by Jane O'Connor
Viking 2002 (48p)
Chinese farmers discovered the tomb of emperor Qin Shihuang, guarded by over seven thousand full-sized terra cotta warriors.

The Buried City of Pompeii
by Shelley Tanaka
Hyperion 1997 (48p)
A steward from the House of the Menander tells of the destruction of Pompeii.

A Gift for Ampatao
by Susan Vande Griek
Groundwood 1999 (112p)
Archaeologists discover the 500-year-old mummy of an Inca girl.

Painters of the Caves
by Patricia Lauber
Nat'l Geo 1998 (49p)
The walls of the Chauvet caves in France show artwork by people from the Ice Age.

 Oracle Bones, Stars, and Wheelbarrows∗
by Frank Ross
Houghton 1990 (192p)
Ancient Chinese inventions and achievements in astronomy, medicine, and science are detailed.

Sirens and Sea Monsters: Tales from the *Odyssey*
by Mary Pope Osborne
Hyperion 2002 (105p)
Osborne retells ten tales based on episodes from Homer's Odyssey, *focusing on those mythical creatures that lived in or near the sea.*

 Stone Age Farmers Beside the Sea
by Caroline Arnold
Clarion 1997 (48p)
The author explores the prehistoric village of Skara Brae in Scotland.

Pyramid∗
by David Macaulay
Houghton 1975 (80p)
This classic reveals how the great pharaohs' burial places were constructed.

∗Included in Classroom Bookshelf, Level 6

Spirit of the Maya

Spirit of the Maya
by Guy Garcia
Walker 1995 (48p)

A twelve-year-old Lacando'n Indian boy examines the Mayan ruins of his people at Palenque.

Galen: My Life in Imperial Rome
by Marissa Moss
Hyperion 2002 (48p)

A twelve-year-old slave describes his life in Rome during the reign of Emperor Augustus.

Cleopatra
by Diane Stanley
Morrow 1994 (48p) also paper

Cleopatra, still one of the most famous names from Egyptian history, dreamed of a world united under Egyptian rule.

The Roman News
by Andrew Langley and Philip De Souza
Candlewick 1999 (32p)

Life in ancient Rome is presented in newspaper format, with editorials, sports, and letters.

Mummies, Tombs, and Treasure *
by Lila Perl
Clarion 1987 (128p)

Perl explains the attempts to safeguard ancient burial sites.

ABOVE LEVEL

Wonders of the Ancient World
by Therese De Angelis
Chelsea 1997 (64p)

Featured are photos and information on twenty-five ancient marvels, including Machu Picchu, Hadrian's Wall, and the Sphinx.

The Dead Sea Scrolls
by Ilene Cooper
Morrow 1997 (64p)

Cooper traces the Dead Sea Scrolls from their discovery by Bedouin shepherds in 1947 to their translations over forty years later.

BOOKS FOR TEACHER READ ALOUD

Greek Myths
retold by Geraldine McCaughrean
McElderry 1993 (96p)

The author has collected sixteen favorite Greek myths, including Jason, Icarus, King Midas, and Arachne.

Quetzal: Sacred Bird of the Cloud Forest
by Dorothy Hinshaw Patent
Morrow 1996 (40p)

This collection contains stories from the Mayan and Aztec traditions about the quetzal, a bird of the rain forest.

Roman Myths, Heroes, and Legends
by Dwayne Pickels
Chelsea 1999 (64p)

Roman myths of twelve gods and goddesses are retold here.

Technology

Computer Software Resources

- **Get Set for Reading CD-ROM Discovering Ancient Cultures**
  Provides background building, vocabulary support, and selection summaries in English and Spanish.
- **Ancient Empires CD-ROM.** *Tom Snyder Productions*
- **Ancient Civilizations: Africa; Egypt and the Fertile Crescent; Greece and Rome; India and China; Middle and South America CD-ROMs.** *Nat'l Geo*

Video Cassettes

- **Who Built the Pyramids?** *Nat'l Geo*
- **Lost City of the Maya** *Nat'l Geo*
- **Ice Tombs of Siberia** *Nat'l Geo*
- **Myths and Legends of Ancient Greece** *Rainbow Educational Media*
- **I Am the Mummy Heb-Nefert** *by Eve Bunting. Spoken Arts*

Audio

- **I Am the Mummy Heb-Nefert** *by Eve Bunting. Spoken Arts*
- **CD-ROM for** *Discovering Ancient Cultures*. *Houghton Mifflin Company*

Technology Resources addresses are on page R32.

Education Place®

www.eduplace.com *Log on to Education Place for more activities relating to* Discovering Ancient Cultures, *including vocabulary support—*
    e • Glossary
    e • WordGame

Book Adventure®

www.bookadventure.org *This Internet reading incentive program provides thousands of titles for students to read.*

Accelerated Reader® Universal CD-ROM

This popular CD-ROM provides practice quizzes for Anthology selections and for many popular children's books.

---

*Included in Classroom Bookshelf, Level 6

Theme Skills Overview

	Selection 1	Selection 2	Selection 3
Pacing Approximately 5–6 weeks	**Lost Temple of the Aztecs** Nonfiction pp. 355A–383R	**The Great Wall** Nonfiction pp. 387I–407R	**The Royal Kingdoms of Ghana, Mali, and Songhay** Nonfiction pp. 407S–427R
Reading **Comprehension** **Information and Study Skills** **Leveled Readers** • Fluency Practice • Independent Reading	Guiding Comprehension 🕹 **Author's Viewpoint** T 🕹 **Evaluate** T **Science Link** How to Adjust Your Rate of Reading Using Multiple Reference Sources **Leveled Readers** *A Brave Past* *Dream Weaver* *Copán, City of the Maya* *The Mighty Maya* Lessons and Leveled Practice	Guiding Comprehension 🕹 **Cause and Effect** T 🕹 **Summarize** T **Technology Link** How to Read a Timeline Note Taking **Leveled Readers** *The Pyramids of Giza* *A Scribe of Ancient China* *The Shape in the Dark: A Story of Hadrian's Wall* *The Pyramids of Ancient Egypt* Lessons and Leveled Practice	Guiding Comprehension 🕹 **Topic, Main Idea, Details** T 🕹 **Monitor/Clarify** T **Social Studies Link** How to Read a Diagram Primary and Secondary Sources **Leveled Readers** *Ancient Baghdad: City at the Crossroads of Trade* *Caravan Boy* *The Kingdom of Kush* *On the Silk Road: Ancient Baghdad* Lessons and Leveled Practice
Word Work **Decoding** **Phonics Review** **Vocabulary** **Spelling**	🕹 **Suffixes -ic, -al, and -ure** T **The /sh/ and /zh/ Sounds** 🕹 **Multiple-Meaning Words** T /sh/ T	🕹 **Suffixes -ion and -ation** T **Sounds for the Letters wh** 🕹 **Synonyms** T Adding -ion or -ation T	🕹 **Unstressed Syllables** T **The ə Sound** 🕹 **Prefixes and Suffixes in a Dictionary** T Unstressed Syllables T
Writing and Oral Language **Writing** **Grammar** **Listening/Speaking/ Viewing**	✏ **Writing an Explanation** Eliminating Unnecessary Words Kinds of Adjectives T Proper Adjectives T Giving a Speech	✏ **Writing a Paragraph of Information** Elaborating with Adjectives T Comparing with Adjectives T Comparing with *good/bad* T Viewing for Information and Details	✏ **Writing a Comparison-and-Contrast Paragraph** Combining Sentences T Kinds of Adverbs T Comparing with Adverbs T Comparing Forms of Information
Cross-Curricular Activities	Responding: Math, Listening and Speaking, Internet Classroom Management Activities	Responding: Science, Viewing, Internet Classroom Management Activities	Responding: Social Studies, Listening and Speaking, Internet Classroom Management Activities

T Skill tested on Theme Skills Test and/or Integrated Theme Test

Target Skills

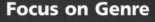
- **Phonics**
- **Comprehension**
- **Vocabulary**
- **Fluency**

Monitoring Student Progress

Check Your Progress
The Lord of the Nile
Legend

The Great Pyramid
Nonfiction

pp. M1–M43

Guiding Comprehension

Theme Connections

🎯 **Comprehension Skills Review** T

🎯 **Summarize** T

Taking Tests: Vocabulary Items

....

Connecting Leveled Readers

🎯 **Structural Analysis Skills Review** T

🎯 **Vocabulary Skills Review** T

Spelling Skills Review T

✏️ **Writing Skills Review** T

Grammar Skills Review T

Cross-Curricular Activities

Classroom Management Activities

Focus on Genre

Myths
pp. 429A–447R

Guiding Comprehension

🎯 **Understanding Myths**

🎯 **Predict/Infer**

Finding Media Resources

....

Leveled Readers

The Quest for Medusa's Head
The Sun's Strength, An Ancient Chinese Myth
Odin's Wisdom
Perseus and Medusa

Lessons and Leveled Practice

🎯 **Prefixes and Suffixes**

Variant Consonant Pronunciations

🎯 **Words from Myths**

Consonant Changes: The Sound of *c*

✏️ **Writing a Myth**
Using Dialogue

Using the Right Word
Using *good* and *well*

Retell an Oral History

Responding: Internet

Classroom Management Activities

Combination Classroom

See the **Combination Classroom Planning Guide** for lesson planning and management support.

Writing Process

Reading-Writing Workshop: Research Report
- Student Writing Model
- Writing Process Instruction
- Writing Traits Focus

Additional Theme Resources

- Leveled Theme Paperbacks Lessons
- Reteaching Lessons
- Challenge/Extension Activities

Technology

Education Place®
www.eduplace.com

Log on to Education Place for more activities relating to *Discovering Ancient Cultures*.

Lesson Planner CD-ROM
Customize your planning for *Discovering Ancient Cultures* with the Lesson Planner CD-ROM.

Independent Activities

Assign these activities at any time during the theme while you work with small groups.

Additional Independent Activities

- Challenge/Extension Activities, Theme Resources, pp. R9, R11, R13

- Theme 4 Assignment Cards 1–10, **Teacher's Resource Blackline Masters,** pp. 73–78

- Classroom Management Activities, pp. 358A–358B, 387Q–387R, 407AA–407BB, M6–M7, 429I–429J

- Language Center, pp. 383M–383N, 407M–407N, 427M–427N, 447M–447N

- **Classroom Management Handbook,** Activity Masters CM4-1–CM4-12

- **Challenge Handbook,** pp. 30–35

Look for more activities in the Classroom Management Kit.

Social Studies

Plan a Time Capsule

👥👥👥 Groups	🕐 45 minutes
Objective	Create a time capsule.

What do you think people in the year 2500 might want to know about your school? What do you think they ought to know? Plan and then create items that you would place in a time capsule. Work with a group.

- Brainstorm a list of things that would help a person in the year 2500 know what life at your school was like, such as class schedules, report cards, class photos.

- Review your list and pick the ten most important items that could fit in a time capsule.

- Working with a partner, write documents such as a daily class schedule or a typical lunch menu.

- Discuss which items would probably last five hundred years and which items might disintegrate.

Daily Schedule Lincoln School
8:30—Bell
8:35—Attendance
8:40—Language Arts
10:00—Break
10:10—Gym

Language Arts

Ancient Pen Pal

👤 Singles	🕐 30 minutes
Objective	Write a journal entry.
Materials	Reference sources

Write a journal entry from the point of view of an ordinary person who lived in ancient Mexico, China, or Ghana. Describe a specific event that you have witnessed. Explain what you see and what effect the event has on you and other people.

You might choose to describe one of these events:

- arrival of Cortés in Tenochtitlán
- construction of the Great Wall
- preparations for the departure of a Ghanaian trading caravan

Publish your journal entry in the classroom reading center.

Consider copying and laminating these activities for use in centers.

Career

Help Wanted

Singles	🕐 30 minutes
Objective	Write a help-wanted ad.
Materials	Examples of newspaper help wanted ads.

An employer who needs to hire workers puts a help-wanted ad in the newspaper. Suppose you are an employer in an ancient culture looking for workers. Design a help-wanted ad that lists the specific skills an employee would need and the tasks he or she would need to perform. Write the ad for one of these jobs:

messenger for the Aztec emperor Moctezuma

construction worker on the Great Wall of China

gold miner in ancient Ghana

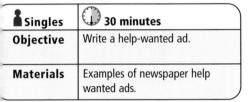

Immediate Openings!
Looking for hard workers
with strong backs.
Knowledge of the building
trade a plus!

Health

Archaeologist Supply List

👥 Pairs	🕐 30 minutes
Objective	Create a supply list for an archaeologist.
Materials	Reference sources

What does an archaeologist need in order to do his or her work? Many archaeologists work in remote areas, with no access to electricity and miles away from stores and hospitals. Work with a partner. Make a supply list of items such as these:

- clothing
- equipment
- medical supplies

Think about the limitations of the work site before you begin planning your list. Read about archaeology in a reference source, if necessary.

Art

Make an Architectural Diagram

👥 Pairs	🕐 45 minutes
Objective	Make a diagram of an ancient structure.
Materials	Reference sources, Internet, posterboard, markers, rulers

Architects and engineers make diagrams when planning the construction of buildings, roads, and other projects. Work with a partner. Think about diagrams you may have seen in museums or in books. Draw a diagram of an ancient structure. Refer to reference sources for text and illustrations of structures such as these:

- the Great Temple of the Aztecs
- part of the Great Wall of China
- part of a city in ancient Ghana

Planning for Assessment

During instruction in Theme 4 . . .

1 SCREENING AND DIAGNOSIS

Screening
- Baseline Group Test

Diagnosis
- Leveled Reading Passages Assessment Kit
- Phonics/Decoding Screening Test
- Lexia Quick Phonics Assessment CD-ROM

2 MONITORING PROGRESS

ONGOING INFORMAL ASSESSMENT

- Guiding Comprehension questions
- Literature Discussion groups
- Comprehension Checks
- Fluency Practice
- Monitoring Student Progress boxes
- Writing Samples
- Observation Checklists
- Skill lesson applications

END-OF-THEME REVIEW AND TEST PREPARATION

Monitoring Student Progress
- emphasizes use of comparing and contrasting critical thinking skills, teaches test-taking strategies as preparation for formal assessments, and reviews tested theme skills and reading strategies.

Assessing Student Progress
- provides suggestions for administering formal assessments, identifies areas of difficulty, and lists program resources for differentiating further instruction.

FORMAL ASSESSMENT

- Selection Tests
- Integrated Theme Tests
- Theme Skills Tests
- Fluency Assessment
- Reading-Writing Workshop

3 MANAGING AND REPORTING

 **Technology**   Record each student's performance on the **Learner Profile® CD-ROM.**

National Test Correlation
Documenting Adequate Yearly Progress

SKILLS for *Discovering Ancient Cultures*	ITBS	Terra Nova (CTBS)	CAT	SAT	MAT
Comprehension Strategies and Skills					
• Strategies: Summarize, Evaluate*	O	O	O	O	O
• Skills: Author's Viewpoint/Bias and Assumption, Cause and Effect, Topic/Main Idea/Details, Categorize and Classify*, Problem Solving*	O	O	O	O	O
Structural Analysis					
• Suffixes *-ic, -ture, -al, -ure*	O	O	O	O	O
• Adding *-ion* or *-ation*	O	O	O	O	
• Unstressed Syllables					
Vocabulary/Dictionary					
• Multiple-Meaning Words	O	O	O	O	O
• Synonyms	O	O	O	O	O
• Prefixes and Suffixes	O	O	O	O	O
Information and Study Skills					
• Paraphrasing and Synthesizing					O
Spelling					
• Spelling /sh/	O	O	O	O	O
• Adding *-ion* or *-ation*	O	O	O	O	O
• Unstressed Syllables			O	O	O
Grammar					
• Adjectives	O	O	O	O	O
• Proper Adjectives	O	O	O		
• Comparing with Adjectives	O			O	
• Adverbs			O		
• Comparing with Adverbs					
Writing					
• Formats: Paragraph of Information, Compare/Contrast Paragraph, Explanation	O	O		O	O
• Elaborating with Adjectives and Adverbs					
• Combining Sentences with Adjectives		O	O	O	
• Reading-Writing Workshop: Research Report	O	O		O	O

*These skills are taught, but not tested, in this theme.

KEY

ITBS Iowa Tests of Basic Skills

Terra Nova (CTBS)
Comprehensive Tests of Basic Skills

CAT California Achievement Tests

SAT Stanford Achievement Tests

MAT Metropolitan Achievement Tests

Launching the Theme

Theme 4

Discovering Ancient Cultures

I should like to rise and go
Where the golden apples grow; . . .
And the rich goods from near and far
Hang for sale in the bazaar;
Where the Great Wall round China goes
And on one side the desert blows,
And with bell and voice and drum,
Cities on the other hum

— *Robert Louis Stevenson*
from "Travel"

354

355

Introducing the Theme: Discussion Options

Combination Classroom

See the **Combination Classroom Planning Guide** for lesson planning and management support.

Read aloud the theme title and the excerpt from a poem by Robert Louis Stevenson on Anthology page 355. Ask:

1 Why do you think Stevenson wants to travel? (to explore new places, to have new adventures, to meet new people)

2 From reading Stevenson's excerpt, where do you think the places he wants to visit are located? (the United States, India, China, and Africa)

3 Why do you think people in the modern world find cultures of long ago fascinating? (The way people lived, their customs and clothes, their beliefs, and their daily lives are so different from the way many people live now.)

4 How and why do we learn about ancient cultures? (from studies done by historians and scientists; to understand the past)

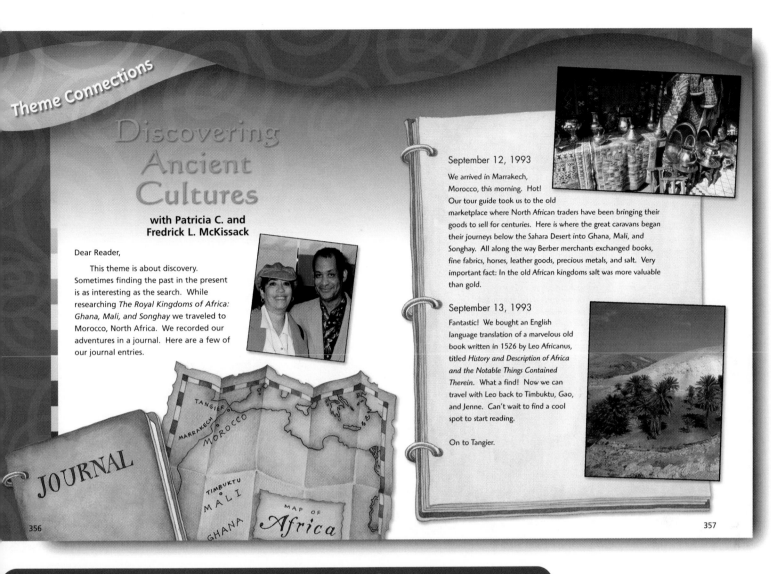

Theme Connections

Discovering Ancient Cultures

with Patricia C. and Fredrick L. McKissack

Dear Reader,

This theme is about discovery. Sometimes finding the past in the present is as interesting as the search. While researching *The Royal Kingdoms of Africa: Ghana, Mali, and Songhay* we traveled to Morocco, North Africa. We recorded our adventures in a journal. Here are a few of our journal entries.

JOURNAL

TANGIER
MARRAKECH
MOROCCO
TIMBUKTU
MALI
GHANA
MAP OF Africa

356

September 12, 1993

We arrived in Marrakech, Morocco, this morning. Hot! Our tour guide took us to the old marketplace where North African traders have been bringing their goods to sell for centuries. Here is where the great caravans began their journeys below the Sahara Desert into Ghana, Mali, and Songhay. All along the way Berber merchants exchanged books, fine fabrics, horses, leather goods, precious metals, and salt. Very important fact: In the old African kingdoms salt was more valuable than gold.

September 13, 1993

Fantastic! We bought an English language translation of a marvelous old book written in 1526 by Leo Africanus, titled *History and Description of Africa and the Notable Things Contained Therein.* What a find! Now we can travel with Leo back to Timbuktu, Gao, and Jenne. Can't wait to find a cool spot to start reading.

On to Tangier.

357

Building Theme Connections

Ask volunteers to read aloud the author's letter on Anthology pages 356, 357, and 358. Tell students that Patricia C. and Fredrick L. McKissack wrote *The Royal Kingdoms of Africa: Ghana, Mali, and Songhay,* a selection they will read in this theme. (See Teacher's Edition page 410 for more information on Patricia C. and Fredrick L. McKissack.) Use the following questions to prompt discussion:

1 What is a caravan? Why did people travel in caravans? (A caravan is a group of vehicles or pack of animals traveling together in single file; for safety or for companionship.)

2 Patricia and Fredrick rode camels on their journey. What method of transportation would you use if you went on a journey? (Sample answer: I would travel by train because it is speedy and comfortable.)

3 If you could choose a place to take a journey to, where would it be? Why? (Sample answer: I would go to Africa because it includes many different countries and cultures and because I'd love to go on a safari.)

Launching the Theme   354N

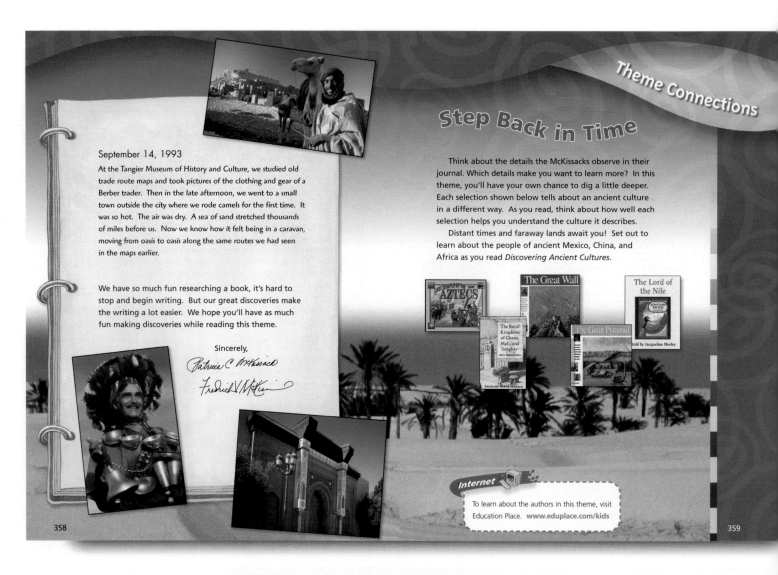

Step Back in Time

September 14, 1993

At the Tangier Museum of History and Culture, we studied old trade route maps and took pictures of the clothing and gear of a Berber trader. Then in the late afternoon, we went to a small town outside the city where we rode camels for the first time. It was so hot. The air was dry. A sea of sand stretched thousands of miles before us. Now we know how it felt being in a caravan, moving from oasis to oasis along the same routes we had seen in the maps earlier.

We have so much fun researching a book, it's hard to stop and begin writing. But our great discoveries make the writing a lot easier. We hope you'll have as much fun making discoveries while reading this theme.

Sincerely,

Patricia C. McKissack
Fredrick L. McKissack

Think about the details the McKissacks observe in their journal. Which details make you want to learn more? In this theme, you'll have your own chance to dig a little deeper. Each selection shown below tells about an ancient culture in a different way. As you read, think about how well each selection helps you understand the culture it describes.

Distant times and faraway lands await you! Set out to learn about the people of ancient Mexico, China, and Africa as you read *Discovering Ancient Cultures*.

Internet

To learn about the authors in this theme, visit Education Place. www.eduplace.com/kids

358

359

Building Theme Connections, continued

Read aloud the paragraph on Anthology page 359.

- Have students brainstorm ideas, images, and words they associate with ancient cultures. Record their thoughts.

- Discuss how students' ideas compare with those of Patricia C. and Fredrick L. McKissack.

Have students finish reading Anthology page 359.

- Explain that the books in the photo are the selections students will read in the theme *Discovering Ancient Cultures*.

- Ask students to predict what ancient cultures will be explored in the selections. Have the students explain their predictions. (Answers will vary.)

- Allow students time to look ahead at the selections and illustrations. Have them revise their original predictions as necessary.

Home Connection

Send home the theme letter for *Discovering Ancient Cultures* to introduce the theme and suggest home activities. (See the **Teacher's Resource Blackline Masters**.)

For other suggestions relating to *Discovering Ancient Cultures*, see **Home/ Community Connections**.

Making Selection Connections

Introduce Selection Connections in the Practice Book.

- Preview the **Graphic Organizers** on pages 1 and 2. Read aloud the directions, column heads, and selection titles. Explain that as they finish reading each selection, students will add to this chart to deepen their understanding of the theme *Discovering Ancient Cultures*.

Classroom Management

At any time during the theme you can assign the independent cross-curricular activities on Teacher's Edition pages 354K–354L while you give differentiated instruction to small groups. For additional independent activities related to specific selections, see the Teacher's Edition pages listed below.

- Week 1: pages 358A–358B, 383M–383N
- Week 2: pages 387Q–387R, 407M–407N
- Week 3: pages 407AA–407BB, 427M–427N
- Week 4: pages M6–M7, M24–M25, M26–M27, M42–M43

Monitoring Student Progress

Monitoring Progress

Throughout the theme, monitor your students' progress by using the following program features in the Teacher's Edition:

- Guiding Comprehension questions
- Literature discussion groups
- Skill lesson applications
- Monitoring Student Progress boxes

Wrapping Up and Reviewing the Theme

Use the two selections and support material in **Monitoring Student Progress** on pages M1–M45 to review theme skills, connect and compare theme literature, and prepare students for the Integrated Theme Test and the Theme Skills Test as well as for standardized tests measuring adequate yearly progress.

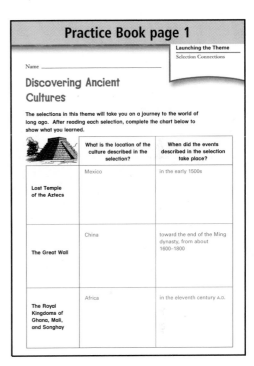

Practice Book page 1

Launching the Theme
Selection Connections

Name _____

Discovering Ancient Cultures

The selections in this theme will take you on a journey to the world of long ago. After reading each selection, complete the chart below to show what you learned.

	What is the location of the culture described in the selection?	When did the events described in the selection take place?
Lost Temple of the Aztecs	Mexico	in the early 1500s
The Great Wall	China	toward the end of the Ming dynasty, from about 1600–1800
The Royal Kingdoms of Ghana, Mali, and Songhay	Africa	in the eleventh century A.D.

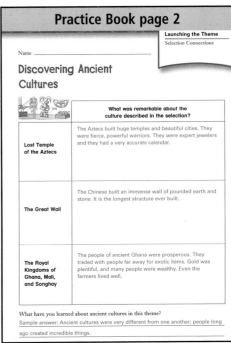

Practice Book page 2

Launching the Theme
Selection Connections

Name _____

Discovering Ancient Cultures

	What was remarkable about the culture described in the selection?
Lost Temple of the Aztecs	The Aztecs built huge temples and beautiful cities. They were fierce, powerful warriors. They were expert jewelers and they had a very accurate calendar.
The Great Wall	The Chinese built an immense wall of pounded earth and stone. It is the longest structure ever built.
The Royal Kingdoms of Ghana, Mali, and Songhay	The people of ancient Ghana were prosperous. They traded with people far away for exotic items. Gold was plentiful, and many people were wealthy. Even the farmers lived well.

What have you learned about ancient cultures in this theme?
Sample answer: Ancient cultures were very different from one another; people long ago created incredible things.

Lesson Overview

Literature

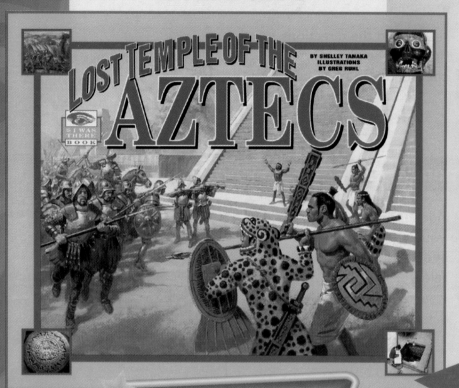

Selection Summary

The 1978 discovery of the Great Temple of the Aztecs, once the center of the city of Tenochtitlán, introduces the story of the Spanish conquest of the wealthy Aztec empire in the sixteenth century.

1 Background and Vocabulary

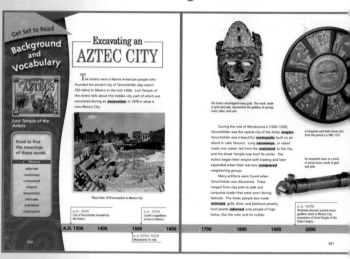

2 Main Selection

Lost Temple of the Aztecs
Genre: Nonfiction

3 Science Link

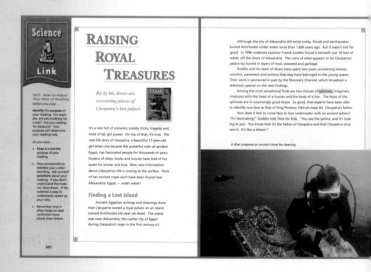

Instructional Support

Planning and Practice

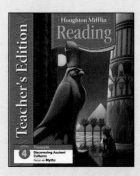

Practice Book

- Planning and classroom management
- Reading instruction
- Skill lessons
- Materials for reaching all learners

- Independent practice for skills, Level 6.2

Teacher's Resource Blackline Masters

Instruction Transparencies/Masters and Strategy Posters

- Transparencies
- Strategy Posters
- Blackline Masters

- Newsletters
- Selection Summaries
- Assignment Cards
- Observation Checklists
- Selection Tests

Reaching All Learners

Intervention Strategies for Extra Support

Instructional Activities for Challenge

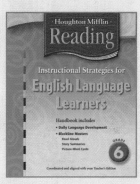

Instructional Strategies for English Language Learners

Independent Activities for Classroom Management

Coordinated lessons, activities, and projects for additional reading instruction

For
- Classroom teacher
- Extended day
- Pull out
- Resource teacher
- Reading specialist

Technology

Audio Selection

Lost Temple of the Aztecs

Get Set for Reading CD-ROM
- Background building
- Vocabulary support
- Selection Summary in English and Spanish

Accelerated Reader®
- Practice quizzes for the selection

www.eduplace.com

Log on to *Education Place®* for more activities related to the selection, including vocabulary support—
- e • Glossary
- e • WordGame

Leveled Books for Reaching All Learners

Leveled Readers and Leveled Practice

- Independent reading for building fluency

- Topic, comprehension strategy, and vocabulary linked to main selection

- Lessons in Teacher's Edition, pages 383O–383R

- Leveled practice for every book

Technology

Leveled Readers
Audio available

Book Adventure®

- Practice quizzes for the Leveled Theme Paperbacks
  www.bookadventure.org

● BELOW LEVEL

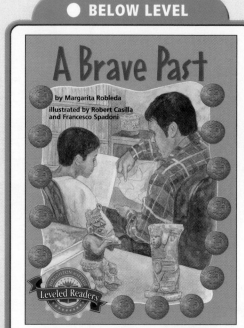

A Brave Past
by Margarita Robleda
illustrated by Robert Casilla and Francesco Spadoni

Leveled Readers

▲ ON LEVEL

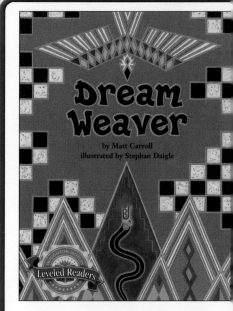

Dream Weaver
by Matt Carroll
illustrated by Stephan Daigle

Leveled Readers

● Below Level Practice

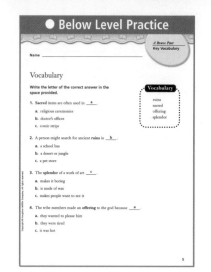

A Brave Past
Key Vocabulary

Name

Vocabulary

Write the letter of the correct answer in the space provided.

Vocabulary
ruins
sacred
offering
splendor

1. Sacred items are often used in ___a___.
   a. religious ceremonies
   b. doctor's offices
   c. comic strips

2. A person might search for ancient **ruins** in ___b___.
   a. a school bus
   b. a desert or jungle
   c. a pet store

3. The **splendor** of a work of art ___c___.
   a. makes it boring
   b. is made of wax
   c. makes people want to see it

4. The tribe members made an **offering** to the god because ___a___.
   a. they wanted to please him
   b. they were tired
   c. it was hot

▲ On Level Practice

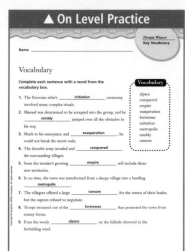

Dream Weaver
Key Vocabulary

Name

Vocabulary

Complete each sentence with a word from the vocabulary box.

Vocabulary
alpaca
conquered
empire
exasperation
fortresses
initiation
metropolis
nimbly
ransom

1. The Peruvian tribe's ___initiation___ ceremony involved many complex rituals.

2. Manuel was determined to be accepted into the group, and he ___nimbly___ jumped over all the obstacles in his way.

3. Much to his annoyance and ___exasperation___, he could not break the secret code.

4. The forceful army invaded and ___conquered___ the surrounding villages.

5. Soon the invader's growing ___empire___ will include three new territories.

6. In no time, the town was transformed from a sleepy village into a bustling ___metropolis___.

7. The villagers offered a large ___ransom___ for the return of their leader, but the captors refused to negotiate.

8. Troops streamed out of the ___fortresses___ that protected the town from enemy forces.

9. Even the wooly ___alpaca___ on the hillside shivered in the forbidding wind.

● Below Level Practice

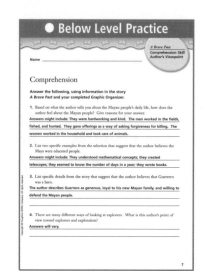

A Brave Past
Comprehension Skill
Author's Viewpoint

Name

Comprehension

Answer the following, using information in the story
A Brave Past and your completed Graphic Organizer.

1. Based on what the author tells you about the Mayan people's daily life, how does the author feel about the Mayan people? Give reasons for your answer.
Answers might include: They were hardworking and kind. The men worked in the fields, fished, and hunted. They gave offerings as a way of asking forgiveness for killing. The women worked in the household and took care of animals.

2. List two specific examples from the selection that suggest that the author believes the Maya were educated people.
Answers might include: They understood mathematical concepts; they created telescopes; they seemed to know the number of days in a year; they wrote books.

3. List specific details from the story that suggest that the author believes that Guerrero was a hero.
The author describes Guerrero as generous, loyal to his new Mayan family, and willing to defend the Mayan people.

4. There are many different ways of looking at explorers. What is this author's point of view toward explorers and exploration?
Answers will vary.

▲ On Level Practice

Dream Weaver
Comprehension Skill
Author's Viewpoint

Name

Comprehension

Answer the following, using information in the selection and your completed Graphic Organizer.

1. What is the author's purpose for writing this story?
Sample answer: To describe the struggle of one Incan girl trying to keep traditions strong at a time when the Incan civilization is about to be conquered.

2. What kinds of facts are included in the selection?
Sample answer: facts about the lives of Quilla and Cori and girls their age; facts about the Incan lifestyle, traditions, and rituals; facts about historic events.

3. What words indicate the author's viewpoint about one of the characters in the story?
Sample answer: The author describes Quilla as patient, talented, and sensitive; these words indicate a positive viewpoint.

4. Consider all the information in the story and describe the author's viewpoint.
Sample answer: The author admires Quilla because she cares for her sister and tries to set a good example. In some ways, she views Quilla as a symbol of Incan civilization. She also views the Spanish invaders negatively.

5. Do you agree with the author's viewpoint? Why or why not?
Answers will vary.

■ ABOVE LEVEL

Houghton Mifflin Leveled Readers

Copán: City of the Maya

by Laura Meredith

◆ LANGUAGE SUPPORT

The Mighty Maya

by Margarita Robleda
illustrated by Robert Casilla
and Francesco Spadoni

Leveled Readers

Leveled Theme Paperbacks

- Extended independent reading in Theme-related trade books
- Lessons in Teacher's Edition, pages R2–R7

KATHRYN LASKY
THE LIBRARIAN WHO MEASURED THE EARTH
ILLUSTRATED BY KEVIN HAWKES

Below Level

■ Above Level Practice

Name _____

Vocabulary

Complete the paragraph below with words from the vocabulary box.

The archaeologist went on an **expedition** to Central America. They traveled to a remote **site** in the jungle, where they began their **excavation**. It wasn't long before they began unearthing ancient **artifacts**. They found pendants and earrings studded with brilliant green **jade**. The archaeologists determined that this jewelry belonged to members of a powerful **dynasty**, whose many **descendants** populated the surrounding areas. They also discovered stones **inscribed** with mysterious writing. The script is so **intricate** that it may be years before it can be **deciphered** by experts.

Vocabulary
artifacts
deciphered
descendants
dynasty
excavation
expedition
inscribed
intricate
jade
site

5

◆ Language Support Practice

Name _____

Build Background

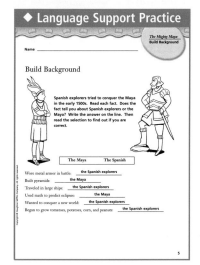

Spanish explorers tried to conquer the Maya in the early 1500s. Read each fact. Does the fact tell you about Spanish explorers or the Maya? Write the answer on the line. Then read the selection to find out if you are correct.

| The Maya | The Spanish |

Wore metal armor in battle: **the Spanish explorers**
Built pyramids: **the Maya**
Traveled in large ships: **the Spanish explorers**
Used math to predict eclipses: **the Maya**
Wanted to conquer a new world: **the Spanish explorers**
Began to grow tomatoes, potatoes, corn, and peanuts: **the Spanish explorers**

5

Aïda
TOLD BY Leontyne Price
ILLUSTRATED BY LEO AND DIANE DILLON

On Level

■ Above Level Practice

Name _____

Comprehension

Answer the following, using information in the selection and your completed Graphic Organizer.

1. What is the author's purpose for writing this story?
Sample answer: to describe the expeditions to the ancient Mayan ruins at Copán and to identify what scientists and scholars have learned by studying these and other sites.

2. What kinds of facts are included in the selection?
There are facts about the expeditions, the explorers, their discoveries, and Mayan communication, beliefs, and lifestyles.

3. What words indicate the author's viewpoint about one of the figures in the story?
Answers will vary. Possible answer: The author views John Lloyd Stephens in a positive way. He is described as successful, and his written work is described as popular.

4. Consider all the clues you've picked up in this selection and evaluate the author's viewpoint.
The author admires the explorers who sought to preserve and study the ruins. She also admires the complexity of the Mayan civilization. This can be concluded from the facts and opinions she includes and specific words she uses.

5. Do you agree with the author's viewpoint? Why or why not?
Answers will vary.

7

◆ Language Support Practice

Name _____

Vocabulary

Read the travel guide. Complete each sentence below with the best word from the box. Use each word only once.

Welcome to the land of the Maya! On our tour, you will learn all about this ancient **culture** that produced so many wonders. You will see the **ruins** of their great city at Chetumal. We will point out the **sites** of battles between the Spanish and the Maya. You will look at the sky through **telescopes** that the Maya invented. Did your family come from Mexico? If so, you may see the city where an **ancestor** of yours lived before the Spanish **conquered** this land!

Vocabulary
ancestor
conquered
culture
ruins
sites
telescopes

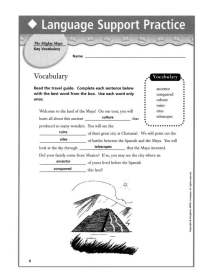

6

Between the
DRAGON
and the
EAGLE

Mical Schneider

Above Level

Daily Lesson Plans

 **Technology**
Lesson Planner CD-ROM allows you to customize the chart below to develop your own lesson plans.

T Skill tested on Theme Skills Test and/or Integrated Theme Test

	DAY 1	DAY 2
50–60 minutes **Reading** **Comprehension** 	**Teacher Read Aloud,** 359A–359B *The Remarkable Voyages of Zheng He* Building Background, 360 **Key Vocabulary,** 361 adorned · empire · momentous causeways · intricate · sites conquered · metropolis · tributes **Reading the Selection,** 362–377 **Comprehension Skill,** 362 Author's Viewpoint **T** **Comprehension Strategy,** 362 Evaluate	**Reading the Selection,** 362–377 Comprehension Check, 377 Responding, 378 Think About the Selection **Comprehension Skill Preview,** 375 Author's Viewpoint **T**

	DAY 1	DAY 2
Leveled Readers • Fluency Practice • Independent Reading	**Leveled Readers** *A Brave Past* *Dream Weaver* *Copán, City of the Maya* *The Mighty Maya*  Lessons and Leveled Practice, 383O–383R	**Leveled Readers** *A Brave Past* *Dream Weaver* *Copán, City of the Maya* *The Mighty Maya* Lessons and Leveled Practice, 383O–383R

| **20–30 minutes**
 Word Work

 Phonics/Decoding
 Vocabulary
 Spelling | **Phonics/Decoding,** 363
 Phonics/Decoding Strategy

 Vocabulary, 362–377
 Selection Vocabulary

 Spelling, 383E
 /sh/ **T** | **Structural Analysis,** 383C
 Suffixes -ure, -ic, and -al **T**

 Vocabulary, 362–377
 Selection Vocabulary

 Spelling, 383E
 /sh/ Review and Practice **T** |

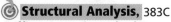

| **20–30 minutes**
 Writing and Oral Language

 Writing
 Grammar
 Listening/Speaking/Viewing | **Writing,** 383K
 Prewriting an Explanation

 Grammar, 383I
 Kinds of Adjectives

 Daily Language Practice
 1. The train statun is on park Street. (station; Park)
 2. At last night's concert, that musicin plays a solo. (musician; played)

 Listening/Speaking/Viewing, 359A–359B, 371
 Teacher Read Aloud, Stop and Think | **Writing,** 383K
 Drafting an Explanation

 Grammar, 383I
 Kinds of Adjectives Practice **T**

 Daily Language Practice
 3. I don't like it when my sister are selfich. (is; selfish.) or (sisters; are; selfish.)
 4. Yesterday, the motin of the ride makes me car-sick. (motion; made)

 Listening/Speaking/Viewing, 377, 378
 Wrapping Up, Responding |

Target Skills of the Week

Phonics	Suffixes -ure, -ic, and -al
Comprehension	Evaluate; Author's Viewpoint
Vocabulary	Multiple-Meaning Words
Fluency	Leveled Readers

DAY 3

Rereading the Selection, 362–377

Comprehension Skill, 383A–383B
Author's Viewpoint **T**

Leveled Readers
A Brave Past
Dream Weaver
Copán, City of the Maya
The Mighty Maya
Lessons and Leveled Practice, 383O–383R

Phonics Review, 383D
The /sh/ and /zh/ Sounds

Vocabulary, 383G
Multiple-Meaning Words **T**

Spelling, 383F
Vocabulary: Analogies; /sh/ Practice **T**

Writing, 383L
Revising an Explanation
Eliminating Unnecessary Words

Grammar, 383J
Proper Adjectives **T**

Daily Language Practice
5. A glacer are an amazing sight. (glacier; is)
6. My father is an officil at the Special olympics. (official; Olympics.)

DAY 4

Reading the Science Link, 380–383
"Raising Royal Treasures"

Skill: How to Adjust Your Rate of Reading

Rereading for Genre, 382
Magazine Articles

Comprehension Skill Review, 369
Topic, Main Idea, and Supporting Details

Leveled Readers
A Brave Past
Dream Weaver
Copán, City of the Maya
The Mighty Maya
Lessons and Leveled Practice, 383O–383R

Phonics/Decoding, 380–383
Apply Phonics/Decoding Strategy to Link

Vocabulary, 383M
Language Center: Building Vocabulary

Spelling, 383F
Spelling Game, Proofreading **T**

Writing, 383L
Proofreading an Explanation

Grammar, 383J
Proper Adjectives Practice **T**

Daily Language Practice
7. In which directin is the nearest canadian town? (direction; Canadian)
8. Who's poorshin of pie is left on the table? (Whose; portion)

Listening/Speaking/Viewing, 383
Discuss the Link

DAY 5

Rereading for Fluency, 365

Responding Activities, 378–379
Write a Letter
Cross-Curricular Activities

Information and Study Skills, 383H
Using Multiple Reference Sources

Comprehension Skill Review, 373
Categorize and Classify

Leveled Readers
A Brave Past
Dream Weaver
Copán, City of the Maya
The Mighty Maya
Lessons and Leveled Practice, 383O–383R

Phonics, 383N
Language Center: Shhhhh!

Vocabulary, 383M
Language Center: Vocabulary Game

Spelling, 383F
Test: /sh/ **T**

Writing, 383L
Publishing an Explanation

Grammar, 383J, 383M
Adjective Position
Language Center: All Kinds of Adjectives

Daily Language Practice
9. I would love to visit an ancint greek temple. (ancient; Greek)
10. Tonight, Mom will helped me sew a special cushin. (help; cushion.)

Listening/Speaking/Viewing, 383N
Language Center: Giving a Speech

Managing Flexible Groups

Leveled Instruction and Leveled Practice

	DAY 1	**DAY 2**
WHOLE CLASS	• Teacher Read Aloud (TE pp. 359A–359B) • Building Background, Introducing Vocabulary (TE pp. 360–361) • Comprehension Strategy: Introduce (TE p. 362) • Comprehension Skill: Introduce (TE p. 362) • Purpose Setting (TE p. 363) **After reading first half of *Lost Temple of the Aztecs*** • Stop and Think (TE p. 371)	**After reading *Lost Temple of the Aztecs*** • Wrapping Up (TE p. 377) • Comprehension Check (Practice Book p. 5) • Responding: Think About the Selection (TE p. 378) • Comprehension Skill: Preview (TE p. 375)
SMALL GROUPS		
Extra Support	**TEACHER-LED** • Preview *Lost Temple of the Aztecs* to Stop and Think (TE pp. 362–371). • Support reading with Extra Support/Intervention notes (TE pp. 363, 365, 367, 368, 369, 370, 373, 376).	**Partner or Individual Work** • Reread first half of *Lost Temple of the Aztecs* (TE pp. 362–371). • Preview, read second half (TE pp. 372–377). • Comprehension Check (Practice Book p. 5)
Challenge	**Individual Work** • Begin "Mapping Mesoamerica" (Challenge Handbook p. 30). • Extend reading with Challenge note (TE p. 376).	**Individual Work** • Continue work on activity (Challenge Handbook p. 30).
English Language Learners	**TEACHER-LED** • Preview vocabulary and *Lost Temple of the Aztecs* to Stop and Think (TE pp. 361–371). • Support reading with English Language Learners notes (TE pp. 360, 364, 366, 372).	**TEACHER-LED** • Review first half of *Lost Temple of the Aztecs* (TE pp. 362–371). ✔ • Preview, read second half (TE pp. 372–377). • Begin Comprehension Check together (Practice Book p. 5).

Independent Activities

- Get Set for Reading CD-ROM
- Journals: selection notes, questions
- Complete, review Practice Book (pp. 3–7) and Leveled Readers Practice Blackline Masters (TE pp. 383O–383R).
- Assignment Cards (Teachers Resource Blackline Masters, pp. 73–74)
- Leveled Readers (TE pp. 383O–383R), Leveled Theme Paperbacks (TE pp. R2–R7), or book from Leveled Bibliography (TE pp. 354E–354F)

✔ Opportunity to informally assess oral reading rate

- Rereading *Lost Temple of the Aztecs* (TE pp. 362–377)
- Comprehension Skill: Main lesson (TE pp. 383A–383B)

- Reading the Science Link (TE pp. 380–383): Skill lesson (TE p. 380)
- Rereading the Science Link: Genre lesson (TE p. 382)
- Comprehension Skill: First Comprehension Review lesson (TE p. 369)

- Responding: Select from Activities (TE pp. 378–379)
- Information and Study Skills (TE p. 383H)
- Comprehension Skill: Second Comprehension Review lesson (TE p. 373)

TEACHER-LED

- Reread, review Comprehension Check (Practice Book p. 5).
- Preview Leveled Reader: Below Level (TE p. 383O), or read book from Leveled Bibliography (TE pp. 354E–354F). ✔

Partner or Individual Work

- Reread the Science Link (TE pp. 380–383).
- Complete Leveled Reader: Below Level (TE p. 383O), or read book from Leveled Bibliography (TE pp. 354E–354F).

TEACHER-LED

- Comprehension Skill: Reteaching lesson (TE p. R8)
- Preview, begin Leveled Theme Paperback: Below Level (TE pp. R2–R3), or read book from Leveled Bibliography (TE pp. 354E–354F). ✔

TEACHER-LED

- Teacher check-in: Assess progress (Challenge Handbook p. 30).
- Preview Leveled Reader: Above Level (TE p. 383Q), or read book from Leveled Bibliography (TE pp. 354E–354F). ✔

Individual Work

- Complete activity (Challenge Handbook p. 30).
- Complete Leveled Reader: Above Level (TE p. 383Q), or read book from Leveled Bibliography (TE pp. 354E–354F).

TEACHER-LED

- Evaluate activity and plan format for sharing (Challenge Handbook p. 30).
- Read Leveled Theme Paperback: Above Level (TE pp. R6–R7), or read book from Leveled Bibliography (TE pp. 354E–354F). ✔

Partner or Individual Work

- Complete Comprehension Check (Practice Book p. 5).
- Begin Leveled Reader: Language Support (TE p. 383R), or read book from Leveled Bibliography (TE pp. 354E–354F).

TEACHER-LED

- Reread the Science Link (TE pp. 380–383) ✔ and review Link Skill (TE p. 380).
- Complete Leveled Reader: Language Support (TE p. 383R), or read book from Leveled Bibliography (TE pp. 354E–354F). ✔

Partner or Individual Work

- Preview, begin book from Leveled Bibliography (TE pp. 354E–354F).

- Responding activities (TE pp. 378–379)
- Language Center activities (TE pp. 383M–383N)
- **Fluency Practice:** Reread *Lost Temple of the Aztecs*. ✔
- Activities relating to *Lost Temple of the Aztecs* at Education Place® www.eduplace.com

Turn the page for more independent activities.

FLEXIBLE GROUPS

Lost Temple of the Aztecs

Managing Flexible Groups 357D

Classroom Management

Assign these activities while you work with small groups.

Differentiated Instruction for Small Groups

- **Handbook for English Language Learners**, pp. 134–143

- **Extra Support Handbook**, pp. 130–139

Independent Activities

- Language Center, pp. 383M–383N

- Challenge/Extension Activities, Theme Resources, pp. R9, R15

- **Classroom Management Handbook**, Activity Masters CM4-1–CM4-4

- **Challenge Handbook**, pp. 30–31

Look for more activities in the Classroom Management Kit.

Social Studies

Leader Comparison Game

 👥 Pairs	🕐 30 minutes
Objective	Identify leaders from written descriptions.
Materials	Index cards

Study the descriptions and illustrations of Cortés and Moctezuma in *Lost Temple of the Aztecs*. Prepare a series of trait cards. Work with a partner.

- Write the name of one of the leaders on one side of an index card.

- On the other side, write one of his traits. Use the traits on the list below and others you think of on your own.

- Prepare several cards for each leader.

- Have your partner read a trait and then guess which leader it refers to.

Possible Traits
- age
- method of reaching a position of power
- leadership skills
- physical traits suggested in the illustrations

Writing

How Did Cortés See It?

 👤 Singles	🕐 30 minutes
Objective	Write a description.

Reread pages 372–375 of *Lost Temple of the Aztecs*. Then follow these steps:

- Review the tips about author's viewpoint below.

- Look for evidence of bias and assumption in the pages you reread.

- Write two to three paragraphs describing the same scene from Cortés's point of view.

Author's Viewpoint: Bias and Assumption
- Viewpoint is an author's attitude toward an individual, group, or issue.
- An author reveals bias by strongly favoring one side in a controversy and not including facts or arguments that support other positions.
- An assumption is a conclusion drawn about an individual, group, or issue, which is based on few or no facts.

Consider copying and laminating these activities for use in centers.

Technology

Aztec Engineering

Groups	🕐 60 minutes
Objective	Research and write about feats of Aztec engineering.
Materials	Reference sources, Internet

n page 365 of *Lost Temple of the Aztecs,* you read that the Aztecs uilt the city of Tenochtitlán on an and in the middle of a lake. esearch this and other feats of ztec technology. Consider choosing ne of the following sets of quesons to explore. Then, as a group, rite a summary of your findings.

What is a causeway? Why and how did the Aztecs build causeways?

What is a canal? How did the Aztecs build canals?

What were *chinampas*? How were they built? How were they related to the Aztecs' canals?

What are aqueducts? Why did the Aztecs need to build them?

What does it mean to irrigate crops?

What irrigation methods did the Aztecs use?

Art

Aztec Art

👤 Singles	🕐 30 minutes
Objective	Trace and color Aztec art.
Materials	Reference sources, Internet, tracing paper, colored pencils, markers

- Trace the stone carving of the Aztec moon goddess Coyolxauhqui shown on page 364 of *Lost Temple of the Aztecs.*

- Research how the Aztecs made these colors and whether specific colors had certain meanings.

- Using what you have learned about Aztec colors, color your tracing with colored pencils or markers.

Science

Digging the Ruins

👥 Pairs	🕐 45 minutes
Objective	Research and write a job description for an archaeologist.
Materials	Internet, encyclopedias, or other research sources

Archaeologists are scientists who study the remains of ancient civilizations. Reread pages 363–365 of *Lost Temple of the Aztecs* and research other sources to learn more about archaeologists. Then with a partner write a brief job description for an archaeologist. Include answers to these questions in your job description:

- Does an archaeologist's job usually require traveling? Explain.

- What is an archaeologist's typical work day like?

- What tools does he or she use?

- How do archaeologists make conclusions about their discoveries?

- What subjects do would-be archaeologists study in school?

Listening Comprehension

Building Background

Tell students that you are going to read aloud a nonfiction article about a sea explorer, Zheng He (jung huh), who lived in China long ago. Discuss what students know about other famous sea explorers.

Fluency Modeling

Explain that as you read aloud, you will be modeling fluent oral reading. Ask students to listen carefully to your phrasing and your expression, or tone of voice and emphasis.

COMPREHENSION SKILL

Author's Viewpoint: Bias and Assumption

Explain that an author's viewpoint reflects the author's attitude, values, or assumptions about the topic. Tell students that an assumption is something that is taken for granted as being true. Explain that bias is a strong feeling for or against something.

Purpose Setting Read the selection aloud, asking students to note clues showing the author's biases and assumptions about Zheng He as they listen. Then use the Guiding Comprehension questions to assess students' understanding. Reread the selection for clarification as needed.

Teacher Read Aloud

The Remarkable Voyages of Zheng He
by Amy Butler Greenfield

Cricket

❶ You probably know all about Christopher Columbus. Maybe you even know something about Ferdinand Magellan or Vasco da Gama. But have you ever heard of Zheng He (jung huh)?

Long before Columbus was born, Zheng He of China was sailing the oceans and exploring the globe. His record-breaking journeys took him all the way to Africa and back.

❷ He was by far the greatest navigator of his day—and yet few people outside China have ever heard of him.

Zheng He was born in Yunnan (YOON-nahn), now a province in southern China, in 1371. When he was still a young boy, Yunnan was invaded by a Chinese army. Zheng He was captured and sent to Nanjing, China's capital at the time. The officials there thought he showed great promise and introduced him into the imperial court. Eventually, Zheng He became a trusted adviser to the emperor, Yongle (yoong-LAW).

The emperor was a strong and ambitious ruler. He believed that China was the most powerful and accomplished country in the world, and in many ways he was right. China had fine silks and teas, great cities and a Great Wall. Its people had invented paper, fireworks, the printing press, the stirrup, and the wheelbarrow.

All this, however, did not satisfy Yongle. He wanted China to be even more impressive and powerful. He sent his armies into neighboring territories and ordered his advisers to build him a fleet so mighty that everyone who saw the ships would be awed by China's wealth and power.

By 1405, the emperor had 62 vessels, and he put them all under Zheng He's command. Then he ordered Zheng He to sail to countries near and far, proclaiming the might of China.

After leaving China, Zheng He first traveled to Java and Sumatra, two islands in the South China Sea. From there, his fleet ventured westward into the Indian Ocean. The fleet reached Ceylon (modern-day Sri Lanka) and India before returning to China in 1407.

On his next voyage (1407–1409), Zheng He sailed to Siam (now Thailand), and on his third voyage (1409–1411), he returned to Ceylon and India. The fleet split up for voyages between 1413 and 1415. Some squadrons went to the East Indies, while others traveled west thousands of miles to the Persian Gulf.

Zheng He's fleet went even farther on his next two voyages (1417–1419 and 1421–1422). While sending some squadrons to the East Indies again, he led others all the way to Africa. Records show that they traveled down the coast to Malindi, a city now in Kenya—a journey of some 8,000 miles! No fleet in recorded history had ever sailed so far before. And Zheng He covered the distance twice—once on the outward voyage and again when he returned to China.

Zheng He's voyages brought fame to China and forged many new alliances for the emperor, but back home many people were unhappy with him. They complained that his voyages were too expensive and that they served no real purpose. In their opinion, China already had everything it needed.

After Yongle died in 1424, the complaints against Zheng He grew stronger. It would be seven years before he was allowed to make another voyage, his seventh and final (1431–1433). His fleet visited many countries and explored more of the African coast, and on the way back to China, his squadrons covered the 1,600 miles between the Persian Gulf and India in only 22 days. But Zheng He became ill soon afterward. He died on the passage home, an explorer to the end.

Guiding Comprehension

1 **AUTHOR'S VIEWPOINT** How might including Zheng He in a list of famous explorers show how the author feels about the Chinese explorer? (Sample answer: The author feels that Zheng He should be counted as a great explorer as well.)

2 **AUTHOR'S VIEWPOINT** What does the sentence *He was by far the greatest navigator of his day* tell you about a possible author bias? (Sample answer: The author thinks Zheng He was great, so she will probably present mostly positive information about Zheng He.)

3 **AUTHOR'S VIEWPOINT** What information does the author include that shows that not everyone thought Zheng He was a great explorer? (Many people in China were unhappy with Zheng He.)

Discussion Options

Personal Response Have students discuss what they think is most interesting about Zheng He and his accomplishments.

⭐ **Connecting/Comparing** Ask students to discuss how well this article fits into a theme called *Discovering Ancient Cultures.*

English Language Learners

Supporting Comprehension

Invite students to share what they know about great explorers or historical figures from their parents' home country. Encourage them to compare what they know about these historical figures with what they have heard about Zheng He.

Building Background

Key Concept: Aztec Culture

Remind students that the selections in this theme tell about people who ruled nations hundreds of years ago. Explain that the next selection tells about the Aztecs, who ruled a great empire in Mexico five centuries ago. Use "Excavating an Aztec City" on Anthology pages 360–361 to build background and introduce key vocabulary.

- Have volunteers read aloud "Excavating an Aztec City."
- Have students study the photographs and timeline as they discuss Aztec art, customs, and skills.

Get Set to Read

Background and Vocabulary

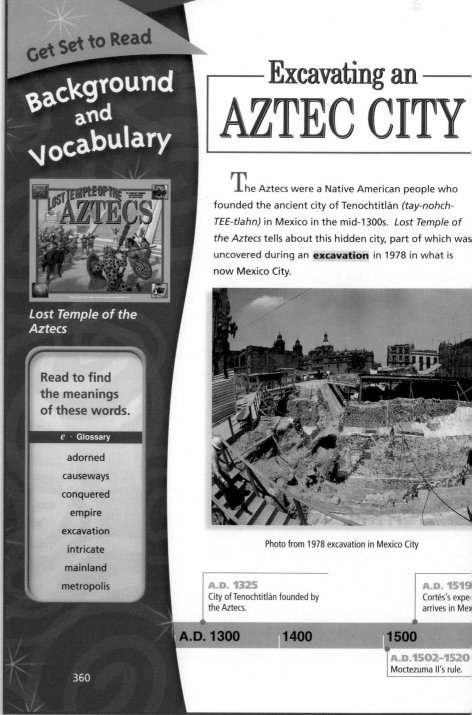

Lost Temple of the Aztecs

Read to find the meanings of these words.

e • Glossary

adorned
causeways
conquered
empire
excavation
intricate
mainland
metropolis

Excavating an AZTEC CITY

The Aztecs were a Native American people who founded the ancient city of Tenochtitlán (tay-nohch-TEE-tlahn) in Mexico in the mid-1300s. *Lost Temple of the Aztecs* tells about this hidden city, part of which was uncovered during an **excavation** in 1978 in what is now Mexico City.

Photo from 1978 excavation in Mexico City

A.D. 1325 City of Tenochtitlán founded by the Aztecs.		A.D. 1519 Cortés's expe arrives in Mex
A.D. 1300	**1400**	**1500**

A.D.1502–1520 Moctezuma II's rule.

360

English Language Learners

Supporting Comprehension

Beginning/Preproduction Have students listen to the article. Next, have them look at the excavation site on page 360 and point to artifacts on page 361. Then have them mime digging up an ancient artifact.

Early Production and Speech Emergence Have students repeat the Key Vocabulary words after you. Ask, What are the names of some ancient empires you know about? Would you like to go to a site where people are working to dig up artifacts? Why or why not?

Intermediate and Advanced Fluency In small groups, have students reread and then restate in their own words the information from the article.

The Aztecs worshipped many gods. This mask, made of gold and jade, represented the goddess of springs, rivers, lakes, and seas.

A turquoise and shell mosaic disc from the period A.D. 900–1521

During the rule of Moctezuma II (1502–1520), Tenochtitlán was the capital city of the Aztec **empire**. Tenochtitlán was a beautiful **metropolis** built on an island in Lake Texcoco. Long **causeways**, or raised roads over water, led from the **mainland** to the city, and the Great Temple rose from its center. The Aztecs began their empire with trading and later expanded when their warriors **conquered** neighboring groups.

Many artifacts were found when Tenochtitlán was discovered. These ranged from clay pots to jade and turquoise masks that were worn during festivals. The Aztec people also made **intricate** gold, silver, and platinum jewelry. Such jewels **adorned** only people of high status, like the ruler and his nobles.

An ornament worn as a mark of social status, made of gold and jade.

A.D. 1978
Workmen discover ancient moon goddess stone in Mexico City; excavation of Great Temple of the Aztecs begins.

| 1700 | 1800 | 1900 | 2000 |

361

Introducing Vocabulary

Key Vocabulary

These words support the Key Concept and appear in the selection.

adorned decorated

causeways raised roadways across water or marshlands

conquered defeated in battle

empire a large area made up of many territories under one government

intricate complicated; made up of many details

metropolis a major city; a center of culture

momentous extremely important

sites places where things are located

tributes gifts given to those in power by people who have been defeated or who want protection

 e • Glossary
e • WordGame

See Vocabulary notes on pages 362, 364, 368, 370, and 372 for additional words to preview.

Transparency 4–1

Words About the Aztec Empire

Welcome to the International Junior Archaeologists web site, your source for the latest word on the earliest civilizations!

- Do you want to learn about how Aztec rulers adorned themselves with jewelry and feathered headdresses?
- Would you like to see a map of Tenochtitlán, the metropolis built by the Aztecs in the middle of a lake?
- Are you interested in the design of the causeways that linked this great city with the surrounding lands?
- Do you want to see how far the Aztec empire extended?
- Would you like to view rare items given as tributes to Aztec rulers by Indian groups they conquered?
- Are you fascinated by the intricate work of ancient artists and craftsmen?
- Would you like to visit archaeological sites in other parts of Mexico?
- Would you like to learn more about the momentous meeting of Cortés and the Aztecs?

Click on the questions you answered yes to, or browse through the fascinating reports and features that follow. Be sure to visit this site often, because we are constantly posting updates on important excavations!

Practice Book page 3

Lost Temple of the Aztecs
Key Vocabulary

Name _____

In the Time of the Aztecs

Words are missing in the sentences. Fill each blank with a word from the box.

Vocabulary
intricate
sites
empire
conquered
momentous
adorned
metropolis
tributes
causeways

1. If you rule over many lands, you rule over an empire **(2 points)**

2. If your city is large, it is a metropolis **(2)** _____

3. If you travel on raised pathways across marshlands, you travel on causeways **(2)** _____.

4. If you have defeated another nation in a war and won control over it, you have conquered **(2)** that nation.

5. If a building has carvings that are carefully done and show great detail, it has intricate **(2)** carvings.

6. If you have decorated an emperor or empress with jewelry, you have adorned **(2)** _____ that person.

7. If you deliver valuable goods to a foreign ruler who holds control of your nation, you give tributes **(2)** _____ to that ruler.

8. If you visit several places where archaeologists have found relics, you have visited archaeological sites **(2)** _____

9. If you witness the first time two cultures meet, you witness a momentous **(2)** _____ event.

Display Transparency 4–1.

- Model figuring out the meaning of *adorned*, using context clues.

- Have students use letter sounds and context clues to figure out the remaining Key Vocabulary words. Have them explain how they figured out each word.

- Ask students to look for these words as they read and to use them as they discuss Aztec culture.

Practice/Homework Assign **Practice Book** page 3.

Introducing Vocabulary **361**

COMPREHENSION STRATEGY
Evaluate

Teacher Modeling Read aloud the Strategy Focus. Explain that students should form opinions about whether the author is doing a good job writing. Have students read the first three paragraphs on page 363. Then model the strategy.

Think Aloud *How does the author begin? First, she shows us modern Mexico City, and then she tells about the unexpected discovery of an ancient stone from the Great Aztec Temple. I think the author does a good job getting me interested quickly.*

✓ **Test Prep** Emphasize that tests can ask for students' opinions and that the Evaluate strategy can help answer these questions.

COMPREHENSION SKILL
Author's Viewpoint

Introduce the Graphic Organizer. Tell students that they will use the chart on **Practice Book** page 4 to recognize the author's viewpoint. Have them note the language used in the selection and the facts and opinions given.

- Display **Transparency 4–2.** Have students read page 365.
- Model the skill, using the first completed row. Monitor students' work as they complete the second row.

Vocabulary

intricate complicated; made up of many details

Selection I

LOST TEMPLE OF THE AZTECS

BY SHELLEY TANAKA
ILLUSTRATIONS
BY GREG RUHL

What it was like when the Spaniards invaded Mexico

362

Strategy Focus

In 1519 the Spanish arrived in Tenochtitlán, capital of the Aztec empire. As you read, **evaluate** how the author portrays Moctezuma, the Aztec leader, and Cortés, the Spanish leader.

Transparency 4–2

Author's Viewpoint Chart

Passage from Selection	Whom It Tells About	Viewpoint
"one of the most famous and tragic rulers in history" (page 365)	Moctezuma	positive
Should they be destroyed or treated as guests? Moctezuma decided to welcome the strangers. (page 365)	Moctezuma	positive
Moctezuma was filled with fear and confusion at these unnatural happenings. (page 370)	Moctezuma	rather negative
Cortés looked at everything they had given him. "Are these your gifts of welcome?" he asked. "Is this all you have brought?" (page 374)	Cortés	negative
Cortés ordered his men to fasten irons around the messengers' ankles and necks. (page 374)	Cortés	negative
"You will do as I say," said Cortés. (page 374)	Cortés	negative
A few months later Moctezuma, against the advice of his chiefs, welcomed Cortés and his army as friends. (page 375)	Moctezuma	negative
The next year the Spaniards seized treasure and attacked the Aztecs during a festival. (page 375)	Cortés	negative
In May 1521 Cortés returned to attack Tenochtitlán and claimed victory after leaving the city in ruins. (page 375)	Cortés	negative

---

Practice Book page 4

Name _____

Lost Temple of the Aztecs
Graphic Organizer Author's Viewpoint

Author's Viewpoint Chart

Passage from Selection	Whom It Tells About	Viewpoint
"one of the most famous and tragic rulers in history" (page 365)	Moctezuma	positive
Should they be destroyed or treated as guests? Moctezuma decided to welcome the strangers. (page 365)	Moctezuma (1 point)	positive (1)
Moctezuma was filled with fear and confusion at these unnatural happenings. (page 370)	Moctezuma (1)	rather negative (1)
Cortés looked at everything they had given him. "Are these your gifts of welcome?" he asked. "Is this all you have brought?" (page 374)	Cortés (1)	negative (1)
Cortés ordered his men to fasten irons around the messengers' ankles and necks. (page 374)	Cortés (1)	negative (1)
"You will do as I say," said Cortés. (page 374)	Cortés (1)	negative (1)
A few months later Moctezuma, against the advice of his chiefs, welcomed Cortés and his army as friends. (page 375)	Moctezuma (1)	negative (1)
The next year the Spaniards seized treasure and attacked the Aztecs during a festival. (page 375)	Cortés (1)	negative (1)
In May 1521 Cortés returned to attack Tenochtitlán and claimed victory after leaving the city in ruins. (page 375)	Cortés (1)	negative (1)

PROLOGUE
February 21, 1978

The zocalo was still dark. The trolley cars crossing the far corner of Mexico City's main square were not yet filled with people on their way to work. Between the cathedral and the presidential palace, workmen were digging ditches for electrical cables, anxious to beat the thick heat and pollution that would wrap around the city by midday.

Suddenly they struck something hard. It was a flat round stone covered with intricate, mysterious carvings.

A team of experts was called. They discovered that the giant disk, almost ten feet (three meters) in diameter, depicted Coyolxauhqui (coy-ohl-ZAH-kee), the ancient moon goddess. Further digging revealed that the stone lay at the foot of some buried steps. Beneath a block of stores and parking lots in the center of Mexico City, they had found the Great Temple of the Aztecs, the cornerstone of what was once the most powerful empire in North America.

Professor Eduardo Matos Moctezuma understood the excavation. He knew that he was witnessing the discovery of a lifetime. A graduate of the Mexican National School of Anthropology, he had long experience in excavating

Professor Eduardo Matos Moctezuma

❶

363

Extra Support/Intervention

Selection Preview

pages 362–367 In 1978, construction workers in Mexico City discovered an ancient buried temple. Five hundred years earlier, it had stood at the center of Tenochtitlán, a great Aztec city built in the middle of a lake.

pages 368–374 In 1519 a group of Spaniards, led by a man named Cortés, came to the realm of the Aztecs by ship. Neither the Aztecs nor their leader, Moctezuma, had seen Europeans before. They thought Cortés was a god and welcomed him with gifts of gold and jade. How do you think Cortés reacted to these gifts?

pages 375–376 The Spaniards overpowered the Aztecs and destroyed Tenochtitlán. Today only ancient artifacts remain of the Aztec empire.

Purpose Setting

- Have students read to find out what happened when the Spaniards and the Aztecs met each other.

- Have students preview the selection and predict what they might learn about Aztec culture.

- Invite students to stop every few pages and evaluate how clear and effective the author's writing is.

- Have students note details in the selection that show how the author feels about the Spaniards and the Aztecs.

- You may want to preview with students the Responding questions on Anthology page 378.

Journal ▶ Students can record the predictions and evaluations they make as they read.

STRATEGY REVIEW

Phonics/Decoding

Remind students to use the Phonics/Decoding strategy as they read.

Modeling Write this phrase on the board: *a headdress of shimmering blue-green quetzal feathers.* Point to *shimmering.*

Think Aloud *I see the letters sh at the beginning of this word and the ending -ing. I'll try dividing the first part of the word between the two m's. The first word part has the vowel i between consonants. I'll try pronouncing it with a short vowel sound, shim. The second syllable has m and er. I'll try pronouncing it mur. When I blend these syllables I get SHIHM-ur-ihng. I know that word, and it makes sense here.*

Reading the Selection 363

CRITICAL THINKING

Guiding Comprehension

❶ **MAKING INFERENCES** Why do you think the professor's find was *the discovery of a lifetime*? (Sample answers: Temple was a building of great importance, in what was once the most powerful empire in North America; Aztecs were his own ancestors.)

❷ **COMPARE AND CONTRAST** In what ways was Tenochtitlán like a modern city? In what ways was it different? (Sample answer: similarities: large population, large buildings, gardens; differences: Aztec city in the middle of a lake, no streets for motor vehicles)

❸ **AUTHOR'S VIEWPOINT** The author uses the word *remarkable* to describe Tenochtitlán. What does this tell you about her viewpoint? (positive word that shows she has a favorable opinion of the city)

The carvings on the great round stone show Coyolxauhqui, the Aztec moon goddess (*above*). An archaeologist carefully records discoveries at the excavation site in Mexico City (*left*).

364

Vocabulary

sites places where things are located

metropolis a major city; a center of culture

causeways raised roadways across water or marshlands

conquered defeated in battle

tributes gifts given to those in power by people who have been defeated or who want protection

REACHING ALL LEARNERS

English Language Learners

Supporting Comprehension

Familiarize students with the organization of the selection.

- Point out the prologue and the date, February 21, 1978.
- Help students find the subtitles heading each section.
- You may want to have students first read and discuss the sections "Who Were the Aztecs?" "The Aztec Year," "Who Was Cortés?" and "Who Was Moctezuma?" before they read the main body of the text.

Aztec sites. But his interest was more than professional. Through his mother's ancestors, his family tree led directly back to one of the most famous and tragic rulers in history. Long before the Europeans came to North America, a very different kind of metropolis stood on the spot where Mexico City is now. It was called Tenochtitlán (teh-NAWCH-tee-TLAHN), and it was the capital city of the Aztec empire.

Five hundred years ago, Tenochtitlán was a city of 250,000 people. It was built on an island in the middle of a sparkling blue lake. Canals crisscrossed the city between blocks of spotless white buildings and lush green gardens. Long causeways led to the mainland, where snowcapped mountains loomed in the distance.

②

The first Europeans who saw Tenochtitlán found the city so beautiful, they thought it must be enchanted.

The Great Temple stood at the heart of this remarkable city. Nine stories high, it faced a huge square surrounded by shrines and palaces. This was where the Aztecs worshipped their gods, where their conquered enemies brought gifts and tributes, and where the Aztec ruler Moctezuma received important guests.

❸

One fateful day in 1519, an unusual group of visitors approached Tenochtitlán. The Aztecs had never seen such people. Their skin was oddly white, their faces were covered with hair, and they wore metal clothing from head to foot. They came with strange, wild-eyed beasts, and they carried heavy weapons that clanked and gleamed in the sun.

Were they friends, or enemies? Should they be destroyed or treated as guests?

Moctezuma decided to welcome the strangers. After all, what could his mighty nation of warriors have to fear here, within the walls of their great city?

365

Fluency Practice

Rereading for Fluency Have students choose a favorite part of the selection to reread to a partner, or suggest that they read the last three paragraphs on page 365. Encourage students to read expressively.

Extra Support/Intervention

Time Shift

Direct students' attention to the first and second full paragraphs on page 365.

- Have a volunteer read these paragraphs aloud.
- Make sure students understand that here the author switches from talking about the discovery of the temple in modern times to discussing the Spanish conquest of the Aztec kingdom that happened many centuries earlier.

CRITICAL THINKING

Guiding Comprehension

4 **MAKING JUDGMENTS** Look at this illustration of Tenochtitlán. Do you think that this city would be easy or difficult for an enemy army to invade? Why? (Sample answers: easy, because an army could cut off the city's access to the mainland; difficult, because an army could not march or sail to the city without being seen)

366

English Language Learners

Language Development

Help students understand the following words and phrases from page 365.

● Point out *family tree* at the top of the page. Draw an example of a family tree.

● Point out *Canals crisscrossed the city* in the first full paragraph. Help students find the canals that crisscross the city in the illustration on pages 366–367.

● Point out *lush green* in the same paragraph. Show a photograph of something lush green, such as a rain forest.

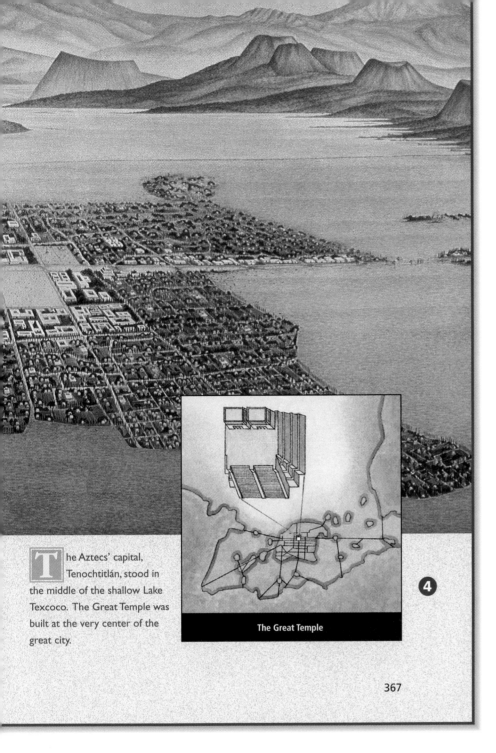

The Great Temple

4

The Aztecs' capital, Tenochtitlán, stood in the middle of the shallow Lake Texcoco. The Great Temple was built at the very center of the great city.

367

Extra Support/Intervention

Strategy Modeling: Evaluate

Use this example to model the strategy.

These pages show an artist's idea of how Tenochtitlán looked. I'll compare it to the author's description of the city on page 365. I see the lake, the island, the causeways, and the temple the author talked about. I think the author and illustrator have done a good job helping readers understand what the Aztec city looked like.

CRITICAL THINKING
Guiding Comprehension

⑤ MAKING INFERENCES What kind of animal are the *huge deer*? What does this phrase tell you about the Aztecs' experience with this kind of animal? (horses; Aztecs had never seen them before.)

⑥ MAKING JUDGMENTS Based on the author's description of Moctezuma, what kind of a person do you think he was? (Sample answers: smart, thoughtful, superstitious)

COMPREHENSION STRATEGY
Evaluate

Teacher/Student Modeling Help students to model evaluating the section "The Strangers Arrive." Use these prompts.

- How well does the author describe the Aztecs' first reactions to the Spaniards? (Sample answer: very well, because she shows how surprised the Aztecs were by the Spaniards' large ships and horses)

- How well does the author explain why Moctezuma believed Cortés was a god? (Sample answer: very well, because she explains that the Aztecs believed the god Quetzalcoatl would return on a boat and that Cortés arrives on a ship in the same year the god was supposed to return)

Vocabulary

momentous extremely important

368

Extra Support/Intervention

Strategy Modeling: Phonics/Decoding

Model the strategy for *mysterious*.

First I'll look for word parts I know. The beginning of the word looks like mystery. *I recognize the ending* -ous. *I'll try saying it:* MIHS-tuh-ree-uhs. *No, that can't be right. Adding the ending must have changed a vowel sound. I'll try using a long e sound:* mih-STEER-ee-uhs. *That's a word I know, and it makes sense in the sentence.*

mysterious
mih-STEER-ee-uhs

THE STRANGERS ARRIVE
April 1519

The ships came from the east. They just appeared on the horizon one day, as if they had dropped from the sky. They were bigger than any boats the people had ever seen, and they floated toward the shore like small mountains.

When Moctezuma's messengers saw the ships, they hurried back to Tenochtitlán.

"Strange people have come to the shores of the great sea," they told their ruler. "They have very light skin and long beards, and their hair only comes down to their ears. They sit on huge deer that carry them wherever they want to go." **5**

Moctezuma listened to the news in silence. His mind raced.

Quetzalcoatl (keht´-zahl-COH-ah-tul) has appeared! he thought. He has come back to reclaim his throne!

It was happening, just as the ancient prophecy had foretold. Long ago, according to legend, Quetzalcoatl, the great god of learning and creation, had sailed east on a raft of serpents to a mysterious land across the ocean. But he had promised to come back, and this was the predicted year of his return.

Moctezuma knew there had already been signs that things were not well with the gods, that some momentous change was about to come to his people. Two years before, a great tongue of fire had streaked across the night sky, like a spear plunged into the very heart **6**

An illustration from a Spanish book of the time shows Cortés's expedition coming ashore near what is today the city of Veracruz, Mexico.

369

Extra Support/Intervention

Sequence of Events

Help students create an informal timeline of events like the one shown below. They may use the timeline in the Get Set as a guide. Encourage students to add other dates to the timeline as they read on.

April 1519
Spaniards arrive.

1502
Moctezuma II
becomes emperor.

1978
Lost temple
discovered

Topic, Main Idea, and Details

Review

- Nonfiction writing is organized by topic, main ideas, and supporting details.

- The topic is what the selection is mostly about. The topic of this selection is the meeting of the Spanish and the Aztecs.

- Main ideas are the most important points made about the topic.

- Supporting details give more information about each main idea.

Practice

- Complete a chart of main ideas and supporting details from pages 369–370.

Main Idea Arrival of Spaniards

Supporting Details

- Aztecs think gods are unhappy.

- Strangers arrive on tall ships.

- Aztecs think god Quetzalcoatl has come.

Apply

- Have partners complete a similar chart for pages 372–375.

Review Skill Trace	
Teach	p. 427A
Reteach	p. R12
▶ Review	p. 369; Theme 2, p. 195; Theme 6, p. 601

CRITICAL THINKING
Guiding Comprehension

❼ CAUSE AND EFFECT Moctezuma thought several unusual events were warnings from Aztec gods. What other explanations could there be?

(Sample answers: *tongue of fire* in sky could be a comet; *boiling* lake could be underwater gases; *woman wailing* could be wind or animals)

of the heavens. At dawn, the sun destroyed the fire, but the next night it appeared again. And so it went on for the better part of a year, and each night the people watched with terror. Would the sun, the source of all life, continue to destroy the fire? Might the sun one day stop rising?

❼ There were other signs of death and ruin. Temples burst into flames. The great lake that surrounded Tenochtitlán swirled and bubbled up as if it were boiling with rage. The nights echoed with the sound of a woman wailing.

Moctezuma was filled with fear and confusion at these unnatural happenings. The gods must be looking unfavorably on the richest and most powerful empire in the land.

And now, it seemed, one of the gods had returned. Quetzalcoatl had arrived.

WHO WERE THE AZTECS?

By the time Cortés arrived in 1519, the Aztecs ruled a great empire in what is now Mexico (*below and inset*). Originally from a land farther north called Aztlán, they arrived on the shores of Lake Texcoco in the fourteenth century. But the people living there wouldn't let them settle. So they created their city right in the lake, on rocky outcroppings and shallow marshes.

(According to legend, the Aztecs' priests had a vision of an eagle eating a snake atop a cactus (*below, right*) and, where they saw the eagle, they built their capital. Today the eagle on a cactus is part of the Mexican flag.) The Aztecs traded with people around the lake, and grew richer. Later, they expanded, creating an empire by defeating their neighbors in war.

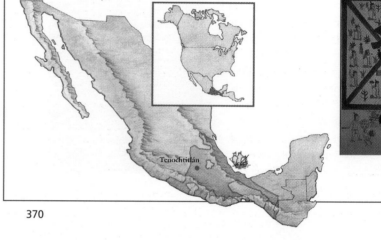

Tenochtitlán

370

Extra Support/Intervention

Review (pages 362–371)

Before students who need extra support join the whole class for Stop and Think on page 371, have them

- review their purpose/predictions
- take turns modeling Evaluate and other strategies they used
- help you add to **Transparency 4–2**
- check and revise their Author's Viewpoint Charts on **Practice Book** page 4, and use them to summarize

Vocabulary

empire a large area made up of many territories under one government

THE AZTEC YEAR

The Aztec calendar was shown as a round disk (*above*), since the Aztecs saw time as being like a wheel, endlessly turning. Each day had a name (rain, crocodile, rabbit, and so forth) and a number from 1 to 13. Every 13 days a new month began, and there were 20 months in the Aztec year — which was only 260 days long. The Aztecs also had a 365-day calendar, which they used to keep track of their many religious cere-monies. Once every 52 years, the first day of the 260-day calendar and the first day of the 365-day calendar were the same. This marked the start of a new "century" or cycle, a very important time in the Aztec world. By coincidence, according to the Aztec calendar, the year Cortés landed happened to be the year given for the possible return of Quetzalcoatl.

371

ASSIGNMENT CARD 2

Literature Discussion

Discuss the following questions and questions of your own with a group of your classmates:

- What is the author's viewpoint toward Moctezuma? Do you agree that he should be viewed this way? Why or why not?

- Do you think Moctezuma acted sensibly in deciding that Cortés was Quetzalcoatl? Why or why not?

- What surprised or interested you about the Aztec civilization?

- What do you think it would have been like to live in Tenochtitlán?

Theme 4: Discovering Ancient Cultures

Stop and Think

Critical Thinking Questions

1. **MAKING INFERENCES** What do you think Cortés's intentions were when he landed at Tenochtitlán? (to see if the Aztecs had treasures he could steal)

2. **DRAWING CONCLUSIONS** What do Moctezuma's reactions to Cortés's arrival suggest about the importance of religion in Aztec culture? (It was very important. People believed in the power of their gods.)

Strategies in Action

Have students take turns modeling Evaluate and other strategies they used.

Discussion Options

You may want to bring the entire class together to do one or more of the activities below.

- **Review Predictions/Purpose** Have students review their predictions about Aztec culture and discuss what they have learned. Have them discuss what they know so far about the Aztecs' and Spaniards' first encounter.

- **Share Group Discussions** Have students share their literature discussions.

- **Summarize** Have students use their Author's Viewpoint Charts to summarize the selection so far.

Monitoring Student Progress

If . . .	Then . . .
students have successfully completed the Extra Support activities on page 370,	have them read the rest of the selection cooperatively or independently.

Reading the Selection 371

CRITICAL THINKING
Guiding Comprehension

8 **MAKING INFERENCES** Why do you think Moctezuma wanted to offer Quetzalcoatl gifts? (Sample answer: so the god wouldn't be angry at them)

9 **WRITER'S CRAFT** Why do you think the author includes the sentence *Surely he was Quetzalcoatl himself!*? (It shows what the messengers were thinking about Cortés.)

July 1519

8 Moctezuma gathered his chiefs around him. "Our lord, Quetzalcoatl, has arrived at last. Hurry to meet him. Tell him that his servant Moctezuma has sent you to welcome him back to his throne, and take him these gifts."

Moctezuma's messengers traveled to the coast. They placed their gifts in canoes and paddled out to where the huge ships floated offshore. The pale-skinned strangers let down a ladder, and the messengers climbed on board. They were taken to the leader, whom the strangers called Cortés. Surely he was Quetzalcoatl himself!

9 The messengers kissed the deck at Cortés's feet. "We bring these gifts from your servant Moctezuma," they told him. "He guards over your kingdom and keeps it safe for your return." Then they adorned Cortés with a serpent mask made of turquoise and a headdress of shimmering blue-green quetzal feathers.

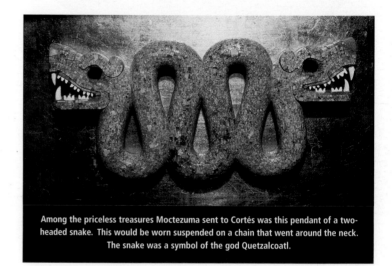

Among the priceless treasures Moctezuma sent to Cortés was this pendant of a two-headed snake. This would be worn suspended on a chain that went around the neck. The snake was a symbol of the god Quetzalcoatl.

372

Vocabulary

adorned decorated

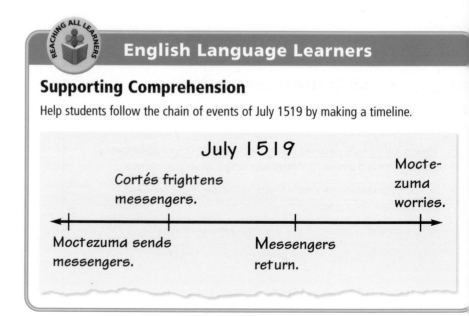

English Language Learners

Supporting Comprehension

Help students follow the chain of events of July 1519 by making a timeline.

July 1519

Cortés frightens messengers.

Moctezuma worries.

Moctezuma sends messengers.

Messengers return.

373

Categorize and Classify

Review

- A category is a group of people, animals, or things that are alike.

- To classify means to put similar items in categories.

- Tell students that they can classify the things Cortés brought.

- Draw a two-column chart on the board. Write the heads *Protective Equipment* and *Weapons*. Explain that these heads are categories.

- Ask, Where does armor belong? (Protective Equipment) Explain that placing an item in a category is classifying.

Protective Equipment	Weapons
armor	swords
helmets	guns
shields	

Practice/Apply

- Work with students to complete the chart as shown above.

- Have partners categorize and classify other things that Cortés brought. (Sample answer: Means of Transportation; horses, ships)

- Compare answers as a class.

Review Skill Trace	
Teach	Theme 6, p. 615A
Reteach	Theme 6, p. R12
▶ Review	p. 373; Theme 6, p. 561

Extra Support/Intervention

Strategy Modeling: Evaluate

Use this example to model the strategy.

At first I felt confused by page 372. The author includes direct quotations from Moctezuma and his messengers. How can she know exactly what they said so long ago? When I thought about it, I realized that the author uses these quotations to show the Aztecs' thoughts and beliefs. The quotations help me understand the Aztecs. I think the author made a good choice to show their feelings in this way.

Reading the Selection 373

CRITICAL THINKING
Guiding Comprehension

10 MAKING INFERENCES Why do you think Cortés fired his gun for the Aztec messengers? (Sample answers: to frighten them; to show his power)

11 TEXT ORGANIZATION How can you tell that the biographical information about Cortés and Moctezuma is not part of the main text? (set off from main text in a shaded box; gives additional information, rather than continuing the story)

TARGET SKILL
COMPREHENSION STRATEGY
Evaluate

Student Modeling Ask students to model evaluating how well the author described the encounter between the Aztec messengers and the Spaniards. You might offer these prompts:

- Did the author's description make these events seem exciting? If so, what did she do that created a sense of excitement?

- Do you think the author could have made these events more realistic? If so, what could she have added?

They draped gold and jade bands around his neck, arms, and legs. They placed a cape of ocelot skin and sandals of glistening black obsidian at his feet, along with the other gifts — serpent-head staffs and spears inlaid with green jade, masks, shields, and fans heavy with gold and turquoise.

Cortés looked at everything they had given him. "Are these your gifts of welcome?" he asked. "Is this all you have brought?"

"Yes, lord," the messengers replied. "This is everything."

Cortés ordered his men to fasten irons around the messengers' ankles and necks. Then he fired a huge gun. The messengers had never seen such a sight. They fainted from fear and fell to the deck.

The strangers revived them.

WHO WAS CORTÉS?

Hernan Cortés was a Spanish landowner who lived on the island of Cuba, which had been visited by Columbus in 1492 and then taken over by the Spanish. Like many men who had moved to the New World, Cortés dreamed of grasping a fortune for himself. With official backing from the governor of Cuba and using some of his own money, Cortés put together an expedition. The governor withdrew his official support, but Cortés left anyway, gambling on the success of his venture.

374

"I have heard about your people," Cortés said. "They say that one Aztec warrior can overpower twenty men. I want to see how strong you are." He gave them leather shields and iron swords. "Tomorrow, at dawn, you will fight, and then we will find out the truth."

"But this is not the wish of our lord and your servant, Moctezuma," the messengers answered. "He has only told us to greet you and bring you gifts."

"You will do as I say," said Cortés. "Tomorrow morning we shall eat. After that you will prepare for combat."

Then Cortés released them. Moctezuma's messengers got back in their boats and paddled away as quickly as they could. Some even paddled with their hands. When they reached land they scarcely stopped to catch their breath before hurrying back to Tenochtitlán to tell Moctezuma about the terrifying things that had happened.

WHO WAS MOCTEZUMA?

Moctezuma was the ninth Aztec emperor or *tlatoani*, an Aztec term that meant "speaker." He was the second ruler to bear the name Moctezuma. He had become emperor in 1502, picked, in the Aztec fashion, by the other nobles. Moctezuma was a little older than Cortés, thirty-eight to the Spaniard's thirty-three.

375

Comprehension Preview

Author's Viewpoint

Teach

- An author's viewpoint is his or her attitude toward a particular individual, group, or issue.

- An author is biased if he or she includes facts that favor only one side in a controversy.

Practice

- Work with students to create a chart like the one shown below.

- Ask, Whom do you think the author likes better, the Aztecs or the Spaniards? Why? (the Aztecs; She makes them seem less warlike and more generous.)

Aztecs' Reactions to Spaniards	Cortés's Behavior Toward Aztecs
welcome Cortés	demands more gifts
bring gifts	puts messengers in irons
faint when gun is fired	fires gun
don't want to fight	wants to fight

Apply

- Have partners find other examples of bias in the selection. Discuss responses.

Target Skill Trace	
Preview; Teach	p. 359A, p. 362, p. 375; p. 383A
Reteach	p. R8
Review	pp. M32–M33; Theme 6, p. 555

Reading the Selection 375

Guiding Comprehension

⑫ WRITER'S CRAFT Why do you think the author chose to end this segment with the sentence *When Moctezuma heard all this, he could not sleep or eat*? (It shows how concerned Moctezuma was about the messengers' report.)

⑬ TEXT ORGANIZATION What information does the summary give that is not included in the main selection? (It explains how Cortés was able to conquer the Aztec city.)

They described the strange sweet food they had eaten and the gun that had sounded to them like deafening thunder.

"A ball of stone comes out shooting sparks and raining fire. It makes smoke that smells of rotten mud. When the ball of stone hits a tree, the trunk splits into splinters, as if it has exploded from the inside.

"They cover their heads and bodies with metal. Their swords are metal, their bows are metal, their shields and spears are metal. Their deer carry them on their backs, making them as tall as the roof of a house."

⑫ When Moctezuma heard all this, he could not sleep or eat.

⑬ A few months later Moctezuma, against the advice of his chiefs, welcomed Cortés and his army as friends. The next year the Spaniards seized treasure and attacked the Aztecs during a festival. After retreating from the Aztecs, the Spaniards escaped. Moctezuma died during the fighting. Smallpox, a disease brought by the Europeans, killed thousands of Tenochtitlán's inhabitants. In May 1521 Cortés returned to attack Tenochtitlán and claimed victory after leaving the city in ruins.

376

REACHING ALL LEARNERS

Extra Support/Intervention	On Level	Challenge

Selection Review

Before students join in Wrapping Up on page 377, have them

- review their purpose/predictions
- take turns modeling Evaluate and other strategies they used
- complete their Author's Viewpoint Charts and help you complete **Transparency 4–2**
- summarize the whole selection

Literature Discussion

Have small groups of students discuss their questions and predictions. They may also discuss the Think About the Selection questions on Anthology page 378.

MEET THE AUTHOR SHELLEY TANAKA

Shelley Tanaka grew up in Toronto, Canada, and attended university in Canada and Germany. She is the author of the "I Was There" series including *The Buried City of Pompeii*, *Discovering the Iceman*, *On Board the Titanic*, and *Secrets of the Mummies*. For more than twenty years she has been an editor of young adult and children's books. She currently lives in rural Ontario, Canada, with her family.

MEET THE ILLUSTRATOR GREG RUHL

Greg Ruhl is also a native Canadian. He graduated from the Ontario College of Art and has worked as a freelance illustrator in Canada for nearly twenty years. Ruhl worked previously with Shelley Tanaka on *The Buried City of Pompeii*.

To find out more about Shelley Tanaka and Greg Ruhl, visit Education Place.
www.eduplace.com/kids

Wrapping Up

Critical Thinking Questions

1. **COMPARE AND CONTRAST** Describe how Moctezuma and Cortés were similar and how they were different. (Sample answers: similar: both were powerful men; different: Moctezuma led an empire, Cortés an expedition.)

2. **MAKING JUDGMENTS** Do you think the author did a good job of describing the events that led to the downfall of the Aztecs? (Answers will vary.)

Strategies in Action

Have students take turns modeling how and where they used the Evaluate strategy.

Discussion Options

Bring the entire class together to do one or more of the activities below.

Review Predictions/Purpose Ask students to discuss what they learned about the Aztecs and what happened when they first met the Spaniards.

Share Group Discussions Have students share their literature discussions.

Summarize Have students use their Author's Viewpoint Charts to help them summarize the selection.

Comprehension Check

Use **Practice Book** page 5 to assess students' comprehension of the selection.

Monitoring Student Progress

If . . .	Then . . .
students score 8 or below on **Practice Book** page 5,	help them find places in the text that describe the Spaniards and the Aztecs.

Responding

READ & COMPREHEND

Think About the Selection

Have students discuss or write their answers. Sample answers are provided; accept reasonable responses.

1. **MAKING INFERENCES** They realized they had discovered something important from an ancient civilization.

2. **MAKING JUDGMENTS** no, because the strangers were hostile and dangerous

3. **DRAWING CONCLUSIONS** He was cruel and was only interested in riches.

4. **EXPRESSING PERSONAL OPINIONS** Answers will vary.

5. **NOTING DETAILS** great city in a difficult-to-reach location; advanced calendar; conquered many peoples and ruled a great empire

6. **MAKING JUDGMENTS** yes, because they provide clues to what life was like in ancient civilizations

7. **Connecting/Comparing** The Aztecs were great builders, ruled a large empire, used an advanced calendar, and had strong religious beliefs. Their civilization was destroyed by Cortés and his troops in 1521.

Responding

Think About the Selection

1. Why did the men working on the electrical cables notify archaeological experts as soon as they discovered the carved stone?

2. Do you think Moctezuma's decision to treat the strangers as friends was a good one? Explain.

3. What does Cortés's treatment of the Aztec messengers reveal about him?

4. What do you think is the most exciting discovery that the archaeologists made while excavating the Great Temple? Explain.

5. The Aztec empire was one of the most advanced and powerful civilizations of its time. What details in the selection support this statement?

6. In your opinion, is it important to preserve artifacts from ancient cities such as Tenochtitlán? Why or why not?

7. **Connecting/Comparing** By reading *Lost Temple of the Aztecs*, what did you discover about the Aztec culture?

Expressing

Write a Letter

Write a letter to a friend describing the Aztec messengers who greeted Cortés. Also describe the gifts they brought with them.

Tips

- Look at the illustrations to help you describe the the messengers.
- Include vivid details in your description.
- Remember to include a date, a greeting, and a closing in your letter.

378

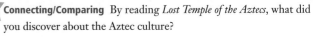

English Language Learners

Supporting Comprehension

Beginning/Preproduction Have students draw what happened to Moctezuma's messengers on Cortés's ship.

Early Production and Speech Emergence Have partners write three sentences about whether they think it was good or bad that Moctezuma treated Cortés as a friend.

Intermediate and Advanced Fluency Have students work in small groups to find details that show the Aztecs were an advanced culture.

Math

Calculate Your Aztec Age

Read the section on the Aztec year on page 371. Then, with a partner, calculate each other's ages in the Aztec 260-day calendar. Make a class chart listing all your classmates' ages in the 260-day Aztec calendar and in our 365-day calendar.

Bonus Calculate how many Aztec cycles, or "centuries," have passed since Cortés's arrival in Tenochtitlán.

	Age in 260-day calendar	Age in 365-day calendar
Bill		
Sara		
Tasha		
Jeremy		

Listening and Speaking

Role-Play a Scene

In a small group, role-play the scene in which the Aztec messengers board Cortés's ship, or the scene in which the messengers report their encounter with Cortés to Moctezuma.

Tips

- Use details from the selection to make the characters' dialogue seem real.
- Speak clearly and use gestures to enliven your performance.

Internet

Post a Review

What did you think of *Lost Temple of the Aztecs*? Would you recommend it to other readers? To post your review, visit Education Place. **www.eduplace.com/kids**

379

Additional Responses

Personal Response Invite students to share their personal responses to the selection.

Journal ▶ Ask students to write in their journals about something that interests them in Aztec culture.

Selection Connections Remind students to add to **Practice Book** pages 1–2.

Practice Book page 1

Name _____

Discovering Ancient Cultures

The selections in this theme will take you on a journey to the world of long ago. After reading each selection, complete the chart below to show what you learned.

	What is the location of the culture described in the selection?	When did the events described in the selection take place?
Lost Temple of the Aztecs	Mexico	in the early 1500s
The Great Wall	China	toward the end of the Ming dynasty, from about 1600–1800
The Royal Kingdoms of Ghana, Mali, and Songhay	Africa	in the eleventh century A.D.

Practice Book page 2

Name _____

Discovering Ancient Cultures

	What was remarkable about the culture described in the selection?
Lost Temple of the Aztecs	The Aztecs built huge temples and beautiful cities. They were fierce, powerful warriors. They were expert jewelers and they had a very accurate calendar.
The Great Wall	The Chinese built an immense wall of pounded earth and stone. It is the longest structure ever built.
The Royal Kingdoms of Ghana, Mali, and Songhay	The people of ancient Ghana were prosperous. They traded with people far away for exotic items. Gold was plentiful, and many people were wealthy. Even the farmers lived well.

What have you learned about ancient cultures in this theme?
Sample answer: Ancient cultures were very different from one another; people long ago created incredible things.

Monitoring Student Progress

End-of-Selection Assessment

Selection Test Use the test on page 131 of the **Teacher's Resource Blackline Masters** to assess selection comprehension and vocabulary.

Student Self-Assessment Have students assess their reading with additional questions such as these:

- Which parts of this selection were difficult? Why?
- What strategies helped me understand the selection?
- Would I like to read more about the Aztec empire? Why or why not?

Science Link

Skill: How to Adjust Your Rate of Reading

- **Introduce** "Raising Royal Treasures," a nonfiction science article from *Time for Kids* magazine.

- **Discuss** the Skill Lesson on Anthology page 380. Tell students that adjusting how quickly or how slowly they read can help them get the most out of their reading.

- **Explain** that students can slow down their reading to understand a difficult article. Tell students that sometimes they may want to look quickly through an article for a particular piece of information.

- **Model** identifying a purpose for reading this article, using the introduction on page 380. Explain that this article contains a lot of information that you want to understand clearly. Ask students how they would adjust their reading rate for this purpose. (read at slower pace)

- **Review** with students what they know about Cleopatra and about ancient Egypt.

- **Set additional purposes** for reading. Tell students to read to find out how the lost palace was discovered, what treasures it has yielded, and what these artifacts reveal about Cleopatra and ancient Egypt. Remind them to use Evaluate and other strategies.

Vocabulary

sphinx (pl. sphinxes) a mythical creature often represented as having the head of a human and the body of a lion

Science Link

Skill: How to Adjust Your Rate of Reading

Before you read . . .

Identify the **purpose** of your reading. For example, are you studying for a test? Are you reading for pleasure? Your purpose will determine your reading rate.

As you read . . .

- Keep in mind the purpose of your reading.

- Stop occasionally to **monitor** your understanding. Ask yourself **questions** about your reading. If you don't understand the material, slow down. If the material is easy to understand, speed up your rate.

- Remember that it often helps to read nonfiction more slowly than fiction.

380

RAISING ROYAL TREASURES

Bit by bit, divers are recovering pieces of Cleopatra's lost palace.

It's a tale full of romance, sneaky tricks, tragedy and, most of all, girl power. On top of that, it's true. The real-life story of Cleopatra, a beautiful 17-year-old girl when she became the powerful ruler of ancient Egypt, has fascinated people for thousands of years. Dozens of plays, books and movies have told of her quest for power and love. Now new information about Cleopatra's life is coming to the surface. Parts of her ancient royal court have been found near Alexandria, Egypt — under water!

Finding a Lost Island

Ancient Egyptian writings and drawings show that Cleopatra owned a royal palace on an island named Antirhodos (An-teer-*uh*-dose). The island was near Alexandria, the capital city of Egypt during Cleopatra's reign in the first century B.C.

English Language Learners

Preview the link with students.

- Have students look at the pictures of divers on pages 381 and 383.

- Make sure that students understand that these divers are archaeologists and that they are recovering objects that have been buried underwater.

- Discuss the photograph on page 382. Point out that this statue is being taken out of the water.

Although the city of Alexandria still exists today, floods and earthquakes buried Antirhodos under water more than 1,600 years ago. But it wasn't lost for good. In 1996 undersea explorer Franck Goddio found it beneath just 18 feet of water, off the shore of Alexandria. The ruins of what appears to be Cleopatra's palace lay buried in layers of mud, seaweed and garbage.

Goddio and his team of divers have spent two years uncovering statues, columns, pavement and pottery that may have belonged to the young queen. Their work is sponsored in part by the Discovery Channel, which broadcast a television special on the new findings.

Among the most sensational finds are two statues of sphinxes, imaginary creatures with the head of a human and the body of a lion. The faces of the sphinxes are in surprisingly good shape. So good, that experts have been able to identify one face as that of King Ptolemy (*Tall*-uh-mee) XII, Cleopatra's father.

How does it feel to come face to face underwater with an ancient sphinx? "It's fascinating!" Goddio told *Time for Kids*. "You see the sphinx, and it's looking at you. You know that it's the father of Cleopatra and that Cleopatra once saw it. It's like a dream."

A diver prepares an ancient stone for cleaning.

Extra Support/Intervention

Educated Guesses

Point out that the writer uses terms such as *probably*, *what appears to be*, and *may have belonged* to show uncertainty about the objects recovered.

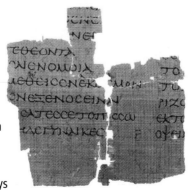

- Explain that sometimes scientists need to study artifacts very carefully before they can be sure what they were or how they were used.

- Tell students that even experts cannot always be sure what objects from an ancient civilization may have been used for.

- When they aren't sure, experts often develop theories, or educated guesses, about what these artifacts were used for.

Magazine Articles

Teach

- Magazines are called periodicals because they are published regularly—often weekly, monthly, or several times a year.

- A magazine usually focuses on a particular area of interest.

Practice

- Ask, What magazine did "Raising Royal Treasures" appear in? (*Time for Kids*) What is the focus or subject of that magazine? (news, current events)

- Have partners discuss magazines they enjoy reading. Have them identify the area of interest each magazine focuses on.

- Discuss what kinds of magazines could be useful for doing research. (magazines about current events, social studies, science, or health)

Apply

- Have students go to the library to find more magazine articles about ancient Egypt.

- Have them share what they discover with the class. Ask them to describe the magazines that they used.

Even without a head, this statue is huge! It was probably made to honor an Egyptian king.

One Queen, Two Love Stories

Cleopatra and her brother Ptolemy XIII began to rule Egypt together in 51 B.C. But Ptolemy did not want to share the throne, and he forced Cleopatra out of the palace.

During this time, another great civilization was rising to power in Rome. Its main leader, Julius Caesar (*See-zer*), traveled to Egypt. In order to meet with him, Cleopatra is said to have sneaked into the palace rolled up in a carpet! Caesar soon fell in love with Cleopatra. He helped her push Ptolemy aside and take control of Egypt.

Romans were angered by Caesar's ties with Egypt's queen. Some feared that he had grown too powerful. Four years after meeting Cleopatra, Caesar was murdered by his enemies.

Three years passed before a new Roman leader, Mark Antony, met Cleopatra. Just like Caesar before him, Antony fell in love with her. He moved into Cleopatra's palace at Antirhodos.

Soon people back in Rome feared that Antony was more interested in Egypt than in his own empire. They turned against him and Egypt. In despair, Cleopatra and Antony took their own lives. Ancient Egypt's last queen died at the age of 39. Soon after her death, the Romans took control of Egypt.

Though her reign ended 2,000 years ago, Cleopatra continues to enchant people everywhere. For that reason, Goddio hopes to set up an underwater museum at the palace site. Visitors would be able to explore and experience Cleopatra's world up close. "To be there, underwater where she reigned and died," says Goddio, "is unbelievable."

382

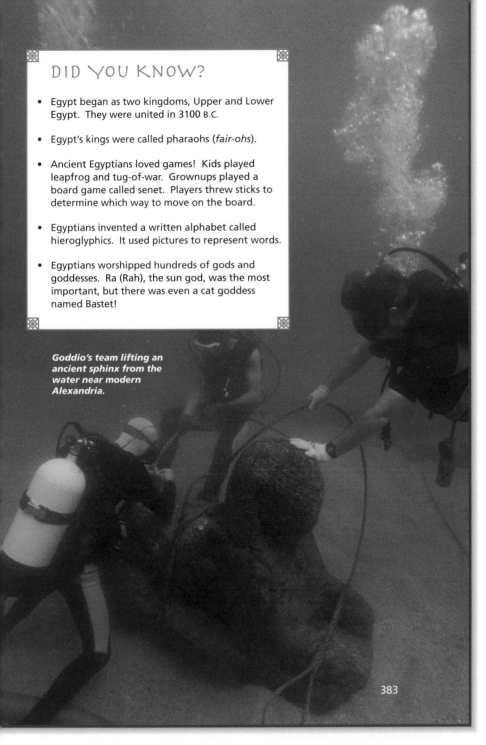

DID YOU KNOW?

- Egypt began as two kingdoms, Upper and Lower Egypt. They were united in 3100 B.C.

- Egypt's kings were called pharaohs (*fair-ohs*).

- Ancient Egyptians loved games! Kids played leapfrog and tug-of-war. Grownups played a board game called senet. Players threw sticks to determine which way to move on the board.

- Egyptians invented a written alphabet called hieroglyphics. It used pictures to represent words.

- Egyptians worshipped hundreds of gods and goddesses. Ra (Rah), the sun god, was the most important, but there was even a cat goddess named Bastet!

Goddio's team lifting an ancient sphinx from the water near modern Alexandria.

383

Challenge

Researching Ancient Empires

Have students search for more information about ancient Egypt or ancient Rome.

- Have them read additional articles or books about Cleopatra, Julius Caesar, or Mark Antony.

- Encourage them to find out how people dressed and adorned themselves in Cleopatra's time.

- Extend the activity by having students dress in costume and present a monologue or dialogue to the class about someone famous from this time period.

Wrapping Up

Critical Thinking Questions

Ask students to use the article to answer these questions.

1. **CAUSE AND EFFECT** Why did Cleopatra's palace remain undiscovered for so long? (Its site was flooded long ago. It was covered by mud, seaweed, and garbage.)

2. **NOTING DETAILS** What have the divers discovered so far? (statues, columns, pottery, pavement)

3. **MAKING INFERENCES** Why do you think people have been so fascinated with Cleopatra over the centuries? (Sample answer: She was an extremely powerful woman ruler in a time when most rulers were men. Two of the greatest Roman emperors fell in love with her.)

4. **DRAWING CONCLUSIONS** Why do you think the author included information about Julius Caesar and Mark Antony? (to show that powerful rulers were interested in Cleopatra and her empire)

5. **Connecting/Comparing** In what ways is the find described in this article similar to the discovery described at the beginning of *Lost Temple of the Aztecs?* In what ways is it different? (Sample answers: similar, because both are important ancient buildings, associated with famous leaders who died tragic deaths; different, because Cleopatra's palace was located by an explorer searching for it, while the Great Temple of the Aztecs was discovered by accident)

OBJECTIVES

- Identify an author's viewpoint or attitude.
- Identify statements in the selection that reveal the author's viewpoint.
- Determine whether an author shows bias in a selection.
- Learn academic language: *viewpoint, bias, assumption.*

Target Skill Trace

Preview; Teach	p. 359A, p. 362, p. 375; p. 383A
Reteach	p. R8
Review	pp. M32–M33; Theme 6, p. 555
See	*Extra Support Handbook,* pp. 132–133; pp. 138–139

Transparency 4–2

Author's Viewpoint Chart

Passage from Selection	Whom It Tells About	Viewpoint
"one of the most famous and tragic rulers in history" (page 365)	Moctezuma	positive
Should they be destroyed or treated as guests? Moctezuma decided to welcome the strangers. (page 365)	Moctezuma	positive
Moctezuma was filled with fear and confusion at these unnatural happenings. (page 370)	Moctezuma	rather negative
Cortés looked at everything they had given him. "Are these your gifts of welcome?" he asked. "Is this all you have brought?" (page 374)	Cortés	negative
Cortés ordered his men to fasten irons around the messengers' ankles and necks. (page 374)	Cortés	negative
"You will do as I say," said Cortés. (page 374)	Cortés	negative
A few months later Moctezuma, against the advice of his chiefs, welcomed Cortés and his army as friends. (page 375)	Moctezuma	negative
The next year the Spaniards seized treasure and attacked the Aztecs during a festival. (page 375)	Cortés	negative
In May 1521 Cortés returned to attack Tenochtitlán and claimed victory after leaving the city in ruins. (page 375)	Cortés	negative

Practice Book page 4

Name _____

Author's Viewpoint Chart

Passage from Selection	Whom It Tells About	Viewpoint
"one of the most famous and tragic rulers in history" (page 365)	Moctezuma	positive
Should they be destroyed or treated as guests? Moctezuma decided to welcome the strangers. (page 365)	Moctezuma (1 point)	positive (1)
Moctezuma was filled with fear and confusion at these unnatural happenings. (page 370)	Moctezuma (1)	rather negative (1)
Cortés looked at everything they had given him. "Are these your gifts of welcome?" he asked. "Is this all you have brought?" (page 374)	Cortés (1)	negative (1)
Cortés ordered his men to fasten irons around the messengers' ankles and necks. (page 374)	Cortés (1)	negative (1)
"You will do as I say," said Cortés. (page 374)	Cortés (1)	negative (1)
A few months later Moctezuma, against the advice of his chiefs, welcomed Cortés and his army as friends. (page 375)	Moctezuma (1)	negative (1)
The next year the Spaniards seized treasure and attacked the Aztecs during a festival. (page 375)	Cortés (1)	negative (1)
In May 1521 Cortés returned to attack Tenochtitlán and claimed victory after leaving the city in ruins. (page 375)	Cortés (1)	negative (1)

COMPREHENSION: Author's Viewpoint

TARGET SKILL

❶ Teach

Review the author's viewpoint in *Lost Temple of the Aztecs*
Remind students that viewpoint is the way an author thinks or feels about his or her subject. Complete the Graphic Organizer on **Transparency 4–2** with students. (Sample answers are shown.) Have students refer to the selection and to **Practice Book** page 4. Discuss how each statement reveals the author's viewpoint toward the Aztecs, Moctezuma, the Spaniards, and Hernan Cortés.

Define bias and assumption. Explain that readers can evaluate an author's viewpoint by looking for assumption and bias.

- Assumption is a belief that is not supported by the facts.
- Bias is a strong slant toward one way of thinking. Authors show bias by leaving out facts or by making statements that don't fit the facts.

Model determining whether an author shows bias. Have students reread pages 372–375. Then model doing additional research to determine whether the author's description of the Aztecs is biased.

Think Aloud *When the author describes how frightened the Aztecs were by Cortés, they seem like a peaceful people. Is this right? I think that the author may be leaving out important facts. I'll look for information about the Aztecs in other sources. I learn that they gained power through conquests. They had an army of more than 200,000 warriors. These facts show that the author's description of the Aztecs is biased. They were more warlike than she suggests.*

❷ Guided Practice

Have students determine whether an author shows bias.
Display the facts about the Aztecs shown below. Then ask students to reread the selection to find statements that seem biased. Have them list these statements and explain why each is biased.

Facts About the Aztecs

- The Aztec army fought constantly, conquering other groups.
- The Aztecs took away children of conquered peoples to be slaves.
- The Aztecs practiced human sacrifice.

❸ Apply

Assign Practice Book pages 6–7. Also have students apply this skill as they read their **Leveled Readers** for this week. You may also select books from the Leveled Bibliography for this theme (pages 354E–354F).

✔️ **Test Prep** Tell students that they are likely to see two types of author's viewpoint questions on reading tests.

- When questions ask why the author wrote the test passage, students should think about the main idea of the passage.

- When questions ask about author's viewpoint, bias, or assumption, students should look for details they can use as clues.

Leveled Readers and Leveled Practice

Students at all levels apply the comprehension skill as they read their Leveled Readers. See lessons on pages 383O–383R.

● BELOW LEVEL — A Brave Past
▲ ON LEVEL — Dream Weaver
■ ABOVE LEVEL — Copán: City of the Maya
◆ LANGUAGE SUPPORT — The Mighty Maya

Reading Traits

Teaching students to think about the author's viewpoint is one way of encouraging them to "read beyond the lines" of a selection. This comprehension skill supports the reading trait **Critiquing for Evaluation**.

Practice Book page 6

Name _____

Lost Temple of the Aztecs
Comprehension Skill
Author's Viewpoint

To Be Fair . . .

Read the passage. Then complete the activity on page 7.

Cabeza de Vaca's Journey

Álvar Núñez Cabeza de Vaca ranks among the greatest explorers who ever lived. In 1528, he joined a Spanish expedition headed to the New World to look for cities filled with gold and other riches.

When the expedition's five ships arrived on the coast of Florida, their leader proposed that they begin an overland exploration. Cabeza de Vaca disagreed with this dangerous and foolish plan but was too proud to stay behind. The landing party never found any cities of gold. Instead, the men lost contact with their ships and became stuck in the Florida swamps. In an effort to find their ships, they built crude boats and set sail. A hurricane separated Cabeza de Vaca's boat from the others and blew it to Texas, where it was destroyed. One by one, his companions died, leaving him alone.

Over the next four years, Cabeza de Vaca survived on his own, a superhuman achievement. He learned to live off the land and helped different native groups trade with each other. Then one day he miraculously came across three other members of the original expedition, who were now enslaved by a native group. He helped these men to escape, and together they wandered through what today is Mexico and the American Southwest. At one point, he healed a Native American man shot by an arrow. News of this feat traveled quickly, and soon many people came to him to be healed. Everywhere he and his companions went, they were welcomed and greeted with gifts.

Finally, the men crossed paths with four Spanish soldiers, who took them to a Spanish city on the Pacific Coast. Cabeza de Vaca returned to Spain to a hero's welcome. He told the king that he would like to go back to the New World. The king asked him to return as an aide to the new governor of Florida, but he refused because he had vowed never again to follow anyone else's orders. By sticking to his principles, he once again showed himself to be a truly great man.

Practice Book page 7

Name _____

Lost Temple of the Aztecs
Comprehension Skill
Author's Viewpoint

To Be Fair . . . *continued*

Answer the questions below about the passage on page 6.

1. What is the author's view of Cabeza de Vaca? The author thinks he is a great explorer, capable of great feats, and a man of principle. **(4 points)**

2. Would you say the author is biased toward Cabeza de Vaca? Why or why not? Yes. The author excessively praises Cabeza de Vaca's personal qualities and accomplishments. **(4)**

3. Do you think the facts in the article support the author's statement that Cabeza de Vaca "showed himself to be a truly great man"? Why or why not? Sample answer: No. The author says that Cabeza de Vaca's greatness is based on his sticking to his principles. But in the beginning of the article, he lets his pride get in the way of his judgment when he joins the overland exploration. **(4)**

4. In his writings, Cabeza de Vaca describes native peoples in an unfavorable way. Why do you think the author does not include this information in the article? The author leaves this information out because it does not support the author's view of Cabeza de Vaca as a great man. **(4)**

Monitoring Student Progress

If . . .	Then . . .
students score 12 or below on **Practice Book** page 7,	use the Reteaching lesson on Teacher's Edition page R8.
students have successfully met the lesson objectives,	have them do the Challenge/Extension activities on Teacher's Edition page R9.

OBJECTIVES

- Read words with suffixes -ic, -al, and -ure.
- Use the Phonics/Decoding Strategy to decode longer words.
- Learn academic language: suffix, base word, word root.

Target Skill Trace

Teach	p. 383C
Reteach	p. R14
Review	pp. M34–M35
See	Handbook for English Language Learners, p. 135; Extra Support Handbook, pp. 130–131; pp. 134–135

Practice Book page 8

Lost Temple of the Aztecs

Structural Analysis Suffixes -ic, -al, -ure

Name _____

Aztec Artifacts

Circle the suffixes *-ic*, *-al*, and *-ure* in the underlined words in the sentences below.

1. The museum had original Aztec artifacts on display for the public. (2)
2. These national treasures of Mexico would only be in the United States for a short time. (1)
3. The arrival of many visitors made the museum crowded by ten o'clock. (1)
4. Visitors could not touch the stone artifacts because they were protected by a rope enclosure. (1)
5. A plaque told of the historic importance of the Aztecs' tragic defeat by Cortés in the year 1521. (2)
6. A letter that showed Cortés's authentic signature was on display in a glass case. (2)
7. A professional archaeologist was also there to answer questions about her work. (1)

Now, choose five underlined words and use them correctly in sentences of your own. Accept responses that use the word correctly. (1 point each)

1. _____
2. _____
3. _____
4. _____
5. _____

Monitoring Student Progress

If . . .	Then . . .
students score 11 or below on **Practice Book** page 8,	use the Reteaching lesson on Teacher's Edition page R14.

STRUCTURAL ANALYSIS/ VOCABULARY: More Suffixes

TARGET SKILL

❶ Teach

Introduce the suffix -ure. Write *The Aztecs regretted their fail-ure to recognize Cortés as a greedy invader.*

- Circle the suffix -ure in *failure*. Point out the base word *fail*.
- Explain that -ure adds the meaning "the act or condition of" to the base word. Explain that the whole word means "the act of failing."

Introduce the suffix -ic. Write *Cortés caused the Aztecs' tragic downfall.*

- Circle -ic in *tragic*. Circle the word part *trag*.
- Help students recognize the root word. Write *tragedy* on the board, and discuss its meaning. (sad, unfortunate)
- Explain that -ic means "characterized by" and that the whole word means "characterized by sadness."

Introduce the suffix -al. Write *Discovering the Great Temple was an emotional experience for archaeologists.*

- Circle -al in *emotional*. Point out the base word *emotion*.
- Explain that -al means "characterized by" and that the whole word means "characterized by emotion."

Model the Phonics/Decoding Strategy. Write *Workers were digging ditches for electrical cables.* Model decoding *electrical*.

Think Aloud
I recognize the suffix -al. I'll cover that and look at the base word. I can divide the base word into syllables and pronounce it, ih-LEHK-trihk. That's a word I know. With the suffix -al it must mean "having to do with electricity." That makes sense in the sentence.

❷ Guided Practice

Have students use the suffixes -ure, -ic, and -al. Display the phrases below. Have partners circle the suffix in each underlined word, decode the word, and figure out its meaning. Discuss students' work.

planned <u>departure</u>   <u>historic</u> discovery

lost their <u>composure</u>   <u>unnatural</u> happenings

❸ Apply

Assign Practice Book page 8.

PHONICS REVIEW:
The /sh/ and /zh/ Sounds

OBJECTIVES

- Read words with /sh/ and /zh/ sounds.
- Use the Phonics/Decoding Strategy to decode longer words.
- Learn academic language: /sh/ sound, /zh/ sound.

❶ Teach

Review the /sh/ and /zh/ sounds. Explain the following points.

- The letters *sh*, *ti*, and *si* can stand for the /sh/ sound, as in these examples: *shining, attention, confession.*

- The letters *s* and *si* can stand for the /zh/ sound, as in these examples: *treasure, illusion.*

Model the Phonics/Decoding Strategy. Write *They were anxious to beat the thick heat and <u>pollution</u> that would wrap around the city by midday.* Then model how to decode *pollution.*

Think Aloud   *I see a word I don't know, so I'll try sounding it out the way it looks,* puh-LOO-tee-uhn. *That isn't a word I've heard before. Maybe the letters* ti *stand for the /sh/ sound in this word. Then it would be* puh-LOO-shuhn. *That is a word I know, and it makes sense in the sentence.*

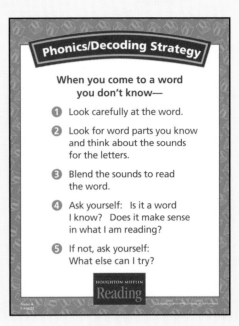

Phonics/Decoding Strategy

When you come to a word you don't know—

❶ Look carefully at the word.

❷ Look for word parts you know and think about the sounds for the letters.

❸ Blend the sounds to read the word.

❹ Ask yourself: Is it a word I know? Does it make sense in what I am reading?

❺ If not, ask yourself: What else can I try?

HOUGHTON MIFFLIN
Reading

❷ Guided Practice

Help students identify words with the /sh/ and /zh/ sounds. Display the sentences below. Have partners circle the letters that stand for the /sh/ or /zh/ sound in each underlined word, pronounce the word, and check to see if it makes sense. Have volunteers model at the board.

1. The Aztec calendar was an amazing <u>invention</u>.

2. His interest was more than <u>professional</u>.

3. Moctezuma was filled with fear and <u>confusion</u>.

4. An <u>unusual</u> group of visitors approached Tenochtitlán.

❸ Apply

Have students identify words with /sh/ and /zh/ sounds. Ask students to find these words in the *Lost Temple of the Aztecs*, decode them, and discuss their meanings.

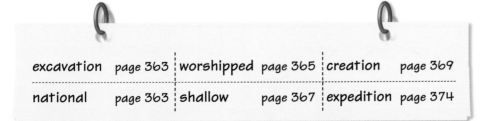

| excavation | page 363 | worshipped | page 365 | creation | page 369 |
| national | page 363 | shallow | page 367 | expedition | page 374 |

PHONICS REVIEW

Lost Temple of the Aztecs

SPELLING: /sh/

OBJECTIVES

- Write Spelling Words that have the /sh/ sound.
- Learn academic language: /sh/ sound.

SPELLING WORDS

Basic

glacier	official*
motion	edition
pressure	musician
direction	mention
caution	mission
partial	portion
ancient*	session
polish	selfish
station	establish
shallow*	cushion

Review	**Challenge**
vanish	expedition*
nation*	diminish
condition	recession
migration	beneficial
confession	technician

Forms of these words appear in the literature.

Extra Support/ Intervention

Basic Word List You may want to use only the left column of Basic Words with students who need extra support.

Challenge

Challenge Word Practice Have students write a definition for each Challenge Word and then write a sentence for each word.

DAY 1 — INSTRUCTION

/sh/

Pretest Use the Day 5 Test sentences.

Teach Write these words on the board: *polish, motion, official, mission.*

- Point to and say each word and have students repeat it. Ask students what sound all four words have in common. (the /sh/ sound)

- Underline *sh* in *polish*, *ti* in *motion*, *ci* in *official*, *ss* in *mission*. Explain that the /sh/ sound is usually spelled with one of these four patterns.

- Erase the board; write *sh, ti, ci,* and *ss* as column heads. Say each Basic Word as you write it in the appropriate column, and have students repeat it. Underline the /sh/ spelling pattern.

Practice/Homework Assign **Practice Book** page 257.

DAY 2 — REVIEW & PRACTICE

Reviewing the Principle

Go over the spelling patterns for the /sh/ sound with students.

Practice/Homework Assign **Practice Book** page 9.

Practice Book page 257

Take-Home Word List	Take-Home Word List	Take-Home Word List
The Great Wall	**Discovering Ancient Cultures** Reading-Writing Workshop	**Lost Temple of the Aztecs**
Adding -ion or -ation connect, connection, situate, situation, admire, admiration	Look for familiar spelling patterns in these words to help you remember their spellings.	The /sh/ Sound /sh/ → polish, motion official, mission
Spelling Words	**Spelling Words**	**Spelling Words**
1. construct 11. admire	1. decent 8. sleek	1. glacier 11. official
2. construction 12. admiration	2. descent 9. alley	2. motion 12. edition
3. connect 13. situate	3. affect 10. ally	3. pressure 13. musician
4. connection 14. situation	4. effect 11. confident	4. direction 14. mention
5. combine 15. examine	5. desert 12. confidant	5. caution 15. mission
6. combination 16. examination	6. dessert 13. hurdle	6. partial 16. portion
7. cooperate 17. contribute	7. slick 14. hurtle	7. ancient 17. session
8. cooperation 18. contribution		8. polish 18. selfish
9. attract 19. explore		9. station 19. establish
10. attraction 20. exploration		10. shallow 20. cushion
Challenge Words	**Challenge Words**	**Challenge Words**
1. negotiate	1. bizarre	1. expedition 4. beneficial
2. negotiation	2. bazaar	2. diminish 5. technician
3. insulate	3. ellipse	3. recession
4. insulation	4. eclipse	
My Study List Add your own spelling words on the back.	**My Study List** Add your own spelling words on the back.	**My Study List** Add your own spelling words on the back.

Take-Home Word List

Practice Book page 9

Lost Temple of the Aztecs
Spelling The /sh/ Sound

Name _____

The /sh/ Sound

The /sh/ sound is usually spelled with two letters. When you hear the /sh/ sound, think of the patterns *sh, ti, ci,* and *s*.

/sh/ polish motion official mission

Write each Spelling Word under its spelling of the /sh/ sound. Order of answers for each category may vary.

sh
polish (1 point)
shallow (1)
selfish (1)
establish (1)
cushion (1)

ci
glacier (1)
ancient (1)
official (1)
musician (1)

ti
motion (1)
direction (1)
caution (1)
partial (1)
station (1)
edition (1)
mention (1)
portion (1)

ss
pressure (1)
mission (1)
session (1)

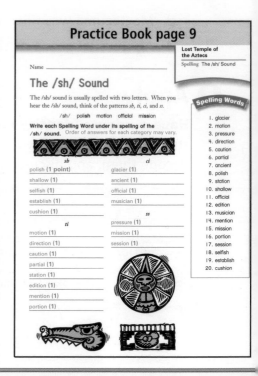

Spelling Words
1. glacier
2. motion
3. pressure
4. direction
5. caution
6. partial
7. ancient
8. polish
9. station
10. shallow
11. official
12. edition
13. musician
14. mention
15. mission
16. portion
17. session
18. selfish
19. establish
20. cushion

VOCABULARY

Analogies

Write the Basic Words on the board.

Dictate the following incomplete analogies, and have students write the Basic Word that completes each one.

– *Thermometer* is to *temperature* as *compass* is to _____. (*direction*)

– *Cast* is to *actor* as *orchestra* is to _____. (*musician*)

– *Gleaming* is to *dull* as *modern* is to _____. (*ancient*)

– *Ounce* is to *ton* as *ice cube* is to _____. (*glacier*)

• Have students use each Basic Word from the board orally in a sentence. (Sentences will vary.)

Practice/Homework For spelling practice, assign **Practice Book** page 10.

Practice Book page 10

Name _____

Lost Temple of the Aztecs
Spelling The /sh/ Sound

Spelling Spree

Adding the /sh/ Sound Write a Spelling Word by adding the correct spelling of the /sh/ sound to the incomplete word in each phrase below.

Spelling Words
1. glacier
2. motion
3. pressure
4. direction
5. caution
6. partial
7. ancient
8. polish
9. station
10. shallow
11. official
12. edition
13. musician
14. mention
15. mission
16. portion
17. session
18. selfish
19. establish
20. cushion

1. the second edi^{ti} (1) on of a book
2. a drop in air pre^{ss} (1) ure
3. the ^{sh} (1) allow end of the pool
4. a large por^{ti} (1) on of food
5. a parti^{ti} (1) al eclipse of the sun
6. a comfortable seat cu^{sh} (1) ion
7. a musi^{ci} (1) an in a band

Word Detective Write a Spelling Word for each clue.

8. a "river" of ice
9. inconsiderate of others
10. a meeting
11. very old
12. where you board a train or bus
13. a synonym for *movement*
14. to found or set up
15. the state of being careful

8. glacier (1)   12. station (1)
9. selfish (1)   13. motion (1)
10. session (1)   14. establish (1)
11. ancient (1)   15. caution (1)

PROOFREADING

Game: What Am I?

Ask students to work in pairs. Tell each pair to make a word card for each Basic and Review Word, shuffle the cards, and stack them face-down.

• Player A draws a card and gives Player B a meaning clue such as this one: "I do not like to share. What am I?" (*selfish*)

• Player B tries to guess and spell the word.

• A player who guesses and spells a word correctly gets to keep the card. If the player guesses the wrong word or misspells it, the card is returned to the bottom of the stack.

• Play proceeds, alternating between partners, until all the words have been guessed and spelled correctly.

• The player with more cards wins.

Practice/Homework For proofreading and writing practice, assign **Practice Book** page 11.

Practice Book page 11

Name _____

Lost Temple of the Aztecs
Spelling The /sh/ Sound

Proofreading and Writing

Proofreading Circle the five misspelled Spelling Words in this letter. Then write each word correctly.

Spelling Words
1. glacier
2. motion
3. pressure
4. direction
5. caution
6. partial
7. ancient
8. polish
9. station
10. shallow
11. official
12. edition
13. musician
14. mention
15. mission
16. portion
17. session
18. selfish
19. establish
20. cushion

To the Royal Governor:
You will be pleased to know that our (mishun) has been successful so far. After leaving Cuba, we sailed in a westerly (direccion) until making landfall. We were quickly able to (astablish) that a great empire lay farther inland. Later, we received some (offical) visitors from this empire. Among their gifts to us were gold and precious stones, which were shined to a very high polish. In return, we demonstrated the power of our guns to them. This they will no doubt (mension) to their lord back in the capital. We believe this country possesses great riches, and are confident of success.
Your servant,
Hernán Cortés

1. mission (1 point)   4. official (1)
2. direction (1)   5. mention (1)
3. establish (1)

Write an Explanation The Aztecs had a calendar just for keeping track of special religious days. Have you ever crossed off on a calendar the days leading up to a holiday? What is your favorite holiday?

On a separate piece of paper, write about your favorite holiday. Remember to name the holiday and tell why it is your favorite. Use Spelling Words from the list. Responses will vary. (5)

ASSESSMENT

Spelling Test

Say each underlined word, read the sentence, and then repeat the word. Have students write only the underlined word.

Basic Words

1. The **glacier** looked like a river of snow.
2. The child likes the **motion** of the swing.
3. The **pressure** will flatten the leaf.
4. I went in the wrong **direction**.
5. Use **caution** as you climb the steps.
6. This **partial** list is missing five names.
7. This **ancient** bone belonged to a dinosaur.
8. Did you **polish** the car with wax?
9. The train pulled into the **station**.
10. We can wade in this **shallow** water.
11. What are the **official** rules?
12. I read a new **edition** of this book.
13. The **musician** plays the drums.
14. Did she **mention** her sister in her letter?
15. The spy went on a secret **mission**.
16. He ate a large **portion** of salad.
17. I missed the first **session** of the class.
18. John is **selfish** and will not lend his books.
19. We will **establish** a tennis team.
20. This chair needs a new **cushion**.

Challenge Words

21. Will you join our **expedition**?
22. Buying a bicycle will **diminish** your savings.
23. The country may soon be in a **recession**.
24. Exercise is **beneficial** to your health.
25. She is a skilled **technician**.

OBJECTIVES

- Identify words that have multiple meanings.
- Use sentence context to identify the intended meaning of a word with multiple meanings.
- Learn academic language: *multiple-meaning words, context.*

Target Skill Trace

Teach	p. 383G
Review	pp. M36–M37
Extend	Challenge/Extension Activities, p. R15
See	*Handbook for English Language Learners,* p. 139

Monitoring Student Progress

If . . .	Then . . .
students score 7 or below on **Practice Book** page 12,	have them work in small groups to correct the items they missed.

TARGET SKILL

VOCABULARY: Multiple-Meaning Words

❶ Teach

Introduce multiple-meaning words. Readers can use context to figure out the intended meaning of most multiple-meaning words.

- Write *Moctezuma was chosen, in the Aztec <u>fashion</u>, by other nobles.* Explain that here *fashion* means "how something is done."
- Write *Men's <u>fashions</u> today are simple compared to the clothing worn by Cortés.* Explain that here *fashion* means "clothing styles."

Model how to figure out words with multiple meanings. Display these sentences: *The Great Temple stood at the <u>heart</u> of this city. Moctezuma had a warm <u>heart</u> when it came to greeting visitors.* Model how to figure out the meanings of *heart.*

Think Aloud *In the first sentence, the word* heart *tells where the Great Temple stood. Here the word must refer to the center of the city. In the second sentence, the word* heart *describes what kind of person Moctezuma was. Here the word must refer to his feelings for other people.*

❷ Guided Practice

Have students figure out words with multiple meanings. Display each pair of sentences shown. Have partners use context clues to figure out the meanings of the underlined words. Discuss students' work.

1. The trolley cars crossed Mexico City's main <u>square</u>. The steps down to the ancient temple were <u>square</u> and dusty.

2. Canals crisscrossed the city between <u>blocks</u> of white buildings. Why didn't Moctezuma <u>block</u> Cortés from entering the city?

❸ Apply

Assign Practice Book page 12.

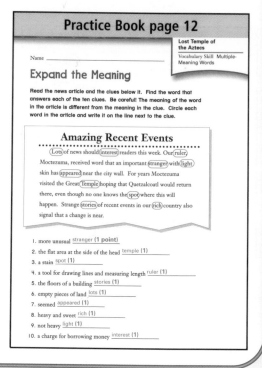

Practice Book page 12

Lost Temple of the Aztecs

Vocabulary Skill Multiple-Meaning Words

Name _____

Expand the Meaning

Read the news article and the clues below it. Find the word that answers each of the ten clues. Be careful! The meaning of the word in the article is different from the meaning in the clue. Circle each word in the article and write it on the line next to the clue.

Amazing Recent Events

(Lots) of news should (interest) readers this week. Our (ruler), Moctezuma, received word that an important (stranger) with (light) skin has (appeared) near the city wall. For years Moctezuma visited the Great (Temple) hoping that Quetzalcoatl would return there, even though no one knows the (spot) where this will happen. Strange (stories) of recent events in our (rich) country also signal that a change is near.

1. more unusual stranger **(1 point)**
2. the flat area at the side of the head temple **(1)**
3. a stain spot **(1)**
4. a tool for drawing lines and measuring length ruler **(1)**
5. the floors of a building stories **(1)**
6. empty pieces of land lots **(1)**
7. seemed appeared **(1)**
8. heavy and sweet rich **(1)**
9. not heavy light **(1)**
10. a charge for borrowing money interest **(1)**

STUDY SKILL: Using Multiple Reference Sources

OBJECTIVES

- Identify types of sources for researching a certain topic.
- Use multiple sources to research a topic.

❶ Teach

Introduce using multiple sources to find information.

- Research reports should always use more than one source.
- This is a good way to check whether information is accurate.

Discuss print sources.

- Nonfiction books present many details on a single subject.
- Encyclopedia entries summarize the major facts about a subject.
- Dictionaries give definitions, pronunciations, and other information about words.
- Atlases contain political and specialized maps.
- Almanacs provide up-to-date facts about geography, sports, current and historical events, and entertainment.

Discuss electronic sources.

- Electronic encyclopedias have the same kind of information as print encyclopedias.
- The Internet gives information about many topics. Students should use sites created by schools or other respected organizations.

Discuss interviews.

- People can provide valuable information and insights.
- An expert can provide background and answer questions. Eyewitnesses to events can tell what they saw.

Model identifying sources for researching Aztecs.

Think Aloud *The first thing I would do is look up* Aztecs *in an encyclopedia. There I might also find suggestions for related topics. I could also look for nonfiction books about the Aztecs or the history of Mexico. I can look at a historical atlas for a map that shows the Aztec empire. I could also do a keyword search for* Aztecs *on the Web or write to an archaeologist.*

❷ Practice/Apply

Have partners use multiple sources to answer one of these research questions.

- How large a kingdom did Cleopatra rule?
- What kind of clothing might Cleopatra have worn?
- How might Cleopatra have traveled from Alexandria to Memphis?

GRAMMAR: Adjectives

GRAMMAR

OBJECTIVES

- Identify and write adjectives, demonstrative adjectives, and the articles *a, an,* and *the.*
- Correctly capitalize and use proper adjectives.
- Proofread and correct sentences with grammar and spelling errors.
- Shift adjectives to improve writing.
- Learn academic language: *adjective, articles, demonstrative adjectives, proper adjectives.*

DAY 1 INSTRUCTION

Kinds of Adjectives

Teach Go over the following:

– An adjective modifies, or describes, a noun or a pronoun. It can tell *what kind, which one,* or *how many.*

– *A, an,* and *the* are special adjectives called articles. *A* and *an* refer to any item in a group; *the* refers to a specific item or items.

– Demonstrative adjectives tell *which one. This* and *these* point out items nearby; *that* and *those,* items farther away. *This* and *that* refer to one item; *these* and *those,* to more than one.

- Display **Transparency 4–4.** Point out the adjectives in the examples.

- Ask volunteers to write the adjectives in Sentences 1–8. Have them underline demonstrative adjectives and circle articles.

Daily Language Practice
Have students correct Sentences 1 and 2 on **Transparency 4–3.**

DAY 2 PRACTICE

Independent Work

Practice/Homework Assign **Practice Book** page 13.

Daily Language Practice
Have students correct Sentences 3 and 4 on **Transparency 4–3.**

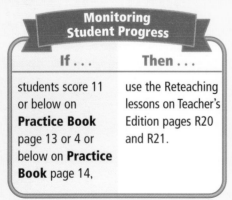

Transparency 4–3

Daily Language Practice

Correct two sentences each day.

1. The train statun is on park Street.
   The train station is on Park Street.

2. At last night's concert, that musicin plays a solo.
   At last night's concert, that musician played a solo.

3. I don't like it when my sister are selfich.
   I don't like it when my sister is selfish.
   Or
   I don't like it when my sisters are selfish.

4. Yesterday, the motin of the ride makes me carsick.
   Yesterday, the motion of the ride made me carsick.

5. A glacer are an amazing sight.
   A glacier is an amazing sight.

6. My father is an officil at the Special olympics.
   My father is an official at the Special Olympics.

7. In which directin is the nearest canadian town?
   In which direction is the nearest Canadian town?

8. Who's poorshin of pie is left on the table?
   Whose portion of pie is left on the table?

9. I would love to visit an ancint greek temple.
   I would love to visit an ancient Greek temple.

10. Tonight, Mom will helped me sew a special cushin.
    Tonight, Mom will help me sew a special cushion.

Monitoring Student Progress

If . . .	Then . . .
students score 11 or below on **Practice Book** page 13 or 4 or below on **Practice Book** page 14,	use the Reteaching lessons on Teacher's Edition pages R20 and R21.

Transparency 4–4

Adjectives

We will study ancient civilizations of the Americas. Some of those civilizations possessed advanced knowledge of astronomy.

1. These colorful photographs were taken at Chichen Itza.
   These, colorful

2. The huge pyramid has a small room inside it.
   The, huge, a, small

3. In that room is a stone statue of a fierce jaguar.
   that, a, stone, a, fierce

4. The large building with a curved dome was an astronomical observatory.
   The, large, a, curved, an, astronomical

5. The ancient Maya were expert astronomers.
   the, ancient, expert

6. This visit was an unforgettable experience.
   This, an, unforgettable

7. The Maya built other fascinating cities in Tikal in Guatemala and Altun Han in Belize.
   The, other, fascinating

8. Many large pyramids of the Maya are today buried under thick mounds of earth.
   Many, large, the, thick

Practice Book page 13

Name _____

Many Ways to Describe

Lost Temple of the Aztecs
Grammar Skill Adjectives

Descriptive adjectives:	what kind, how many, which one	Visitors, old and young, are awed by ancient ruins.
Demonstrative adjectives:	which one	These postcards show those sites. This photograph was taken at that place.
Articles:		The people built a temple. It was uncovered in an excavation.

Adjectives Identify the adjectives in each sentence. Write each adjective on the correct line under each sentence. Hint: Every sentence does not contain every kind of adjective, and some sentences may contain more than one of a kind.

1. The Aztecs used a circular stone calendar.
   descriptive adjectives: circular, stone (1 point)
   articles: the, a (1)   demonstrative adjectives: (none) (1)

2. They created a great empire.
   descriptive adjectives: great (1)
   articles: a (1)   demonstrative adjectives: (none) (1)

3. Those workers found that temple and made an important discovery.
   descriptive adjectives: important (1)
   articles: an (1)   demonstrative adjectives: those, that (1)

4. It was a magnificent building.
   descriptive adjectives: magnificent (1)
   articles: a (1)   demonstrative adjectives: (none) (1)

5. That temple was in the capital city.
   descriptive adjectives: capital (1)
   articles: the (1)   demonstrative adjectives: that (1)

383I THEME 4: Discovering Ancient Cultures

Proper Adjectives

Teach Go over the following:

– A proper adjective is an adjective formed from a proper noun.

– Proper adjectives are always capitalized.

Display the example sentences at the top of **Transparency 4–5.** Identify *Brazilian* and *Chilean* as proper adjectives.

Rewrite Sentence 1 so that it contains a proper adjective. Then ask volunteers to rewrite Sentences 2–10 so that each one contains a proper adjective.

Independent Work

Practice/Homework Assign **Practice Book** page 14.

Adjective Position

Teach Tell students that a good writer may change the position of adjectives to make sentences more effective.

- Model changing the position of adjectives to improve a sentence:

  – The air was hot and humid, and it made Steffen uneasy.

  – *Improved:* The <u>hot, humid</u> air made Steffen uneasy.

- Have students examine a piece of their own writing to see whether they could improve any sentences by shifting adjectives from one position to another. Invite them to share their improved sentences with the class.

Practice/Homework Assign **Practice Book** page 15.

Daily Language Practice

Have students correct Sentences 5 and 6 on **Transparency 4–3.**

Daily Language Practice

Have students correct Sentences 7 and 8 on **Transparency 4–3.**

Daily Language Practice

Have students correct Sentences 9 and 10 on **Transparency 4–3.**

Transparency 4–5

Proper Adjectives

We will visit villages in the Brazilian rain forest. We will also visit a Chilean town in the Atacama Desert.

1. The band in the park played music from Mexico.
   The band in the park played Mexican music.

2. Alberta is a province of Canada.
   Alberta is a Canadian province.

3. Robert dreamed of vacationing at a resort in Jamaica.
   Robert dreamed of vacationing at a Jamaican resort.

4. Have you experienced a winter in Alaska?
   Have you experienced an Alaskan winter?

5. My sister prepared a delicious stew from a recipe from Brazil.
   My sister prepared a delicious stew from a Brazilian recipe.

6. We listened to a speech given by a diplomat from Turkey.
   We listened to a speech given by a Turkish diplomat.

7. This is a basket from Guatemala.
   This is a Guatemalan basket.

8. I like food from Vietnam.
   I like Vietnamese food.

9. At a restaurant in Japan, you can eat sushi.
   At a Japanese restaurant, you can eat sushi.

10. Let's visit the beautiful beaches of Morocco.
    Let's visit the beautiful Moroccan beaches.

Practice Book page 14

Name _____

Lost Temple of the Aztecs
Grammar Skill Proper Adjectives

It's Only Proper!

A **proper adjective** is formed from a proper noun and always begins with a capital letter.

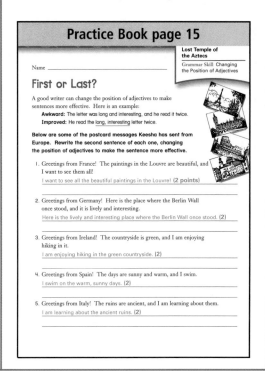

Proper noun	Ending	Proper adjective
Germany	-an	German poetry
Chile	-an	Chilean fruit
China	-ese	Chinese art
Japan	-ese	Japanese language
Sweden	-ish	Swedish bread
Ireland	-ish	Irish music

Proper Adjectives Complete each sentence. Write the proper adjective formed from the proper noun in parentheses. Use a dictionary if you need to.

1. Nancy read about an Alaskan **(1 point)** _____ sled race. (Alaska)

2. Tim prepared an Italian **(1)** _____ meal for us. (Italy)

3. A trifle is an English **(1)** _____ dessert. (England)

4. Our class saw African **(1)** _____ art at the museum. (Africa)

5. This Chinese **(1)** _____ vase is extremely old. (China)

6. The design on that Portuguese **(1)** _____ dish is lovely. (Portugal)

Practice Book page 15

Name _____

Lost Temple of the Aztecs
Grammar Skill Changing the Position of Adjectives

First or Last?

A good writer can change the position of adjectives to make sentences more effective. Here is an example:

Awkward: The letter was long and interesting, and he read it twice.
Improved: He read the long, interesting letter twice.

Below are some of the postcard messages Keesha has sent from Europe. Rewrite the second sentence of each one, changing the position of adjectives to make the sentence more effective.

1. Greetings from France! The paintings in the Louvre are beautiful, and I want to see them all!
   I want to see all the beautiful paintings in the Louvre! **(2 points)**

2. Greetings from Germany! Here is the place where the Berlin Wall once stood, and it is lively and interesting.
   Here is the lively and interesting place where the Berlin Wall once stood. **(2)**

3. Greetings from Ireland! The countryside is green, and I am enjoying hiking in it.
   I am enjoying hiking in the green countryside. **(2)**

4. Greetings from Spain! The days are sunny and warm, and I swim.
   I swim on the warm, sunny days. **(2)**

5. Greetings from Italy! The ruins are ancient, and I am learning about them.
   I am learning about the ancient ruins. **(2)**

WRITING: Explanation

OBJECTIVES

- Identify the characteristics of a good explanation.
- Write an explanation.
- Eliminate unnecessary words.
- Learn academic language: *explanation*.

Writing Traits

Ideas As students draft their explanations on Day 2, emphasize the importance of using exact details. Share these examples.

Without Exact Details The Aztecs built a city in the middle of a lake because <u>of trouble they were having</u>. The water helped <u>keep them safe.</u>

With Exact Details The Aztecs built a city in the middle of a lake because <u>they were fighting with other groups.</u> The water helped <u>protect them from attack.</u>

DAY 1 — PREWRITING

Introducing the Format

Define an explanation.

- An explanation can tell who or what something is.
- It can tell what is or was important about something or someone.
- It can tell how something works.
- It can explain the steps of a process.
- It can tell why something happens or happened.
- Some topics may require research in an encyclopedia or other resource.

Start students thinking about writing an explanation.

- Display the question shown below.
- Tell students to list details that answer the question.
- Have students save their notes.

> Why did Moctezuma decide to welcome the strangers as friends rather than treat them as enemies?

DAY 2 — DRAFTING

Discussing the Model

Display Transparency 4–6. Ask:

- What is being explained? (what the ancient Incans built) Which sentence states this topic? (first sentence)
- What examples support the topic? (Sample answers: aqueducts and irrigation canals; fortress above city of Cuzco, Peru)
- What details support each example? (Sample answer: aqueducts: pumped water uphill, farmed on terraces; fortress: huge stone blocks and each fitted perfectly)
- How is the explanation organized? (details grouped with examples)
- What is the conclusion? (*Clearly, the Incans were very advanced builders.*)

Display Transparency 4–7, and discuss the guidelines.

Have students draft an explanation.

- Have them use their notes from Day 1.
- Assign **Practice Book** page 16 to help students organize their writing.
- See Writing Traits on this page.
- Provide support as needed.

Transparency 4–6

An Explanation

Introduction/Topic Sentence
The ancient Inca civilization is known for its mysteries and marvels of construction and engineering. At its height, the Inca empire stretched along the Andes range in South America for 3,000 miles, taking in parts of the present-day countries of Peru, Bolivia, Ecuador, Chile, and Argentina. Somehow, without using wheels or harnessed animals, Inca builders constructed a system of roads that extended 10,000 miles, networking across the Andes from one end of the empire to the other.

Example 1 and supporting details

Grouped examples and supporting details
The Inca also built aqueducts and irrigation canals, pumped water uphill, and farmed on terraces hewn into the sides of steep mountains. These constructions can still be seen at places such as Machu Picchu, one of the most famous Inca ruins, at 8,000 feet high in the Andes. The building of suspension bridges was also perfected by the Inca and continues in the same manner today.

Example and supporting details
High above the city of Cuzco, in Peru, is yet another Inca wonder, the remains of a fortress over 500 years old. This fortress, known as Sacsahuaman, is mysterious in at least two ways. First, the stone blocks used to construct its walls are huge! Some are 25 feet high (three times the size of a tall person) and weigh up to 200 tons. The second fact that continues to astonish observers is that each stone was fitted together so perfectly, using only bronze and stone tools, that even today a knife blade cannot be inserted between them.

Conclusion
Clearly, the Inca were very advanced builders.

TRANSPARENCY 4–6 TEACHER'S EDITION PAGE 383K

Transparency 4–7

Guidelines for Writing an Explanation

- Pick a topic you know well or would like to know about.
- If you have chosen an unfamiliar topic, do any necessary research before you begin to draft.
- Begin with a topic sentence that tells what you will explain.
- Include examples or steps that explain your topic.
- Include details that explain each example or step.
- Group details with the examples or steps that they support.
- Keep your language simple and clear. Define all terms likely to be unfamiliar, including any technical terms, the first time you use them.

TRANSPARENCY 4–7 TEACHER'S EDITION PAGE 383K

Practice Book page 16

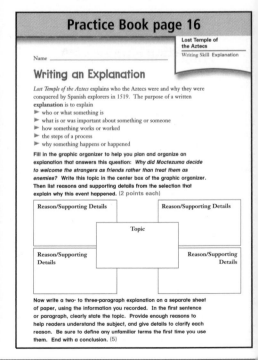

Lost Temple of the Aztecs
Writing Skill Explanation

Name _____

Writing an Explanation

Lost Temple of the Aztecs explains who the Aztecs were and why they were conquered by Spanish explorers in 1519. The purpose of a written **explanation** is to explain

- ▶ who or what something is
- ▶ what is or was important about something or someone
- ▶ how something works or worked
- ▶ the steps of a process
- ▶ why something happens or happened

Fill in the graphic organizer to help you plan and organize an explanation that answers this question: *Why did Moctezuma decide to welcome the strangers as friends rather than treat them as enemies?* Write this topic in the center box of the graphic organizer. Then list reasons and supporting details from the selection that explain why this event happened. (2 points each)

Reason/Supporting Details		Reason/Supporting Details
	Topic	
Reason/Supporting Details		Reason/Supporting Details

Now write a two- to three-paragraph explanation on a separate sheet of paper, using the information you recorded. In the first sentence or paragraph, clearly state the topic. Provide enough reasons to help readers understand the subject, and give details to clarify each reason. Be sure to define any unfamiliar terms the first time you use them. End with a conclusion. (5)

Improving Writing: Unnecessary Words

Explain eliminating unnecessary words.

Write, *The glass dropped and fell on the floor.* Ask, Which words repeat ideas? (*dropped, fell*)

Tell students that good writers delete words that repeat ideas. These unnecessary words can make writing awkward or unclear.

Display Transparency 4–8.

Have a volunteer read Example 1.

Then read Example 2. Have partners compare the passages and identify the words and phrases that were deleted.

Discuss how Example 2 is clearer and easier to read than Example 1.

Assign Practice Book page 17.

Have students revise their drafts.

Display **Transparency 4–7** again. Have students use it to revise their explanations.

Have partners hold writing conferences.

Ask students to revise any parts of their explanations that still need work. Have them eliminate unnecessary words.

Checking for Errors

Have students proofread for errors in grammar, spelling, punctuation, or usage.

- Students can use the proofreading checklist on **Practice Book** page 273 to help them proofread their explanations.

- Students can also use the chart of proofreading marks on **Practice Book** page 274.

Sharing Explanations

Consider these publishing options.

- Ask students to read their explanations or some other piece of writing from the Author's Chair.

- Make a Class Book of Knowledge, featuring students' explanations.

Portfolio Opportunity

Save students' explanations as samples of their writing development.

Transparency 4–8

Eliminating Unnecessary Words

Example 1

The ancient Maya were expert astronomers. Their keen observations of the sun and moon up in the sky enabled them to create an accurate calendar that was amazingly exact. In fact, the Maya developed two calendars, a festival calendar of 260 days, and a second one, a solar calendar of 365 days.

When the Aztecs gained control and dominance over central Mexico, they used these two calendars too. The priests used the 260-day calendar to do something that was really important to them, which was to determine which days were lucky for building houses, planting crops, going to war, and other activities too numerous to mention. They also used this calendar to schedule religious ceremonies.

The other calendar was a solar calendar. It was based on the movement of the earth around the sun, which takes 365 days. The solar year had 18 months in it; each month had 20 days in it. In addition to all those months and days, the calendar also had five extra days, to make the total be 365.

Example 2

The ancient Maya were expert astronomers. Their keen observations of the sun and moon enabled them to create an accurate calendar. In fact, they developed two calendars, a festival calendar of 260 days and a solar calendar of 365 days.

When the Aztecs gained control over central Mexico, they used these two calendars too. The priests used the 260-day calendar to determine which days were lucky for building houses, planting crops, going to war, and other activities. They also used it to schedule religious ceremonies.

The other calendar was a solar calendar. It was based on the movement of the earth around the sun. The solar year had 18 months in it; each month had 20 days. The calendar also had five extra days, to make the total 365.

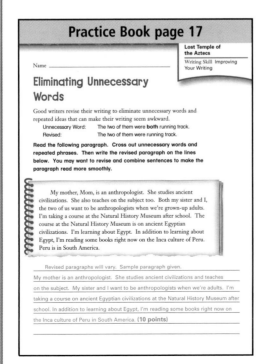

Practice Book page 17

Lost Temple of the Aztecs

Writing Skill Improving Your Writing

Name _____

Eliminating Unnecessary Words

Good writers revise their writing to eliminate unnecessary words and repeated ideas that can make their writing seem awkward.

Unnecessary Word: The two of them were **both** running track.
Revised: The two of them were running track.

Read the following paragraph. Cross out unnecessary words and repeated phrases. Then write the revised paragraph on the lines below. You may want to revise and combine sentences to make the paragraph read more smoothly.

My mother, Mom, is an anthropologist. She studies ancient civilizations. She also teaches on the subject too. Both my sister and I, the two of us want to be anthropologists when we're grown-up adults. I'm taking a course at the Natural History Museum after school. The course at the Natural History Museum is on ancient Egyptian civilizations. I'm learning about Egypt. In addition to learning about Egypt, I'm reading some books right now on the Inca culture of Peru. Peru is in South America.

Revised paragraphs will vary. Sample paragraph given.

My mother is an anthropologist. She studies ancient civilizations and teaches on the subject. My sister and I want to be anthropologists when we're adults. I'm taking a course on ancient Egyptian civilizations at the Natural History Museum after school. In addition to learning about Egypt, I'm reading some books right now on the Inca culture of Peru in South America. **(10 points)**

Monitoring Student Progress

If . . .	Then . . .
students' writing does not follow the guidelines on **Transparency 4–7,**	work with students to improve specific parts of their writing.

LANGUAGE CENTER

VOCABULARY

Descriptive Words

👤 Singles	🕐 20 minutes
Objective	Create a descriptive-words web.

The ancient city of Tenochtitlán is described in *Lost Temple of the Aztecs* as *beautiful, enchanted,* and *remarkable.* Look through the selection to find other examples of vivid descriptive words. Then create a word web with them. Start by answering these questions:

- What words describe the discovery of the temple stone in 1978?

- What words does the author use to describe the strange occurrences before the Spaniards arrived?

- How do Moctezuma's messengers describe the visitors?

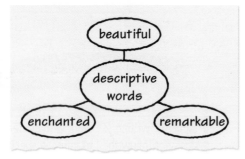

GRAMMAR

All Kinds of Adjectives

👤 Singles	🕐 30 minutes
Objective	Identify various types of adjectives.

Here is a diary entry written by one of Moctezuma's messengers about Cortés's arrival.

- Copy the diary entry onto a sheet of paper.

- Underline every adjective in the entry.

- Then list the adjectives in columns with these headings: Descriptive Adjectives, Demonstrative Adjectives, Articles, Proper Adjectives.

This morning, Moctezuma sent us to visit the pale-skinned strangers and their mysterious leader. We brought numerous, expensive gifts to give to that odd man. But when he had looked at the gifts, he seemed to expect much more. He did frightening things to us and demanded to find out how strong Aztec men are. He wanted us to fight his men, but he released us reluctantly. We came back quickly and told Moctezuma all these things.

VOCABULARY

Vocabulary Game

👥 Pairs	🕐 30 minutes
Objective	Create a Key Vocabulary words puzzle.
Materials	Activity Master 4–1, 2 copies

Work with a partner to complete the mystery sentence on Activity Master 4–1. Follow these steps:

- Read each numbered sentence. Then, in the blanks that follow, write the Key Vocabulary word that best completes the sentence.

- When you have filled in all the blanks, unscramble the letters that appear in boxes to discover the mystery word.

- Write the mystery word in the sentence at the bottom.

Consider copying and laminating these activities for use in centers.

LISTENING/SPEAKING

Giving a Speech

🧍 Sings	🕐 45 minutes
Objective	Prepare and deliver a speech.
Materials	Reference sources, note cards

A speech is a talk given for the purpose of informing, persuading, or entertaining. Prepare, rehearse,
and deliver a speech, using the guidelines below at
an appropriate time. Here are some possible topics:

- Inform listeners about an ancient culture, such as
  that of the Aztecs.

- Inform listeners about the discovery of
  Cleopatra's lost palace.

- Persuade listeners of the value of traveling to
  learn about other cultures.

Guidelines for Giving a Speech
- Choose a topic that will interest the
  audience.
- Use formal or informal language, as is
  appropriate to your audience.
- Find all the information you need to include.
  Use multiple sources.
- Prepare an interesting beginning and ending,
  and arrange the information so that one
  idea leads logically to the next.
- Practice the speech until you know it well.
  Write key words on note cards as cues.

PHONICS/SPELLING

Shhhhh!

🧍 Sings	🕐 30 minutes
Objective	Identify and spell words with the /sh/ sound.

You are consulting a guidebook about writing
research papers. Follow these steps:

- Copy the passage below onto a sheet of paper. In
  each blank, write down a Spelling Word that uses
  the /sh/ sound. The letter combination that spells
  the /sh/ sound in the Spelling Word is indicated in
  parentheses. See **Practice Book** page 257 for the
  complete Spelling Word list.

- Use context clues to make sure the word you pick
  makes sense.

When writing about _____(ci)_____ cultures, be
sure to _____(sh)_____ that your details and
conclusions are correct. Use _____(ti)_____ as
you do your research. Check that you have a
current _____(ti)_____ of each book you look at.
Sources published by _____(ci)_____ agencies of
the government or by universities are
considered authoritative. You may feel
_____(ss)_____ to include Internet sources that are
not reliable, but that would defeat your _(ss)_.
Avoid _____(sh)_____ generalizations in favor of
in-depth analysis.

Shhh!	caution	pressure
ancient	edition	mission
establish	official	shallow

Leveled Readers

LEVELED READERS

A Brave Past

Summary *Texas schoolboy Victor Guerrero discovers that there was a Spanish explorer who shared his last name and who tried to save the Maya from invading conquistadors. Victor decides to research the life of Gonzalo Guerrero and the ancient Maya. He reads about Mayan achievements and customs and about the Maya's struggles with the Spanish. He learns that no one is sure why the Mayan civilization faded, and he also learns that the culture's strong heritage survives.*

Vocabulary

Introduce the Key Vocabulary and ask students to complete the BLM.

ruins partial remains of buildings, *p. 3*

sacred holy, for religious use, *p. 10*

offering a gift or contribution, *p. 11*

splendor powerful, beautiful appearance, *p. 21*

Building Background and Vocabulary

Share that this story tells about a boy who researches a Spanish explorer after discovering that he and the explorer have the same last name. Ask students what they know about the Mayan civilization. Guide students through the text, using some of the vocabulary from the story.

Comprehension Skill: Author's Viewpoint

Have students read the Strategy Focus on the book flap. Remind students to use the strategy and to think about the author's viewpoint as they read the book. (See the Leveled Readers Teacher's Guide for **Vocabulary and Comprehension Practice Masters.**)

Responding

Have partners discuss how to answer the questions on the inside back cover.

Think About the Selection Sample answers:

1. He probably admired their achievements in math, science, architecture, and art.

2. Since he is proud of Gonzalo Guerrero, Victor would like to know he is related.

3. The Maya. She presents Guerrero as a hero, saving the Maya from the greedy Spanish conquerors; she describes the glory of the Mayan civilization.

4. Answers will vary.

Making Connections Answers will vary.

Building Fluency

Model Read aloud the caption on page 8. Point out to students that the caption explains the picture above it.

Practice Have small groups find and read aloud other examples of picture captions in the story (pages 9, 10, 16, etc.).

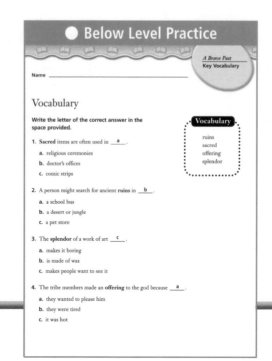

● Below Level Practice

A Brave Past
Key Vocabulary

Name _____

Vocabulary

Write the letter of the correct answer in the space provided.

Vocabulary
ruins
sacred
offering
splendor

1. Sacred items are often used in ___a___ .
   a. religious ceremonies
   b. doctor's offices
   c. comic strips

2. A person might search for ancient **ruins** in ___b___ .
   a. a school bus
   b. a desert or jungle
   c. a pet store

3. The **splendor** of a work of art ___c___ .
   a. makes it boring
   b. is made of wax
   c. makes people want to see it

4. The tribe members made an **offering** to the god because ___a___ .
   a. they wanted to please him
   b. they were tired
   c. it was hot

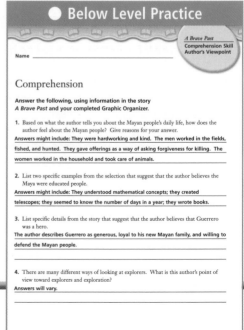

● Below Level Practice

A Brave Past
Comprehension Skill
Author's Viewpoint

Name _____

Comprehension

Answer the following, using information in the story *A Brave Past* **and your completed Graphic Organizer.**

1. Based on what the author tells you about the Mayan people's daily life, how does the author feel about the Mayan people? Give reasons for your answer.
   Answers might include: They were hardworking and kind. The men worked in the fields, fished, and hunted. They gave offerings as a way of asking forgiveness for killing. The women worked in the household and took care of animals.

2. List two specific examples from the selection that suggest that the author believes the Maya were educated people.
   Answers might include: They understood mathematical concepts; they created telescopes; they seemed to know the number of days in a year; they wrote books.

3. List specific details from the story that suggest that the author believes that Guerrero was a hero.
   The author describes Guerrero as generous, loyal to his new Mayan family, and willing to defend the Mayan people.

4. There are many different ways of looking at explorers. What is this author's point of view toward explorers and exploration?
   Answers will vary.

▲ ON LEVEL

Dream Weaver
by Marc Carroll
illustrated by Stephan Daigle

Dream Weaver

Summary *Cori and Quilla are about to reach milestones in their lives. When a messenger comes to their Incan village, the sisters and the other villagers learn that invading Spanish soldiers have just captured their emperor. Their whole way of life is about to change.*

Vocabulary

Introduce the Key Vocabulary and ask students to complete the BLM.

alpaca a shaggy, camel-like animal, *p. 3*

exasperation frustration, *p. 4*

nimbly with agility, *p. 6*

initiation introduction, *p. 9*

empire* a large area made up of many territories under one government, *p. 11*

metropolis* a major city; a center of culture, *p. 11*

fortress strongholds, *p. 12*

ransom payoff, *p. 18*

conquered* defeated in battle, *p. 18*

*Forms of these words are Anthology Key Vocabulary words.

Building Background and Vocabulary

Help students locate Peru and the Andes Mountains on a map. Tell them that hundreds of years ago, a people called the Inca lived in this region. Guide students through the text, using some of the vocabulary from the story.

Comprehension Skill: Author's Viewpoint

Have students read the Strategy Focus on the book flap. Remind students to use the strategy and to think about the author's viewpoint as they read the book. (See the Leveled Readers Teacher's Guide for **Vocabulary and Comprehension Practice Masters.**)

Responding

Have partners discuss how to answer the questions on the inside back cover.

Think About the Selection Sample answers:

1. She's afraid she may be sent away to become a Chosen Woman.
2. She daydreams about Incan history, and it inspires her art.
3. The stories have a soothing and cheering effect, and help her family members forget their troubles.
4. Answers will vary.

Making Connections Answers will vary.

Building Fluency

Model Read aloud page 7. Explain that the story Quilla tells is an example of folklore.

Practice Ask students to read aloud other examples of folklore elements in the story (pages 10, 20). Have them explain what folkloric details these examples contain (talking animals, gods and goddesses).

▲ On Level Practice

Dream Weaver
Key Vocabulary

Name _____

Vocabulary

Complete each sentence with a word from the vocabulary box.

Vocabulary
alpaca
conquered
empire
exasperation
fortresses
initiation
metropolis
nimbly
ransom

1. The Peruvian tribe's _____initiation_____ ceremony involved many complex rituals.

2. Manuel was determined to be accepted into the group, and he _____nimbly_____ jumped over all the obstacles in his way.

3. Much to his annoyance and _____exasperation_____, he could not break the secret code.

4. The forceful army invaded and _____conquered_____ the surrounding villages.

5. Soon the invader's growing _____empire_____ will include three new territories.

6. In no time, the town was transformed from a sleepy village into a bustling _____metropolis_____.

7. The villagers offered a large _____ransom_____ for the return of their leader, but the captors refused to negotiate.

8. Troops streamed out of the _____fortresses_____ that protected the town from enemy forces.

9. Even the wooly _____alpaca_____ on the hillside shivered in the forbidding wind.

▲ On Level Practice

Dream Weaver
Comprehension Skill
Author's Viewpoint

Name _____

Comprehension

Answer the following, using information in the selection and your completed Graphic Organizer.

1. What is the author's purpose for writing this story?
Sample answer: To describe the struggle of one Incan girl trying to keep traditions strong at a time when the Incan civilization is about to be conquered.

2. What kinds of facts are included in the selection?
Sample answer: facts about the lives of Quilla and Cori and girls their age; facts about the Incan lifestyle, traditions, and rituals; facts about historic events.

3. What words indicate the author's viewpoint about one of the characters in the story?
Sample answer: The author describes Quilla as patient, talented, and sensitive; these words indicate a positive viewpoint.

4. Consider all the information in the story and describe the author's viewpoint.
Sample answer: The author admires Quilla because she cares for her sister and tries to set a good example. In some ways, she views Quilla as a symbol of Incan civilization. She also views the Spanish invaders negatively.

5. Do you agree with the author's viewpoint? Why or why not?
Answers will vary.

Copán: City of the Maya

Summary *In 1839, explorers discovered the ancient Mayan ruins at Copán. Unfortunately, some valuable evidence has been lost. But tourists still flock to Copán to view the site of a civilization that was much like our own.*

Vocabulary

Introduce the Key Vocabulary and ask students to complete the BLM.

intricate* complicated; made up of many details, *p. 5*

inscribed written upon, *p. 5*

site* place where something was, is, or will be located, *p. 5*

excavation a dig to uncover evidence, *p. 7*

expedition trip, mission, *p. 9*

descendants people whose descent can be traced, *p. 9*

artifacts relics, *p. 13*

deciphered decoded, *p. 13*

dynasty period of rule, *p. 14*

jade a stone commonly carved or used for jewelry, *p. 18*

*Forms of these words are Anthology Key Vocabulary words.

■ ABOVE LEVEL

Building Background and Vocabulary

Invite volunteers to locate Central America on a map. Ask students what an archaeologist does and what it might be like to discover an unknown site. Guide students through the text, using some of the vocabulary from the story.

◉ Comprehension Skill: Author's Viewpoint

Have students read the Strategy Focus on the book flap. Remind students to use the strategy and to think about the author's viewpoint as they read the book. (See the Leveled Readers Teacher's Guide for **Vocabulary and Comprehension Practice Masters**.)

Responding

Have partners discuss how to answer the questions on the inside back cover.

Think About the Selection Sample answers:

1. They made careful measurements, and Catherwood drew pictures.
2. The modern language spoken by the Maya who still live in the region; and the work of the Spanish monk Diego de Landa.
3. They believed that they could prosper only if there were balance and harmony in the universe, which could only be achieved if the gods' needs were satisfied.
4. Answers will vary.

Making Connections Answers will vary.

◉ Building Fluency

Model Explain to students that the first paragraph on page 8 is an example of opinion or theory, while the second paragraph contains factual information.

Practice Ask students to find and read aloud examples of fact (pages 11, 14, 15) and opinion (pages 7, 20, 21) from the story.

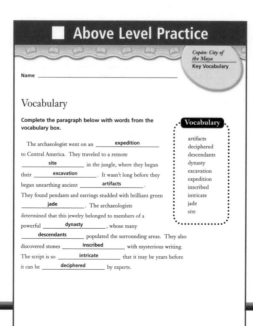

Leveled Readers

The Mighty Maya

Summary *Victor is not interested in his Mayan people's past until he hears about an explorer named Gonzalo Guerrero, who lived with the Maya and loved their culture. Thinking he might be related to the explorer, Victor dedicates himself to learning about Mayan culture.*

Vocabulary

Introduce the Key Vocabulary and ask students to complete the BLM.

ruins the remains of something that has collapsed, *p. 3*

conquered* defeated in battle, *p. 4*

culture all the results of human work and thought that belong to a people, *p. 4*

ancestor a person from whom one is descended, *p. 4*

telescopes devices to make distant objects appear closer, *p. 8*

sites* places where things were, are, or will be located, *p. 20*

*Forms of these words are Anthology Key Vocabulary words.

◆ LANGUAGE SUPPORT

Building Background and Vocabulary

Tell students they will be reading about the ancient Mayan culture in Mexico. Have students help you create a word web to show what they already know about the Mayan culture in Mexico. Then distribute the **Build Background Practice Master,** read it aloud, and have students complete it in pairs.

Comprehension Skill: Author's Viewpoint

Have students read the Strategy Focus on the book flap. Remind students to use the strategy and to think about the author's viewpoint as they read the book. (See the Leveled Readers Teacher's Guide for **Build Background, Vocabulary,** and **Graphic Organizer Masters.**)

Responding

Have partners discuss how to answer the questions on the inside back cover.

Think About the Selection Sample answers:

1. He learns that he may be related to someone who helped the Maya.
2. The ruins hold clues about an interesting group of people and how those people lived long ago.
3. His wife and children were Maya, and the Mayan people had treated him well.
4. Answers will vary.

Making Connections Answers will vary.

Building Fluency

Model Have students follow along in their books as they listen to the recording of pages 3–4 on the audio CD.

Practice Have students read aloud with the recording until they are able to read the text on their own accurately and with expression.

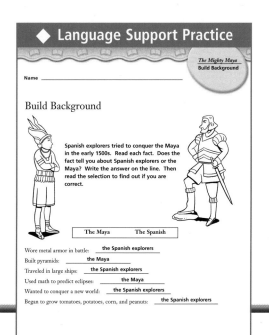

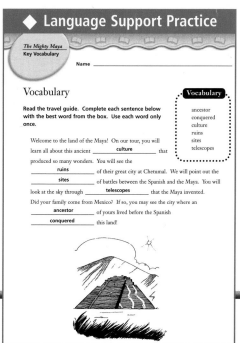

Reading-Writing Workshop

Research Report

In the Reading-Writing Workshop for Theme 4, *Discovering Ancient Cultures,* students read Stephanie's research report, "The Ancient Culture of the Inca," on Anthology pages 384–387. Then they follow the five steps of the writing process to write a research report.

Meet the Author

Stephanie S.
Grade: six
State: New York
Hobbies: movies, crafts, and reading
What she'd like to be when she grows up: a teacher

Theme Skill Trace

Writing
- Eliminating Unnecessary Words, 383L
- Elaborating with Adjectives, 407L
- Combining Sentences with Adjectives, 427L

Grammar
- Changing the Position of Adjectives, 383J
- Using the Correct Form of Adjectives, 407J
- Using Adjectives and Adverbs Correctly, 427J

Spelling
- The /sh/ Sound, 383E
- Adding *-ion* or *-ation*, 407E
- Unstressed Syllables, 427E

Pacing the Workshop

Here is a suggestion for how you might pace the workshop within one week or on five separate days across the theme.

DAY 1 PREWRITING

Students
- read the student model, 384–387
- choose a topic for their research report, 387A
- organize their report, 387B
- locate and evaluate information for their report, 387C

Spelling Frequently Misspelled Words, 387F; *Practice Book,* 257

DAY 2 DRAFTING

Students
- outline and draft their report, 387D

Spelling *Practice Book,* 20

Focus on Writing Traits: Research Report

The workshop for this theme focuses on the traits of organization, conventions, and presentation. However, students should think about all of the writing traits during the writing process.

ORGANIZATION Have students write questions about their topic on separate note cards and then use the cards to organize their information.

- Point to a specific question, and ask, Which facts answer this question?

- Point to specific facts, and ask, Which question does this fact answer?

- If a fact doesn't fit a question, discuss deleting the fact. If several facts don't fit, discuss adding a new question.

CONVENTIONS AND PRESENTATION Your students will likely fall into two groups: One group will spend too much time on conventions and presentation, and the other will spend too little.

- One group will want to fix mistakes during prewriting and drafting. Emphasize that at these stages they should be thinking about what they want to say.

- The other group will hand in their final copy without thought for their mistakes. Remind them that mistakes prevent others from understanding their ideas.

Tips for Teaching the Writing Traits

- Teach one trait at a time.

- Discuss examples of the traits in the literature students are reading.

- Encourage students to talk about the traits during a writing conference.

- Encourage students to revise their writing for one trait at a time.

DAY 3 REVISING

Students

- evaluate their research report, 387E

- revise their report, 387E

- have a writing conference, 387E

- improve their writing by using exact adjectives, 387E

Spelling *Practice Book,* 21

DAY 4 PROOFREADING

Students

- proofread their research report, 387E

- correct frequently misspelled words in their report, 387F

Spelling *Practice Book,* 22

DAY 5 PUBLISHING

Students

- publish their research report, 387G

- reflect on their writing experience, 387G

Spelling Assessment, 387F

Research Report

Discussing the Guidelines

Display **Transparency RWW4–1,** and discuss what makes a great research report.

- Remember that students should think about all the writing traits as they write: ideas, organization, voice, word choice, sentence fluency, conventions, and presentation.

Discussing the Model

Have students read the Student Writing Model on Anthology pages 384–387.

- Discuss with students what the writer did to make her research report interesting to read.

- Use the Reading As a Writer questions on page 387.

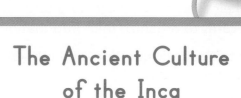

Student Writing Model

A Research Report

A research report presents facts about a particular topic. Use this student's writing as a model when you write a research report of your own.

The Ancient Culture of the Inca

The first paragraph of a research report usually **introduces** the topic.	The ancient Inca culture of Peru formed a vast and powerful empire that extended from northern Ecuador to central Chile. The Inca Empire began in the 1100s and ended in the 1500s, when the Spanish army took control.
Topic sentences present the **main idea** of a report.	The Inca people were considered an empire, but in fact they were really a confederation of many nations located in South America. The Inca Empire was made up of what are today Peru, Ecuador, Bolivia, and parts of Argentina and Chile. These different nations were treated well as long as they followed the Inca leader and obeyed the laws.

384

Transparency RWW4–1

What Makes a Great Research Report?

A research report presents facts about a particular topic.

When you write your research report, remember to follow these guidelines.

- Choose an engaging, thought-provoking topic. Make sure it is neither too broad nor too narrow.
- Do research. Use more than one reliable source.
- Take notes and make an outline. Use the outline to write the report.
- Write an introduction that tells your topic.
- Write at least one paragraph for each main idea. Support each topic sentence with facts.
- Use your own words. Don't copy from your sources.
- Write a meaningful conclusion at the end of the report.
- Include an accurate list of sources.

ANNOTATED VERSION   RESEARCH REPORT   Reading-Writing Workshop: Research Report

TRANSPARENCY RWW 4–1
TEACHER'S EDITION PAGE 384

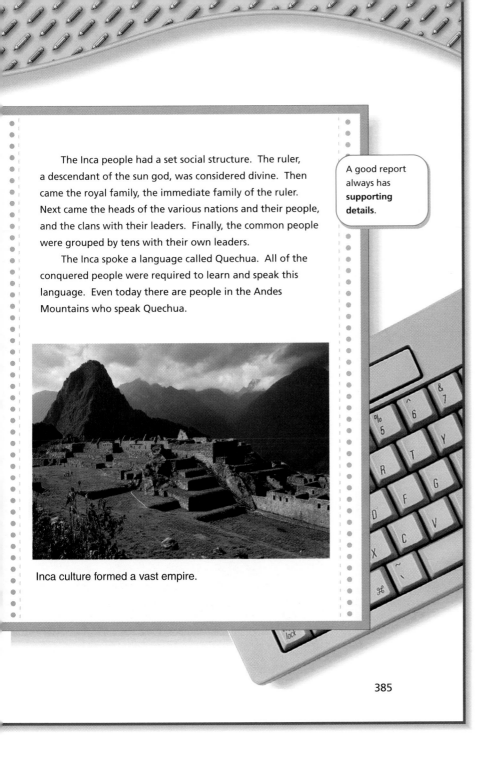

The Inca people had a set social structure. The ruler, a descendant of the sun god, was considered divine. Then came the royal family, the immediate family of the ruler. Next came the heads of the various nations and their people, and the clans with their leaders. Finally, the common people were grouped by tens with their own leaders.

The Inca spoke a language called Quechua. All of the conquered people were required to learn and speak this language. Even today there are people in the Andes Mountains who speak Quechua.

> A good report always has **supporting details**.

Inca culture formed a vast empire.

385

The Inca were good engineers. They were able to build huge forts, using perfectly cut stone that fit together so well that mortar was not needed. In fact, their forts are still standing today. They also built roads and tunnels through the mountains. They built bridges as well. The ability to perform all of these skills is amazing, since the Inca didn't have the tools and machinery that we have today. They were also able to make mountainous terrain into usable farmland on which they grew corn and potatoes and raised animals such as llama and alpaca.

The Inca raised animals, like this llama.

386

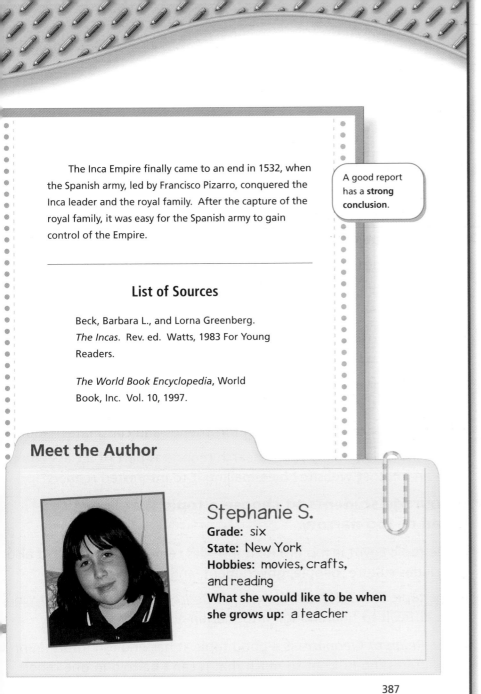

The Inca Empire finally came to an end in 1532, when the Spanish army, led by Francisco Pizarro, conquered the Inca leader and the royal family. After the capture of the royal family, it was easy for the Spanish army to gain control of the Empire.

> A good report has a **strong conclusion**.

List of Sources

Beck, Barbara L., and Lorna Greenberg. *The Incas*. Rev. ed. Watts, 1983 For Young Readers.

The World Book Encyclopedia, World Book, Inc. Vol. 10, 1997.

Meet the Author

Stephanie S.
Grade: six
State: New York
Hobbies: movies, crafts, and reading
What she would like to be when she grows up: a teacher

387

Reading As a Writer

1. What is the topic of this research report? (the ancient Inca culture)

2. What is the topic sentence of the third paragraph? What facts support the topic sentence? (Topic sentence: *The Inca people had a set social structure*; Facts: ruler considered divine; below ruler—royal family, then heads of various nations, then leaders of clans; common people at the bottom)

3. What is the topic sentence of the fifth paragraph? What facts support the topic sentence? (Topic sentence: *The Inca were good engineers*; Facts: able to build huge forts using perfectly cut stone; built roads and tunnels through the mountains; built bridges)

4. Where did the author get the information for this report? How do you know? (from a book called *The Incas* and from *The World Book Encyclopedia*; list of sources at the end of the report)

Choosing a Topic

❶ Tell students they will write a research report. Have studen[ts] list three or more ideas for a research report that they could write. Offer the following prompts.

- Is there a subject discussed in newspapers you find interesting?

- What is your favorite animal? time in history? science subject?

- Which people, either from the present or from history, do you admire?

❷ Have students answer these questions, either in a writing journal or on a sheet of paper, as they choose a topic.

- What is your main purpose: to inform? to shed light on an important topic? to set the record straight about past events?

- What audience are you writing for: friends and classmates? adults?

- How will you publish your research report: as part of a class book? on an Internet website? by e-mailing it to interested readers?

❸ Encourage students to choose a topic that is not too broad or too narrow.

- The topic *Egypt* is too broad. It includes centuries of history. It also includes culture, people, government, and so on.

- The topic *The Design of Cleopatra's Bedroom* is too narrow. It woul[d] be difficult to find enough information about this topic.

- *The Reign of Cleopatra* is a good topic. It has enough information t[o] be interesting but not so much that it can't be told in one report.

❹ Have students discuss their ideas with a partner and decide which topic would be the best one to write about. Then review these tips with students.

Tips for Getting Started With a Topic

- Discuss your topic with a partner. Is your topic too broad or too narrow?

- What questions does your partner have? Where could you find answers?

- Talk with an expert who is knowledgeable about your topic.

- Does your topic still interest you? If not, you might choose another topic.

Organizing and Planning

1 Explain planning a research report. Go over these points.

- Organize what you know about your topic.
- Plan what you want to learn about your topic.
- Think about possible source materials.

2 Display Transparency RWW4–2. Model filling it out, using the Student Writing Model on page 384–387. (Sample answers are shown below.) Explain that this is how Stephanie might have filled out her questionnaire before researching her topic.

Research Report Questionnaire

What is your subject? The ancient Inca culture

Explain your subject in one sentence. The Inca were an ancient people who ruled an empire.

How much do you already know about this subject? I know they lived in South America a long time ago.

What source materials will you use? An encyclopedia and a book; could also use websites, magazines

What are some possible titles for your subject? The Ancient Culture of the Inca, The People Who Spoke Quechua

Why did you choose this subject? The Inca fascinate me.

What will your readers learn from this report? How the Inca ruled; what they were like

---

3 Duplicate and distribute Transparency RWW4–2. Have students fill it out. They can write additional questions they want to answer on the back.

4 Tell students how to take notes on what they learn. Go over these points.

- Use your questions and what you already know to guide your research.
- Write your questions about your topic on separate note cards.
- Record interesting facts that answer each question.
- Use your own words. Don't copy. Write the source and the page number or website address next to each fact.

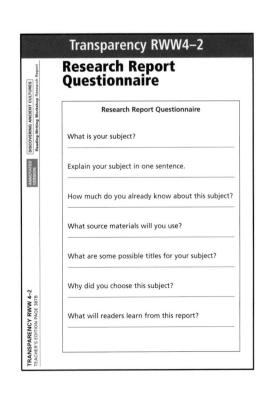

Locating and Evaluating Information

1 Introduce using sources. Tell students there are many sources for finding information about a topic. Go over these points.

- Review the kind of information available in encyclopedias, almanacs, atlases, newspapers, and magazines. Use the chart below.

- Recommend that students also consider talking to experts to answer questions about a topic.

- Students can also use technology when they research their topic.

Research Question	Possible Source
Which is the smallest continent?	atlas; encyclopedia
What was Mozart's childhood like?	biography; encyclopedia
Do all birds migrate?	Audubon Society; nonfiction book

2 Explain strategies for evaluating information.

- Write down only facts, not opinions. Facts can be proven. Opinions are thoughts or beliefs.

- Only write down information that will help explain your topic.

- Use more than one source to make sure that the information you find is accurate. Speak with a librarian for additional ideas.

- Use only information from reputable sources. For instance, if the source is an Internet site, it should be created by a respected school or organization.

3 Display Transparency RWW4–3. Explain that some examples will have more than one correct answer.

- Discuss the correct answer to the first question (b). Explain that the time periods of answers a, c, and d are not during the sixteenth century.

- Ask what kind of information would be found in the other books. (Sample answers: (a) Historical information from before the Aztecs, (c) Mexico during the 1800s, (d) lifestyle of Mexican artists today)

- Work with students to complete the rest of the transparency.

4 Have students research their topic. Remind them to take notes in their own words.

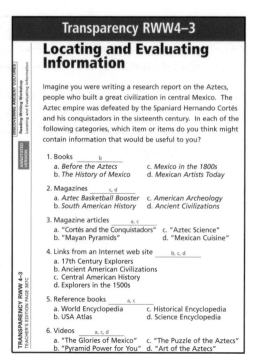

Transparency RWW4–3

Locating and Evaluating Information

Imagine you were writing a research report on the Aztecs, people who built a great civilization in central Mexico. The Aztec empire was defeated by the Spaniard Hernando Cortés and his conquistadors in the sixteenth century. In each of the following categories, which item or items do you think might contain information that would be useful to you?

1. Books ___b___
   a. *Before the Aztecs* c. *Mexico in the 1800s*
   b. *The History of Mexico* d. *Mexican Artists Today*

2. Magazines ___c, d___
   a. *Aztec Basketball Booster* c. *American Archeology*
   b. *South American History* d. *Ancient Civilizations*

3. Magazine articles ___a, c___
   a. "Cortés and the Conquistadors" c. "Aztec Science"
   b. "Mayan Pyramids" d. "Mexican Cuisine"

4. Links from an Internet web site ___b, c, d___
   a. 17th Century Explorers
   b. Ancient American Civilizations
   c. Central American History
   d. Explorers in the 1500s

5. Reference books ___a, c___
   a. World Encyclopedia c. Historical Encyclopedia
   b. USA Atlas d. Science Encyclopedia

6. Videos ___a, c, d___
   a. "The Glories of Mexico" c. "The Puzzle of the Aztecs"
   b. "Pyramid Power for You" d. "Art of the Aztecs"

Using an Outline

Writing Traits

ORGANIZATION Explain that a good research report is well organized. Go over these steps for writing and using outlines.

- List all of the points you plan to cover.
- List main topics first. Use Roman numerals (I, II, III, and so on). Then list subtopics. Use capital letters (A, B, C, and so on).

❶ Display Transparency RWW4–4. Model completing main topic I. Work with students to complete main topics II and III.

❷ Discuss writing a paragraph for each main topic in an outline. Keep **Transparency RWW4–4** displayed, and model writing a paragraph based on the first main topic. Discuss these points.

- The topic sentence tells the main topic. It usually comes first.
- The other sentences tell the subtopics.

> Congress is the legislative branch of the United States government. Making laws is its main job, or function. Congress is made up of the House of Representatives and the Senate. Each has some unique duties. It is the job of the House to approve government spending. The Senate, on the other hand, must ratify treaties.

❸ Have students draft their research report.

- Remind them to use their own words.
- Encourage them to use questions as well as statements.
- Tell students to begin the report with a paragraph that states the topic of the report and to end with a concluding paragraph that sums up the report.

❹ Remind students to include a list of sources. Point out Stephanie's list of sources on page 387. Review proper formatting.

- When they write the title of a book, magazine article, or newspaper article, students should capitalize the first, last, and each important word.
- Point out the use of italics, or slanted type, for the book titles. When handwritten, titles should be underlined. Titles of magazine articles and book chapters should be enclosed in quotation marks.

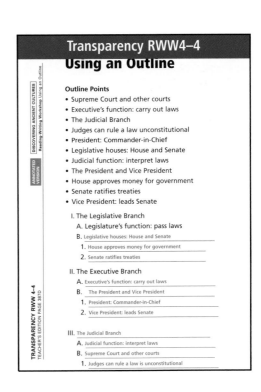

Transparency RWW4–4
Using an Outline

DISCOVERING ANCIENT CULTURES
Reading-Writing Workshop Using an Outline

ANNOTATED VERSION

Outline Points
- Supreme Court and other courts
- Executive's function: carry out laws
- The Judicial Branch
- Judges can rule a law unconstitutional
- President: Commander-in-Chief
- Legislative houses: House and Senate
- Judicial function: interpret laws
- The President and Vice President
- House approves money for government
- Senate ratifies treaties
- Vice President: leads Senate

I. The Legislative Branch
   A. Legislature's function: pass laws
   B. Legislative houses: House and Senate
      1. House approves money for government
      2. Senate ratifies treaties

II. The Executive Branch
   A. Executive's function: carry out laws
   B. The President and Vice President
      1. President: Commander-in-Chief
      2. Vice President: leads Senate

III. The Judicial Branch
   A. Judicial function: interpret laws
   B. Supreme Court and other courts
      1. Judges can rule a law is unconstitutional

TRANSPARENCY RWW 4–4
TEACHER'S EDITION PAGE 387D

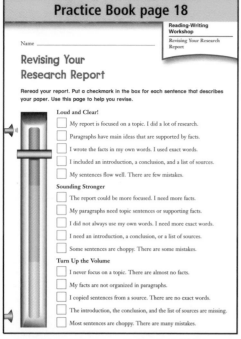

Practice Book page 18

Reading-Writing Workshop
Revising Your Research Report

Name _____

Revising Your Research Report

Reread your report. Put a checkmark in the box for each sentence that describes your paper. Use this page to help you revise.

Loud and Clear!

☐ My report is focused on a topic. I did a lot of research.

☐ Paragraphs have main ideas that are supported by facts.

☐ I wrote the facts in my own words. I used exact words.

☐ I included an introduction, a conclusion, and a list of sources.

☐ My sentences flow well. There are few mistakes.

Sounding Stronger

☐ The report could be more focused. I need more facts.

☐ My paragraphs need topic sentences or supporting facts.

☐ I did not always use my own words. I need more exact words.

☐ I need an introduction, a conclusion, or a list of sources.

☐ Some sentences are choppy. There are some mistakes.

Turn Up the Volume

☐ I never focus on a topic. There are almost no facts.

☐ My facts are not organized in paragraphs.

☐ I copied sentences from a source. There are no exact words.

☐ The introduction, the conclusion, and the list of sources are missing.

☐ Most sentences are choppy. There are many mistakes.

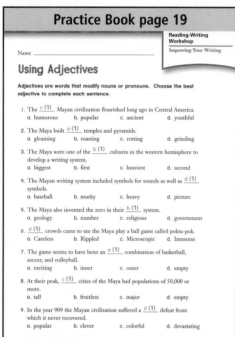

Practice Book page 19

Reading-Writing Workshop
Improving Your Writing

Name _____

Using Adjectives

Adjectives are words that modify nouns or pronouns. Choose the best adjective to complete each sentence.

1. The __c (1)__ Mayan civilization flourished long ago in Central America.
   a. humorous   b. popular   c. ancient   d. youthful

2. The Maya built __a (1)__ temples and pyramids.
   a. gleaming   b. roasting   c. rotting   d. grinding

3. The Maya were one of the __b (1)__ cultures in the western hemisphere to develop a writing system.
   a. biggest   b. first   c. heaviest   d. second

4. The Mayan writing system included symbols for sounds as well as __d (1)__ symbols.
   a. baseball   b. murky   c. heavy   d. picture

5. The Maya also invented the zero in their __b (1)__ system.
   a. geology   b. number   c. religious   d. government

6. __d (1)__ crowds came to see the Maya play a ball game called pokta-pok.
   a. Careless   b. Rippled   c. Microscopic   d. Immense

7. The game seems to have been an __a (1)__ combination of basketball, soccer, and volleyball.
   a. exciting   b. inner   c. outer   d. empty

8. At their peak, __c (1)__ cities of the Maya had populations of 50,000 or more.
   a. tall   b. fruitless   c. major   d. empty

9. In the year 909 the Mayan civilization suffered a __d (1)__ defeat from which it never recovered.
   a. popular   b. clever   c. colorful   d. devastating

Transparency RWW4–5

Using Adjectives

1. To hide from the Spanish conquerors, the Inca people built a(n) ____d____ city called Machu Picchu.
   a. natural   c. ruined
   b. ordinary   d. secret

2. Machu Picchu was built on a ____a____ peak high in the Andes Mountains.
   a. majestic   c. busy
   b. swampy   d. sandy

3. The rugged terrain and ____c____ location kept the city safe from invaders.
   a. central   c. remote
   b. fertile   d. coastal

4. The people cut terraces in the ____a____ mountainsides in order to grow crops.
   a. steep   c. green
   b. rolling   d. level

5. The city's ____b____ houses were built of stone blocks.
   a. wooden   c. flimsy
   b. sturdy   d. rickety

6. At the center of the city was a huge and ____b____ palace where the ruler lived.
   a. barren   c. forlorn
   b. splendid   d. cramped

7. Life in the city came to a ____c____ end when the people left abruptly.
   a. glorious   c. sudden
   b. triumphant   d. happy

TRANSPARENCY RWW 4-5
TEACHER'S EDITION PAGE 387E

DISCOVERING ANCIENT CULTURES
Reading-Writing Workshop Using Adjectives

ANNOTATED VERSION

Revising

Have students use **Practice Book** page 18 to help them evaluate and then revise their research report. Students should also discuss their drafts in a writing conference with one or more classmates. (Distribute the Conference Master on page R30. Discuss the sample thoughts and questions before students have their conferences.) Remind students to keep in mind their listeners' comments and questions when they revise.

Improving Writing: Using Adjectives

Explain that a successful research report uses adjectives to make vivid descriptions. Adjectives are words that modify nouns or pronouns. Adjectives modify by describing the following.

- What size: *The fox has <u>large</u> ears.*

- How many: *The fox has <u>two</u> ears.*

- What color: *The fox has <u>red</u> ears.*

- What kind: *The fox has <u>beautiful</u> ears.*

- What shape: *The fox has <u>pointed</u> ears.*

Display **Transparency RWW4–5.**

- Model the first exercise. Explain that (d) is the most exact adjective.

- Then have students complete the transparency on a sheet of paper.

- Encourage students to explain their choices.

Assign **Practice Book** page 19. Then have students reread their research reports to find places where they can add adjectives.

Proofreading

Writing Traits

CONVENTIONS Explain that students should pay attention to conventions to make it easy for others to read what they have written. Have students proofread their papers to correct capitalization, punctuation, spelling, and usage. They can use the proofreading checklist and proofreading marks on **Practice Book** pages 273–274.

Frequently Misspelled Words

Write the Spelling Words on the board, or distribute the list on **Practice Book** page 257. Help students identify the part of the word likely to be misspelled.

Spelling Pretest/Test

Basic Words

1. The equipment is **decent**.
2. The **descent** is steep.
3. What would **affect** his game?
4. He has a positive **effect**.
5. The floor was **desert** sand.
6. Their dinners include **dessert**.
7. The horses' flanks were **slick**.
8. Each animal's coat was **sleek**.
9. They entered from an **alley**.
10. No one could count on an **ally**.
11. We were **confident** of winning.
12. I whispered to a **confidant**.
13. The horse jumped the **hurdle**.
14. They **hurtle** down the track.

Challenge Words

15. The **bizarre** colors clashed.
16. He bought a pin at the **bazaar**.
17. She skated an **ellipse** on the ice.
18. My skating will **eclipse** his.

Practice Book page 20

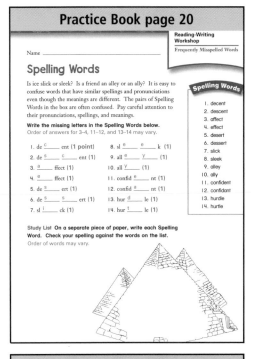

Reading-Writing Workshop
Frequently Misspelled Words

Name _____

Spelling Words

Is ice slick or sleek? Is a friend an alley or an ally? It is easy to confuse words that have similar spellings and pronunciations even though the meanings are different. The pairs of Spelling Words in the box are often confused. Pay careful attention to their pronunciations, spellings, and meanings.

Write the missing letters in the Spelling Words below.
Order of answers for 3–4, 11–12, and 13–14 may vary.

1. de <u>c</u> ent (1 point)
2. de <u>s</u> <u>c</u> ent (1)
3. <u>a</u> ffect (1)
4. <u>e</u> ffect (1)
5. de <u>s</u> ert (1)
6. de <u>s</u> <u>s</u> ert (1)
7. sl <u>i</u> ck (1)
8. sl <u>e</u> <u>e</u> k (1)
9. all <u>y</u> (1)
10. all <u>y</u> (1)
11. confid <u>e</u> nt (1)
12. confid <u>a</u> nt (1)
13. hur <u>d</u> le (1)
14. hur <u>t</u> le (1)

Spelling Words
1. decent
2. descent
3. affect
4. effect
5. desert
6. dessert
7. slick
8. sleek
9. alley
10. ally
11. confident
12. confidant
13. hurdle
14. hurtle

Study List On a separate piece of paper, write each Spelling Word. Check your spelling against the words on the list.
Order of words may vary.

Practice Book page 21

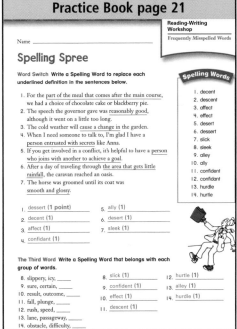

Reading-Writing Workshop
Frequently Misspelled Words

Name _____

Spelling Spree

Word Switch Write a Spelling Word to replace each underlined definition in the sentences below.

1. For the part of the meal that comes after the main course, we had a choice of chocolate cake or blackberry pie.
2. The speech the governor gave was reasonably good, although it went on a little too long.
3. The cold weather will cause a change in the garden.
4. When I need someone to talk to, I'm glad I have a person entrusted with secrets like Anna.
5. If you get involved in a conflict, it's helpful to have a person who joins with another to achieve a goal.
6. After a day of traveling through the area that gets little rainfall, the caravan reached an oasis.
7. The horse was groomed until its coat was smooth and glossy.

1. dessert (1 point)
2. decent (1)
3. affect (1)
4. confidant (1)
5. ally (1)
6. desert (1)
7. sleek (1)

The Third Word Write a Spelling Word that belongs with each group of words.

8. slippery, icy, _____
9. sure, certain, _____
10. result, outcome, _____
11. fall, plunge, _____
12. rush, speed, _____
13. lane, passageway, _____
14. obstacle, difficulty, _____

8. slick (1)
9. confident (1)
10. effect (1)
11. descent (1)
12. hurtle (1)
13. alley (1)
14. hurdle (1)

Spelling Words
1. decent
2. descent
3. affect
4. effect
5. desert
6. dessert
7. slick
8. sleek
9. alley
10. ally
11. confident
12. confidant
13. hurdle
14. hurtle

Practice Book page 257

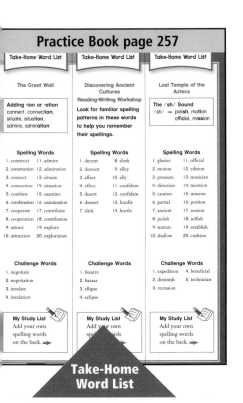

Take-Home Word List	Take-Home Word List	Take-Home Word List
The Great Wall	**Discovering Ancient Cultures**	**Lost Temple of the Aztecs**
Adding -ion or -ation connect, connection, situate, situation, admire, admiration	Reading-Writing Workshop Look for familiar spelling patterns in these words to help you remember their spellings.	The /sh/ Sound /sh/ → polish, motion official, mission

Spelling Words	**Spelling Words**	**Spelling Words**
1. construct 11. admire	1. decent 8. sleek	1. glacier 11. official
2. construction 12. admiration	2. descent 9. alley	2. motion 12. edition
3. connect 13. situate	3. affect 10. ally	3. pressure 13. musician
4. connection 14. situation	4. effect 11. confident	4. direction 14. mention
5. combine 15. examine	5. desert 12. confidant	5. caution 15. mission
6. combination 16. examination	6. dessert 13. hurdle	6. partial 16. portion
7. cooperate 17. contribute	7. slick 14. hurtle	7. ancient 17. session
8. cooperation 18. contribution		8. polish 18. selfish
9. attract 19. explore		9. station 19. establish
10. attraction 20. exploration		10. shallow 20. cushion

Challenge Words	**Challenge Words**	**Challenge Words**
1. negotiate	1. bizarre	1. expedition 4. beneficial
2. negotiation	2. bazaar	2. diminish 5. technician
3. insulate	3. ellipse	3. recession
4. insulation	4. eclipse	

My Study List
Add your own spelling words on the back. →

My Study List
Add your own spelling words ...

My Study List
Add your own spelling words on the back. →

Take-Home Word List

Practice Book page 22

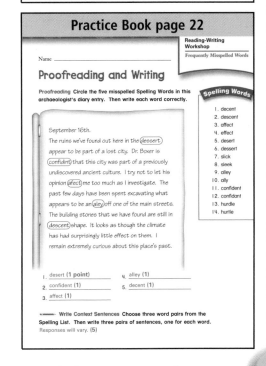

Reading-Writing Workshop
Frequently Misspelled Words

Name _____

Proofreading and Writing

Proofreading Circle the five misspelled Spelling Words in this archaeologist's diary entry. Then write each word correctly.

September 16th.
The ruins we've found out here in the (dessert) appear to be part of a lost city. Dr. Boxer is (confidint) that this city was part of a previously undiscovered ancient culture. I try not to let his opinion (afect) me too much as I investigate. The past few days have been spent excavating what appears to be an (aley) off one of the main streets. The building stones that we have found are still in (descent) shape. It looks as though the climate has had surprisingly little effect on them. I remain extremely curious about this place's past.

1. desert (1 point)
2. confident (1)
3. affect (1)
4. alley (1)
5. decent (1)

Write Context Sentences Choose three word pairs from the Spelling List. Then write three pairs of sentences, one for each word.
Responses will vary. (5)

Spelling Words
1. decent
2. descent
3. affect
4. effect
5. desert
6. dessert
7. slick
8. sleek
9. alley
10. ally
11. confident
12. confidant
13. hurdle
14. hurtle

📁 Portfolio Opportunity

Save students' final copy of their research report as an example of the development of their writing skills.

Publishing

Writing Traits

PRESENTATION Tell students to arrange their sentences and paragraphs in a way that will be easy for others to read. Encourage them to use neat handwriting or to type carefully when working on a computer.

Have students publish their research reports.

- Ask them to look back at the publishing ideas they noted when they chose a topic. Discuss the Ideas for Sharing box below.
- Then ask students to decide how they want to publish their writing.
- Tell them to make a neat final copy of their reports.

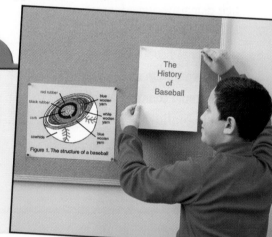

Ideas for Sharing

Write It

- Collect your research reports in a class *Book of Knowledge*.
- Submit your report to the school newspaper.

Say It

- Present your report orally.
- In a small group, tape-record your reports as a radio show. Introduce each speaker.

Show It

- Create an electronic multimedia presentation.
- Make a visual display.

Tips for Creating a Visual Display

- Create large visuals for your report.
- Include quotations, a diorama, or objects related to your topic.
- Arrange your visuals on posterboard, on the bulletin board, or as a "museum exhibit" of objects and resources.

Monitoring Student Progress

Student Self-Assessment

- Did your topic interest you? Did it interest your readers?
- What was the most outstanding part of your research report?
- What did you learn from writing this report about organization? about finding sources?
- What will you do differently next time you write a research report?

Evaluating

Have students write responses to the Student Self-Assessment questions.

Evaluate your students' writing, using the Writing Traits Scoring Rubric. The Scoring Rubric is based on the criteria in this workshop and reflects the criteria students used in Revising Your Research Report on **Practice Book** page 18.

Research Report

Writing Traits Scoring Rubric

4

IDEAS	The report is factual and well researched. It is focused on an interesting topic that is neither too broad nor too narrow. The list of sources is complete and accurate.
ORGANIZATION	Main ideas are stated in topic sentences. Facts and examples are grouped in paragraphs to support each main idea. The introduction and conclusion are effective.
VOICE	The writer used his or her own words.
WORD CHOICE	Words are precise, active, and descriptive.
SENTENCE FLUENCY	The writing flows well. Sentence length and structure vary.
CONVENTIONS	There are almost no errors in grammar, capitalization, spelling, or usage.
PRESENTATION	The final copy is neat and legible.

3

IDEAS	The report is well researched, although the topic may be too broad or too narrow. Facts or details are needed in some places. The list of sources may be incomplete.
ORGANIZATION	The introduction or conclusion may be weak. Some paragraphs may need topic sentences. Some details may be in the wrong paragraphs.
VOICE	The writer mostly used his or her own words.
WORD CHOICE	The writer could have used more exact, interesting words.
SENTENCE FLUENCY	The essay would benefit from greater sentence variety.
CONVENTIONS	There are a few mistakes, but they do not affect understanding.
PRESENTATION	The final copy is messy in a few places but still legible.

2

IDEAS	The report may not be clearly focused on a single topic. Many additional facts or details are needed. Facts are mixed with opinions. The list of sources is incomplete.
ORGANIZATION	Facts and details are not well organized into paragraphs with clear main ideas. There are few topic sentences. The report begins and ends abruptly.
VOICE	The writer often did not use his or her own words.
WORD CHOICE	Word choice is limited and repetitive.
SENTENCE FLUENCY	The essay lacks sentence variety.
CONVENTIONS	Mistakes sometimes make the essay hard to understand.
PRESENTATION	The final copy is messy. It may be illegible in a few places.

1

IDEAS	The report does not have a clear focus. The paper shows little research. There are almost no supporting details. There is no list of sources.
ORGANIZATION	Ideas and facts are disorganized, unclear, or just listed.
VOICE	The writer copied many sentences from a source.
WORD CHOICE	Word choice is vague or uninteresting. It may be confusing.
SENTENCE FLUENCY	Sentences are short, unclear, or repetitive.
CONVENTIONS	Many mistakes make the paper hard to understand.
PRESENTATION	The final copy is messy. It may be illegible in many places.

Lesson Overview

Literature

The Great Wall

The story of thousands of miles of earth and stone that turned a nation into a fortress

By Elizabeth Mann

Selection Summary

For centuries, the Chinese built the Great Wall as a form of defense against the Mongol warriors.

1 Background and Vocabulary

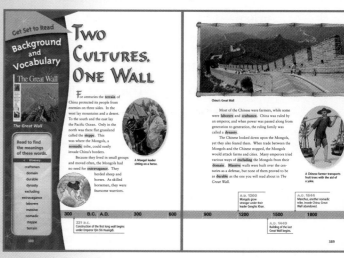

2 Main Selection

The Great Wall
Genre: Nonfiction

3 Technology Link

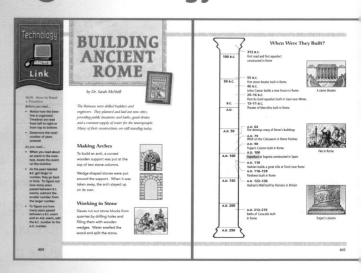

Instructional Support

Planning and Practice

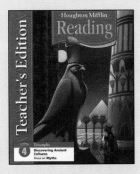

- Planning and classroom management
- Reading instruction
- Skill lessons
- Materials for reaching all learners

- Independent practice for skills, Level 6.2

- Transparencies
- Strategy Posters
- Blackline Masters

- Newsletters
- Selection Summaries
- Assignment Cards
- Observation Checklists
- Selection Tests

Reaching All Learners

Coordinated lessons, activities, and projects for additional reading instruction

For
- Classroom teacher
- Extended day
- Pull out
- Resource teacher
- Reading specialist

Technology

Audio Selection
The Great Wall

Get Set for Reading CD-ROM
- Background building
- Vocabulary support
- Selection Summary in English and Spanish

Accelerated Reader®
- Practice quizzes for the selection

www.eduplace.com
Log on to *Education Place*® for more activities related to the selection, including vocabulary support—
e • **Glossary**
e • **WordGame**

Leveled Books for Reaching All Learners

Leveled Readers and Leveled Practice

- Independent reading for building fluency
- Topic, comprehension strategy, and vocabulary linked to main selection
- Lessons in Teacher's Edition, pages 407O–407R
- Leveled practice for every book

Technology

Leveled Readers
Audio available

Book Adventure®

- Practice quizzes for the Leveled Theme Paperbacks
  www.bookadventure.org

● BELOW LEVEL

THE PYRAMIDS OF GIZA
BY STANFORD MAKISHI
ILLUSTRATED BY FRANCESCO SPADONI AND LORENZO CECCHI

Leveled Readers

● Below Level Practice

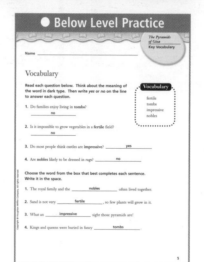

● Below Level Practice

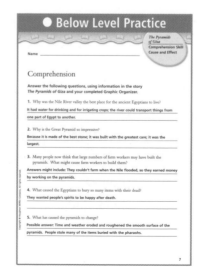

▲ ON LEVEL

A SCRIBE OF ANCIENT CHINA
by Jane Prassit
illustrated by Oki Han

Leveled Readers

▲ On Level Practice

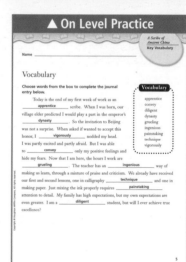

▲ On Level Practice

■ ABOVE LEVEL

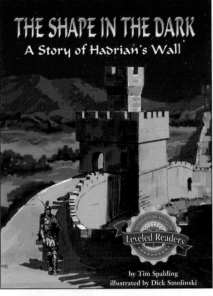

THE SHAPE IN THE DARK
A Story of Hadrian's Wall

Houghton Mifflin
Leveled Readers

by Tim Spalding
illustrated by Dick Smolinski

◆ LANGUAGE SUPPORT

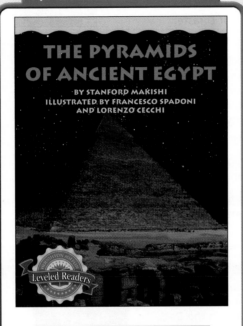

THE PYRAMIDS OF ANCIENT EGYPT

BY STANFORD MAKISHI
ILLUSTRATED BY FRANCESCO SPADONI
AND LORENZO CECCHI

Houghton Mifflin
Leveled Readers

Leveled Theme Paperbacks

- Extended independent reading in Theme-related trade books
- Lessons in Teacher's Edition, pages R2–R7

KATHRYN LASKY
THE LIBRARIAN WHO MEASURED THE EARTH

ILLUSTRATED BY KEVIN HAWKES

Below Level

■ Above Level Practice

The Shape in the Dark: A Story of Hadrian's Wall
Key Vocabulary

Name _____

Vocabulary

Choose words from the box to complete the journal entry below.

For the past two years, I've been helping to build the new **aqueduct** that will bring much-needed water to our growing city. It is nearly complete. Our population is **massive** and growing bigger every day. Our powerful **empire** not only controls the Mediterranean Sea, but also boasts outposts as distant as Britain. My brother has the job I really want: guarding our lands against the **barbarians** in Britain. But here I am, working alongside the other **laborers** here in Rome. My father says he is proud that I am helping to build something **durable**, something that will last through the ages, rather than guarding land that may not always be our own. But if there is one more report about a **revolt** by one of the British tribes, I will be joining my brother. The **terrain** in the north doesn't scare me. I know I have the courage to push beyond Hadrian's Wall and help **conquer** more lands for the Emperor.

Vocabulary
aqueduct
barbarians
conquer
durable
empire
laborers
massive
revolt
terrain

5

◆ Language Support Practice

The Pyramids of Ancient Egypt
Build Background

Name _____

Build Background

The kings of ancient Egypt filled their pyramids with items that were important to them. Design your own pyramid. Draw it in the frame. Then tell how you would build it and tell what you would put inside the pyramid. Answers will vary.

How I would build it	What I would put in it

5

Aïda
TOLD BY
Leontyne Price

ILLUSTRATED BY
LEO AND DIANE DILLON

On Level

■ Above Level Practice

The Shape in the Dark: A Story of Hadrian's Wall
Comprehension Skill
Cause and Effect

Name _____

Comprehension

Answer the following, using information in the story and your completed Graphic Organizer.

1. Describe the central cause-effect relationship in the fictional part of the story.
Answers will vary. Possible answer: Because Lucius was guarding the wall alone at night, he became very nervous and jumpy, thereby losing his effectiveness as a guard.

2. What kinds of questions help the reader identify cause-and-effect relationships?
Why did something happen? What led up to an event? What followed an event?

3. Describe a cause in the story that led to many effects.
Answers will vary. Possible answer: The Roman invasion and conquest of the southern part of Britain was a cause that led to many effects.

4. Describe an effect in the story that led to another event, condition, or circumstance.
Possible answer: Even though the Romans were under attack from the north, the emperor was unwilling to hold all of Britain because it would require too many soldiers. As a result, he decided to build a wall to protect the south.

5. How does understanding cause-effect relationships add to the reader's appreciation of the events in the story or the actions of the characters?
Answers will vary.

7

◆ Language Support Practice

The Pyramids of Ancient Egypt
Key Vocabulary

Name _____

Vocabulary

Read the report. Fill in each blank with the correct word from the box.

The pyramids were built to be **tombs** for Egyptian kings. Many **experts** have studied the pyramids. The pyramids are amazing **structures** that have stood for centuries. Historians know that the stone blocks were cut from large **quarries**. Thousands of hard-working **laborers** moved the blocks. The workers probably moved the blocks up **ramps**.

Vocabulary
experts
laborers
quarries
ramps
structures
tombs

6

Between the
Dragon
and the
Eagle

Mical Schneider

Above Level

Daily Lesson Plans

 **Technology**
Lesson Planner CD-ROM allows you to customize the chart below to develop your own lesson plans.

T Skill tested on Theme Skills Test and/or Integrated Theme Test

 50–60 minutes  The Great Wall

Reading
Comprehension

Leveled Readers
- Fluency Practice
- Independent Reading

 20–30 minutes

Word Work
Phonics/Decoding
Vocabulary
Spelling

 20–30 minutes

Writing and Oral Language
Writing
Grammar
Listening/Speaking/Viewing

DAY 1 The Great Wall

Teacher Read Aloud, 387S–387T
The Day of Disaster

Building Background, 388

Key Vocabulary, 389

craftsmen	excluding	nomadic
domain	extravagance	steppe
durable	laborers	terrain
dynasty	massive	

Reading the Selection, 390–401

Comprehension Skill, 390
Cause and Effect **T**

Comprehension Strategy, 390
Summarize **T**

Leveled Readers
The Pyramids of Giza
A Scribe of Ancient China
The Shape in the Dark
The Pyramids of Ancient Egypt

Lessons and Leveled Practice, 407O–407R

Phonics/Decoding, 391
Phonics/Decoding Strategy

Vocabulary, 390–401
Selection Vocabulary

Spelling, 407E
Adding *-ion* or *-ation* **T**

Writing, 407K
Prewriting a Paragraph of Information

Grammar, 407I
Comparing with Adjectives **T**

Daily Language Practice
1. My brother can construt a biggest sandcastle than I can. (construct; bigger)
2. Last week we visit the main attracsin at the museum. (visited; attraction)

Listening/Speaking/Viewing, 387S–387T, 397
Teacher Read Aloud, Stop and Think

DAY 2 The Great W

Reading the Selection, 390–401

Comprehension Check, 401

Responding, 402
Think About the Selection

Comprehension Skill Preview, 399
Cause and Effect **T**

Leveled Readers
The Pyramids of Giza
A Scribe of Ancient China
The Shape in the Dark
The Pyramids of Ancient Egypt

Lessons and Leveled Practice, 407O–407R

Structural Analysis, 407C
Suffixes *-ion* and *-ation* **T**

Vocabulary, 390–401
Selection Vocabulary

Spelling, 407E
Adding *-ion* or *-ation* Review and Practice **T**

Writing, 407K
Drafting a Paragraph of Information

Grammar, 407I
Comparing with Adjectives Practice **T**

Daily Language Practice
3. This examinasun was more harder than the one last week. (examination; more)
4. The twins Dan and Jen does not cooperite with each other. (do; cooperate)

Listening/Speaking/Viewing, 401, 402
Wrapping Up, Responding

Target Skills of the Week

Phonics	Suffixes -ion and -ation
Comprehension	Summarize; Cause and Effect
Vocabulary	Synonyms
Fluency	Leveled Readers

DAY 3

Rereading the Selection, 390–401

Comprehension Skill, 407A–407B
Cause and Effect **T**

Leveled Readers
The Pyramids of Giza
A Scribe of Ancient China
The Shape in the Dark
The Pyramids of Ancient Egypt

Lessons and Leveled Practice, 407O–407R

Phonics Review, 407D
Sounds for the Letters wh

Vocabulary, 407G
Synonyms **T**

Spelling, 407F
Vocabulary: Clipped Words; Adding -ion or -ation Practice **T**

Writing, 407L
Revising a Paragraph of Information
Elaborating with Adjectives **T**

Grammar, 407J
Comparing with good/bad **T**

Daily Language Practice
5. Let's explour the roman exhibit at the museum.(explore; Roman)
6. I have great admirasun for professor Suarez. (admiration; Professor)

DAY 4

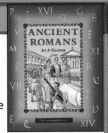

Reading the Technology Link, 404–407
"Building Ancient Rome"

Skill: How to Read a Timeline

Rereading for Visual Literacy, 406
Graphic Aids

Comprehension Skill Review, 393
Noting Details

Leveled Readers
The Pyramids of Giza
A Scribe of Ancient China
The Shape in the Dark
The Pyramids of Ancient Egypt

Lessons and Leveled Practice, 407O–407R

Phonics/Decoding, 404–407
Apply Phonics/Decoding Strategy to Link

Vocabulary, 407M
Language Center: Building Vocabulary

Spelling, 407F
Spelling Game, Proofreading **T**

Writing, 407L
Proofreading a Paragraph of Information

Grammar, 407J
Comparing with good/bad Practice **T**

Daily Language Practice
7. Karens constructun of a gingerbread house is amazing. (Karen's; construction)
8. Forecasting this weather situasion is more difficulter than forecasting the one last week. (situation; difficult)

Listening/Speaking/Viewing, 407
Discuss the Link

DAY 5

Rereading for Fluency, 395

Responding Activities, 402–403
Write a Story
Cross-Curricular Activities

Information and Study Skills, 407H
Note Taking

Comprehension Skill Review, 395
Drawing Conclusions

Leveled Readers
The Pyramids of Giza
A Scribe of Ancient China
The Shape in the Dark
The Pyramids of Ancient Egypt

Lessons and Leveled Practice, 407O–407R

Phonics, 407M
Language Center: Word Detective

Vocabulary, 407M
Language Center: Vocabulary game

Spelling, 407F
Test: Adding -ion or -ation **T**

Writing, 407L
Publishing a Paragraph of Information

Grammar, 407J, 407M
Correct Adjective Forms
Language Center: Comparative and Superlative Adjectives

Daily Language Practice
9. Mr. Brown are happy with the cooperasun in his classroom. (is; cooperation)
10. An explorasun of the ancient mayan culture is fascinating. (exploration; Mayan)

Listening/Speaking/Viewing, 407N
Language Center: Viewing for Information and Details

Managing Flexible Groups

Leveled Instruction and Leveled Practice

	DAY 1	**DAY 2**
WHOLE CLASS	• Teacher Read Aloud (TE pp. 387S–387T) • Building Background, Introducing Vocabulary (TE pp. 388–389) • Comprehension Strategy: Introduce (TE p. 390) • Comprehension Skill: Introduce (TE p. 390) • Purpose Setting (TE p. 391) **After reading first half of *The Great Wall*** • Stop and Think (TE p. 397)	**After reading *The Great Wall*** • Wrapping Up (TE p. 401) • Comprehension Check (Practice Book p. 25) • Responding: Think About the Selection (TE p. 402) • Comprehension Skill: Preview (TE p. 399)
SMALL GROUPS		
Extra Support	**TEACHER-LED** • Preview *The Great Wall* to Stop and Think (TE pp. 390–397). • Support reading with Extra Support/Intervention notes (TE pp. 391, 393, 395, 396, 399, 400).	**Partner or Individual Work** • Reread first half of *The Great Wall* (TE pp. 390–397). • Preview, read second half (TE pp. 398–401). • Comprehension Check (Practice Book p. 25)
Challenge	**Individual Work** • Begin "A Model Wall" (Challenge Handbook p. 32). • Extend reading with Challenge note (TE p. 400).	**Individual Work** • Continue work on activity (Challenge Handbook p. 32).
English Language Learners	**TEACHER-LED** • Preview vocabulary and *The Great Wall* to Stop and Think (TE pp. 389–397). • Support reading with English Language Learners notes (TE pp. 388, 394, 396, 401).	**TEACHER-LED** • Review first half of *The Great Wall* (TE pp. 390–397). ✔ • Preview, read second half (TE pp. 398–401). • Begin Comprehension Check together (Practice Book p. 25).

Independent Activities

- Get Set for Reading CD-ROM
- Journals: selection notes, questions
- Complete, review Practice Book (pp. 23–27) and Leveled Readers Practice Blackline Masters (TE pp. 407O–407R).
- Assignment Cards (Teachers Resource Blackline Masters, pp. 75–76)
- Leveled Readers (TE pp. 407O–407R), Leveled Theme Paperbacks (TE pp. R2–R3), or book from Leveled Bibliography (TE pp. 354E–354F)

✔ **Opportunity to informally assess oral reading rate**

Rereading *The Great Wall* (TE pp. 390–401)

Comprehension Skill: Main lesson
(TE pp. 407A–407B)

- Reading the Technology Link
(TE pp. 404–407): Skill lesson (TE p. 404)
- Rereading the Technology Link: Visual
Literacy lesson (TE p. 406)
- Comprehension Skill: First Comprehension
Review lesson (TE p. 393)

- Responding: Select from Activities
(TE pp. 402–403)
- Information and Study Skills (TE p. 407H)
- Comprehension Skill: Second
Comprehension Review lesson (TE p. 395)

TEACHER-LED

Reread, review Comprehension Check
(Practice Book p. 25).

Preview Leveled Reader: Below Level
(TE p. 407O), or read book from Leveled
Bibliography (TE pp. 354E–354F). ✔

Partner or Individual Work

- Reread the Technology Link
(TE pp. 404–407).
- Complete Leveled Reader: Below Level
(TE p. 407O), or read book from Leveled
Bibliography (TE pp. 354E–354F).

TEACHER-LED

- Comprehension Skill: Reteaching lesson
(TE p. R10)
- Reread Leveled Theme Paperback: Below
Level (TE pp. R2–R3), or read book from
Leveled Bibliography (TE pp. 354E–354F). ✔

TEACHER-LED

Teacher check-in: Assess progress (Challenge
Handbook p. 32).

Preview Leveled Reader: Above Level
(TE p. 407Q), or read book from Leveled
Bibliography (TE pp. 354E–354F). ✔

Individual Work

- Complete activity (Challenge Handbook
p. 32).
- Complete Leveled Reader: Above Level
(TE p. 407Q), or read book from Leveled
Bibliography (TE pp. 354E–354F).

TEACHER-LED

- Evaluate activity and plan format for sharing
(Challenge Handbook p. 32).
- Reread Leveled Theme Paperback: Above
Level (TE pp. R6–R7), or read book from
Leveled Bibliography (TE pp. 354E–354F). ✔

Partner or Individual Work

Complete Comprehension Check (Practice
Book p. 25).

Begin Leveled Reader: Language Support
(TE p. 407R), or read book from Leveled
Bibliography (TE pp. 354E–354F).

TEACHER-LED

- Reread the Technology Link
(TE pp. 404–407) ✔ and review
Link Skill (TE p. 404).
- Complete Leveled Reader: Language Support
(TE p. 407R), or read book from Leveled
Bibliography (TE pp. 354E–354F). ✔

Partner or Individual Work

- Reread book from Leveled Bibliography
(TE pp. 354E–354F).

- Responding activities (TE pp. 402–403)
- Language Center activities (TE pp. 407M–407N)
- **Fluency Practice:** Reread *Lost Temple of the Aztecs, The Great Wall.* ✔
- Activities relating to *The Great Wall* at Education Place® www.eduplace.com

**Turn the page for more
independent activities.**

Managing Flexible Groups   387P

Classroom Management

Assign these activities while you work with small groups.

Differentiated Instruction for Small Groups

- **Handbook for English Language Learners**, pp. 144–153

- **Extra Support Handbook**, pp. 140–149

Independent Activities

- Language Center, pp. 407M–407N

- Challenge/Extension Activities, Theme Resources, pp. R11, R17

- **Classroom Management Handbook**, Activity Masters CM4-5–CM4-8

- **Challenge Handbook**, pp. 32–33

Look for more activities in the Classroom Management Kit.

Social Studies

A Vision of the Past

Groups	⏱ 45 minutes
Objective	Create a timeline.
Materials	Encyclopedia, butcher paper, colored pencils, or markers

Create a timeline of ancient Chinese history.

- Use an encyclopedia or the Internet to find out about ancient Chinese history.

- Divide periods of Chinese history among group members. Each member will create a segment of the timeline.

- Take notes on your period. Decide which dates and events are important enough to include on your portion of the timeline.

- Divide and label your timeline in equal segments (such as periods of 100 years).

- Add the dates of specific events and label them.

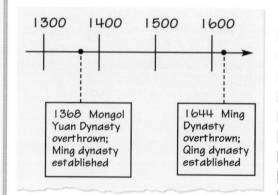

Art

Map the Wall

👤 Singles	⏱ 45 minutes
Objective	Create a map of the Great Wall.
Materials	Historical atlas or encyclopedia, tracing paper, colored pencils

Create a map of the Great Wall of China as it looked at the end of the Ming dynasty (A.D. 1644). Using a historical atlas or encyclopedia as a reference, follow these steps:

- Draw or trace an outline map of China.

- Locate and label major cities during the Ming dynasty.

- Draw the course of the Great Wall.

- Note special geographical features at different points along the wall.

- Include the major rivers and regions of China on your map.

- Include a compass rose and scale.

Consider copying and laminating these activities for use in centers.

Technology

How Did They Do It?

Groups	🕐 45 minutes
Objective	Research building methods used on the Great Wall.
Materials	Internet or other reference sources

n *The Great Wall*, you read a little bout materials and techniques used n the construction of the Great Wall. Research this topic further. ind answers to some of the follow-ng questions, and then summarize our findings in a brief report.

How were the stones quarried?

How were the kilns for making bricks built? How were they used to make the bricks?

How were the stones and the bricks transported from the quar-ries and the kilns to the building site?

How were the stones and bricks held together on the wall?

How did building materials and techniques vary from region to region?

Writing

Working on the Wall

🧍 Singles	🕐 30 minutes
Objective	Write a short story.

Tens of thousands of workers labored on the wall over centuries. Write a short story describing the construction of the wall from one worker's point of view.

- Review the description of workers' roles on pages 393–397.

- Write your story as if the narrator were a worker. Use the pronoun *I*.

- Include details about the worker's background, family, and particular role in building the wall.

- Also include details about the worker's thoughts and feelings.

Wall of Sweat

Work on the wall was very hard. My fellow workers and I awoke long before the sun was up, and we worked until long after the sun had set.

Social Studies

Two Historic Projects

👥 Pairs	🕐 45 minutes
Objective	Compare and contrast the Egyptian pyramids with the Great Wall.
Materials	Internet, encyclopedias, and other reference sources

The Egyptian pyramids of Giza, like the Great Wall of China, are won-ders of architecture. Working with a partner, research the pyramids. Then compare and contrast facts about the pyramids with facts about the Great Wall. Create a chart like the one below, and fill it in with details about the following characteristics of the two structures.

- purpose
- size
- materials
- number of workers
- workers' backgrounds
- length of time to build
- dates started and finished

	Great Wall of China	Pyramids of Giza
Purpose		
Size		
Materials		

Listening Comprehension

Building Background

Tell students that you are going to read aloud a selection about two cities buried by a gigantic volcanic eruption.

● Help students locate Italy, the Bay of Naples, and Mt. Vesuvius on a map. Explain that Pompeii and Herculaneum were two cities that existed in Italy during the time of the Roman Empire.

Fluency Modeling

Explain that as you read aloud, you will be modeling fluent oral reading. Ask students to listen carefully to your phrasing and your expression, or tone of voice and emphasis.

COMPREHENSION SKILL

Cause and Effect

Explain that the reason why something happens is called a cause. Tell students that the event that happens as a result is called an effect. Point out that clue words such as *because* or *as a result of* may signal cause-and-effect relationships.

Purpose Setting Read the selection aloud, asking students to note causes and effects as they listen. Then use the Guiding Comprehension questions to assess students' understanding. Reread the selection for clarification as needed.

Teacher Read Aloud

The Day of Disaster
by Michael Burgan

Found: **Two Lost Cities**

Without warning, Vesuvius exploded on the morning of August 24, 79 A.D. Until then the volcano had been silent for more than eight hundred years. Located six miles northwest of the city of Pompeii, Italy, Vesuvius sent a massive black cloud of ash and rock twelve miles into the air. The sky turned as dark as midnight. Pumice (PUH mihs), a type of volcanic rock, fell on Pompeii like hail.

❶ During the eruption, people panicked trying to escape the downfall. Some rushed into buildings, and others tried to flee the city. Pumice and ash fell at the rate of six inches an hour. Within a few hours, roofs collapsed under the weight of the pumice, trapping those inside. Then the air became searingly hot.

Around midnight the nature of the eruption changed into what scientists call a surge cloud of glowing avalanche. Now the volcano unleashed a wave of burning ash, rock, and dust particles that rolled down the mountainside instead of rising sky-high. The materials in such an avalanche can reach temperatures of a thousand degrees Fahrenheit and move at speeds of more than sixty miles an hour. For the next eight hours, Vesuvius spewed out six major glowing avalanches.

❷ The first one roared westward into the seaside town of Herculaneum. This avalanche and others surged over the stone buildings and tore tiles off roofs. Some people ran toward the Bay of Naples, but they couldn't escape the deadly heat. They died, and volcanic rocks covered them. Another avalanche moved south and ripped through Pompeii. Later that day, when the erup-

---

tion finally ended, Herculaneum lay underneath more than twenty feet of rock; Pompeii lay under many layers of ash and pumice.

For more than fifteen hundred years there was no trace of the ancient cities. People built houses and farmed the land at those sites with no idea of what lay beneath the surface. Then in 1594 an Italian architect uncovered inscribed stones. About one hundred fifty years later, people found evidence that the stones had come from Pompeii. Since then archaeologists have excavated buildings, streets, and skeletons in the cities. The volcanic materials from Vesuvius had actually preserved them. As digging continues today, each unearthed treasure reveals something about everyday life in the Roman Empire nearly two thousand years ago.

Ancient Lives Revealed

The discoveries at Pompeii and Herculaneum, frozen in time in 79 A.D., provide many clues about daily life in the Roman Empire.

People saved gold coins such as the aureus. It shows the head of the emperor Nero, who ruled Rome from 54 to 68 A.D.

As they do today, bakers made round loaves of bread. An ancient loaf was found in an oven in Pompeii. Over the years it blackened and turned to charcoal.

Like many ancient peoples, the Romans owned slaves. Boys who were not slaves wore a bulla, a piece of jewelry, until they became adults. Women wore earrings and necklaces and gold pins for fastening cloths.

The town of Herculaneum was named for the Greek god Hercules, its legendary founder. The Romans worshipped many gods and often built statues of them. A bronze bust of Hercules was excavated at the Villa dei Papiri.

CRITICAL THINKING
Guiding Comprehension

1 **CAUSE AND EFFECT** What caused roofs to collapse in Pompeii, trapping people inside buildings? (falling pumice and ash from the eruption)

2 **CAUSE AND EFFECT** What were the effects of the glowing avalanches? (They covered buildings, tore tiles off roofs, and killed people with heat. They buried Herculaneum under more than twenty feet of rock and Pompeii under layers of ash and pumice.)

3 **CAUSE AND EFFECT** What effect do you think excavations of these cities have had on scientists? (Excavations have given archaeologists a better understanding of what daily life was like in the Roman Empire.)

Discussion Options

Personal Response Discuss with students what they find most interesting about the discoveries at Pompeii and Herculaneum.

⭐ **Connecting/Comparing** Ask students to compare the discovery of the lost temple in *Lost Temple of the Aztecs* with the discovery of the ruins of Pompeii and Herculaneum.

English Language Learners

Supporting Comprehension

Invite volunteers to share what they know about archaeological sites and discoveries in their parents' home countries. Encourage students to note similarities and differences between discoveries at those sites and discoveries at Pompeii and Herculaneum.

Building Background

Key Concept: Great Wall of China

Remind students that this theme explores cultures that flourished long ago. Explain that the next selection is about ancient China and one of the greatest structures ever built—the Great Wall of China. Use "Two Cultures, One Wall" on Anthology pages 388–389 to build background and introduce key vocabulary.

- Have a volunteer read aloud "Two Cultures, One Wall."

- Have students look at the illustrations and the timeline. Have them discuss what they know about the Great Wall.

Background and Vocabulary

The Great Wall

The Great Wall

Read to find the meanings of these words.

e • Glossary

craftsmen
domain
durable
dynasty
excluding
extravagance
laborers
massive
nomadic
steppe
terrain

388

TWO CULTURES, ONE WALL

For centuries the **terrain** of China protected its people from enemies on three sides. In the west lay mountains and a desert. To the south and the east lay the Pacific Ocean. Only in the north was there flat grassland called the **steppe**. This was where the Mongols, a **nomadic** tribe, could easily invade China's borders.

Because they lived in small groups and moved often, the Mongols had no need for **extravagance**. They herded sheep and horses. As skilled horsemen, they were fearsome warriors.

A Mongol leader sitting on a horse.

300	B.C.	A.D.		300

221 B.C.
Construction of the first long wall begins under Emperor Qin Shi Huangdi.

English Language Learners

Supporting Comprehension

Beginning/Preproduction Have students listen to the article. Then ask them to point to China on the map on page 388 and to the Great Wall in the photograph on page 389. Have them draw someone climbing the Great Wall or standing at the bottom of it.

Early Production and Speech Emergence Have students repeat the Key Vocabulary words after you. Have them mime how laborers or craftsmen might work on the wall. Discuss examples of structures that are massive and durable, such as skyscrapers or bridges.

Intermediate and Advanced Fluency In small groups, have students read and then restate in their own words the information provided in the article.

China's Great Wall

Most of the Chinese were farmers, while some were **laborers** and **craftsmen**. China was ruled by an emperor, and when power was passed along from generation to generation, the ruling family was called a **dynasty**.

The Chinese looked down upon the Mongols, yet they also feared them. When trade between the Mongols and the Chinese stopped, the Mongols would attack farms and cities. Many emperors tried various ways of **excluding** the Mongols from their **domain**. **Massive** walls were built over the centuries as a defense, but none of them proved to be as **durable** as the one you will read about in *The Great Wall*.

A Chinese farmer transports fruit trees with the aid of a yoke.

A.D. 1200
Mongols grow stronger under their leader Genghis Khan.

A.D. 1644
Manchus, another nomadic tribe, invade China; Great Wall abandoned.

| 900 | 1200 | 1500 | 1800 |

A.D. 1449
Building of the last Great Wall begins.

389

Introducing Vocabulary

Key Vocabulary

These words support the Key Concept and appear in the selection.

craftsmen skilled workers

domain the territory ruled by a government

durable sturdy and long-lasting

dynasty a line of rulers from one family

excluding keeping someone or something out

extravagance wasteful spending on luxuries

laborers workers who do tasks that do not require special skills

massive large and solid

nomadic moving from place to place

steppe a vast, dry, grassy plain

terrain the physical features of an area of land

e • Glossary
e • WordGame

See Vocabulary notes on pages 392, 396, 398, and 400 for additional words to preview.

Transparency 4–9

Great Wall Words

The Great Wall of China is the longest structure ever built by humans. It runs for more than 2,100 miles, and is so long and <u>massive</u> it can be seen from outer space. The wall was built upon many kinds of <u>terrain</u>, including rolling hills, rugged mountains, and the flat, grassy plains called the <u>steppe</u>.

Although construction on the wall may have begun as early as 600 B.C., most of the wall we see today was built during the Ming <u>dynasty</u>, a period of rule that began in 1386 and lasted for about 300 years. The goal of the Chinese emperors was to protect China's <u>domain</u> from the <u>nomadic</u> Mongol warriors who wandered the surrounding plains.

In regions where stone was scarce, the wall was made of packed dirt. Not much skill was needed to build earth walls, just many <u>laborers</u> who could work very, very hard. These portions of the wall crumbled over time. The most <u>durable</u> parts of the wall were built of stone or brick. Skilled <u>craftsmen</u> were needed for this work.

The hard, simple life of the workers and soldiers was far different from the <u>extravagance</u> in the Ming dynasty's royal court. In time, the Ming rulers would learn that their Great Wall would not protect them from enemies outside China's borders. They would also learn that <u>excluding</u> the Mongol warriors would not protect them from their enemies within.

Practice Book page 23

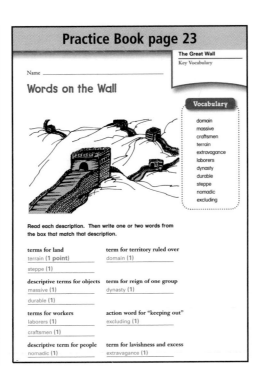

The Great Wall
Key Vocabulary

Name

Words on the Wall

Vocabulary

domain
massive
craftsmen
terrain
extravagance
laborers
dynasty
durable
steppe
nomadic
excluding

Read each description. Then write one or two words from the box that match that description.

terms for land
terrain **(1 point)**
steppe **(1)**

term for territory ruled over
domain **(1)**

descriptive terms for objects
massive **(1)**
durable **(1)**

term for reign of one group
dynasty **(1)**

terms for workers
laborers **(1)**
craftsmen **(1)**

action word for "keeping out"
excluding **(1)**

descriptive term for people
nomadic **(1)**

term for lavishness and excess
extravagance **(1)**

Display Transparency 4–9.

- Model how to figure out the meaning of the word *massive* from the context.

- Ask students to use letter sounds and context clues to figure out the other Key Vocabulary words. Have them explain how they figured out each word.

- Ask students to look for these words as they read and to use them as they discuss why the Chinese felt they needed to build the Great Wall.

Practice/Homework Assign **Practice Book** page 23.

Introducing Vocabulary **389**

COMPREHENSION STRATEGY
Summarize

Teacher Modeling Have a volunteer read aloud the Strategy Focus. Remind students that summing up important ideas can help them understand and remember what they read. Have students read the introduction and the first four paragraphs on pages 392–393. Then model the strategy.

Think Aloud *I can summarize the beginning of the selection. For two hundred years, Chinese rulers built a huge wall in order to keep the Mongol warriors out of China. Craftsmen and laborers worked on the wall, using materials such as mud, brick, and stone.*

✓ **Test Prep** Students can quickly summarize a test passage before they start to answer questions. Creating this kind of mental "outline" will help them decide where to look for the answer.

COMPREHENSION SKILL
Cause and Effect

Introduce the Graphic Organizer.
Tell students that a Cause and Effect Chart can help them understand the history of the Great Wall. Explain that as they read, students will fill in the chart on **Practice Book** page 24.

- Display **Transparency 4–10.** Have students read Anthology page 392.
- Model how to fill in the first Effect box on the chart.
- Have students complete the chart as they read.
- Monitor their work as needed.

MEET THE AUTHOR
Elizabeth Mann

Elizabeth Mann was a public school teacher in New York City before she wrote her first nonfiction book. One day, while teaching her second grade students about the Brooklyn Bridge, she noticed how bored they all looked. The next day, she told them an extraordinary story about a family that spent fourteen years building the bridge. Suddenly, everyone was excited. That story became part of her first book, *The Brooklyn Bridge.* Mann has also written books about the Great Pyramid, the Panama Canal, and the Roman Colosseum.

MEET THE ILLUSTRATOR
Alan Witschonke

Alan Witschonke is an award-winning illustrator who has worked with Elizabeth Mann on *The Great Wall* and *The Brooklyn Bridge.* He lives in Belmont, Massachusetts, with his wife, Judith, who is also an illustrator, and their two sons.

Internet

To find out more about Elizabeth Mann and Alan Witschonke, visit Education Place. **www.eduplace.com/kids**

390

Transparency 4–10
Cause and Effect Chart

Cause	Effect
Mongol warriors threatened to overpower the Chinese.	Chinese emperors constructed a wall to keep the Mongols out.
Stone was scarce in western China.	Laborers built the western part of the Great Wall from packed dirt.
The Great Wall had to be guarded against the Mongols.	Forts for soldiers to live in were built all along the wall.
The Great Wall demanded great sacrifices of the Chinese people, yet their leaders lived extravagant lives.	The Chinese people became angry with their leaders and began to rebel against them.
The Ming dynasty had been disliked by its own people.	The Manchus easily won support for the new Qing dynasty.
The Manchus drove the Mongols away. The Qing emperors ruled both sides of the Great Wall.	The Great Wall was no longer needed for defense.

DISCOVERING ANCIENT CULTURES: The Great Wall
Graphic Organizer Cause and Effect Chart

ANNOTATED VERSION

TRANSPARENCY 4–10
TEACHER'S EDITION PAGES 390 AND 407A

Practice Book page 24

The Great Wall
Graphic Organizer
Cause and Effect

Name _____

Cause and Effect Chart

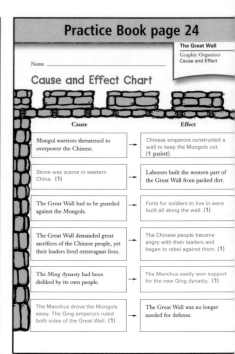

Cause	Effect
Mongol warriors threatened to overpower the Chinese.	Chinese emperors constructed a wall to keep the Mongols out. (1 point)
Stone was scarce in western China. (1)	Laborers built the western part of the Great Wall from packed dirt.
The Great Wall had to be guarded against the Mongols.	Forts for soldiers to live in were built all along the wall. (1)
The Great Wall demanded great sacrifices of the Chinese people, yet their leaders lived extravagant lives.	The Chinese people became angry with their leaders and began to rebel against them. (1)
The Ming dynasty had been disliked by its own people.	The Manchus easily won support for the new Qing dynasty. (1)
The Manchus drove the Mongols away. The Qing emperors ruled both sides of the Great Wall. (1)	The Great Wall was no longer needed for defense.

Selection 2

The Great Wall

The story of thousands of miles of earth and stone that turned a nation into a fortress

By Elizabeth Mann

Strategy Focus

The Chinese built a wall thousands of miles long to protect themselves from invaders. As you read, **summarize** how the wall was built.

391

Extra Support/Intervention

Selection Preview

pages 391–395 The Chinese built the Great Wall to keep out nomadic warriors called Mongols. It took hundreds of years and thousands of workers to build.

pages 396–397 Nearly a million soldiers lived on and patrolled the wall over a span of thousands of miles. What are some things a soldier or a worker on the wall might have to do every day?

pages 398–401 The Chinese people grew angry at being taxed so much and revolted against the Ming government. A powerful group of warriors, the Manchus, came to the rescue of the Ming leaders but instead took over the government. The Great Wall was no longer as important as it had once been.

Purpose Setting

- Have students read to find out whether it was easy or difficult to build the Great Wall.

- Have students preview the selection, looking at the illustrations. Have them predict what they might learn about the Great Wall.

- Invite students to stop every few pages and summarize why the Great Wall was built and how it was done.

- Have students identify what caused the building of the Great Wall and what effects the wall's construction may have had on China.

- You may want to preview with students the Responding questions on Anthology page 402.

Journal ▸ Have students use their journals to record reasons why the Chinese emperors wanted to build the Great Wall.

STRATEGY REVIEW

Phonics/Decoding

Remind students to use the Phonics/ Decoding Strategy as they read.

Modeling Write this sentence from *The Great Wall* on the board: *Many different kinds of <u>fortifications</u> were built along the wall.* Point to *fortifications.*

Think Aloud *I recognize this word's ending, -tions, which is pronounced shuhnz. I'll try breaking the word into syllables and sounding it out: FAWR-ty-fy-KAY-shuhnz. That doesn't sound right. I'll try it agan with short vowel sounds for the middle syllables: FAWR-tuh-fih-KAY-shuhnz. That sounds right, but what does it mean? I know that forts are places where soldiers stay to keep watch over an area. Maybe this word has something to do with fighting. That makes sense in this paragraph. I'll look it up to learn more.*

CRITICAL THINKING
Guiding Comprehension

❶ DRAWING CONCLUSIONS What does the author mean by *There was no masterplan or blueprint for a Great Wall?* (no overall plan to follow)

❷ NOTING DETAILS Why might an eastern part of the Great Wall look different from a western part? (western: built with pounded earth; eastern: with stone and brick)

COMPREHENSION STRATEGY
Summarize

Teacher/Student Modeling List these important details from the last two paragraphs on page 393: *thousands of workers; soldiers, peasants, criminals; forts for guarding the wall.* Then ask students to summarize these paragraphs. (Thousands of soldiers, peasants, and criminals helped to build the Great Wall. Soldiers lived in forts to guard the wall.)

Vocabulary

terrain the physical features of an area of land

craftsmen skilled workers

laborers workers who do tasks that do not require special skills

dynasty a line of rulers from one family

durable sturdy and long-lasting

stonemasons persons who prepare and lay stones in buildings

massive large and solid

For thousands of years, fierce Mongol warriors threatened China from the north. In 221 B.C., the Chinese began to build a thousand-mile-long wall to protect their farms and cities from the Mongols. Over the centuries, the wall crumbled. Other walls were built, but still the raids went on.

In A.D. 1449, the Mongol army grew much stronger. More and more Chinese soldiers were killed. After one devastating defeat, a young Chinese emperor, Zhu Qizhen, was kidnapped by a Mongol prince. When news of the kidnapping reached the Chinese government, the people were seized by fear. Too weak to fight back, they decided to build a stronger wall. The building of the Great Wall, the last long wall, went on for the next two centuries.

392

ASSIGNMENT CARD 6
Invent a Code

Math Connection

The number of cannon shots and smoke plumes the soldiers set off were a code that signaled how many Mongol warriors were approaching. With a partner, work out what that code might have been like. You might figure out a cannon and smoke code that could communicate this information:

- Ten riders are approaching.

- Two groups of fifteen riders each are approaching.

- An army of a hundred riders is approaching.

Theme 4: Discovering Ancient Cultures

Teacher's Resource BLM page 76

---

1 There was no masterplan or blueprint for a Great Wall. Each emperor built when and where he thought the Mongol threat was the greatest. Construction across northern China continued for the next two centuries. The routes through mountain passes that the Mongols used most often to reach China were blocked with walls. Those walls were then connected with other sections of wall.

In the western part of the country, walls were built of pounded earth, an ancient building technique. Peasants' homes, city walls, even Qin Shi Huangdi's first long wall had been made of pounded earth. In the dry, desert **2** terrain of western China, earth was the only building material available in great quantity. It was simple to build with pounded earth. No skilled craftsmen were needed, just many, many laborers.

Toward the end of the Ming dynasty much building was done in the eastern mountains to protect the capital city, Peking. Builders began using bricks and blocks of stone instead of pounded earth. Walls built of stone and brick didn't erode in wind and rain. They didn't need constant repair as earth walls did.

Stone and brick walls were strong and durable, but they were more complicated to build. Progress was slow. Stone had to be dug from quarries, cut into blocks, and transported to the wall. Bricks were made from mud and then baked in kilns. Workers with special skills — stonemasons and brickmakers — were needed to handle the new materials.

Tens of thousands of workers were involved in building the Great Wall. The army provided many laborers. Soldiers became construction workers and generals became architects and engineers. Peasants were required to work on the wall. They worked for months at a time for little or no pay. Criminals served their sentences doing hard labor on the wall.

Even the most massive wall needed soldiers to patrol it. The Mongols were a determined enemy. If the wall was not guarded, they would find a way to get through. Many different kinds of fortifications were built along the wall for soldiers to live in. Some forts were large enough for one thousand soldiers. Watchtowers, built right into the wall, were sometimes so small they barely held twelve soldiers.

393

Extra Support/Intervention

Strategy Modeling: Phonics/Decoding

Model the strategy for *quarries.*

I know that the letters qu *stand for the* kw *sound in words like* quack *and* quart. *I also recognize the ending* -ies, *which is usually pronounced* eez. *I can try blending these sounds with the letters* arr *in the middle of the word:* KWAWR-eez. *That sounds right. Quarries are places where stones are cut from the earth.*

> quarries
> KWAWR-eez

Noting Details

Review

- A nonfiction selection may include many details.
- Readers need to find and remember the most important details—details that support a main idea.

Practice/Apply

- Have students reread page 393.
- Display the chart shown below. Help students complete the first section. Then have partners complete the chart.
- Bring the class together to compare charts and discuss which details are the most important.

Materials Used to Build the Wall
western wall: pounded earth
eastern wall: stone and brick

Workers on the Wall
architects, engineers
laborers, stonemasons, builders, brickmakers

Soldiers on the Wall
helped build wall
patrolled and defended wall

Review Skill Trace	
Teach	Theme 1, p. 47A
Reteach	Theme 1, p. R8
Review	p. 393; Theme 1, p. 85; Theme 2, p. 173; Theme 3, p. 279; Theme 5, p. 503

Guiding Comprehension

❸ NOTING DETAILS What details in the illustration on pages 394–395 help you understand how the wall was attacked and defended? (Sample answers: Mongol soldiers using catapults; Chinese soldiers with spears; bows and arrows)

394

English Language Learners

Supporting Comprehension

Work with students to make a chart listing the people who worked on the wall and what their jobs were.

Name	Job
laborers	moved earth
builders	used brick and stone
stonemasons	cut stones
soldiers	guarded and built wall

395

Drawing Conclusions

Review

- When an author does not state something directly, readers need to draw conclusions by "adding up" details.

Practice/Apply

- Have students turn to page 393. Point out that the author does not state directly how the peasants felt about working on the wall.

- Work with students to add up details about how the peasant workers felt.

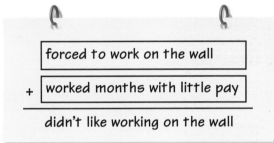

forced to work on the wall

+ worked months with little pay

didn't like working on the wall

- Have students make a similar equation showing how the soldiers who lived on the wall felt.

Review Skill Trace	
Teach	Theme 6, p. 639A
Reteach	Theme 6, p. R14
▶ Review	p. 395; Theme 2, p. 155; Theme 5, p. 507

Extra Support/Intervention

Strategy Modeling: Summarize

Model summarizing the first two paragraphs on page 397.

Because they had horses, Mongol warriors could launch an attack at any time. This gave them an advantage over the Chinese soldiers, who were spread thinly across the thousands of miles of the wall. To defend themselves, the Chinese built guard towers along the wall and sent smoke-signal warnings whenever they saw Mongols approaching.

Fluency Practice

Rereading for Fluency Have students choose a favorite part of the selection to reread to a partner, or suggest that they read the last two paragraphs on page 393. Encourage students to read expressively.

Guiding Comprehension

4 MAKING INFERENCES What does the author mean by saying that the Mongols *flowed like water across the steppe*? (Sample answer: They moved quickly and easily.)

5 CAUSE AND EFFECT What did smoke signals do to help the Chinese defend themselves against Mongol warriors? (They warned soldiers elsewhere on the wall that the Mongols were approaching.)

6 WRITER'S CRAFT What comparison does the author make to help readers picture the Great Wall? (She compares the wall to a dragon twisting and turning over the hills.)

396

Vocabulary

steppe a vast, dry, grassy plain

ingenious clever and original

insurmountable impossible to overcome

grueling physically exhausting

Extra Support/Intervention

Review (pages 391–397)

Before students who need extra support join the whole class for Stop and Think on page 397, they should

- review their purpose/predictions
- take turns modeling Summarize and other strategies they used
- help you add to **Transparency 4–10**
- check and revise their Cause and Effect Charts on **Practice Book** page 24, and use them to summarize

English Language Learners

Language Development

Help students understand these terms and expressions from page 397.

- Use math manipulatives or other objects to model the meaning of *outnumbered*.
- Draw a picture to illustrate a *plume of smoke*.
- Model the meaning of *code*.

The wall and the soldiers who guarded it were part of an elaborate defense system across northern China. Nearly a million soldiers patrolled the Great Wall, but they were spread thinly across thousands of miles. The Mongol warriors were outnumbered, but they had an advantage. Thanks to their swift horses, they flowed like water across the steppe. They could assemble anywhere, at any time to launch an attack and then disappear just as quickly back into the steppe. To defend against their fast-moving enemy the Chinese used an ingenious system of communication to gather soldiers together for battle.

Stone platforms, called signal towers, were built on high ground near the wall. When Mongol horsemen were spotted, a smoky fire was built on top of the nearest signal tower. The smoke was visible for miles, and when guards at the next tower saw it they built their own fire, passing the signal along. Sometimes loud cannon shots accompanied the plumes of smoke. The number of smoke plumes and cannon shots was a code indicating how many enemy riders were approaching.

The wall was shaped to fit the landscape it passed through. In flat desert areas it ran in a straight line. In hilly areas it twisted and turned like a dragon. The Chinese took advantage of the terrain to make the wall even more insurmountable. They built along the crests of tall hills and mountain peaks. The wall plunged down into rivers and then continued on the far bank. At the eastern end it ran into the sea.

By 1644, the Great Wall ran from Jiayuguan in the west, past the Gobi Desert, across the Yellow River, past Peking, all the way to Shanhaiguan on the Bohai Sea in the east. A Mongol warrior could ride for miles in its shadow without coming to a gate. And work was still being done on it.

The wall demanded great sacrifices of the Chinese people. The workers who built it were separated from their families for long periods of time. Many didn't survive the grueling work and harsh conditions.

Life was no easier for the soldiers who guarded the wall. Winters in northern China were punishingly cold and the summers were dry and hot. They were paid very little, and had to grow their own food in order to survive. Farming was difficult in the dry climate, but they had no choice.

Even though soldiers were poorly paid, the wall was very expensive. Adding to it, repairing it, and patrolling it cost more every year. To pay for it, the Ming government taxed the people of China.

397

ASSIGNMENT CARD 5

Literature Discussion

Discuss the following questions and questions of your own with a group of your classmates:

- Do you think it was wise or foolish of the Chinese emperors to build the Great Wall? Why?

- Based on details in the first part of the selection, what conclusions can you draw about the leaders of the Ming dynasty?

- Compare the Mongol horsemen with the Chinese soldiers who lived and worked on the Great Wall. How were they alike? How were they different?

- What do you think it was like to be a laborer or craftsman on the Great Wall? A soldier? A peasant? A Mongol? A member of the royal Ming Dynasty?

Theme 4: Discovering Ancient Cultures

Teacher's Resource BLM page 75

Stop and Think

Critical Thinking Questions

1. **MAKING JUDGMENTS** Chinese people made many sacrifices to build the Great Wall. Do you think the sacrifices were worth it? (Sample answers: yes, because the wall defended the country; no, because the work was hard and separated people from their families)

2. **SEQUENCE OF EVENTS** Describe what the Chinese soldiers did to communicate when Mongol warriors were spotted. (First, soldiers would light a fire in a signal tower. Next, guards at another tower would see the smoke and build their own fire. In this way, the message would be passed along the wall.)

Strategies in Action

Have students take turns modeling Summarize and other strategies they used while reading.

Discussion Options

You may want to bring the entire class together to do one or more of the activities below.

- **Review Predictions/Purpose** Have students share something they learned about the Great Wall or how it was built that surprised them.

- **Share Group Discussions** Have students share their literature discussions.

- **Summarize** Have students use their Cause and Effect Charts to summarize the selection so far.

Monitoring Student Progress

If . . .	Then . . .
students have successfully completed the Extra Support activities on page 396,	have them read the rest of the selection cooperatively or independently.

Reading the Selection 397

Guiding Comprehension

7 **CAUSE AND EFFECT** In what way did the Great Wall help end the rule of the Ming dynasty? (It was expensive to build, which made taxes high.)

8 **MAKING JUDGMENTS** Was it wise of the Ming government to open its gates to the Manchus? Why or why not? (Sample answer: no, because the Manchus took over the government)

At the same time, the cost of supporting the Ming government was increasing. Tens of thousands of people were part of the court, and more were being added all the time. Officals and advisors, well-fed and dressed in silk, spent their days quarreling and endlessly vying for the emperor's favor. Paying for the extravagance inside the Forbidden City, or the palaces of the Ming emperors, placed another burden on Chinese taxpayers.

7

People grew angry at the extravagance and corruption in the Ming court, and at the taxes that were being imposed on them. Once again, peasants began to rebel against government officials. The Ming dynasty, which had been founded by a peasant, was now threatened by its own people. In 1644, an opportunity arose. A group of Chinese rebels stormed the Forbidden City and overthrew the last Ming emperor.

The world outside China was changing.

Once again lacking strong leadership, the Mongols were growing weaker and less united. Meanwhile, another nomadic tribe, the Manchus, had been gathering strength for years. They controlled a large area north and east of Peking and had conquered Mongol lands to the west. It was only a matter of time before they tried to expand their domain into China.

The Manchus waited. When rebels attacked the Forbidden City, they seized the opportunity. They quickly offered to come to the rescue of the Ming dynasty.

8

The Ming army gratefully threw open the gates and the Manchu forces marched through the Great Wall and on into Peking. The Manchus chased the rebels out of the Forbidden City, but they did not restore power to the Ming. Instead, they seized the throne and established their own dynasty, the Qing (ching).

Because the Ming dynasty had been disliked by many of its own people, it was easy for the Manchus to win Chinese support for the Qing dynasty. The combined Manchu and Chinese forces were far stronger than the Mongols. Subdued, the Mongols withdrew to distant parts of the steppe. Their fierce army, which had once so terrified the Chinese, was just a memory.

The Qing emperors ruled the land on both sides of the Great Wall. The Mongols were not a threat. The wall no longer marked a border, and it wasn't needed for defense. Construction stopped and the watchtowers were abandoned. Traders and travelers passed freely through gates that never closed.

398

Vocabulary

vying competing

extravagance careless, wasteful spending on luxuries

imposed placed

nomadic moving from place to place

domain the territory ruled by a government

Gossiping and scheming, as the two men at the lower left of this painting show, were as much a part of court life as beautiful silk robes and portrait painting.

399

Extra Support/Intervention

Strategy Modeling: Summarize

Model the strategy for the first two paragraphs on page 398.

I'll think about the most important details and summarize these paragraphs. The Ming government was corrupt, and its officials spent money extravagantly. People grew angry at the government, and rebels attacked the Forbidden City. They overthrew the emperor, removing the last Ming ruler from power.

TARGET SKILL
Cause and Effect

Teach

- A cause is an event that makes another event happen. An effect is the result of another event.

- Authors who write about historical events often describe causes and effects.

- They do not always use clue words such as *because* or *as a result of* to signal causes and effects.

- Readers must think carefully about how one event led to another.

Practice

- Have students reread page 398. Ask, What caused the Chinese people to become angry with the Ming dynasty? (taxes, forced labor, extravagance)

- Ask, What did the people do as a result? (rebelled against the government)

Apply

- Ask partners to identify three more pairs of causes and effects in the selection.

- Have partners write cause-and-effect statements using signal words such as *because* or *as a result of*. Share these as a class.

Target Skill Trace	
Preview; Teach	p. 387S, p. 390, p. 399; p. 407A
Reteach	p. R10
Review	pp. M32–M33; Theme 1, p. 41; Theme 3, p. 261

Reading the Selection 399

CRITICAL THINKING
Guiding Comprehension

9 MAKING INFERENCES Why does the author say it was as though the Great Wall *didn't exist at all* for the Manchus? (By playing a trick, they were able to pass right through it and take over the Ming dynasty.)

10 WRITER'S CRAFT Why do you think the author asks the questions on page 400? (to make the reader think about how a different solution might have been better for protecting China)

COMPREHENSION STRATEGY
Summarize

Student Modeling Call on volunteers to summarize pages 398–400. Offer these prompts:

- What happened to the Ming government? (Chinese rebels overthrew it, and the Manchus took it over.)

- Why did this happen? (The government lacked support; its leaders fell for a trick by the Manchus.)

- What was the result of the Manchus' takeover? (Construction stopped on the Great Wall, which was no longer needed for defense.)

Vocabulary

unity togetherness; working as one

excluding keeping someone or something out

9 In 1644 the Great Wall was longer, stronger, and better guarded than it had ever been before, but for the Manchus it was as though it didn't exist at all. They walked through it without a struggle and readily conquered China. The wall was meaningless.

10 But was it suddenly meaningless or had it been that way for a long time? Was it the wall or the Mongols' own lack of unity that prevented them from conquering China again during the Ming rule? Was excluding the Mongols the best, or the only, way of preventing their raids? Would negotiating peaceful trade with them have been effective? Or even possible? We will never know. We can only imagine the fear that the Ming emperors felt when facing the

400

REACHING ALL LEARNERS

Extra Support/ Intervention	On Level	Challenge

Selection Review

Before students join the whole class for Wrapping Up on page 401, they should

- review their purpose/predictions

- take turns modeling Summarize and other strategies they used

- complete their Cause and Effect Charts and help you complete **Transparency 4–10**

- summarize the whole selection

Literature Discussion

In mixed-ability small groups, have students discuss their purposes for reading, their own questions, and the Think About the Selection questions on Anthology page 402.

Mongols, and how that fear influenced the choices they made in defending against them.

Looking at the Great Wall today we are amazed at its length, at how difficult it was to build, at the expense and effort that went into its construction. It was an extraordinary feat and the Great Wall has emerged as the most famous and enduring creation of the Ming dynasty. We are also aware that building it severely weakened the Ming government. Ironically, the greatest accomplishment of the Ming dynasty was an important cause of its downfall.

401

Wrapping Up

Critical Thinking Questions

1. **PROBLEM SOLVING AND DECISION MAKING** What else besides building a wall might the Chinese emperors have done to protect their country from invaders? (Answers will vary.)

2. **MAKING GENERALIZATIONS** What words would you use to describe the building of the Great Wall of China? (Sample answers: *ambitious, expensive, wasteful, incredible*)

Strategies in Action

Have students model Summarize and other strategies they used while reading.

Discussion Options

Review Predictions/Purpose Ask students what interested them most about the building of the Great Wall. Discuss the reasons why it was built.

Share Group Discussions Have students share their literature discussions.

Summarize Ask students to use their completed Cause and Effect Charts to help them summarize the selection.

Comprehension Check

Use **Practice Book** page 25 to assess students' comprehension of the selection.

English Language Learners

Supporting Comprehension

Students may have difficulty with the series of questions on page 400.

Point out the sentence *We will never know.* Emphasize that the author is asking these questions because she isn't sure of the answers.

Discuss the first question. Explain that the author wonders whether the wall was ever really protecting China.

Practice Book page 25

Name _____

The Great Wall
Comprehension Check

The People Behind the Great Wall

Each entry below names a group of people who were important in the history of the Great Wall. Next to each entry write a sentence or two telling about that group and its role.

Ming Leaders They built most of the Great Wall under their 300-year rule. Many Chinese people were not happy with them. **(2 points)**

Mongols They were nomadic warriors. The Chinese built the wall to keep them out. **(2)**

Laborers and Craftsmen Unskilled laborers built the parts of the wall made of packed earth. Skilled craftsmen built the parts made of stone. **(2)**

Chinese Soldiers They guarded, helped build, and even lived on the wall. **(2)**

Chinese People They were taxed by the Ming government to pay for the wall and forced to work on it. They eventually rebelled against the Ming rulers. **(2)**

Manchus They were a powerful nomadic tribe who took over the Ming throne when the Chinese people rebelled. **(2)**

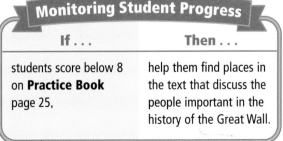

Monitoring Student Progress

If . . .	Then . . .
students score below 8 on **Practice Book** page 25,	help them find places in the text that discuss the people important in the history of the Great Wall.

Responding

Think About the Selection

Have students discuss or write their answers. Sample answers are provided; accept reasonable responses.

1. **CAUSE AND EFFECT** The Chinese people rebelled against the Ming leaders and stormed the Forbidden City. When this happened, the Manchus were able to trick the government and take over.

2. **PREDICTING OUTCOMES** no, because a wall wouldn't be a good defense against modern-day technology

3. **NOTING DETAILS** Life was hard because families were split apart when people were forced to work on the wall. Also, workers received very little pay. In addition, people were taxed to pay for the wall as well as for the extravagance of the Ming court.

4. **CAUSE AND EFFECT** It caused great hardship. It caused people to become angry with the government and to rebel.

5. **EXPRESSING PERSONAL OPINIONS** Answers will vary.

6. **MAKING JUDGMENTS** Strong barriers can't protect weak government; you shouldn't lead an extravagant life while your people live in poverty.

7. **Connecting/Comparing** The Chinese and the Mongols had been warring for a long time and understood each other's tactics well. The Aztecs thought Cortés was a god, and they had never before seen the weapons the Spanish used. Fighting was much more unequal between the Aztecs and the Spanish than it was between the Chinese and the Mongols.

Responding

Think About the Selection

1. What unexpected circumstance led to the defeat of the Ming dynast

2. Do you think a nation would build a wall like the Great Wall of Ch today? Explain.

3. Describe what life was like for the Chinese people during the Ming dynasty. List specific examples from the selection.

4. What effects did the construction of the Great Wall have on the pe of China?

5. Would you want to visit the Great Wall? Why or why not?

6. What lessons could a modern leader learn from the story of the Gr Wall?

7. **Connecting/Comparing** Compare the conflict between the Mongols the Chinese with the conflict between the Aztecs and the Spanish i *Lost Temple of the Aztecs.* How were their relationships alike, an how were they different?

Narrating

Write a Story

The selection provides many details about the lives of people who worked on the Great Wall. Write a short story about a typical day in the life of a soldier who guarded the wall.

Tips
- Use dialogue to show what your character thinks or feels.
- Use details from the selection to describe your character, the setting, and the day's events.

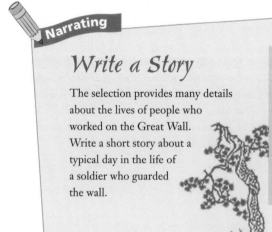

402

English Language Learners

Supporting Comprehension

Beginning/Preproduction Have students draw soldiers using smoke signals to send a message along the Great Wall.

Early Production and Speech Emergence Have partners discuss whether they think it was fair that the Chinese people were forced to build the wall by their government.

Intermediate and Advanced Fluency Have students work in small groups to find details that show how much the ancient Chinese knew about building.

cience

Make a Poster

iew the different building methods
materials used by the builders of
Great Wall. Then make a poster
wing the materials they used and
antages and disadvantages of each.

The Great Wall
Building Materials

	Advantages	Disadvantages
1. pounded earth		
2. stone		
3. brick		

Viewing

Compare an Illustration and a Photograph

Look closely at the illustration of the
Great Wall on page 396. Compare this
to the photograph of the wall in "Two
Cultures, One Wall" on page 389. What
different things do you learn about
the wall from each view? Discuss with
a partner.

Go on a Web Field Trip

Visit Education Place to take an online field trip. **www.eduplace.com/kids**

403

Additional Responses

Personal Response Invite volunteers
to share their personal responses to the
selection.

Journal ► Have students write in their
journals about whether or not they would like
to have lived in ancient China.

Selection Connections Remind students to add to **Practice Book** pages 1–2.

Monitoring Student Progress

End-of-Selection Assessment

Selection Test Use the test on page 133 in the
Teacher's Resource Blackline Masters to
assess selection comprehension and vocabulary.

Student Self-Assessment Have students assess
their reading with additional questions such as these:

● What parts of this selection were difficult for
me? Why?

● What strategies helped me understand the
selection?

● Would I like to read more about the Chinese
Empire or the Great Wall of China? Why or
why not?

Practice Book page 1

Name _____

Discovering Ancient Cultures

The selections in this theme will take you on a journey to the world of
long ago. After reading each selection, complete the chart below to
show what you learned.

	What is the location of the culture described in the selection?	When did the events described in the selection take place?
Lost Temple of the Aztecs	Mexico	in the early 1500s
The Great Wall	China	toward the end of the Ming dynasty, from about 1600–1800
The Royal Kingdoms of Ghana, Mali, and Songhay	Africa	in the eleventh century A.D.

Practice Book page 2

Name _____

Discovering Ancient Cultures

	What was remarkable about the culture described in the selection?
Lost Temple of the Aztecs	The Aztecs built huge temples and beautiful cities. They were fierce, powerful warriors. They were expert jewelers and they had a very accurate calendar.
The Great Wall	The Chinese built an immense wall of pounded earth and stone. It is the longest structure ever built.
The Royal Kingdoms of Ghana, Mali, and Songhay	The people of ancient Ghana were prosperous. They traded with people far away for exotic items. Gold was plentiful, and many people were wealthy. Even the farmers lived well.

What have you learned about ancient cultures in this theme?
Sample answer: Ancient cultures were very different from one another; people long
ago created incredible things.

Technology Link

Skill: How to Read a Timeline

- **Introduce** "Building Ancient Rome," a nonfiction article.

- **Discuss** the Skill Lesson on Anthology page 404. Tell students that the timeline on page 405 can show them when some of the Romans' most famous structures were built.

- **Explain** that each bar on this timeline represents 50 years and that the whole timeline spans 350 years. Point out the transition between B.C. and A.D. Show how to find how many years passed between a B.C. date and an A.D. date by adding the years.

- **Model** locating the dates of specific events and calculating spans of time, using the timeline.

- **Ask** students to find what happened first, the building of the first stone theater or the fire that destroyed Rome. (first stone theater) How many years passed between the building of Trajan's Column and the completion of Hadrian's Wall? (40 years)

- **Set a purpose** for reading. Discuss with students what they know about ancient Rome. Then have them read to find out what purpose some of the Romans' structures had. Remind them to use Summarize and other strategies as they read.

Vocabulary

aqueducts pipes or channels that carry water from a distant source

---

Skill: How to Read a Timeline

Before you read...

- Notice how the timeline is organized. Timelines are read from left to right or from top to bottom.

- Determine the total number of years covered.

As you read...

- When you read about an event in the main text, locate the event on the timeline.

- As the years labeled **B.C.** get larger in number, they go back in time. To figure out how many years passed between B.C. events, subtract the smaller number from the larger number.

- To figure out how many years passed between a B.C. event and an **A.D.** event, add the B.C. number to the A.D. number.

404

BUILDING ANCIENT ROME

by Dr. Sarah McNeill

The Romans were skilled builders and engineers. They planned and laid out new cities, providing public lavatories and baths, good drains and a constant supply of water for the townspeople. Many of their constructions are still standing today.

Making Arches

To build an arch, a curved wooden support was put at the top of two stone columns.

Wedge-shaped stones were put around the support. When it was taken away, the arch stayed up on its own.

Working in Stone

Slaves cut out stone blocks from quarries by drilling holes and filling them with wooden wedges. Water swelled the wood and split the stone.

English Language Learners

Supporting Comprehension

Demonstrate how to read the timeline. Show students how to figure out the number of years between events.

- Have them work in pairs, asking each other which year certain events happened and the length of time between pairs of events.

- Bring the class back together to answer similar questions as a group.

When Were They Built?

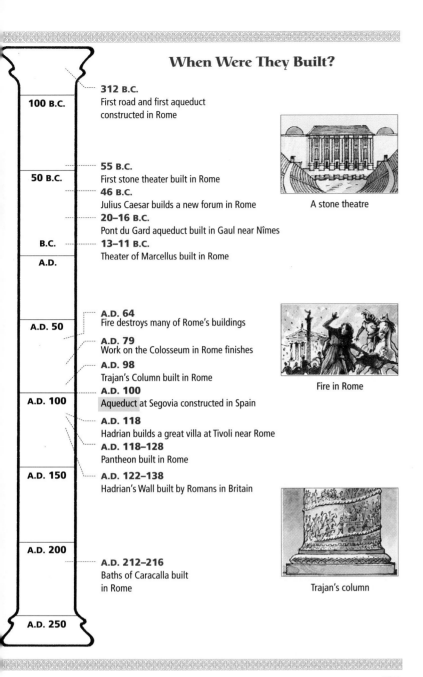

312 B.C.
First road and first aqueduct constructed in Rome

100 B.C.

55 B.C.
First stone theater built in Rome

50 B.C.

46 B.C.
Julius Caesar builds a new forum in Rome

20–16 B.C.
Pont du Gard aqueduct built in Gaul near Nîmes

B.C.

13–11 B.C.
Theater of Marcellus built in Rome

A.D.

A stone theatre

A.D. 64
Fire destroys many of Rome's buildings

A.D. 50

A.D. 79
Work on the Colosseum in Rome finishes

A.D. 98
Trajan's Column built in Rome

A.D. 100
Aqueduct at Segovia constructed in Spain

A.D. 100

Fire in Rome

A.D. 118
Hadrian builds a great villa at Tivoli near Rome

A.D. 118–128
Pantheon built in Rome

A.D. 150

A.D. 122–138
Hadrian's Wall built by Romans in Britain

A.D. 200

A.D. 212–216
Baths of Caracalla built in Rome

Trajan's column

A.D. 250

405

Extra Support/Intervention

Paraphrasing Information

Paraphrasing will help students understand each section. Have them make a numbered list, like the one shown, for "Making Arches" and "Working in Stone."

Making Arches

Step 1 Place curved wooden support at top.

Step 2 Place wedge-shaped stones around support.

Step 3 Remove support.

Graphic Aids

Teach

- Illustrations in an article help readers to understand what the author is describing.

- Illustrations are especially useful when an article is explaining the steps in a process.

Practice

- Have students reread the section called "Aqueducts and Bridges" on page 407, looking at the illustrations.

- Ask, How were the circles of wooden stakes used? Work with students to list on the board details that are made clearer by the illustrations.

Wooden Stakes

- what the circles of stakes looked like
- how close the stakes were to each other
- how stone columns were built inside them

Apply

- Have students reread the section "Roads," looking at the illustrations.

- Have partners list details that are made clearer by the illustrations. (what a groma looked like; how the stakes were laid out; what the trench looked like)

Vocabulary

amphitheater an oval or round structure with rows of seats rising gradually outward from an open space at the center

READ & COMPREHEND

Biggest Buildings

The Colosseum, in Rome, was an enormous amphitheater built to stage gladiator fights. It seated crowds of up to 50,000 people and took ten years to build.

The Colosseum

The Pantheon was a temple with a large, circular hall. It was one of the most famous buildings of ancient times because of its vast domed roof, 141 feet in diameter. Built between A.D. 118 and 128, it has been used as a place of worship ever since.

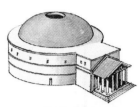

The Pantheon

The Baths of Caracalla in Rome were built on a grand scale. The main hall was enormous, over 100 x 25 yards in size. The baths could take up to 1,600 bathers every day. The buildings included shops, offices, libraries, gymnasiums and sports facilities.

Hadrian's Wall, a fortified wall 75 miles long, was built by Romans across ancient Britain to keep out warring tribes. The wall was of stone, up to 10 feet thick, with fortified positions along its length.

Hadrian's Wall

Central Heating

Wealthy Romans enjoyed central heating thanks to underfloor heating systems called hypocausts. Floors were supported on piles of bricks, with space underneath for air to circulate. A fire sent hot air into this space, warming the rooms above. Hypocausts were used in public baths as well as private houses.

Aqueducts and Bridges

The Romans were very skilled at building aqueducts and bridges. Aqueducts brought water to cities from springs and lakes in the hills. The Romans realized that they could use gravity to bring the water down to towns at lower levels. Eleven aqueducts brought water to Rome, from up to 30 miles away. Over 300 million gallons of water were brought to the city every day to supply fountains, baths and private houses.

1. To make a river crossing, first a temporary bridge was laid across a row of boats.

2. Then circles of wooden stakes were sunk into the river bed and the water pumped out of the space inside.

3. These spaces were filled with columns of stone blocks.

4. A wooden frame was lifted onto the columns by cranes to form the bridge.

Roads

Engineers built 50,000 miles of roads, to link all parts of the Empire to Rome. The roads enabled soldiers to move about the Empire, but they were also used by merchants. Roman roads took the shortest, straightest routes possible. Some roads involved tunneling through hills and cutting across valleys.

1. First, surveyors used a *groma* to make sure the land was level and marked out the road with stakes.

2. Then workmen dug a trench, up to 40 feet wide, and laid curbstones along the edges.

3. The trench was packed with sand, then stones, then rubble. These layers formed the foundation of the road.

4. The top layer of stone slabs, the road's surface, was curved to allow rain to drain off.

407

Wrapping Up

Critical Thinking Questions

Ask students to read aloud the parts of the selection that support their answers to these questions.

1. **MAKING GENERALIZATIONS** What are some generalizations you can make about the ancient Romans, based on this selection? (Sample answers: They were clever; they valued culture and the arts; they did not value equality because they had slaves.)

2. **MAKING JUDGMENTS** Which structure do you think would have been more valuable to an ancient culture such as the Romans or the Chinese, a road for travel and trade or a wall for defense? Why? (Answers will vary.)

3. **COMPARE AND CONTRAST** What modern-day structures are similar to those built by the Romans? (some modern bridges; modern stadiums similar to the Colosseum and the Pantheon; many modern buildings with columns and arches)

4. **Connecting/Comparing** Considering what you know about the Great Wall, how well do you think Hadrian's Wall kept warring tribes out of Roman lands? Why? (probably not very effectively, because the Great Wall was much longer, and it didn't keep China's enemies out)

Challenge

Build Your Own Roman Structure

Using materials available in your school, students can try to create a Roman arch or a working model of an aqueduct.

- If students choose the aqueduct, they may want to do more research in the library.

- If students choose to build an arch, they should do so without glue; blocks could be made from clay or cut from Styrofoam.

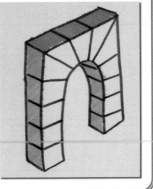

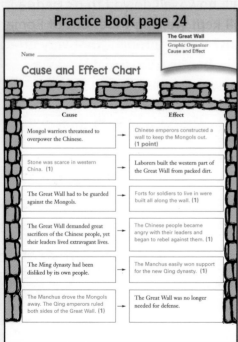

COMPREHENSION: Cause and Effect

❶ Teach

Review cause and effect in *The Great Wall*. Remind students that a cause is what makes something happen and an effect is a result of something that happened. Complete the Graphic Organizer on **Transparency 4–10** with students. (Sample answer are shown.) Have students refer to the selection and to **Practice Book** page 24. Then discuss these points.

- Sometimes authors state cause-and-effect relationships directly, using clue words such as *because* or *as a result of*.

- Sometimes causes and effects are unstated. Then readers must figure out the relationship by thinking about the order of ever and by asking themselves questions such as, What led up to thi

Model identifying an unstated cause-and-effect relationshi Have students reread the last two paragraphs on page 398. Then display **Transparency 4–10** while you think aloud.

Think Aloud *The Great Wall was no longer needed for defense. What led to this? I'll review the events that came right before this. Wi the Chinese army, the Manchus drove the Mongols away so the wall wasn't nee ed for defense. After that, the Qing emperors of China ruled both sides of the Gr Wall so the wall wasn't needed as a border. Now I understand—because the wa was no longer needed for defense or as a border, it became useless.*

❷ Guided Practice

Have students identify unstated causes and effects. Ask partners to complete a diagram like the one below by identifying causes that led to an effect. (Sample answers are shown.)

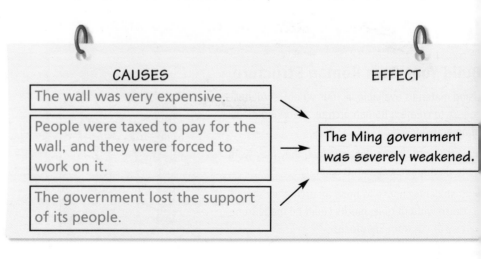

CAUSES | EFFECT

The wall was very expensive.

People were taxed to pay for the wall, and they were forced to work on it.

The government lost the support of its people.

The Ming government was severely weakened.

Apply

Assign Practice Book pages 26–27. Also have students apply this skill as they read their **Leveled Readers** for this week. You may also select books from the Leveled Bibliography for this theme (pages 354E–354F).

Test Prep When answering multiple-choice questions about cause and effect, students should circle the key word or phrase that tells them whether the question is asking about a cause or an effect. This will help them avoid wrong answer choices.

Leveled Readers and Leveled Practice

Students at all levels apply the comprehension skill as they read their Leveled Readers. See lessons on pages 407O–407R.

● BELOW LEVEL — THE PYRAMIDS OF GIZA — BY STANFORD MAKISHI, ILLUSTRATED BY FRANCESCO SPADONI AND LORENZO CECCHI

▲ ON LEVEL — A SCRIBE OF ANCIENT CHINA — by Jane Prassit, illustrated by Oki Han

■ ABOVE LEVEL — THE SHAPE IN THE DARK — A Story of Hadrian's Wall — by Tim Spalding, illustrated by Dick Smolinski

◆ LANGUAGE SUPPORT — THE PYRAMIDS OF ANCIENT EGYPT — BY STANFORD MAKISHI, ILLUSTRATED BY FRANCESCO SPADONI AND LORENZO CECCHI

Reading Traits

Teaching students to recognize and describe cause-and-effect relationships is one way of encouraging them to "read between the lines" of a selection. This comprehension skill supports the reading trait **Integrating for Synthesis**.

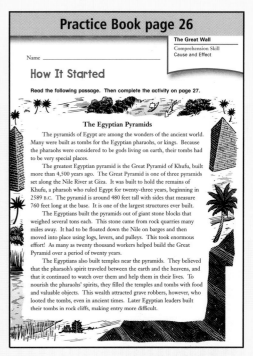

Practice Book page 26

The Great Wall
Comprehension Skill
Cause and Effect

Name _____

How It Started

Read the following passage. Then complete the activity on page 27.

The Egyptian Pyramids

The pyramids of Egypt are among the wonders of the ancient world. Many were built as tombs for the Egyptian pharaohs, or kings. Because the pharaohs were considered to be gods living on earth, their tombs had to be very special places.

The greatest Egyptian pyramid is the Great Pyramid of Khufu, built more than 4,500 years ago. The Great Pyramid is one of three pyramids set along the Nile River at Giza. It was built to hold the remains of Khufu, a pharaoh who ruled Egypt for twenty-three years, beginning in 2589 B.C. The pyramid is around 480 feet tall with sides that measure 760 feet long at the base. It is one of the largest structures ever built.

The Egyptians built the pyramids out of giant stone blocks that weighed several tons each. This stone came from rock quarries many miles away. It had to be floated down the Nile on barges and then moved into place using logs, levers, and pulleys. This took enormous effort! As many as twenty thousand workers helped build the Great Pyramid over a period of twenty years.

The Egyptians also built temples near the pyramids. They believed that the pharaoh's spirit traveled between the earth and the heavens, and that it continued to watch over them and help them in their lives. To nourish the pharaohs' spirits, they filled the temples and tombs with food and valuable objects. This wealth attracted grave robbers, however, who looted the tombs, even in ancient times. Later Egyptian leaders built their tombs in rock cliffs, making entry more difficult.

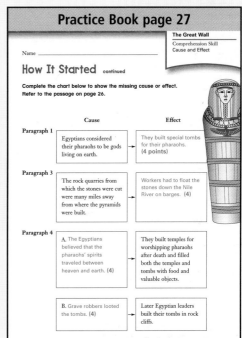

Practice Book page 27

The Great Wall
Comprehension Skill
Cause and Effect

Name _____

How It Started continued

Complete the chart below to show the missing cause or effect. Refer to the passage on page 26.

	Cause	Effect
Paragraph 1	Egyptians considered their pharaohs to be gods living on earth.	They built special tombs for their pharaohs. (4 points)
Paragraph 3	The rock quarries from which the stones were cut were many miles away from where the pyramids were built.	Workers had to float the stones down the Nile River on barges. (4)
Paragraph 4	A. The Egyptians believed that the pharaohs' spirits traveled between heaven and earth. (4)	They built temples for worshipping pharaohs after death and filled both the temples and tombs with food and valuable objects.
	B. Grave robbers looted the tombs. (4)	Later Egyptian leaders built their tombs in rock cliffs.

Monitoring Student Progress

If . . .	Then . . .
students score 12 or below on **Practice Book** page 27,	use the Reteaching lesson on Teacher's Edition page R10.
students have successfully met the lesson objectives,	have them do the Challenge/Extension activities on Teacher's Edition page R11.

OBJECTIVES

- Read words with suffixes *-ion* and *-ation*.
- Use the Phonics/Decoding Strategy to decode longer words.
- Learn academic language: *suffix, base word, noun suffix*.

Target Skill Trace

Teach	p. 407C
Reteach	p. R16
Review	pp. M34–M35
See	*Handbook for English Language Learners*, p. 145; *Extra Support Handbook*, pp. 140–141; pp. 144–145

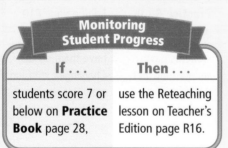

Practice Book page 28

Name _____

Suffix Search

Circle the suffixes *-ion* and *-ation* in the underlined words in the blocks.

1. The Great Wall marked the separation between the Ming and the Mongol territories. (1 point)
2. A huge gate was the place of connection between two sections of the Great Wall. (2)
3. The Ming government got money to build the Great Wall through years of taxation of the Chinese people. (1)
4. The Chinese people finally staged a rebellion because they were tired of the Ming government's lying and corruption. (2)

Now, use four of the underlined words above in sentences of your own.

Accept sentences that use the words correctly. (4)

Monitoring Student Progress

If . . .	Then . . .
students score 7 or below on **Practice Book** page 28,	use the Reteaching lesson on Teacher's Edition page R16.

Spelling · Connection

STRUCTURAL ANALYSIS/ VOCABULARY: More Suffixes

❶ Teach

Discuss the noun suffixes *-ion* and *-ation*. Write <u>Construction</u> *across northern China continued for the next two centuries.*

- Underline the suffix *-ion* in *construction*. Explain that it can mean "action or process" or "state or condition."
- Discuss the meaning of the base word, *construct*. ("to build") Explain that the whole word means "the process of building."
- Ask, What part of speech is *construction*? (noun) What part of speech is *construct*? (verb)
- Tell students that the suffix *-ion* is called a noun suffix because it is often used to form a noun from a verb.
- Explain that the suffix *-ation* is also a noun suffix that can mean "process" or "condition." Discuss this example: *relax* and *relaxation*.

Model the Phonics/Decoding Strategy. Write *There were many* <u>complications</u> *involved in such a massive project.* Then model decoding *complications*.

> **Think Aloud** *I recognize the suffix -ion. I know it is used to form a noun from a verb. I don't recognize the base word. I'll try pronouncing it, KAHM-plih-kat. That doesn't sound familiar. Maybe the word ended in an e that was dropped when the suffix was added. That would make the base word KAHM-plih-kayt. That's a verb that means "to make difficult." The whole word is a noun that must mean "difficulties." That makes sense in the sentence.*

❷ Guided Practice

Have students use noun suffixes. Display the phrases and sentences below. Tell partners to circle the suffix in each underlined word, decode the word, and figure out its meaning. Call on volunteers to model at the board.

1. an ingenious system of <u>communication</u>
2. The project took <u>determination</u>.
3. <u>Fortifications</u> were built along the wall.
4. <u>cooperation</u> helped

❸ Apply

Assign Practice Book page 28.

PHONICS REVIEW:
Sounds for the Letters *wh*

OBJECTIVES
- Read words with the letters *wh*.
- Use the Phonics/Decoding Strategy to decode longer words.

❶ Teach

Review different sounds for the letters *wh*. Explain these points.

- The letters *wh* can stand for the /w/ sound as in *where*.
- The letters *wh* can stand for the /h/ sound as in *whose*.
- The letters *wh* can stand for the /hw/ sound as in *whale*.

Model the Phonics/Decoding Strategy. Write *It was difficult for the soldiers to grow* <u>*wholesome*</u> *food on the harsh steppe.* Then model how to decode *wholesome*.

Think Aloud *I recognize the word* some *in the second part of this word. In the first part, I see the letters* wh, *so I'll try pronouncing the first part with the /hw/ sound,* HWOHL-suhm. *That definitely doesn't sound right. The* wh *in this word must stand for the /h/ sound. The word is* HOHL-suhm. *It means "good for you" or "healthy." That makes sense in the sentence.*

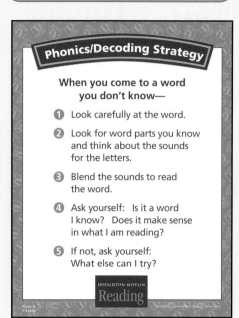

Phonics/Decoding Strategy

When you come to a word you don't know—

❶ Look carefully at the word.

❷ Look for word parts you know and think about the sounds for the letters.

❸ Blend the sounds to read the word.

❹ Ask yourself: Is it a word I know? Does it make sense in what I am reading?

❺ If not, ask yourself: What else can I try?

HOUGHTON MIFFLIN
Reading

❷ Guided Practice

Help students decode words with different sounds for the letters *wh*. Display the sentences below. Have partners circle the letters *wh* in each underlined word, pronounce the word, and check to see if it makes sense in the sentence. Call on individuals to model at the board.

1. I know <u>which</u> dynasty came after the Ming.
2. Tell <u>whoever</u> needs to know.
3. They lit smoke signals <u>whenever</u> the Mongols approached.

❸ Apply

Have students decode words with different sounds for the letters *wh*. Ask students to find these words in *The Great Wall*, decode them, and discuss their meanings.

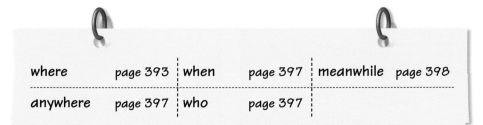

where	page 393	when	page 397	meanwhile	page 398
anywhere	page 397	who	page 397		

SPELLING: Adding *-ion* or *-ation*

OBJECTIVES

- Write verbs and the nouns formed by adding the suffix *-ion* or *-ation* to the verbs.
- Learn academic language: *suffix.*

SPELLING WORDS

Basic

construct*	admire
construction*	admiration
connect*	situate
connection*	situation
combine*	examine
combination*	examination
cooperate	contribute
cooperation	contribution
attract	explore
attraction	exploration

Review	Challenge
inspect	negotiate*
inspection	negotiation*
create*	insulate
creation*	insulation

Forms of these words appear in the literature.

Extra Support/Intervention

Basic Word List You may want to use only the left column of Basic Words with students who need extra support.

Challenge

Challenge Word Practice Have students use the Challenge Words to write quotes from a conversation between a builder and a person who wants to build a home.

DAY 1 INSTRUCTION

Adding *-ion* or *-ation*

Pretest Use the Day 5 Test sentences.

Teach Write these word pairs on the board: *connect/connection, situate/situation, admire/admiration.*

- Say each word; have students repeat it. Tell them that each pair includes a verb and a noun, and that the noun was formed by adding the suffix *-ion* or *-ation* to the verb.

- Explain that the final *e* of a verb is dropped before *-ion* or *-ation* is added because both suffixes begin with vowels.

- List the remaining Basic Words, and have students repeat them. Ask students to identify any spelling changes that took place when the suffixes were added.

Practice/Homework Assign **Practice Book** page 257.

Practice Book page 257

Take-Home Word List	Take-Home Word List	Take-Home Word List
The Great Wall	**Discovering Ancient Cultures** Reading-Writing Workshop	**Lost Temple of the Aztecs**
Adding *-ion* or *-ation* connect, connection, situate, situation, admire, admiration	Look for familiar spelling patterns in these words to help you remember their spellings.	**The /sh/ Sound** /sh/ → polish, motion official, mission
Spelling Words	**Spelling Words**	**Spelling Words**
1. construct 11. admire	1. decent 8. sleek	1. glacier 11. official
2. construction 12. admiration	2. descent 9. alley	2. motion 12. edition
3. connect 13. situate	3. affect 10. ally	3. pressure 13. musician
4. connection 14. situation	4. effect 11. confident	4. direction 14. mention
5. combine 15. examine	5. desert 12. confidant	5. caution 15. mission
6. combination 16. examination	6. dessert 13. hurdle	6. partial 16. portion
7. cooperate 17. contribute	7. slick 14. hurtle	7. ancient 17. session
8. cooperation 18. contribution		8. polish 18. selfish
9. attract 19. explore		9. station 19. establish
10. attraction 20. exploration		10. shallow 20. cushion
Challenge Words	**Challenge Words**	**Challenge Words**
1. negotiate	1. bizarre	1. expedition 4. beneficial
2. negotiation	2. bazaar	2. diminish 5. technician
3. insulate	3. ellipse	3. recession
4. insulation	4. eclipse	
My Study List Add your own spelling words on the back.	**My Study List** Add your own spelling words on the back.	**My Study List** Add your own spelling words on the back.

Take-Home Word List

DAY 2 REVIEW & PRACTICE

Reviewing the Principle

Go over the spelling principle for adding *-ion* or *-ation* with students.

Practice/Homework Assign **Practice Book** page 29.

Practice Book page 29

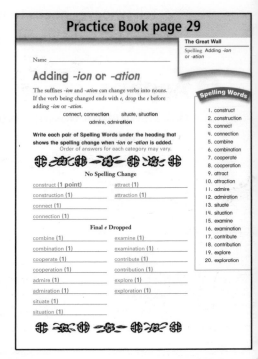

The Great Wall
Spelling Adding *-ion* or *-ation*

Name _____

Adding *-ion* or *-ation*

The suffixes *-ion* and *-ation* can change verbs into nouns. If the verb being changed ends with *e*, drop the *e* before adding *-ion* or *-ation*.

connect, connection   situate, situation
admire, admiration

Write each pair of Spelling Words under the heading that shows the spelling change when *-ion* or *-ation* is added.
Order of answers for each category may vary.

No Spelling Change

construct (1 point)	attract (1)
construction (1)	attraction (1)
connect (1)	
connection (1)	

Final *e* Dropped

combine (1)	examine (1)
combination (1)	examination (1)
cooperate (1)	contribute (1)
cooperation (1)	contribution (1)
admire (1)	explore (1)
admiration (1)	exploration (1)
situate (1)	
situation (1)	

Spelling Words
1. construct
2. construction
3. connect
4. connection
5. combine
6. combination
7. cooperate
8. cooperation
9. attract
10. attraction
11. admire
12. admiration
13. situate
14. situation
15. examine
16. examination
17. contribute
18. contribution
19. explore
20. exploration

DAY 3 VOCABULARY

lipped Words

rite *exam* on the board. Tell stu-nts that this is a clipped, or short-ed, form of *examination*.

Point out that many familiar words are actually clipped words.

Write these words on the board, and ask students to identify their longer forms: *flu, gym, tux, ref, memo, photo, stereo, deli, ad, lab.* (*influenza, gymnasium, tuxedo, ref-eree, memorandum, photograph, stereophonic, delicatessen, adver-tisement, laboratory*)

List the Basic Words on the board. Have students use each word orally in a sentence. (Sentences will vary.)

actice/Homework For spelling actice, assign **Practice Book** ge 30.

DAY 4 PROOFREADING

Game: Twenty Questions

Ask students to form groups of 3 to 5, and give each group a list of this lesson's Basic and Review Words.

- To play, players take turns thinking of a word on the list.

- The other players take turns asking questions to help them guess the word.

- Players can ask questions such as "Does it have a short *a* sound in it?" "Is it a noun?" or "Is it a synonym for *build*?"

- A player can ask a question and make a guess in the same turn. The player must then spell the word correctly to score a point.

- If the player misspells the word, the next player may try to score a point by spelling it correctly.

Practice/Homework For proofread-ing and writing practice, assign **Practice Book** page 31.

DAY 5 ASSESSMENT

Spelling Test

Say each underlined word, read the sentence, and then repeat the word. Have students write only the under-lined word.

Basic Words

1. They will **construct** a new house.
2. The school is under **construction.**
3. You can **connect** those two puzzle pieces.
4. There is a **connection** between old friends.
5. I will **combine** the milk and the flour.
6. This paste is a **combination** of flour and water.
7. Let's **cooperate** on this project.
8. Your **cooperation** helped the team win.
9. That sign will **attract** his attention.
10. The next **attraction** at the theater is a play.
11. I **admire** your handwriting.
12. Actors love the **admiration** of the crowd.
13. Try to **situate** yourself in the room.
14. When our ship sank, the **situation** was grave.
15. Please **examine** my work for mistakes.
16. His doctor gave him an **examination.**
17. I will **contribute** money to the fund.
18. Your food **contribution** was helpful.
19. We want to **explore** the cave.
20. In our cave **exploration,** we found a gem.

Challenge Words

21. Can we **negotiate** the price of the car?
22. The contract **negotiation** is going well.
23. My heavy coat will **insulate** me from the cold.
24. She put **insulation** in the walls.

Practice Book page 30

Name _____

Spelling Spree

Questions Write a Spelling Word to answer each question.

1. What does a magnet have for iron?
2. What do people do when they want to work well together?
3. What does a teacher give you to test your knowledge of a subject?
4. What is the opposite of *repel*?
5. When you hear static during a telephone call, you have a bad what?
6. What do you have for your favorite role model?
7. What is another word for *build*?

1. attraction **(1 point)**	5. connection **(1)**
2. cooperate **(1)**	6. admiration **(1)**
3. examination **(1)**	7. construct **(1)**
4. attract **(1)**	

Syllable Scramble Rearrange the syllables to write a Spelling Word. There is one extra syllable in each numbered item.

Example: de tion in spec *inspection*

8. nect ble con connect **(1)**
9. bu con ant tion tri contribution **(1)**
10. plo at ex ra tion exploration **(1)**
11. bine dent com combine **(1)**

The Third Word Write the Spelling Word that belongs with each group of words.

12. like, appreciate, ___ admire **(1)**
13. teamwork, collaboration, ___ cooperation **(1)**
14. investigate, examine, ___ explore **(1)**
15. place, locate, ___ situate **(1)**

Spelling Words
1. construct
2. construction
3. connect
4. connection
5. combine
6. combination
7. cooperate
8. cooperation
9. attract
10. attraction
11. admire
12. admiration
13. situate
14. situation
15. examine
16. examination
17. contribution
18. contribution
19. explore
20. exploration

Practice Book page 31

Name _____

Proofreading and Writing

Proofreading Circle the five misspelled Spelling Words in this proclamation. Then write each word correctly.

The imperial architect is pleased to announce that the construcktion of our Emperor's wall is going splendidly. However, much work remains to be done. The combanation of building materials must be just right. Then we must connect all the separate parts into one solid barrier. The Chinese people are now called upon to contribuet more labor to this effort. The Mongol situashun on our northern border continues to worsen. The barbarians constantly examin our defenses to find weaknesses. Therefore, we must build a wall that has none. Let all people unite in this glorious endeavor!

1. construction **(1 point)**	4. situation **(1)**
2. combination **(1)**	5. examine **(1)**
3. contribute **(1)**	

Spelling Words
1. construct
2. construction
3. connect
4. connection
5. combine
6. combination
7. cooperate
8. cooperation
9. attract
10. attraction
11. admire
12. admiration
13. situate
14. situation
15. examine
16. examination
17. contribute
18. contribution
19. explore
20. exploration

—— Write a Report You are on an inspection tour of the Great Wall. You must write a report to the chief architect on the conditions along the wall. How would you describe the usefulness of the wall against Mongol attacks? Are there any suggestions you would make?

On a separate sheet of paper, write a report giving an update on the state of affairs along the Great Wall. Use Spelling Words from the list.
Responses will vary. **(5)**

OBJECTIVES

- Identify synonyms as words that have almost the same meaning.
- Use synonyms to add variety and interest to writing.
- Learn academic language: *synonyms*.

Target Skill Trace

Teach	p. 407G
Review	pp. M36–M37
Extend	Challenge/Extension Activities, p. R17
See	*Handbook for English Language Learners*, p. 149

VOCABULARY: Synonyms

TARGET SKILL

❶ Teach

Introduce synonyms. Tell students that words with the same or nearly the same meaning are called synonyms.

- Discuss these examples: *strong* and *durable; warn* and *caution.*
- Explain that synonyms can have slightly different meanings. For example, *talk* and *chat* are synonyms, but *talk* suggests a more serious conversation than *chat.*
- Writers should keep shades of meaning in mind when choosing a synonym. It often helps to look up synonyms in a dictionary.

Model choosing synonyms when writing. Tell students that writers use synonyms to keep their writing interesting.

Think Aloud *Let's say I'm writing a report about how the Great Wall of China was built. Instead of repeating certain words such as* built *again and again, I can vary my sentences by using synonyms. Synonyms for* built *might include* constructed, raised, *and* created. *I could use* build *in the first sentence and* construct *in the second sentence.*

❷ Guided Practice

Give students practice in choosing synonyms. Display the paragraph and the words below. Have students rewrite each sentence using the synonyms. Discuss their answers.

The mountain <u>routes</u> that the Mongols <u>usually</u> used to <u>invade</u> China were <u>blocked</u> with walls. Those walls were <u>connected</u> with other <u>sections</u> of the Great Wall.

Synonyms joined; pathways; parts; attack; obstructed; normally

❸ Apply

Assign Practice Book page 32.

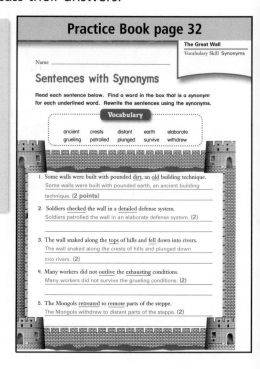

Practice Book page 32

The Great Wall
Vocabulary Skill Synonyms

Name _____

Sentences with Synonyms

Read each sentence below. Find a word in the box that is a *synonym* for each underlined word. Rewrite the sentences using the synonyms.

Vocabulary

ancient   crests   distant   earth   elaborate
grueling   patrolled   plunged   survive   withdrew

1. Some walls were built with pounded <u>dirt</u>, an <u>old</u> building technique.
   Some walls were built with pounded earth, an ancient building technique. **(2 points)**

2. Soldiers <u>checked</u> the wall in a <u>detailed</u> defense system.
   Soldiers patrolled the wall in an elaborate defense system. (2)

3. The wall snaked along the <u>tops</u> of hills and <u>fell</u> down into rivers.
   The wall snaked along the crests of hills and plunged down into rivers. (2)

4. Many workers did not <u>outlive</u> the <u>exhausting</u> conditions.
   Many workers did not survive the grueling conditions. (2)

5. The Mongols <u>retreated</u> to <u>remote</u> parts of the steppe.
   The Mongols withdrew to distant parts of the steppe. (2)

Monitoring Student Progress

If . . .	Then . . .
students score 7 or below on **Practice Book** page 32,	have them work in small groups to correct the items they missed.

STUDY SKILL: Note Taking

OBJECTIVES

- Take notes on a nonfiction selection.
- Organize notes under topic headings.
- Record all source information necessary for a bibliography.

❶ Teach

Introduce taking notes.

- When you take notes, you list important facts and details that you want to remember about a topic.
- Taking notes helps you to do research and organize information.

Discuss these tips for taking notes.

- As you read, look for main ideas. Write each main idea as a heading.
- Use an index card or a separate sheet of paper for each main idea. Write a heading for each card or sheet of paper.
- Write important facts below the heading where it belongs.
- Write words and phrases or complete sentences.
- Use your own words unless you are quoting words exactly.
- When you quote words exactly, use quotation marks.
- Record the title of the source and the page number where you found each fact. Keep a record of each source's full title, its author or editor, and its publisher for your bibliography.

Display Transparency 4–11 and model how to take notes.

Think Aloud *I will take notes on page 393 of* The Great Wall. *I reread this page, looking for the main ideas. One main idea is how the Great Wall of China was built, so the heading on my first note card will be* Building the Great Wall. *I'll jot down these details:* no master plan; purpose was to keep out Mongols; western part—built with pounded earth; eastern part—built with stone and bricks—needed skilled craftsmen for this. *Another main idea is who built the Great Wall. The heading on my second note card will be* People Who Built the Great Wall. *I'll jot down details under that.*

❷ Practice/Apply

Give students practice in taking notes.

- Have partners take notes on the remaining pages of The Great Wall. Then ask, What headings did you use? What facts did you record? What other information did you include in your notes?
- Assign students an article from an encyclopedia or other reference source about the Great Wall of China, the Roman Colosseum, or another topic that interests them. Have them take notes about what they read.

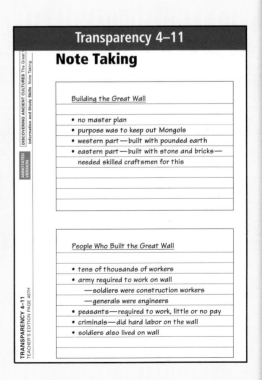

Transparency 4–11

Note Taking

Building the Great Wall

- no master plan
- purpose was to keep out Mongols
- western part—built with pounded earth
- eastern part—built with stone and bricks— needed skilled craftsmen for this

People Who Built the Great Wall

- tens of thousands of workers
- army required to work on wall
    —soldiers were construction workers
    —generals were engineers
- peasants—required to work, little or no pay
- criminals—did hard labor on the wall
- soldiers also lived on wall

GRAMMAR: Comparing with Adjectives

OBJECTIVES

- Write comparative and superlative forms of adjectives.
- Write comparative and superlative forms of *good* and *bad*.
- Proofread and correct sentences with grammar and spelling errors.
- Use the correct forms of comparative and superlative adjectives to improve writing.
- Learn academic language: *adjective, comparative form, superlative form, irregular form.*

Transparency 4–12
Daily Language Practice

Correct two sentences each day.

1. My brother can construt a biggest sandcastle than I can.
   My brother can construct a bigger sandcastle than I can.
2. Last week we visit the main attracsin at the museum.
   Last week we visited the main attraction at the museum.
3. This examinasun was more harder than the one last week.
   This examination was harder than the one last week.
4. The twins Dan and Jen does not cooperite with each other.
   The twins Dan and Jen do not cooperate with each other.
5. Let's explour the roman exhibit at the museum.
   Let's explore the Roman exhibit at the museum.
6. I have great admirasun for professor Suarez.
   I have great admiration for Professor Suarez.
7. Karens constructun of a gingerbread house is amazing.
   Karen's construction of a gingerbread house is amazing.
8. Forecasting this weather situasion is more difficulter than forecasting the one last week.
   Forecasting this weather situation is more difficult than forecasting the one last week.
9. Mr. Brown are happy with the cooperasun in his classroom.
   Mr. Brown is happy with the cooperation in his classroom.
10. An explorasun of the ancient mayan culture is fascinating.
    An exploration of the ancient Mayan culture is fascinating.

TRANSPARENCY 4–12
TEACHER'S EDITION PAGE 407I

Monitoring Student Progress

If . . .	Then . . .
students score 4 or below on **Practice Book** page 33 or 34,	use the Reteaching lessons on Teacher's Edition pages R22 and R23.

DAY 1 INSTRUCTION

Comparing with Adjectives

Teach Go over these rules:

- Use the comparative form of an adjective to compare two things. Add *-er* to most adjectives to compare two things; use *more* with long adjectives.

- Use the superlative form to compare three or more things. Add *-est* to most adjectives to compare three or more things; use *most* with long adjectives.

- Display the example sentences on **Transparency 4–13.** Point out *-er* added to *fierce* to compare two things and *-est* added to compare many things. Note that *more* and *most* are used with *aggressive.*

- Ask volunteers to change each adjective in parentheses to the correct comparative or superlative form in Sentences 1–6.

Daily Language Practice
Have students correct Sentences 1 and 2 on **Transparency 4–12.**

Transparency 4–13
Comparing with Adjectives

The Mongol soldiers of the fourteenth century were fiercer than those of the seventeenth century.
The soldiers in Genghis Khan's army may have been the fiercest soldiers of all.
In the seventeenth century, the Manchus were more aggressive than the Mongols.
Did they send their most aggressive legions to take control of the Forbidden City?

1. The emperors of China built additions to the Great Wall in places where the likelihood of attack was the (great) _greatest_
2. Earthen walls were (weak) _weaker_ than walls of brick.
3. Building a brick wall was (complicated) _more complicated_ than building an earthen wall.
4. The stonemasons and bricklayers were the (skillful) _most skillful_ workers of all.
5. The watchtowers were the (small) _smallest_ of all the fortifications.
6. The Great Wall was the (significant) _most significant_ accomplishment of the Ming dynasty.

TRANSPARENCY 4–13
TEACHER'S EDITION PAGE 407I

DAY 2 PRACTICE

Independent Work

Practice/Homework Assign **Practice Book** page 33.

Daily Language Practice
Have students correct Sentences 3 and 4 on **Transparency 4–12.**

Practice Book page 33

The Great Wall
Grammar Skill Comparing with Adjectives

Name _____

Compare Us!

Comparing with Adjectives Use the **comparative** form (*-er* or *more*) of an adjective to compare two persons, places, ideas, or things. Use the **superlative** form (*-est* or *most*) to compare three or more. Look at this chart of spelling changes that happen when *-er* or *-est* is added to some words.

Spelling changes with *-er* and *-est*			
▶ Do not add another *e* to adjectives ending in *e*.	nice	nicer	nicest
▶ You usually double the final consonant of **adjectives that end in a consonant after a single vowel.**	flat	flatter	flattest
▶ Change the final *y* to *i* in adjectives ending in *y*.	busy	busier	busiest

Complete each sentence with the correct form of the adjective in parentheses. Remember to use *more* or *most* with long adjectives.

1. My family built a _larger_ (1 point) _____ snow fort this year than last year. (large)
2. Our neighbors tried to build a _bigger_ (1) _____ one than ours. (big)
3. We made the fort on the _coldest_ (1) _____ day of the year. (cold)
4. It was the _most fantastic_ (1) _____ snow fort ever built! (fantastic)
5. I hope tomorrow is not _sunnier_ (1) _____ than today. (sunny)
6. If the snow melts, we'll lose the _most ambitious_ (1) _____ snow fort we've ever made! (ambitious)

DAY 3 — INSTRUCTION

omparing with *good/bad*

each Go over these rules:

- The adjectives *good* and *bad* have irregular comparative and superlative forms.

- Use *better* to compare two things and *best* to compare three or more.

- Use *worse* to compare two things and *worst* to compare three or more.

Display the example sentences at the top of **Transparency 4–14**. Point out that *better* and *worse* are used to compare two things, and *best* and *worst* are used to compare more than two.

Ask volunteers to write the appropriate comparative or superlative form of *good* or *bad* in Sentences 1–6.

aily Language Practice
ave students correct Sentences 5 nd 6 on **Transparency 4–12**.

Transparency 4–14

Comparing with *good* and *bad*

The Mongol warriors were <u>better</u> horsemen than their neighbors.
Their horses were the <u>best</u> in all of Asia.
Were the Ming emperors in the early seventeenth century <u>worse</u> rulers than previous emperors?
Working on the Great Wall was perhaps the <u>worst</u> fate that could happen to a peasant.

1. Winter was the (bad) <u>worst</u> time to work on the Great Wall.
2. Which is (bad) <u>worse</u> a snowstorm or an ice storm?
3. Summer was not much (good) <u>better</u> than winter.
4. The people who had the (good) <u>best</u> accommodations were probably the leaders.
5. What is the (good) <u>best</u> time to visit the Great Wall?
6. Is hot, humid weather (good) <u>better</u> or (bad) <u>worse</u> than cold, snowy weather?

DAY 4 — PRACTICE

Independent Work

Practice/Homework Assign **Practice Book** page 34.

Daily Language Practice
Have students correct Sentences 7 and 8 on **Transparency 4–12**.

Practice Book page 34

The Great Wall
Grammar Skill Comparing with *good* and *bad*

Name _____

Good News or Bad?

Comparing with *good* and *bad* The adjectives *good* and *bad* are irregular. They do not take the endings *-er* or *-est*, and the words *more* or *most* are not added to them. Study their special comparative forms in this chart.

	Positive	Negative
Adjective:	I have **good** news.	I have **bad** news.
Comparative form:	The news is **better** today.	Today's news is **worse**.
Superlative form:	This is the **best** news I've ever heard.	This is the **worst** news I've ever heard.

Fill in the blank with the correct form of *good* if the word in parentheses ( ) is *positive* and the correct form of *bad* if the word in parentheses is *negative*.

1. Signal fires were once a <u>good (1 point)</u> means of communication. (positive)
2. Now we have <u>better (1)</u> ways of getting in touch than ever before. (positive)
3. This is the <u>worst (1)</u> telephone connection I've ever had! (negative)
4. Receiving a scrambled message is <u>worse (1)</u> than no message at all. (negative)
5. Sending electronic mail is the <u>best (1)</u> way of all to keep in touch with friends who live far away. (positive)
6. No one likes to get <u>bad (1)</u> news. (negative)

DAY 5 — IMPROVING WRITING

Correct Adjective Forms

Teach Tell students that a good writer is careful to use the correct comparative and superlative forms of adjectives.

- Model correcting a sentence in which an incorrect form is used:
  - If the Ming emperors had been more kinder, people might not have revolted.
  - *Corrected:* If the Ming emperors had been <u>kinder</u>, people might not have revolted.

- Ask students to proofread a piece of their own writing for correct forms of adjectives.

Practice/Homework Assign **Practice Book** page 35.

Daily Language Practice
Have students correct Sentences 9 and 10 on **Transparency 4–12**.

Practice Book page 35

The Great Wall
Grammar Skill Using the Correct Forms of Adjectives

Name _____

What Good Form!

Using the Correct Forms of Adjectives It is important for a good writer to use the correct form of an adjective. Here are examples of some common mistakes writers make with adjectives:

Error: As the years went by, they found a **more better** way to build the wall.
Correct: As the years went by, they found a **better** way to build the wall.

Error: Some rulers were **benevolenter** than others.
Correct: Some rulers were **more benevolent** than others.

Error: What is the **older** place you have ever seen?
Correct: What is the **oldest** place you have ever seen?

Beth has written a draft of a letter to her friend Nell about an enjoyable visit to the art museum. In her enthusiasm, she has made some mistakes with her adjectives. Find the five incorrect adjective forms in her letter, and write them correctly on the lines below. Order of answers may vary.

Dear Nell,

Yesterday I visited the greater art museum I've ever seen. It was gooder than the one we went to last month. The works from China were the impressivest ones. Many of the works are very old. A beautifuler statue of a young man with two birds was more than 2000 years old! Can you imagine seeing anything ancienter? If an American statue is 200 years old, we think that is amazing.

1. greatest (1 point)
2. better (1)
3. most impressive (1)
4. beautiful (1)
5. more ancient (1)

WRITING: Paragraph of Information

OBJECTIVES

- Identify the characteristics of a good paragraph of information.
- Write a paragraph of information.
- Elaborate with adjectives.

Writing Traits

Word Choice As students revise their paragraphs on Day 3, encourage them to add adjectives that say exactly what they mean. Share these examples.

Vague We went to a <u>cool</u> movie. Then I bought some <u>nice</u> pants.

Exact We went to an <u>exciting action</u> movie. Then I bought some <u>brick-red</u> pants.

DAY 1 · PREWRITING

Introducing the Format

Introduce paragraph of information.

- A paragraph of information gives facts.
- An informational paragraph should include only facts, not opinions.
- Facts can be proven. Opinions tell how the writer thinks or feels.

Start students thinking about writing an informational paragraph.

- Remind students that they have learned many facts about structures built by the Chinese and the ancient Romans.
- Ask students to list three human-built structures that they might write about.
- They might list structures from *The Great Wall* or "Building Ancient Rome." They might also list other structures.
- Have students save their notes.

DAY 2 · DRAFTING

Discussing the Model

Display Transparency 4–15. Ask:

- What is the topic of the paragraph? (three largest buildings in ancient Rome)
- Which sentence states the topic? (the first sentence)
- What information do the supporting sentences give about the Colosseum? (huge amphitheater; seated 50,000 people)
- What information do the supporting sentences give about the Pantheon? (temple; domed roof 141 feet in diameter)
- What information do the supporting sentences give about the Baths of Caracella? (could fit 1,600 people; main hall about the size of a football field; libraries, shops)

Display Transparency 4–16, and discuss the guidelines.

Have students draft a paragraph of information.

- Have them use their notes from Day 1.
- Assign **Practice Book** page 36 to help students organize their writing.
- Provide support as needed.

Transparency 4–15

DISCOVERING ANCIENT CULTURES *The Great Wall* — Writing Skill Paragraph of Information

ANNOTATED VERSION

Writing a Paragraph of Information

Three of the largest buildings constructed in ancient Rome were the Pantheon, the Colosseum, and the Baths of Caracalla. The Colosseum was a huge amphitheater where up to 50,000 people could sit and watch gladiators do battle. The Pantheon was a large temple that had a domed roof 141 feet in diameter. In ancient times, the size of this dome was very famous. The structure is still used as a house of worship, even though it is almost 2,000 years old. As many as 1,600 people could take a bath in the Baths of Caracalla complex. The main hall was as large as a modern-day football field, about 100 yards long and 25 yards wide. The Baths of Caracalla was almost like a city itself. It contained libraries, shops, offices, and sports facilities in addition to bathing areas.

TRANSPARENCY 4–15
TEACHER'S EDITION PAGE 407K

Transparency 4–16

DISCOVERING ANCIENT CULTURES *The Great Wall* — Writing Skill Paragraph of Information

Guidelines for Writing a Paragraph of Information

- Select an interesting topic that you know something about.
- Include a topic sentence that tells what the whole paragraph is about. The topic sentence is usually the first sentence in the paragraph.
- Include several supporting sentences that give more information about the topic. Make sure your sentences are in a logical order.
- Leave out any sentences that don't give more information about your topic.
- Include facts only—don't include your opinions.
- Remember to indent the first sentence of the paragraph.

TRANSPARENCY 4–16
TEACHER'S EDITION PAGE 407K

Practice Book page 36

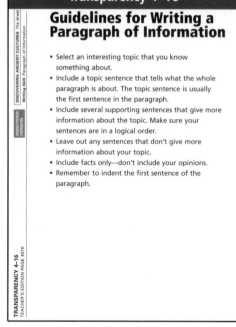

The Great Wall
Writing Skill Paragraph of Information

Name _____

Writing a Paragraph of Information

In *The Great Wall*, you learned about the building of China's Great Wall. A **paragraph of information** like this one from the selection presents facts in a logical order.

Tens of thousands of workers were involved in building the Great Wall. The army provided many laborers. Soldiers became construction workers, and generals became architects and engineers. Peasants were required to work on the wall. They worked for months at a time for little or no pay. Criminals served their sentences doing hard labor on the wall.

Use this graphic organizer to build your own paragraph of information about another human structure.

Topic
(2 points)

Topic Sentence
(2)

Supporting Sentences
(4)

Now write your paragraph of information on a separate sheet of paper. Include a topic sentence, usually the first sentence in the paragraph, that tells what the entire paragraph is about. Arrange several supporting sentences in a logical order, and make sure all of the sentences contain facts about the topic. (4)

Improving Writing: Elaborating with Adjectives

Explain elaborating with adjectives.

Explain that adding adjectives can make writing clearer and more vivid.

Write *I ate my food* and *I ate my delicious Mexican food.*

Ask, Which sentence gives a clearer picture? Why? (second; adjectives)

Display Transparency 4–17.

Have different volunteers read aloud the examples. Discuss how the adjectives in Example 2 create a clearer picture.

Help students add adjectives to the practice sentences on the transparency.

Assign Practice Book page 37.

Have students revise their drafts.

Display **Transparency 4–16** again. Have students use it to revise their paragraphs.

See Writing Traits on page 407K.

Have partners hold writing conferences.

Ask students to revise any parts of their paragraphs that still need work. Have them look for places to add adjectives.

Transparency 4–17

Elaborating with Adjectives

Example 1:
In some areas, the wall ran in a line.

Example 2:
In flat, treeless desert areas, the ever-expanding wall ran in an endless, straight line.

Practice Sentences
Answers will vary.

1. Laborers worked on the wall through summers and winters.
_____

2. The warriors rode horses and made attacks without warning.
_____

3. The wall was built along hills and mountains, across rivers, and through valleys.
_____

Checking for Errors

Have students proofread for errors in grammar, spelling, punctuation, or usage.

- Students can use the proofreading checklist on **Practice Book** page 273 to help them proofread their paragraphs.

- Students can also use the chart of proofreading marks on **Practice Book** page 274.

Practice Book page 37

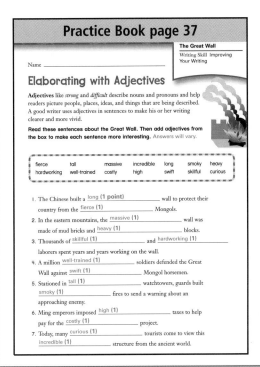

The Great Wall
Writing Skill Improving Your Writing

Name _____

Elaborating with Adjectives

Adjectives like *strong* and *difficult* describe nouns and pronouns and help readers picture people, places, ideas, and things that are being described. A good writer uses adjectives in sentences to make his or her writing clearer and more vivid.

Read these sentences about the Great Wall. Then add adjectives from the box to make each sentence more interesting. Answers will vary.

| fierce | tall | massive | incredible | long | smoky | heavy |
| hardworking | well-trained | costly | high | swift | skilful | curious |

1. The Chinese built a long (1 point) _____ wall to protect their country from the fierce (1) _____ Mongols.

2. In the eastern mountains, the massive (1) _____ wall was made of mud bricks and heavy (1) _____ blocks.

3. Thousands of skillful (1) _____ and hardworking (1) _____ laborers spent years and years working on the wall.

4. A million well-trained (1) _____ soldiers defended the Great Wall against swift (1) _____ Mongol horsemen.

5. Stationed in tall (1) _____ watchtowers, guards built smoky (1) _____ fires to send a warning about an approaching enemy.

6. Ming emperors imposed high (1) _____ taxes to help pay for the costly (1) _____ project.

7. Today, many curious (1) _____ tourists come to view this incredible (1) _____ structure from the ancient world.

Sharing Writing

Consider these publishing options.

- Ask students to read their paragraphs or some other piece of writing from the Author's Chair.

- Encourage students to publish their paragraphs in a class book about buildings. They might want to add photographs or other illustrations.

Portfolio Opportunity

Save students' paragraphs of information as samples of their writing development.

Monitoring Student Progress

If . . .	Then . . .
students' writing does not follow the guidelines on **Transparency 4–16,**	work with students to improve specific parts of their writing.

Language Center

VOCABULARY

Using a Thesaurus

👤 Singles	🕐 20 minutes
Objective	Use a thesaurus.
Materials	Thesaurus, dictionary

One way you can improve your writing and build word power is to consult a thesaurus to find synonyms for common words.

- Look in a thesaurus to find synonyms for three of these common words: *bad, big, go, good, home, small.*

- The synonyms listed in a thesaurus often have different connotations—meanings the word suggests in addition to its literal or exact meaning. If you don't know the connotation of a synonym, look it up in a dictionary.

- Write sentences using five of the synonyms you found.

Thesaurus

brave *adjective*
Having or showing courage: *a brave effort to rescue the drowning child.*

Syns: audacious, bold, courageous, dauntless, doughty, fearless, fortitudinous, gallant, game, gutsy

GRAMMAR

Comparative and Superlative Adjectives

👤 Singles	🕐 20 minutes
Objective	Use comparative and super-lative forms of adjectives.

Suppose you and your family are visiting the Great Wall of China during summer vacation. You are writing a letter to a friend back home.

- Read the letter below, then copy it onto a sheet of paper.

- Replace each adjective in parentheses with its comparative or superlative form, as appropriate.

Today was a (cool) day than yesterday, but that is (good) news than it might seem, because we took the (tiring) walk yet. This part of the Great Wall is (tall) than any other and the watchtowers are (numerous) than we've seen. The (good) part of our trip is still ahead, because we will visit Beijing soon—the (exciting) city in all of China.

VOCABULARY

Vocabulary Game

👥 Pairs	🕐 30 minutes
Objective	Identify Key Vocabulary words from their definitions
Materials	Activity Master 4–2, scissors, dictionary

With a partner, make a set of Key Vocabulary flash cards by following these steps:

- Cut out all the word cards on Activity Master 4–2 and divide the cards equally between yourselves.

- On the back of each card write the definition of the word printed on the front. Use a dictionary if you need help.

- Mix up the finished cards and place them on the table, definition side up.

- Take turns picking a card, reading a definition, and naming the Key Vocabulary word defined. Then use the word in a sentence.

- For a variation, place the Key Vocabulary word side upward and take turns giving the definition of the word.

Consider copying and laminating these activities for use in centers.

VIEWING

Viewing for Information and Details

👤 Singles	🕐 25 minutes
Objective	Examine different elements of an article.

A nonfiction article may present information in several ways. Look again at "Building Ancient Rome" (pages 404–407). In it you can find information in the title, introductory text, subheadings, main text, timeline, captions, and diagrams. Find the answer to these questions in the article:

- What shape were the stones that were used on the surface of the road?
- Was Hadrian's Wall built on flat land or on hills?
- How many people could visit the Baths of Caracalla in one day?
- What did the Pantheon's roof look like?

Noting Information and Details
- Identify how information is presented.
- Scan titles, subheadings, and graphics to get a sense of the main ideas.
- Study visuals in a systematic way, such as top to bottom or left to right.
- Read captions to understand illustrations and other visuals.
- Read sections of the main text straight through, referring to other features only when they pertain to the main text.

PHONICS/SPELLING

Word Detective

👤 Singles	🕐 30 minutes
Objective	Identify words using clues, and spell them correctly in writing.

Read each definition below. Write the Spelling Word defined. (Hint: See the Spelling Words on **Practice Book** page 257.) Then on a sheet of paper write a sentence using the word.

- an emotion you might feel for your favorite musician or teacher
- what you do when you follow an unknown path to see where it leads
- what you do when you tie two ropes together to make one long rope
- something you have made or built
- what you get when you mix different things together
- what you do with someone when you both work together
- what you do when you build something
- the act of working together with someone

Leveled Readers

The Pyramids of Giza

Summary *This nonfiction selection describes the lush Nile Valley, where the ancient Egyptians buried their pharaohs in mighty pyramids some 4,500 years ago. The Great Pyramid was built as a tomb for King Khufu. Two other pyramids were built for kings Khafre and Menkaure. The selection details the pyramids' construction and explains how they have endured over the ages, outlasting all the other Wonders of the Ancient World.*

Building Background and Vocabulary

Ask students what they know about ancient Egypt, the Nile River, and the pyramids. Briefly explain that there are Seven Wonders of the Ancient World. Guide students through the text, using some of the vocabulary from the story.

Comprehension Skill: Cause and Effect

Have students read the Strategy Focus on the book flap. Remind students to use the strategy and to think about causes and effects as they read the book. (See the Leveled Readers Teacher's Guide for **Vocabulary and Comprehension Practice Masters.**)

Responding

Have partners discuss how to answer the questions on the inside back cover.

Think About the Selection Sample answers:

1. They are impressive buildings that have outlasted other ancient wonders.
2. People needed water to live; the valley was lush and fertile.
3. Quarried stone was strong and lasted, but it took a lot of work to dig out, transport, and assemble.
4. Answers will vary.

Making Connections Answers will vary.

Building Fluency

Model Read aloud page 9. Explain to students that words like *best, greatest,* and *largest* are examples of superlative adjectives, which indicate a description of the highest degree.

Practice Ask students to read aloud other sentences that contain examples of superlatives (pages 3, 4, 5).

Vocabulary

Introduce the Key Vocabulary and ask students to complete the BLM.

fertile good for plants to grow in, *p. 3*

tombs graves or burial chambers, *p. 4*

impressive creating a powerful effect, *p. 9*

nobles people of high rank, *p. 16*

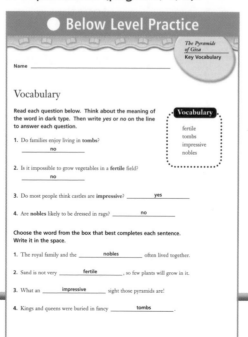

Leveled Readers

A Scribe of Ancient China

Summary *Wu Chen is learning the Chinese art of calligraphy. His teacher gives him an unusual assignment: to compose and write a poem. Wu Chen decides to write a tribute to the workers who are building the Great Wall of China.*

Vocabulary

Introduce the Key Vocabulary and ask students to complete the BLM.

apprentice trainee, *p. 3*

technique method, *p. 4*

diligent hardworking and careful, *p. 4*

dynasty* a line of rulers from one family, *p. 8*

painstaking thorough, *p. 9*

ingenious clever, *p. 10*

convey put into words, *p. 12*

grueling demanding, *p. 12*

vigorously energetically, forcefully, *p. 14*

*Forms of these words are Anthology Key Vocabulary words.

Building Background and Vocabulary

Explain that the position of a scribe, a person who recorded what happened at the Royal Court, was a very important job in ancient China. Invite students to share what they know about the Great Wall of China. Guide students through the text, using some of the vocabulary from the story.

Comprehension Skill: Cause and Effect

Have students read the Strategy Focus on the book flap. Remind students to use the strategy and to think about causes and effects as they read the book. (See the Leveled Readers Teacher's Guide for **Vocabulary and Comprehension Practice Masters.**)

Responding

Have partners discuss how to answer the questions on the inside back cover.

Think About the Selection Sample answers:

1. The scribe keeps records of the imperial family, copies official documents, and records every word the emperor speaks.

2. the inkstick, the inkstone, the writing brush, and paper

3. He thinks it is both a magnificent and challenging topic.

4. Answers will vary.

Making Connections Answers will vary.

Building Fluency

Model Read aloud the second sentence of the last paragraph on page 4. Explain that this is a compound sentence, or two sentences combined into one.

Practice Ask small groups to find other examples of compound sentences in the story (pages 5, 6, 13).

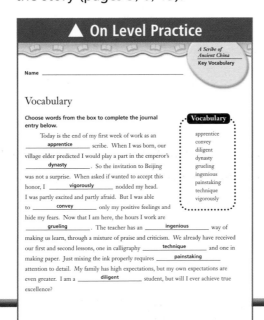

▲ On Level Practice

A Scribe of Ancient China
Key Vocabulary

Name _____

Vocabulary

Choose words from the box to complete the journal entry below.

Today is the end of my first week of work as an _____apprentice_____ scribe. When I was born, our village elder predicted I would play a part in the emperor's _____dynasty_____. So the invitation to Beijing was not a surprise. When asked if wanted to accept this honor, I _____vigorously_____ nodded my head. I was partly excited and partly afraid. But I was able to _____convey_____ only my positive feelings and hide my fears. Now that I am here, the hours I work are _____grueling_____. The teacher has an _____ingenious_____ way of making us learn, through a mixture of praise and criticism. We already have received our first and second lessons, one in calligraphy _____technique_____ and one in making paper. Just mixing the ink properly requires _____painstaking_____ attention to detail. My family has high expectations, but my own expectations are even greater. I am a _____diligent_____ student, but will I ever achieve true excellence?

Vocabulary
apprentice
convey
diligent
dynasty
grueling
ingenious
painstaking
technique
vigorously

▲ On Level Practice

A Scribe of Ancient China
Comprehension Skill
Cause and Effect

Name _____

Comprehension

Answer the following, using information in the story and your completed Graphic Organizer.

1. Describe a central cause-effect relationship in the story.

Answers will vary. Possible answer: The Great Wall of China inspired Wu Chen to write a poem honoring the workers.

2. Describe a cause in the story that led to many effects.

Answers will vary. Possible answer: Wu Chen's skills and talents were the causes of many of the events in the story.

3. Describe an effect in the story that led to another event.

Answers will vary. Possible answer: Master Chang's assignment led to Wu Chen's poem, which led to the job offer of assistant to the master scribe of the Great Wall.

4. How does understanding cause-effect relationships add to the reader's appreciation of the events in a story?

Answers will vary.

Leveled Readers

The Shape in the Dark: A Story of Hadrian's Wall

Summary *Two soldiers, Marcus and Aristander, take off on a mysterious mission, leaving the youngest guard, Lucius, all alone to guard Hadrian's Wall. Lucius sees a dark figure coming toward him. Is it an invader? No, it's Marcus, tri-umphantly returning with a feast!*

Vocabulary

Introduce the Key Vocabulary and ask students to complete the BLM.

barbarians fierce people, *p. 3*

empire territory, realm, *p. 4*

aqueduct water channel, *p. 7*

conquer defeat, *p. 8*

massive* large and solid, *p. 10*

revolt rebellion, mutiny, *p. 10*

terrain* the physical features of an area of land, *p. 12*

laborers* workers who do tasks that do not require special skills, *p. 12*

durable* sturdy and long-lasting, *p. 16*

*Forms of these words are Anthology Key Vocabulary words.

■ ABOVE LEVEL

Building Background and Vocabulary

Ask students to locate Great Britain on a map. Explain that in ancient times, walls were frequently built to guard territory and to prevent an attack. The Great Wall of China and Hadrian's Wall are among the largest and most famous walls ever built. Guide students through the text, using some of the vocabulary from the story.

Comprehension Skill: Cause and Effect

Have students read the Strategy Focus on the book flap. Remind students to use the strategy and to think about causes and effects as they read the book. (See the Leveled Readers Teacher's Guide for **Vocabulary and Comprehension Practice Masters.**)

Responding

Have partners discuss how to answer the questions on the inside back cover.

Think About the Selection Sample answers:

1. He built it to guard the northern border of the Roman Empire against invaders.
2. He fears that northern tribesmen or Britons from the south might attack.
3. It would have required too many soldiers, and Scotland was far too aggressive.
4. Answers will vary.

Making Connections Answers will vary.

Building Fluency

Model Read aloud page 6. Demonstrate that thoughts should be read differently than descriptions or spoken dialogue.

Practice Have students find other examples of Lucius's thoughts. Ask them to read the examples aloud, making sure they read them appropriately.

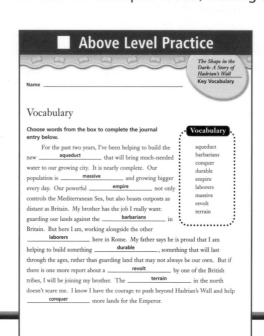

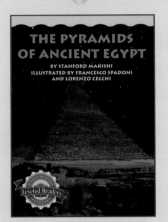

The Pyramids of Ancient Egypt

Summary *The famous pyramids of Giza have stood outside Cairo for thousands of years. Their remarkable durability serves as a testament to the scope of the technological prowess of ancient Egypt.*

Vocabulary

Introduce the Key Vocabulary and ask students to complete the BLM.

tombs structures for holding dead bodies, *p. 4*

laborers* workers who do tasks that do not require special skills, *p. 9*

experts people who have great knowledge or skill in a special area, *p. 9*

structures things, such as buildings or bridges, that have been built, *p. 9*

quarries open pits from which stone is extracted by digging, cutting, or blasting, *p. 10*

ramps sloping passages or roadways that lead from one level to another, *p. 11*

*Forms of these words are Anthology Key Vocabulary words.

◆ LANGUAGE SUPPORT

Building Background and Vocabulary

Display the cover picture, and ask students what they think of when they look at the pyramid. Explain that the Egyptians built pyramids as tombs for their rulers. Distribute the **Build Background Practice Master,** read aloud the directions, and have students complete the activity.

Comprehension Skill: Cause and Effect

Have students read the Strategy Focus on the book flap. Remind students to use the strategy and to look for causes and effects as they read the book. (See the Leveled Readers Teacher's Guide for **Build Background, Vocabulary,** and **Graphic Organizer Masters.**)

Responding

Have partners discuss how to answer the questions on the inside back cover.

Think About the Selection Sample answers:

1. They're made of large, heavy blocks of stone.
2. The smooth white covering has worn off, and the pyramid is shorter than it used to be.
3. Experts have different opinions, but most experts believe the pyramids were built by farmers who worked during the flood season.
4. Answers will vary.

Making Connections Answers will vary.

Building Fluency

Model Read aloud the text and caption on page 5 as students follow along in their books. Review the number words by writing them out on the board.

Practice Have partners look through the selection for other sentences with numbers and practice reading them aloud.

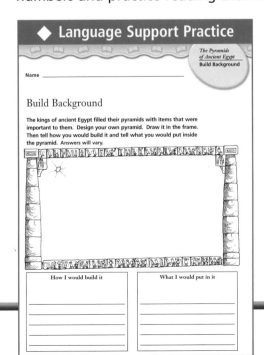

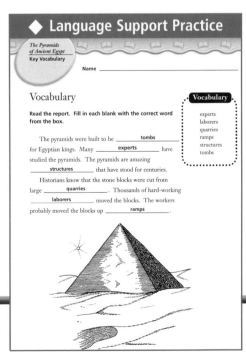

Lesson Overview

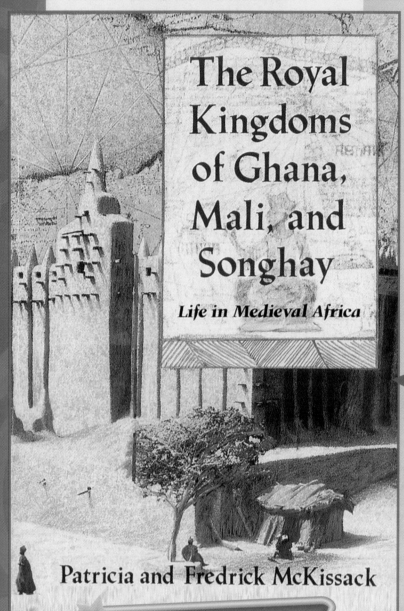

The Royal Kingdoms of Ghana, Mali, and Songhay

Life in Medieval Africa

Patricia and Fredrick McKissack

Selection Summary

From A.D. 700–1000, Ghana was the dominant power in Western Africa, due largely to its successful gold and salt trade.

1 Background and Vocabulary

2 Main Selection

The Royal Kingdoms of Ghana, Mali, and Songhay
Genre: Nonfiction

3 Social Studies Link

Instructional Support

Planning and Practice

- Planning and classroom management
- Reading instruction
- Skill lessons
- Materials for reaching all learners

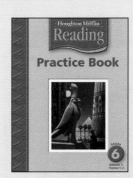

- Independent practice for skills, Level 6.2

- Newsletters
- Selection Summaries
- Assignment Cards
- Observation Checklists
- Selection Tests

- Transparencies
- Strategy Posters
- Blackline Masters

Reaching All Learners

Coordinated lessons, activities, and projects for additional reading instruction

For
- Classroom teacher
- Extended day
- Pull out
- Resource teacher
- Reading specialist

Technology

Audio Selection

The Royal Kingdoms of Ghana, Mali, and Songhay

Get Set for Reading CD-ROM
- Background building
- Vocabulary support
- Selection Summary in English and Spanish

Accelerated Reader®
- Practice quizzes for the selection

www.eduplace.com

Log on to *Education Place®* for more activities related to the selection, including vocabulary support—
- e•Glossary
- e•WordGame

Leveled Books for Reaching All Learners

Leveled Readers and Leveled Practice

- Independent reading for building fluency
- Topic, comprehension strategy, and vocabulary linked to main selection
- Lessons in Teacher's Edition, pages 427O–427R
- Leveled practice for every book

Technology

Leveled Readers
Audio available

Book Adventure®
- Practice quizzes for the Leveled Theme Paperbacks
  www.bookadventure.org

● BELOW LEVEL

Ancient Baghdad:
City at the Crossroads of Trade

by George Capaccio
illustrated by L. R. Galante

● Below Level Practice

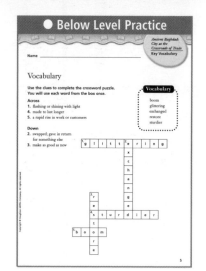

● Below Level Practice

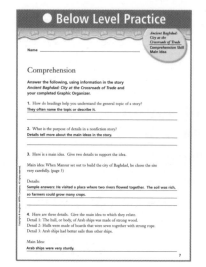

▲ ON LEVEL

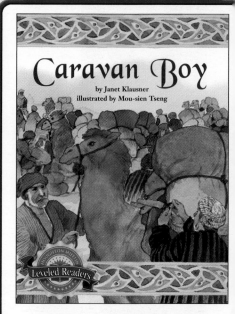

Caravan Boy
by Janet Klausner
illustrated by Mou-sien Tseng

▲ On Level Practice

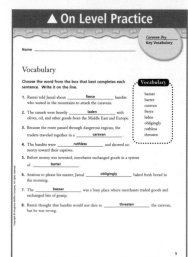

▲ On Level Practice

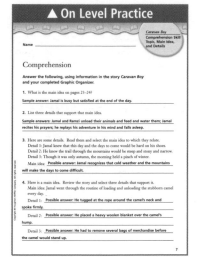

■ ABOVE LEVEL

The Kingdom of Kush

by Harley Farewell

◆ LANGUAGE SUPPORT

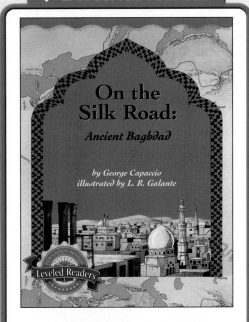

On the Silk Road: *Ancient Baghdad*

by George Capaccio
illustrated by L. R. Galante

Leveled Theme Paperbacks

- Extended independent reading in Theme-related trade books
- Lessons in Teacher's Edition, pages R2–R7

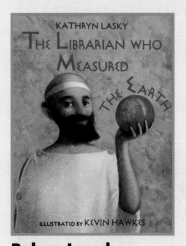

KATHRYN LASKY
THE LIBRARIAN WHO MEASURED THE EARTH

ILLUSTRATED BY KEVIN HAWKES

Below Level

Aïda
TOLD BY Leontyne Price

ILLUSTRATED BY LEO AND DIANE DILLON

On Level

Between the DRAGON and the EAGLE

Mical Schneider

Above Level

■ Above Level Practice

The Kingdom of Kush
Key Vocabulary

Name _____

Vocabulary

Choose the word from the box that best completes each sentence. Write it on the line.

Vocabulary
affiliation
apprenticeship
caravans
flourish
foundries
irrigating
ornate
prosperity
renowned
sophisticated

1. The people had ample water for ___**irrigating**___ their crops.

2. Kings and queens were buried in ___**ornate**___ tombs, decorated with fancy carvings of animals and deities.

3. Because the kingdom was relatively inaccessible, traders traveled to Meroë in ___**caravans**___.

4. Some ornaments and carvings suggest religious ___**affiliation**___, or connection, with the god Amun.

5. In Kush, gifted craftspeople and bountiful agricultural products helped the economy ___**flourish**___.

6. For many years, the kingdom of Kush enjoyed ___**prosperity**___ due to its rich agricultural lands and abundant water and mineral resources.

7. Iron was smelted in ___**foundries**___ and used to make tools, which were much in demand.

8. Potters were ___**renowned**___ for their skill at crafting and decorating beautiful objects.

9. Young people learned a craft or trade by serving an ___**apprenticeship**___, during which they studied with a master.

10. Scholars believe that the culture of ancient Kush was as ___**sophisticated**___ and highly developed as that of ancient Egypt.

5

◆ Language Support Practice

On the Silk Road:
Ancient Baghdad
Build Background

Name _____

Build Background

Suppose you are looking for a place to build a great city. Circle the best places for your city.

The best place for a city is

between two great rivers | near rich farmland
far from rivers | near the sea
on a mountain top | far from the sea
in a desert | near heavily traveled roads

Write 3 or 4 sentences to explain the choices you made for your city.
Answers will vary.

5

■ Above Level Practice

The Kingdom of Kush
Comprehension Skill
Topic, Main Idea, and Details

Name _____

Comprehension

Answer the following, using information in the story *The Kingdom of Kush* and your completed Graphic Organizer.

1. What is the main idea on pages 4–6 of the selection?
Egypt and Nubia were similar in many ways.

2. List three details that support that main idea.
Sample answers: Both Egypt and Nubia were located in the Nile Valley; most people survived by farming or raising cattle and sheep; the most powerful god was Amun.

3. Here are some details. Select the main idea to which they relate.
Detail 1: Kush lay between six stretches of cataracts on the Nile.
Detail 2: To reach the kingdom of Kush, traders had to come by caravan, over land.
Detail 3: The people built walls around their cities.
Main idea: Possible answer: Kush was well protected from enemies by geography as well as by human effort.

4. Here is a main idea. Review the story and select three details that support it.
Main idea: The Nubians possessed many unusual skills that helped them survive and flourish for many years.
Detail 1: Possible answer: They knew how to smelt iron and make tools.
Detail 2: Possible answer: They were renowned for their use of the bow and arrow.
Detail 3: Possible answer: They were skilled craftspeople and jewelers.

7

◆ Language Support Practice

On the Silk Road:
Ancient Baghdad
Key Vocabulary

Name _____

Vocabulary

Read the conversation between a trader from Baghdad and a trader from China. Fill in each blank with the Vocabulary word that fits best.

Vocabulary
caravans
incense
magnificent
ports
route
traded

Chinese Trader: I am sure your ___**incense**___ smells wonderful. But I said I wanted rose oil!

Baghdad Trader: I am sorry. My ship stopped at many ___**ports**___ before I came here. I sold all the rose oil.

Chinese Trader: Well, your ___**caravans**___ must have brought many glass beads or jewels!

Baghdad Trader: I have ___**traded**___ all my jewels and beads for horses. Would you like to buy some ___**magnificent**___ Arabian horses?

Chinese Trader: Finally, you have something I want! I'd like some camels, too, because the ___**route**___ to my next stop goes through the desert.

6

Daily Lesson Plans

T Skill tested on Theme Skills Test and/or Integrated Theme Test

 50–60 minutes

Reading
Comprehension

Leveled Readers
• Fluency Practice
• Independent Reading

 20–30 minutes

Word Work
Phonics/Decoding
Vocabulary
Spelling

 20–30 minutes

Writing and Oral Language
Writing
Grammar
Listening/Speaking/Viewing

DAY 1

Teacher Read Aloud, 407CC–407DD
Our Gifts from the Greeks

Building Background, 408

Key Vocabulary, 409

bartering	flourishing	primary
caravans	goods	vicinity
entourage	oasis	

Reading the Selection, 410–423

Comprehension Skill, 410
Topic, Main Idea, and Supporting Details **T**

Comprehension Strategy, 410
Monitor/Clarify

Leveled Readers
Ancient Baghdad
Caravan Boy
The Kingdom of Kush
On the Silk Road

Lessons and Leveled Practice, 427O–427R

Phonics/Decoding, 411
Phonics/Decoding Strategy

Vocabulary, 410–423
Selection Vocabulary

Spelling, 427E
Unstressed Syllables **T**

Writing, 427K
Prewriting a Comparison-and-Contrast Paragraph

Grammar, 427I
Kinds of Adverbs **T**

Daily Language Practice
1. The ambulince raced quick to the hospital. (ambulance; quickly)
2. We always have our car repaired at henderson's Gareage. (Henderson's; Garage.)

Listening/Speaking/Viewing, 407CC–407DD, 417
Teacher Read Aloud, Stop and Think

DAY 2

Reading the Selection, 410–423

Comprehension Check, 423

Responding, 424
Think About the Selection

Comprehension Skill Preview, 415
Topic, Main Idea, and Supporting Details **T**

Leveled Readers
Ancient Baghdad
Caravan Boy
The Kingdom of Kush
On the Silk Road

Lessons and Leveled Practice, 427O–427R

Structural Analysis, 427C
Unstressed Syllables **T**

Vocabulary, 410–423
Selection Vocabulary

Spelling, 427E
Unstressed Syllables Review and Practice **T**

Writing, 427K
Drafting a Comparison-and-Contrast Paragraph

Grammar, 427I
Kinds of Adverbs Practice **T**

Daily Language Practice
3. My dogs awack more frequent than I do at night. (awake; frequently)
4. The school's policey on tardiness is enforced strict. (policy; strictly.)

Listening/Speaking/Viewing, 423, 424
Wrapping Up, Responding

Target Skills of the Week

Phonics	Unstressed Syllables
Comprehension	Monitor/Clarify; Topic, Main Idea, and Supporting Details
Vocabulary	Prefixes and Suffixes in a Dictionary
Fluency	Leveled Readers

DAY 3

Rereading the Selection, 410–423

Comprehension Skill, 427A–427B
Topic, Main Idea, and Supporting Details **T**

Leveled Readers
Ancient Baghdad
Caravan Boy
The Kingdom of Kush
On the Silk Road

Lessons and Leveled Practice, 427O–427R

Phonics Review, 427D
The /ə/ Sound

Vocabulary, 427G
Prefixes and Suffixes in a Dictionary **T**

Spelling, 427F
Vocabulary, Antonyms; Unstressed Syllables Practice **T**

Writing, 427L
Revising a Comparison-and-Contrast Paragraph
Combining Sentences **T**

Grammar, 427J
Comparing with Adverbs **T**

Daily Language Practice
5. This problim was solved more faster than the one last week. (problem; more)
6. Admiril jones will receive an award today. (Admiral; Jones)

DAY 4

Reading the Social Studies Link, 426–427
"Daily Life in Ancient Greece"

Skill: How to Read a Diagram

Comprehension Skill Review, 419
Problem Solving

Leveled Readers
Ancient Baghdad
Caravan Boy
The Kingdom of Kush
On the Silk Road

Lessons and Leveled Practice, 427O–427R

Phonics/Decoding Longer Words, 426–427
Apply Phonics/Decoding Strategy to Link

Vocabulary, 427M
Language Center: Building Vocabulary

Spelling, 427F
Unstressed Syllables Game, Proofreading **T**

Writing, 427L
Proofreading a Comparison-and-Contrast Paragraph

Grammar, 427J
Comparing with Adverbs Practice **T**

Daily Language Practice
7. The historical ducument were very interesting to read. (document; was) or (documents)
8. Please don't ignour the rules, peter. (ignore; Peter.)

Listening/Speaking/Viewing, 427
Discuss the Link

DAY 5

Rereading for Fluency, 413

Responding Activities, 424–425
Write an Advertisement
Cross-Curricular Activities

Information and Study Skills, 427H
Primary and Secondary Sources

Comprehension Skill Review, 421
Text Organization

Leveled Readers
Ancient Baghdad
Caravan Boy
The Kingdom of Kush
On the Silk Road

Lessons and Leveled Practice, 427O–427R

Phonics, 427N
Language Center: Words in Hiding

Vocabulary, 427M
Language Center: Vocabulary game

Spelling, 427F
Test: Unstressed Syllables **T**

Writing, 427L
Publishing a Comparison-and-Contrast Paragraph

Grammar, 427J, 427M
Adjective or Adverb?
Language Center: Adverbs in Fine Form

Daily Language Practice
9. This summer I'm going to work for the johnson Paint Compiny. (Johnson; Company.)
10. I am proud of my brothers sucess at chess competitions. (brother's; success)

Listening/Speaking/Viewing, 427N
Language Center: Comparing Forms of Information

DAILY LESSON PLANS

The Royal Kingdoms of Ghana, Mali, and Songhay

Daily Lesson Plans **407X**

Managing Flexible Groups

Leveled Instruction and Leveled Practice

	DAY 1	**DAY 2**
WHOLE CLASS	• Teacher Read Aloud (TE pp. 407CC–407DD) • Building Background, Introducing Vocabulary (TE pp. 408–409) • Comprehension Strategy: Introduce (TE p. 410) • Comprehension Skill: Introduce (TE p. 410) • Purpose Setting (TE p. 411) **After reading first half of *The Royal Kingdoms*** • Stop and Think (TE p. 417)	**After reading *The Royal Kingdoms*** • Wrapping Up (TE p. 423) • Comprehension Check (Practice Book p. 40) • Responding: Think About the Selection (TE p. 424) • Comprehension Skill: Preview (TE p. 415)
SMALL GROUPS		
Extra Support	**TEACHER-LED** • Preview *The Royal Kingdoms* to Stop and Think (TE pp. 410–417). • Support reading with Extra Support/Intervention notes (TE pp. 411, 412, 413, 416, 420, 422).	**Partner or Individual Work** • Reread first half of *The Royal Kingdoms* (TE pp. 410–417). • Preview, read second half (TE pp. 418–423). • Comprehension Check (Practice Book p. 40)
Challenge	**Individual Work** • Begin "Your Story of Medieval Africa" (Challenge Handbook p. 34). • Extend reading with Challenge note (TE p. 422).	**Individual Work** • Continue work on activity (Challenge Handbook p. 34).
English Language Learners	**TEACHER-LED** • Preview vocabulary and *The Royal Kingdoms* to Stop and Think (TE pp. 409–417). • Support reading with English Language Learners notes (TE pp. 408, 414, 416, 423).	**TEACHER-LED** • Review first half of *The Royal Kingdoms* (TE pp. 410–417). ✔ • Preview, read second half (TE pp. 418–423). • Begin Comprehension Check together (Practice Book p. 40).

Independent Activities

• Get Set for Reading CD-ROM
• Journals: selection notes, questions
• Complete, review Practice Book (pp. 38–42) and Leveled Readers Practice Blackline Masters (TE pp. 427O–427R).
• Assignment Cards (Teachers Resource Blackline Masters, pp. 77–78)
• Leveled Readers (TE pp. 427O–427R), Leveled Theme Paperbacks (TE pp. R2–R7), or book from Leveled Bibliography (TE pp. 354E–354F)

✔ Opportunity to informally assess oral reading rate

- Rereading *The Royal Kingdoms* (TE pp. 410–423)

- Comprehension Skill: Main lesson (TE pp. 427A–427B)

- Reading the Social Studies Link (TE pp. 426–427): Skill lesson (TE p. 426)

- Rereading the Social Studies Link (TE pp. 426–427)

- Comprehension Skill: First Comprehension Review lesson (TE p. 419)

- Responding: Select from Activities (TE pp. 424–425)

- Information and Study Skills (TE p. 427H)

- Comprehension Skill: Second Comprehension Review lesson (TE p. 421)

TEACHER-LED

- Reread, review Comprehension Check (Practice Book p. 40).

- Preview Leveled Reader: Below Level (TE p. 427O), or read book from Leveled Bibliography (TE pp. 354E–354F). ✔

Partner or Individual Work

- Reread the Social Studies Link (TE pp. 426–427).

- Complete Leveled Reader: Below Level (TE p. 427O), or read book from Leveled Bibliography (TE pp. 354E–354F).

TEACHER-LED

- Comprehension Skill: Reteaching lesson (TE p. R12)

- Reread Leveled Theme Paperback: Below Level (TE pp. R2–R3), or read book from Leveled Bibliography (TE pp. 354E–354F). ✔

TEACHER-LED

- Teacher check-in: Assess progress (Challenge Handbook p. 34).

- Preview Leveled Reader: Above Level (TE p. 427Q), or read book from Leveled Bibliography (TE pp. 354E–354F). ✔

Individual Work

- Complete activity (Challenge Handbook p. 34).

- Complete Leveled Reader: Above Level (TE p. 427Q), or read book from Leveled Bibliography (TE pp. 354E–354F).

TEACHER-LED

- Evaluate activity and plan format for sharing (Challenge Handbook p. 34).

- Reread Leveled Theme Paperback: Above Level (TE pp. R6–R7), or read book from Leveled Bibliography (TE pp. 354E–354F). ✔

Partner or Individual Work

- Complete Comprehension Check (Practice Book p. 40).

- Begin Leveled Reader: Language Support (TE p. 427R), or read book from Leveled Bibliography (TE pp. 354E–354F).

TEACHER-LED

- Reread the Social Studies Link (TE pp. 426–427) ✔ and review Link Skill (TE p. 426).

- Complete Leveled Reader: Language Support (TE p. 427R), or read book from Leveled Bibliography (TE pp. 354E–354F). ✔

Partner or Individual Work

- Reread book from Leveled Bibliography (TE pp. 354E–354F).

- Responding activities (pp. 424–425)
- Language Center activities (TE pp. 427M–427N)
- **Fluency Practice:** Reread *Lost Temple of the Aztecs, The Great Wall, The Royal Kingdoms of Ghana, Mali, and Songhay.* ✔
- Activities relating to *The Royal Kingdoms of Ghana, Mali, and Songhay* at Education Place® www.eduplace.com

Turn the page for more independent activities.

FLEXIBLE GROUPS

The Royal Kingdoms of Ghana, Mali, and Songhay

Classroom Management

Independent Activities

Assign these activities while you work with small groups.

Differentiated Instruction for Small Groups

- **Handbook for English Language Learners,** pp. 154–163
- **Extra Support Handbook,** pp. 150–159

Independent Activities

- Language Center, pp. 427M–427N
- Challenge/Extension Activities, Theme Resources, pp. R13–R19
- **Classroom Management Handbook,** Activity Masters CM4-9–CM4-12
- **Challenge Handbook,** pp. 34–35

Look for more activities in the Classroom Management Kit.

Art

A Vast Continent

👥 Pairs	🕐 30 minutes
Objective	Create a map of Africa.
Materials	Atlas, poster board or art paper, colored pencils, markers

Create a poster illustrating Africa's geographical features. Work with a partner. First, use an atlas to learn geographical facts about Africa. Create an outline map of the continent. Then map its basic geography, using symbols and colors of your choice. Include the following features:

- mountain ranges
- major valleys
- major rivers and lakes
- major deserts

Label all the features clearly, and include a key to the symbols and colors you have used.

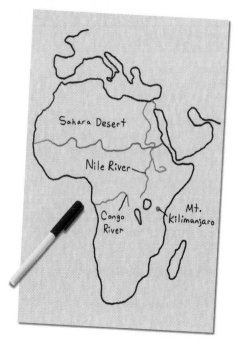

Social Studies

Kingdoms of Africa

👥 Pairs	🕐 45 minutes
Objective	Create flash cards about historic African civilizations.
Materials	Historical atlas or encyclopedia, index cards or tagboard

Using a historical atlas or an encyclopedia, identify civilizations that existed in Africa between 3000 B.C. and A.D. 1200 in addition to ancient and medieval Ghana. For example, the dynasty of Nubia, along the Nile River, was at its glory from about 920 B.C. to A.D. 350. With a partner, complete the following steps.

- Make a chart of the kingdoms you find. Organize it by region, and include the approximate dates of each kingdom's existence.
- Create flash cards with the name of each civilization on one side and its region on the other.
- Quiz each other on the names and locations of these civilizations.

Ancient African Civilization	Region Where Found
Egypt	Lower Nile Valley
Ancient Ghana	West Africa

Consider copying and laminating these activities for use in centers.

Writing

Travel Back in Time

🧍 Singles	🕐 60 minutes
Objective	Write an adventure story.
Materials	Historical atlas, encyclopedia, other reference sources

Skim *The Royal Kingdoms of Ghana, Mali, and Songhay,* noting all the regions that traded with Ghana. Locate them on a map. Then suppose that you are a Ghanaian trader preparing for a journey. Choose a region and find out the answers to these questions:

What items did people in this region or city want from Ghana?

What items did people in Ghana want from this region or city?

In what manner were these items traded?

How were the goods transported to and from this region or city?

Now, write a short story about your adventure. Include as many details as possible. Make sure your story has a beginning, middle, and end, that it has characters, and that it includes a conflict and resolution.

Science

It's a Camel's Life

🧍🧍 Pairs	🕐 45 minutes
Objective	Research facts about camels.
Materials	Encyclopedia, other reference sources

Make a camel fact file. Work with a partner. Consider these questions, as well as your own:

- How are camels born and how do their parents take care of them?
- How long do camels stay with their parents or in their original environment?
- What skills do the parents teach young camels?
- How does a cameleer learn how to handle a camel?
- How long does a camel live?

Working with your partner, decide what sort of chart would be most helpful for presenting your findings, and use that chart to present your information.

Technology

Desert Journeying

🧍 Singles	🕐 60 minutes
Objective	Research methods of travel across the Sahara Desert.
Materials	Reference sources, Internet

Trade routes across the Sahara Desert have existed since at least 1000 B.C. Research how people have traveled across the Sahara in ancient and modern times.

- What preparations did ancient travelers make?
- What did they do to survive the harsh climate?
- How long did caravan journeys take?
- What were the major caravan routes? Why were these routes selected?
- How has modern technology changed travel in the Sahara?
- Have routes across the Sahara changed in modern times? How?

Write a brief summary of your findings and illustrate it with drawings of the technology of Saharan travel.

Listening Comprehension

* Listen to identify the topic, main ideas, and supporting details.

Building Background

Tell students that you are going to read aloud a nonfiction article about some aspects of modern life that have their origins in the world of the ancient Greeks.

Fluency Modeling

Explain that as you read aloud, you will be modeling fluent oral reading. Ask students to listen carefully to your phrasing and your expression, or tone of voice and emphasis.

COMPREHENSION SKILL

Topic, Main Idea, and Details

Explain that the topic of a passage or paragraph is what most or all of the sentences tell about. Tell students that a main idea is an important idea about the topic. It may be stated in a sentence or inferred from details. Point out that details support the main idea.

Purpose Setting Read the selection aloud, asking students to think about the selection's topic, main ideas, and supporting details as they listen. Use the Guiding Comprehension questions to assess students' understanding. Reread the selection for clarification as needed.

Teacher Read Aloud

Our Gifts from the Greeks

by Ann Jordan

APPLESEEDS
A Cobblestone Publication

CHILDREN OF ANCIENT ATHENS

① Which flavor of gum do you prefer—grape, spearmint, or mastic? The children of ancient Athens didn't have a choice. They collected resin (sticky sap) from the mastic tree and chewed it. Chewing gum is something you do today, like children did 2,500 years ago.

Imagine playing in the shadow of the largest temple in Greece. In ancient Athens, children could look up from their yo-yos or their dolls and see the white columns of the Parthenon. The Athenians built this temple on top of the Acropolis, the hill overlooking the city. They dedicated it to the goddess Athena. The architects designed 46 huge marble columns to support the large porch around the temple. Architects all over the world have copied Greek designs.

Have you ever been to a theater where live plays were performed? In ancient Greece, there were huge open-air theaters that held more than 10,000 people. Drama was a Greek invention. The word *drama* comes from the Greek word for "action." Greek writers wrote the first tragedies (sad plays) and comedies (funny plays). Some of those ancient plays are still performed today.

② Our system of democracy (rule by the people) also has its roots in Athens. The Athenians believed it was important for all citizens to be involved in their government. However, only men 18 years old or older were allowed to be citizens. The Athenian assembly met three or four times a month to make decisions, such as changing laws. All citizens could gather to cast their votes. Today, the United States has a democracy, too. When you turn 18, you can vote in local, state, and national elections.

Have you watched the Olympic Games or seen a marathon race? The first Olympic Games were held more than 2,500 years ago in Olympia, in western Greece. The games were held every four years to honor the great god Zeus.

The first marathon was a communication event, not a sporting event. Messages in ancient Greece were carried by men who could run the long distances between cities. Phidippides, a famous Athenian messenger, ran about 26 miles from Marathon to Athens with an important message. Today's marathon races were named for this amazing run. Perhaps you will train to run a marathon race someday. When you do, remember the gifts of the Greeks.

CRITICAL THINKING

Guiding Comprehension

❶ TOPIC, MAIN IDEA, AND DETAILS
What do you think the topic of the selection is? (customs in ancient Athens that still exist today)

❷ TOPIC, MAIN IDEA, AND DETAILS
What is one main idea in this selection? (Sample answer: Modern democracy has its roots in ancient Athens.) Which details support this main idea? (Sample answer: In ancient Athens, men who were 18 years old or older could vote. In the United States today, citizens also participate in government and must be at least 18 years old to vote.)

❸ TOPIC, MAIN IDEA, AND DETAILS
What details explain how the modern-day marathon was named and how its length was established? (An Athenian messenger ran 26 miles from Marathon to Athens. This explains why the modern-day version is called a *marathon* and how long it is.)

Discussion Options

Personal Response Have students tell what information about ancient Athens they found most surprising or interesting, and why.

⭐ **Connecting/Comparing** Ask students to discuss how the accomplishments of ancient Athens are similar to or different from those of ancient China or the Aztec empire.

English Language Learners

Language Development

Remind students that *democracy* names a form of government used in both ancient Athens and today in the United States. Invite students to share what they know about aspects of democracy in the United States, such as voting.

Building Background

Key Concept: Ghana's Medieval Trading Empire

Point out that the next selection is about Ghana, an ancient culture that was one of Africa's great trading empires in the third century A.D. Discuss how trade with other countries might have influenced such elements of Ghana's culture as music, art, mode of dress, and wealth. Then use "The Rise of Ghana" on Anthology pages 408–409 to build background and introduce key vocabulary.

- Preview the article by having students point to the illustrations, map, and time line as you read aloud the captions.

- Have a volunteer read aloud "The Rise of Ghana."

- Guide students as they study the photographs, read the captions, and discuss the ancient civilization of Ghana.

Background and Vocabulary

The Royal Kingdoms of Ghana, Mali, and Songhay

Read to find the meanings of these words.

e · Glossary

caravans

flourishing

goods

primary

vicinity

408

The Rise of Ghana

FROM A.D. 500 TO 1700, civilization in western Africa was **flourishing**. In this selection from *The Royal Kingdoms of Ghana, Mali, and Songhay*, you'll discover the people and culture of ancient Ghana. The first great empire in Ghana was created by a group called the Soninke, a people who spoke the Mande language.

We know much about ancient Ghana from *griots* (GREE-ohs) — storytellers who pass along the Soninke people's oral history from generation to generation. Their musical and dramatic performances are the earliest accounts of Ghana's origin.

Aboure tribe elder telling tribal stories

A.D. 200	300	400

A.D. 200
Ghana first established by Soninke people of northwest Africa

English Language Learners

Supporting Comprehension

Beginning/Preproduction As students listen to the article, have them point to the storyteller, the caravan, a musical instrument, and the year on the timeline in which Ghana was first established.

Early Production and Speech Emergence Have students repeat the Key Vocabulary words after you. Use the photograph on page 409 to discuss caravans. Mime bartering by trading objects with a student.

Intermediate and Advanced Fluency Pair students with more proficient speakers of English to prepare an oral presentation in which they restate the important information in the article.

The ancient kingdom of Ghana was located in present-day Mali and Mauritania in western Africa, in the **vicinity** of the Sahara desert. With its fertile land, Ghana quickly became a wealthy area with advanced methods of iron and gold work, carpentry, and pottery. The kingdom's **primary** source of wealth came from trading **goods** with surrounding areas. Trade wouldn't have been possible without the **caravans** that transported these goods.

A Samburu tribesman (above) leads a camel caravan through the wilderness.

A musical instrument from Ghana, made from a dried gourd and covered by seeds woven into a net

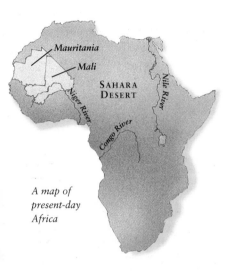
A map of present-day Africa

Mauritania
Mali
SAHARA DESERT
Niger River
Congo River
Nile River

A.D. 990
Ghana, at height of its power, captures the Muslim city of Awdoghast.

A.D. 1050
Invasion of Ghana; wide disruption of trade

700 800 900 1000

A.D. 700–1000
Ghana is dominant power in Western Sudan

A.D. 1000
Al-Bakri writes history of Old Kingdom of Ghana.

409

Introducing Vocabulary

Key Vocabulary
These words support the Key Concept and appear in the selection.

bartering the trading of goods without the exchange of money

caravans files of vehicles or pack animals traveling together

entourage a group of followers

flourishing growing extremely well

goods items for sale

oasis a green spot in a desert, where water can be found

primary main; basic

vicinity the region within close range of a place

 e • Glossary
e • WordGame

See Vocabulary notes on pages 412, 414, 416, 418, 420, and 422 for additional words to preview.

Display Transparency 4–18.

- Model how to figure out the meaning of the word *bartering* by using context clues.

- Ask students to use what they know about letter sounds and context clues to figure out the remaining Key Vocabulary words. Have volunteers explain how they figured out the meaning of each word.

- Ask students to look for these words as they read and to use them as they discuss Ghana's medieval trading empire.

Practice/Homework Assign **Practice Book** page 38.

Transparency 4–18

Words at the Market

Fast-Breaking News!

Reporter: I'm coming to you live from the central Koumbi Saleh marketplace, where the Prince has just entered the marketplace gates. Just minutes ago, shoppers were bartering for low prices on the goods brought in by donkey and camel caravans. Now, every person in the vicinity can't help staring at the Prince and his full entourage of servants, attendants, and followers. It is quite a sight to see! I hear that the Prince's primary reason for coming is to eat and stop at the nearby oasis for water. I am sure he is happy to be back in our flourishing city after his long, dry trip across the desert.

Practice Book page 38

The Royal Kingdoms of Ghana, Mali, and Songhay
Key Vocabulary

Name _____

A Desert Journey

Use these desert words to complete the journal entry below.

Vocabulary

oasis   entourage   vicinity   primary
flourishing   bartering   goods   caravans

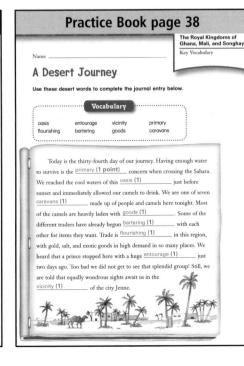

Today is the thirty-fourth day of our journey. Having enough water to survive is the primary (1 point) _____ concern when crossing the Sahara. We reached the cool waters of this oasis (1) _____ just before sunset and immediately allowed our camels to drink. We are one of seven caravans (1) _____ made up of people and camels here tonight. Most of the camels are heavily laden with goods (1) _____. Some of the different traders have already begun bartering (1) _____ with each other for items they want. Trade is flourishing (1) _____ in this region, with gold, salt, and exotic goods in high demand in so many places. We heard that a prince stopped here with a huge entourage (1) _____ just two days ago. Too bad we did not get to see that splendid group! Still, we are told that equally wondrous sights await us in the vicinity (1) _____ of the city Jenne.

COMPREHENSION STRATEGY
Monitor/Clarify

Teacher Modeling Have a volunteer read the Strategy Focus aloud. Remind students to pause to check their understanding. They can clear up any confusion by looking at illustrations, rereading, or reading ahead. Have students read the introduction on page 412. Then model the strategy.

Think Aloud *Wait. Do I understand what I've just read? Actually, I'm not sure when ancient Ghana existed. So I reread the introduction, and I find the answer in the first sentence. Ghana was established in the third century A.D.*

✓ **Test Prep** Remind students that many reading tests are timed, but caution them not to rush. Students should take time to monitor and clarify their understanding of what they are reading.

COMPREHENSION SKILL
Topic, Main Idea, and Details

Introduce the Graphic Organizer. Tell students that a chart can help them focus on the topic, the main idea, and the supporting details of a nonfiction selection. Explain that as they read, students will complete the Topic, Main Idea, and Details Chart on **Practice Book** page 39.

- Display **Transparency 4–19.** Have students read Anthology page 413.

- Model how to identify the main idea and key details of Section 1.

- Have students complete the chart as they read. Monitor their work.

410   **THEME 4: Discovering Ancient Cultures**

Meet the Authors Fredrick and Patricia McKissack

A life together: Fredrick and Patricia McKissack both grew up in Nashville, Tennessee, and attended the same university.
Beginnings: While working as a teacher, Patricia couldn't find good books about African Americans for her students. This led her to write her first biography.
Prolific writers: The McKissacks have published nearly a hundred books about the history of African Americans, including *Red-Tail Angels: The Story of the Tuskegee Airmen of World War II* and *African American Inventors.*
Their mission: "We try to enlighten, to change attitudes, to form new attitudes — to build bridges with books."

Meet the Illustrator Rob Wood

Southern roots: Like the McKissacks, Rob Wood grew up in Tennessee.
Artist's intuition: Wood says he "always wanted to become an illustrator." In the fourth grade, his teacher was an artist and encouraged him to follow his dream.
Hobbies: Sailing in the Chesapeake Bay, snorkeling, diving, and watching the stars and planets through his telescope

 **Internet**

To find out more about Fredrick and Patricia McKissack and Rob Wood, visit Education Place. **www.eduplace.com/kids**

410

Transparency 4–19
Topic, Main Idea, and Details Chart

Topic: Life in the medieval Kingdom of Ghana

Section 1
Main Idea: Ghana's secret gold mines produced gold for use and trade.
Key Details: 1. Gold was common and plentiful in Ghana.
2. The location of the gold mines was kept secret.
3. Archaeologists are still searching for the mines.

Section 2
Main Idea: Wangaran miners used dumb bartering to protect their gold.
Key Details: 1. Merchants and miners traded without speaking.
2. Miners chose death over betraying the location of the mines.
3. Trade was Ghana's lifeblood, so soldiers protected caravans.

Section 3
Main Idea: Trade caravans carried goods through Ghana and beyond.
Key Details: 1. Camels were essential for desert travel.
2. Traveling in large groups provided safety and resources.
3. Caravans traveled during the coolest parts of the day.

Section 4
Main Idea: Daily life in the city differed from life in small villages.
Key Details: 1. City people had expensive belongings and ate exotic food.
2. Eighty percent of people lived in small farming compounds.
3. The whole community was one big extended family.

TRANSPARENCY 4–19
TEACHER'S EDITION PAGES 410 AND 427A

DISCOVERING ANCIENT CULTURES: Royal Kingdom
Graphic Organizer Topic, Main Idea, and Details Ch

ANNOTATED VERSION

Practice Book page 39

The Royal Kingdoms of Ghana, Mali, and Songhay
Graphic Organizer Topic, Main Idea, and Details Chart

Name _____

Topic, Main Idea, and Details Chart

Topic: Life in the medieval Kingdom of Ghana **(2 points)**

Section 1
Main Idea: Ghana's secret gold mines produced gold for use and trade. (1)
Key Details: 1. Gold was common and plentiful in Ghana. (1)
2. The location of the gold mines was kept secret. (1)
3. Archaeologists are still searching for the mines. (1)

Section 2
Main Idea: Wangaran miners used dumb bartering to protect their gold. (1)
Key Details: 1. Merchants and miners traded without speaking. (1)
2. Miners chose death over betraying the location of the mines. (1)
3. Trade was Ghana's lifeblood, so soldiers protected caravans. (1)

Section 3
Main Idea: Trade caravans carried goods through Ghana and beyond. (1)
Key Details: 1. Camels were essential for desert travel. (1)
2. Traveling in large groups provided safety and resources. (1)
3. Caravans traveled during the coolest parts of the day. (1)

Section 4
Main Idea: Daily life in the city differed from life in small villages. (1)
Key Details: 1. City people had expensive belongings and ate exotic food. (1)
2. Eighty percent of people lived in small farming compounds. (1)
3. The whole community was one big extended family. (1)

Selection 3

The Royal Kingdoms of Ghana, Mali, and Songhay

Life in Medieval Africa

Patricia and Fredrick McKissack

Strategy Focus

The people of ancient Ghana traded with peoples in faraway lands. As you read, **monitor** how well you understand the information. **Clarify** parts you don't understand by rereading or reading ahead.

411

Extra Support/Intervention

Selection Preview

pages 411–415 Although traders came from across Africa to exchange goods for gold, miners in ancient Ghana kept the locations of the mines a secret. Why do you think they did this?

pages 415–417 Camels made travel across the Sahara Desert possible for the traders. What qualities do you think a camel needed to make this journey?

pages 418–419 Trade caravans crossing the Sahara needed experienced guides to lead them to their destinations. Why do you think this was so?

pages 420–423 Most Ghanaians lived in groups outside cities. People in these small farming communities lived like large, extended families.

Purpose Setting

- Have students read to find out why Ghana is known as the first great empire of northwest Africa.

- Have students preview the selection by looking at the illustrations. Ask them to predict what they might learn about Ghana's trading empire.

- Remind students to pause when they're confused and to reread, read ahead, or use the illustrations to help their understanding.

- Tell students that noting the topic, main idea, and supporting details will help them remember information.

- You may want to preview with students the Responding questions on Anthology page 424.

Journal ▶ Students can use their journals to record what they learn about Ghana as they read.

STRATEGY REVIEW

Phonics/Decoding

Remind students to use the Phonics/Decoding Strategy as they read.

Modeling Display this sentence part from the selection: *Ordinary people <u>adorned</u> themselves with golden jewelry …* Point to *adorned*.

Think Aloud *I recognize the ending, -ed. The first part of the word looks like one that I know,* adore. *If I blend those sounds together with the* n *sound, I get* uh DAWRND. *From clues in the sentence, I think it means "decorated with jewelry or other fancy things."*

CRITICAL THINKING
Guiding Comprehension

❶ DRAWING CONCLUSIONS Why did the authors explain that ordinary people wore golden jewelry? (to show that gold was plentiful in Ghana)

❷ MAKING INFERENCES Why did the Wangaran miners keep the location of their mines a secret? (to keep outsiders from stealing their wealth)

COMPREHENSION STRATEGY
Monitor/Clarify

Teacher/Student Modeling Help students model the strategy. Use this prompt.

- Suppose you didn't understand why the people of Wangara received things from distant countries of the world. What would you do? (reread, then read ahead to find out more about Ghana's trade)

Vocabulary

Sudan a region of northern Africa south of the Sahara Desert and north of the equator, stretching from the Atlantic coast to Ethiopia

caravans files of vehicles or pack animals traveling together

medieval the period in history from about A.D. 500 to A.D. 1450

vicinity the region within close range of a place

flourishing growing extremely well

floodplain flat land along a river made up of soil left by floods

bartering the trading of goods without the exchange of money

In the third century A.D., the Soninke people of northwest Africa established Ghana, the first great empire of the western Sudan.
Ancient Ghana grew rich from its iron and gold ore. The Berbers, tribesmen from North Africa, led camel caravans across the Sahara Desert and between North Africa and the western Sudan. They exchanged salt for Ghanaian gold and named a green area along the Sahara the Sahel, or shore of the desert sea.
Al-Bakri, an eleventh-century Arabic historian, has left the fullest description of medieval Ghana.

412

Extra Support/Intervention

Phonics/Decoding Strategy

Use this example to model the strategy for *established*.

I'll try dividing this word into syllables. I think the first syllable divides between the s and the t, and the second between the b and the l: es-tab. I recognize the familiar ending -ed, and the letters sh make the /sh/ sound. I think the last syllable is pronounced lihshd. When I blend all the sounds together, I get ehs-TAB-lishd. I know that word means "to begin or set up." That makes sense in the sentence.

> established
> ehs-TAB-lishd

Gold for Salt

Ghana (GAH-nuh) had more than enough gold. Ordinary people adorned themselves with golden jewelry and wore cloth spun with strands of golden thread. Al-Bakri claimed that the king's hitching post was a gold nugget weighing close to forty pounds!

 1

Everybody knew the location of the salt mines, but the exact location of the gold mines was a well-guarded secret. People assumed that the mines were located in the vicinity of Wangara.

2

An Arabic commentator, named al-Idrisi, described the city of Wangara as he saw it in the twelfth century:

> *In Wangara there are flourishing towns and famous fortresses. Its inhabitants are rich. They possess gold in abundance, and receive productions which are brought to them from the most distant countries of the world.*

Al-Idrisi also noted that Wangara was an island that was often flooded. When the water receded, gold could be found lying on top of the ground. Some scholars think that Bambuk, located on the headwaters of the Senegal River, and Bure (byur), at the headwaters of the Niger (NY-juhr) in modern-day Guinea, were the sites of Wangaran gold mines. Modern archeologists have found mine shafts, some as deep as fifty feet, at Bambuk and Bure. But not all archeologists are convinced that these are the remains of the mines that supplied old Ghana, and they are continuing to search the floodplain of the middle Niger for other possible sites.

By limiting outside contacts, the Wangaran miners protected the secret of their mines. According to a widespread tale, they even traded their gold dust for salt and other goods through a special, silent form of trade called dumb bartering.

413

Fluency Practice

Rereading for Fluency Have students choose a favorite part of the selection to reread to a partner, or suggest that they read the first two paragraphs on page 413. Encourage students to read expressively.

Extra Support/Intervention

Strategy Modeling: Monitor/Clarify

Use this example to model the strategy.

When I read the description of Wangara on page 413, I didn't understand why the writers said the towns were flourishing. I know that this word means "growing extremely well," but what does this have to do with gold? To clear up my confusion, I read ahead and found out that people came from all over the world to trade goods for the gold. Then I understood. The cities were growing because there were a lot of people there as well as a lot of gold.

Guiding Comprehension

③ NOTING DETAILS Why did the authors call the Wangaran miners *shy*? (because they hid from view)

④ MAKING INFERENCES Were you surprised to learn that dumb bartering usually worked quickly and smoothly? Explain. (Sample answer: yes, because it seems as if communicating without speaking would have been difficult)

Dumb Bartering

Al-Musadi, a tenth-century writer from Baghdad, reported that dumb bartering took place in this way: Their donkeys ladened with grains, leather, cloth, and salt, traders arrived at Wangara, where men lived in holes (no doubt, mines). There the traders spread out their goods along a stream or near a thicket. Then they announced their presence by beating on a special drum called a *deba*. The merchants went away.

③

The shy Wangaran miners crept from their hiding places and laid out a measure of gold dust. They, too, departed. Some time later the traders returned, and, if the amount of gold dust was acceptable, they took it and left. If not, they went away again and the Wangarans came back and made a counteroffer. Each group went back and forth until an agreement was satisfactory to both sides. Through years of experience, both sides had a general idea of what exchange would be acceptable, so the system generally moved quickly and smoothly. The silent miners inspired a lot of curiosity by trading in this manner. But, even if they were captured, as sometimes they were, the Wangaran miners chose death over betraying the location of the mines.

④

414

Vocabulary

ladened weighed down with heavy things

goods items for sale

thicket a dense growth of shrubs

primary main; basic

livestock animals raised and kept on a farm

English Language Learners

Supporting Comprehension

- Use the map on page 419 to help students locate Bambuk, on the headwaters of the Senegal River, and Bure, on the headwaters of the Niger River, the believed sites of the Wangaran gold mines.

- Assign one group of students the role of miners and another group the role of traders. Have students pantomime dumb bartering as you read page 414 aloud.

The Wangaran miners were secretive, but no less eager to trade. Trade was the lifeblood of Ghana. The king employed a standing, well-disciplined army whose primary responsibility was to defend his empire. The soldiers' peacetime duty was to protect the steady flow of caravans that came into the kingdom and the Berber traders who were Ghana's allies in the sub-Saharan trade system.

4:42

The Trade Caravans

Gold and salt weren't the only items traded in Ghana. Local donkey caravans arrived daily from all points in the empire, bringing slaves, honey, jewelry, tools, metal and leather goods, rare birds, livestock, horses, special cloth called *chigguyiya*, and, of course, news. Caravans also left Koumbi Saleh (KOOM-bee SAL-ay) and other large trading cities in the kingdom going to points north.

The arrival of a trans-Saharan camel caravan was a special event. Traders brought rare and wonderful treasures like jewels, silk, and furs from everywhere in the Islamic world, including Egypt, Arabia, Palestine, and even from as far away as central Asia.

415

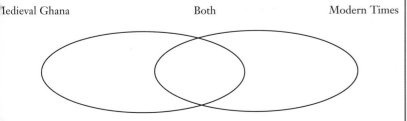

ASSIGNMENT CARD 9

Did You Hear About This?

Compare and Contrast

With a partner, create a Venn diagram to compare and contrast the spread of news in medieval Ghana to the spread of information today. Use what you have read in the selection and what you know about present-day life. Present your diagram to the class.

The Spread of News

Medieval Ghana   Both   Modern Times

Teacher's Resource BLM page 78

TARGET SKILL

Topic, Main Idea, and Details

Teach

- The topic is what most of the selection is about. The topic of this selection is medieval Ghana.

- The main ideas are the important ideas about the topic.

- The supporting details are facts that further explain each main idea.

Practice

- Help students identify the main idea and supporting details on page 414.

- Record their responses in a chart like the one below.

Main Idea
Dumb bartering method

Supporting Details
1. Traders laid out goods and left.
2. Miners left gold and went away.
3. Traded until agreement reached.

Apply

- Have partners read the second paragraph on page 415 or the last paragraph on page 417. Then ask them to make a chart like the one above.

- Discuss charts as a class.

Target Skill Trace	
Preview; Teach	p. 407CC, p. 410, p. 415; p. 427A
Reteach	p. R12
Review	pp. M32–M33; p. 369; Theme 2, p. 195; Theme 6, p. 601

CRITICAL THINKING
Guiding Comprehension

⑤ NOTING DETAILS Why do you think the authors described a camel caravan as *colorful*? (Sample answers: colorful dress; colorful goods being transported; interesting variety of people; unpredictable behavior of camels)

⑥ COMPARE AND CONTRAST Tell what the authors mean by this analogy: *The camel was to the Berbers what the bison was to the Native American.* (Each kind of animal was vitally important to the lives of the people in each group.)

⑦ DRAWING CONCLUSIONS What details show that journey by camel caravan was difficult and complicated? (Sample answers: Difficult-to-manage camels required a crew; caravans needed *safety in numbers.*)

During the period of old Ghana, caravans departed from Koumbi Saleh and usually took the western route through Awdoghast. Caravans from North Africa came through Sijilmasa in Morocco and down to the market towns of Awdoghast and Walata. From there the caravans split up and took short routes along the Senegal and Niger rivers.

⑤ The makeup of a long-distance caravan was as complex as it was colorful. Everything centered around the camels, which made trans-Saharan travel possible.

⑥ The camel was to the Berbers what the bison was to the Native American. The animal provided transportation, milk, wool, hides, and meat. These oddly shaped creatures adapted to desert travel so well because they have a double row of eyelashes, hairy ear openings, and the ability to close their nostrils to protect themselves from the sun and sand. Camels can endure the dry heat better than any other beast of burden. They can drink up to twenty-five gallons of water at a time, then go several days without food.

416

Extra Support/ Intervention

Review (pages 411–417)

Before students who need extra support join the whole class for Stop and Think on page 417, have them

- review their purpose/predictions
- take turns modeling Monitor/Clarify and other strategies they used
- help you add to **Transparency 4–19**
- check and revise their Topic, Main Idea, and Details Charts on **Practice Book** page 39, and use them to summarize

English Language Learners

Supporting Comprehension

Check understanding of these terms and phrases: *adapted to desert travel* and *car endure* (page 416); *ill-tempered* and *famously stubborn* (page 417). Then have students complete a T-chart like the one shown.

Camels	
Helpful	Unhelpful

Vocabulary

endure to carry on despite hardships

entourage a group of followers

That's where praise for the camel ends. They are famous for being ill-tempered and make traveling in a caravan very difficult. They bite, spit, kick, run away, or refuse to move. Famously stubborn, camels cannot be handled by just anybody, so caravan leaders usually hired a full-time cameleer and crew to manage them.

Generally, several merchants pooled their resources to form a caravan. There was safety in numbers, too. On the day of departure, as many as a hundred camels were loaded with merchandise and supplies. An official made a strict accounting of all the goods for tax purposes. Then each merchant and his entourage assembled and were assigned their positions. Finally, when all the merchants, slaves, bodyguards, scholars, ambassadors, poets, and musicians had mounted their camels, the overland journey began.

7

417

Stop and Think

Critical Thinking Questions

1. **PREDICTING OUTCOMES** What might have happened if outsiders had found the gold mines? (main source of wealth for Ghana taken over; empire weakened or destroyed)

2. **MAKING INFERENCES** Describe what crossing the Sahara in a camel caravan might have been like. (Sample answers: difficult; exciting; entertaining)

Strategies in Action

Have students model the Monitor/Clarify strategy and other strategies they used as they read.

Discussion Options

You may want to bring the entire class together to do one or more of the activities below.

- **Review Predictions/Purpose** Have students review their predictions and purpose. Have them discuss what they have learned about why Ghana was the first great empire of northwest Africa.

- **Share Group Discussions** Have students share their literature discussions.

- **Summarize** Have students use their Topic, Main Idea, and Details Charts to summarize the selection so far.

ASSIGNMENT CARD 8

Literature Discussion

Discuss the following questions and your own questions with a group of classmates:

- What role do you think the gold mines and Ghana's location in Africa played in helping Ghana to become "the first great empire of western Sudan"?

- Why do you think the people of Ghana traded their gold for salt?

- Archaeologists are still curious about the location of Wangara's secret gold mines. Why do you think this is so?

- Why might the arrival of a trade caravan in medieval Ghana have been exciting for the local people?

- If you could journey back in time and wander through the market towns of ancient Ghana, what things would you want to buy? Why?

Theme 4: Discovering Ancient Cultures

Monitoring Student Progress

If . . .	Then . . .
students have successfully completed the Extra Support Activities on page 416,	have them read the rest of the selection cooperatively or independently.

CRITICAL THINKING

Guiding Comprehension

8 CAUSE AND EFFECT Why did the caravans move so slowly across the desert? (Sample answers: shifting sands, thieves, heat, required prayer periods, camels for transportation)

9 COMPARE AND CONTRAST In what ways do you think caravanserai might have been similar to modern-day roadside rest stops? (Sample answers: Travelers were resting and talking; refreshments were available; resting camels might have looked a little like parked cars.)

There were four major trade routes that the caravans coming from the east could have traveled. Following an experienced guide, the caravan made its way through the ever-changing Saharan sands, clocking about three miles an hour, stopping only to observe the required prayer periods.

Mile after mile, day after day, the caravan pushed west and then south. Occasionally they must have been greeted by a lizard, a scorpion, or a snake, but no other life could endure the desert. The caravan moved from one oasis to another before the sun rose too high and temperatures soared to 130°F. During the hot part of the day the travelers rested at Berber-run caravanserai, much like our modern-day roadside rest stops.

Sometimes the caravan moved a few more miles at night by using the stars as their guide. More often, everyone slept, while guards stood watch for thieves, which were a real threat. But once a caravan reached the borders of Ghana, they were safe, for the king's soldiers guarded the area. Royal patrols maintained order and guaranteed safe passage to all visitors.

418

Vocabulary

oasis a green spot in the desert where water can be found

caravanserai an inn with a large outdoor area where caravans would stay

A typical caravan from Arabia to the Sahel took about forty days to complete. Coming out of the desert at a major city in Ghana must have been a wonderful sight to desert travelers who had endured such a long, hot journey.

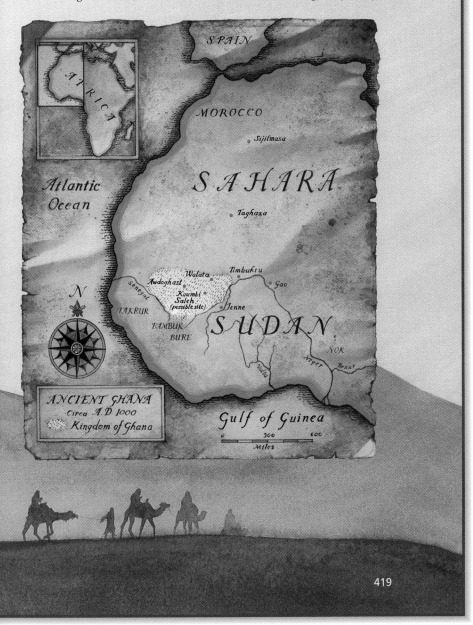

419

Problem Solving

Review

- Remind students that defining problems and evaluating solutions helps them understand an author's message.

- Guide students to identify travelers' problems on page 418 and evaluate the solutions. Write them on a chart.

Problem	→	Solution
ever-changing sands		followed experienced guide
130°F temperatures		rested at hottest time of day
thieves		guards stood watch

- Model evaluating the travelers' solution to follow an experienced guide.

- Note that maps wouldn't be accurate if the sands kept changing and that following someone who knew the desert was probably the best solution.

Practice/Apply

- Have partners make similar charts for problems and solutions described on pages 420–423.

- Discuss students' evaluation of solutions.

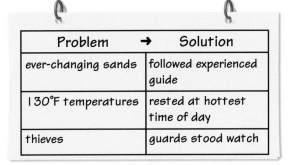

Review Skill Trace	
Teach	Theme 3, p. 351A
Reteach	Theme 3, p. R14
▶ Review	p. 419; Theme 3, p. 263

Reading the Selection 419

CRITICAL THINKING

Guiding Comprehension

10 **MAKING INFERENCES** What can you infer from the detail that most small towns *were surrounded by walls with moats or pits in front of them*? (probably needed to defend themselves against attackers)

11 **DRAWING CONCLUSIONS** Why do you think the authors give more details about life in Ghana's villages than in its cities? (Most people lived in farming villages.)

TARGET SKILL

COMPREHENSION STRATEGY

Monitor/Clarify

Student Modeling Have students model the strategy. You might use these prompts.

- Was there any information on the past few pages that you didn't understand?

- Did you find it helpful to reread or read ahead at any point? Where?

Vocabulary

compounds groups of houses or other buildings, enclosed by a wall or fence

allocated set aside for a particular purpose

grievance a complaint based on a real or imagined wrong

irrigation bringing water to farmland by streams, ditches, or pipes

Daily Life

Whether or not it was the capital of Ghana, Koumbi Saleh was certainly an important city, and there is growing evidence that there were other large trading centers on the Niger and Senegal rivers. By about A.D. 800, Jenne (JEHN-nay) alone had about 20,000 inhabitants, archeologists assure us. Most Soninke towns, though, had about 500 to 1,500 residents. These smaller towns were surrounded by walls with moats or pits in front of them.

10 City dwellers wore expensive clothing, owned objects of art, swords, copper utensils, foreign products, and ate exotic foods, especially citrus fruit, but a majority of the people didn't live that way.

420

REACHING ALL LEARNERS

Extra Support/Intervention

Strategy Modeling: Monitor/Clarify

Use this example to model the strategy.

In the first paragraph on page 421, there are a lot of details about how people in farming communities lived. After reading it, I went back and read it again to make sure I understood everything. It helped me to make a list of the important details in the paragraph, too.

Eighty percent of the population lived outside the towns, in small farming compounds, where a man and his sons' and daughters' families worked cooperatively. Several compounds of the same clan made up a village, but according to custom the land couldn't be bought or sold. Village leaders, appointed by the local king, allocated land to each family according to need. One family might be given the right to farm a piece of land, while another family might be given the right to harvest the fruit from the trees grown on the same land. If there was a dispute, each party could take their grievance to the local king, and even to the great king in the capital.

Anthropologists who have studied Soninke village life have discovered that eighth-century Mande people had advanced farming skills. They probably used dikes and earthen dams for irrigation, and their use of land was so well managed, farmers even grew enough to support the larger cities.

Ghana's major crops included millet, sorghum, cotton, ground nuts, rice, cow peas, okra, pumpkins, watermelons, kola nuts, sesame seeds, and shea nuts — butternuts — from which they made a spread.

Even in the villages, trade was an important aspect of daily life. A village that grew millet and cotton might trade with another that grew butternuts and watermelons. This local trading system helped unite the various groups who lived within the empire.

Men and women shared the workload, each taking responsibility for various chores. The men hunted and did most of the farming. The women were responsible for harvesting and processing the food for storage and sale. Women made pots and baskets and tended chickens. During the harvest season, men built houses, made tools, or spent a month on border duty in the military.

421

ASSIGNMENT CARD 10

An Outline of Village Life

Create an Outline

Making an outline is a good way to organize and remember information. Reread page 421. Find the main idea of the first paragraph and write it next to the Roman numeral I. Write each detail that supports the main idea next to a capital letter. Do the same for paragraphs 2-5 (Roman numerals II, III, IV, and V). Use the example below as a guide. When you have finished, compare your outline with a classmate's.

Village Life

I. _____
   A. _____
   B. _____

Theme 4: Discovering Ancient Cultures

Teacher's Resource BLM page 78

Text Organization

Review

- Remind students that paragraphs or groups of paragraphs in a nonfiction article can be organized by main ideas and details.

- Explain that paragraphs can also be organized into comparisons and contrasts.

Practice

- Have volunteers read aloud the last paragraph on page 420 and the first paragraph on page 421.

- Ask, How are these paragraphs organized? (comparison and contrast) Why? (tell differences between lives of city dwellers and villagers)

- Have a volunteer read aloud the last paragraph on page 421.

- Ask, How is this paragraph organized? (main idea and details) Why? (main idea in first sentence; other sentences give details)

Apply

- Have partners reread pages 416–417 and 422–423.

- Ask, Which paragraphs are organized by main idea and details? Which are organized by comparison and contrast?

Review Skill Trace	
Teach	Theme 2, p. 213A
Reteach	Theme 2, p. R12
Review	p. 421

CRITICAL THINKING
Guiding Comprehension

12 DRAWING CONCLUSIONS What does the Soninke proverb mean? (Family ties are stronger and last longer than a relationship with a king.)

13 MAKING INFERENCES What does the proverb show about the Soninke? (Family is very important to them.)

14 AUTHOR'S VIEWPOINT Why did the authors end this selection with the words to a poem? (Poems were and are an important part of Soninke culture; it shows the Soninke's values; it reveals the authors' appreciation of the Soninke culture.)

Because each man was expected to serve in the military for at least one month every year and to bring his own weapons, time was set aside for him to make bows and arrows and spears. At other times the men shared in making axes, hoes, and scythes. Women and men made baskets, pots, and utensils. Grinding stones for making meal from millet and sorghum were made by both men and women pooling their talents and resources.

Village houses were made of sun-dried mud or acacia wood and stone. Because of the hot climate, they were used mostly for sleeping and storage while a great many activities took place outside. Since the people were, in fact, a large family, the women cooked, ate, worked, and entertained together, and the men hunted and worked the fields together.

Inside furnishings were few and personal belongings were fewer still. The average household contained one sleeping mat or cot per person, rugs, and a stool. There might be a wooden or woven storage chest. The climate also made a lot of clothing unnecessary. Farmers wore woven cotton breeches, tunics, and sandals. Women wrapped their heads and draped themselves in cloth. Their diet was simple but adequate. Visitors were always welcome to share a meal, which most of the time consisted of rice stuffed in green peppers, milk, fruits, and wild game.

12 Although a farmer's possessions may seem meager by today's standards, he was not poor. Successful farmers had a good standard of living and they also had a respected place in society.

13 The Soninke people loved stories and poetry, and they still do today. An often-repeated theme in Mande proverbs is family. This one dates back to the old kingdom: *Kings may come and go, but the family endures.*

422

Vocabulary

adequate enough

game wild animals, birds, or fish hunted for food

meager lacking in amount or richness

paternal related through one's father

maternal related through one's mother

dissent disagreement

belligerence a warlike, unfriendly attitude

REACHING ALL LEARNERS

Extra Support/ Intervention	On Level	Challenge

Selection Review

Before students join the whole class for Wrapping Up on page 423, have them

- review their purpose/predictions
- take turns modeling the reading strategies they used
- complete their Topic, Main Idea, and Details Charts and help you complete **Transparency 4–19**
- summarize the whole selection

Literature Discussion

Have small groups of students discuss the selection, using their own questions or the questions in Think About the Selection on Anthology page 424.

Among the Mande, family relationships were not defined as they are today. A child's oldest paternal uncle was her big father. Her youngest paternal uncle was her little father. A child's maternal aunt was his big mother and so on. Cousins were brothers and sisters. Therefore, there were no orphans or homeless people within their society. An elder surrounded and cared for by a big family was considered rich beyond measure. That's why the birth of a child was celebrated with feasting, dancing, and singing.

"Song of the Turtle" is a poem that dates back to the Ghanaian period:

We lived in freedom
Before man appeared:
Our world was undisturbed,
One day followed the other joyfully.
Dissent was never heard.
Then man broke into our forest,
With cunning and belligerence.
He pursued us
With greed and envy:
Our freedom vanished.

14

4231

Wrapping Up

Critical Thinking Questions

1. **MAKING INFERENCES** "Song of the Turtle" expresses disapproval of greed and envy. How did the Soninke demonstrate these values in daily life? (shared the workload; welcomed visitors; valued community ties more than wealth)

2. **DRAWING CONCLUSIONS** How might Soninke villagers have contributed to the strength of Ghana's empire? (had advanced farming skills and grew enough crops to support cities; trading system helped unite groups of people)

Strategies in Action

Have students take turns modeling how and where they used the Monitor/Clarify strategy.

Discussion Options

Bring the entire class together to do one or more of the activities below.

Review Predictions/Purpose Have students discuss what they predicted and what they learned about Ghana's trading empire.

Share Group Discussions Have students share their literature discussions.

Summarize Have students use their completed Topic, Main Idea, and Details Charts to summarize the main ideas in the selection.

Comprehension Check

Use **Practice Book** page 40 to assess students' comprehension of the selection.

English Language Learners

Supporting Comprehension

Help students understand Soninke family relationships as you discuss the terms *maternal, paternal, orphan,* and *elder,* as well as the expression *rich beyond measure.*

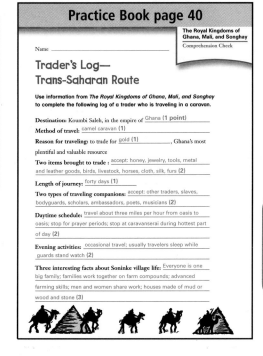

Practice Book page 40

The Royal Kingdoms of Ghana, Mali, and Songhay
Comprehension Check

Name _____

Trader's Log—
Trans-Saharan Route

Use information from *The Royal Kingdoms of Ghana, Mali, and Songhay* to complete the following log of a trader who is traveling in a caravan.

Destination: Koumbi Saleh, in the empire of Ghana **(1 point)**
Method of travel: camel caravan **(1)**
Reason for traveling: to trade for gold **(1)**, Ghana's most plentiful and valuable resource
Two items brought to trade: accept: honey, jewelry, tools, metal and leather goods, birds, livestock, horses, cloth, silk, furs **(2)**
Length of journey: forty days **(1)**
Two types of traveling companions: accept: other traders, slaves, bodyguards, scholars, ambassadors, poets, musicians **(2)**
Daytime schedule: travel about three miles per hour from oasis to oasis; stop for prayer periods; stop at caravanserai during hottest part of day **(2)**
Evening activities: occasional travel; usually travelers sleep while guards stand watch **(2)**
Three interesting facts about Soninke village life: Everyone is one big family; families work together on farm compounds; advanced farming skills; men and women share work; houses made of mud or wood and stone **(3)**

Monitoring Student Progress

If . . .	Then . . .
students score 11 or below on **Practice Book** page 40,	help them find sections in the text that will clarify their understanding.

Reading the Selection **423**

Responding

Think About the Selection

Have students discuss or write their answers. Sample answers are provided; accept reasonable responses.

Responding

Think About the Selection

The Royal Kingdoms of Ghana, Mali, and Songhay
Life in Medieval Africa

Patricia and Fredrick McKissack

READ & COMPREHEND

1. **DRAWING CONCLUSIONS** Trade was Ghana's lifeblood, and gold was the most important source of wealth.

2. **NOTING DETAILS** Locations of the gold mines were protected; the king's soldiers at the borders guarded merchants; traders came from all over.

3. **MAKING JUDGMENTS** no, because people today are used to the speed and convenience of using money; yes, because people who have goods or services to share could barter with each other

4. **NOTING DETAILS** mined gold in the area; used rivers and camels to trade; grew crops for food and trade; built homes out of mud and acacia wood

5. **EXPRESSING PERSONAL OPINIONS** Answers will vary.

6. **TOPIC, MAIN IDEA, AND DETAILS** Villagers lived as members of an extended family. Men and women shared the workload. Villagers spent their time farming and making what they needed. They traded with other villages. Men were soldiers for part of each year.

7. **Connecting/Comparing** Ghanaian farmers had plenty to eat, a warm climate to live in, and a government that protected them and solved disputes fairly. The Chinese soldiers lived a hard, cold, lonely life and were separated from their families.

1. Why do you think the workers at the Wangaran gold mine refused to reveal the mine's location even when threatened with death?

2. What details support the main idea that trade was the "lifeblood of Ghana"?

3. Do you think that the ancient practice of bartering would be a success way of doing business in today's world? Why or why not?

4. In what ways did the people of ancient Ghana make good use of the resources they had? Give specific examples.

5. Would you have liked to be part of a trans-Saharan camel caravan? If not, why not? If so, describe the role you would have wanted on the trip.

6. Based on information in the selection, describe the daily life in a Soninke village.

7. **Connecting/Comparing** Compare the life of a soldier guarding the Great Wall of China to the life of a farmer in Ghana. Which life wou you prefer? Why?

Persuading

Write an Advertisement

Make a poster advertising the arrival of a camel caravan in the ancient city of Koumbi Saleh. Try to persuade people to come to greet the caravan and view the goods.

Tips
- Think of a head line that will gr readers' interes
- Use imperative sentences to ur people to atten
- Include vivid details.

424

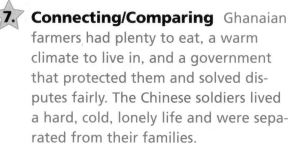

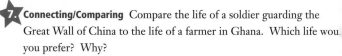
English Language Learners

Supporting Comprehension

Beginning/Preproduction Have students create and label a series of drawings that show the sequence of the dumb bartering between miners and traders.

Early Production and Speech Emergence Have students work in pairs to review the illustrations in the selection. For each illustration, ask them to write a sentence that explains an important fact.

Intermediate and Advanced Fluency Have students work with partners or in small groups to find and list phrases that show trade was the *lifeblood of Ghana*.

Social Studies

Compare Lifestyles

Make a chart that compares how village and city dwellers lived in ancient Ghana. Include the following categories in the chart: food and clothing; possessions; occupations; and family life.

	Village Life	City Life
Food & Clothing		
Possessions		
Occupations		
Family life		

Listening and Speaking

Conduct a Trade

With a partner, act out a trade between a member of a trans-Saharan caravan and a city merchant. In the conversation, each person should describe what he or she has to trade and use bargaining skills to try to get the best deal possible.

Bonus Imagine that the traders speak different languages. Act out another version of the trade. Use movements and props instead of words.

Internet

Send an E-Postcard

Tell a friend about one or more of the ancient cultures you've read about in this theme. To send your friend an e-postcard, visit Education Place. **www.eduplace.com/kids**

425

Additional Responses

Personal Response Invite volunteers to share their personal responses to the selection.

Journal ▶ Remind students about the colorful caravans described in this selection. Have them write in their journals about a journey they took once.

Selection Connections Remind students to add to **Practice Book** pages 1 and 2.

Practice Book page 1

Name _____

Launching the Theme
Selection Connections

Discovering Ancient Cultures

The selections in this theme will take you on a journey to the world of long ago. After reading each selection, complete the chart below to show what you learned.

	What is the location of the culture described in the selection?	When did the events described in the selection take place?
Lost Temple of the Aztecs	Mexico	in the early 1500s
The Great Wall	China	toward the end of the Ming dynasty, from about 1600–1800
The Royal Kingdoms of Ghana, Mali, and Songhay	Africa	in the eleventh century A.D.

Practice Book page 2

Name _____

Launching the Theme
Selection Connections

Discovering Ancient Cultures

	What was remarkable about the culture described in the selection?
Lost Temple of the Aztecs	The Aztecs built huge temples and beautiful cities. They were fierce, powerful warriors. They were expert jewelers and they had a very accurate calendar.
The Great Wall	The Chinese built an immense wall of pounded earth and stone. It is the longest structure ever built.
The Royal Kingdoms of Ghana, Mali, and Songhay	The people of ancient Ghana were prosperous. They traded with people far away for exotic items. Gold was plentiful, and many people were wealthy. Even the farmers lived well.

What have you learned about ancient cultures in this theme?
Sample answer: Ancient cultures were very different from one another; people long ago created incredible things.

Monitoring Student Progress

End-of-Selection Assessment

Selection Test Use the test on page 135 in the **Teacher's Resource Blackline Masters** to assess selection comprehension and vocabulary.

Student Self-Assessment Have students assess their reading with additional questions such as the following:

- What parts of this selection were easy for me to understand?

- What strategies helped me clarify any confusion I had while reading?

- Would I like to read more about medieval African empires? Why or why not?

Social Studies Link

Skill: How to Read a Diagram

- **Introduce** "Daily Life in Ancient Greece," a nonfiction article.

- **Explain** that diagrams reveal the special features of an object or place; many show how something works, and some give a sequence of steps.

- **Model** reading a diagram by following the steps on Anthology page 426. Identify the type of diagram. (cut-away view) Read and discuss each caption. Then compare the diagram to the text.

- **Set a purpose** for reading. Have students interpret the diagram as they read the article on pages 426–427. Ask, What does the diagram show that the text doesn't? (Sample answer: what furniture looked like) Remind students to use the Monitor/Clarify and Question strategies as they read.

- **Extend** the discussion by asking students, What labels could be added to the diagram to improve understanding?

Vocabulary

tunics long, simple, straight shirts belted loosely about the waist

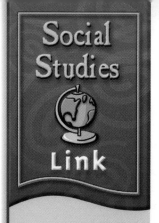

Social Studies Link

Skill: How to Read a Diagram
Interpreting a Diagram

- Identify whether the diagram shows a **cross-section**, a **cut-away view**, or a view from above.

- Read **labels** to identify different items or parts of the diagram. Ask yourself: Are the labels clear? What do they add to my understanding?

- Compare the diagram to the text. Ask yourself: What does the diagram add to the text? How is the diagram useful? Should more information be included?

426

Daily Life in Ancient Greece

by Robert Nicholson

A GREEK HOME

Most Greeks were farmers or craftsmen living in simple houses. Businesses were family run with a few slaves to help out.

Greek houses were arranged around a courtyard with an altar in the middle. Ordinary Greek houses were made from mud bricks dried in the sun. It was easy to dig through the walls, so burglars were known as wall diggers.

The living rooms were on the ground floor, with bedrooms above. Often men and women had separate living areas and spent most of their time apart. Food was cooked over open fires in the kitchen. The smoke escaped through a hole in the roof.

Inside a typical Greek house, walls were plain with just a few hangings. Chests were used for storage.

Parts of this house have been cut away so you can see inside.

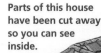

CLOTHES

Men's tunics were made from wool or linen. A plain square of material called a **chiton** was fastened over one or both shoulders and belted around the waist. Women wore a long tunic called a **peplos** or a long chiton. Wealthier people had tunics made from decorated material, while slaves had plain tunics. In classical times, it was fashionable for men to have short hair and a beard. Cloaks and shawls would be worn outside in colder weather and for traveling. Many people went barefoot most of the time. Shoes were leather sandals or boots.

Although Greek cities always had public baths, there was no soap, so the Greeks rubbed their bodies with olive oil to get clean. Then they would scrape the oil and dirt off with a tool called a **strigil**.

At the front of most houses stood a statue of the god Hermes — a **herm** — thought to act as a guard for the house.

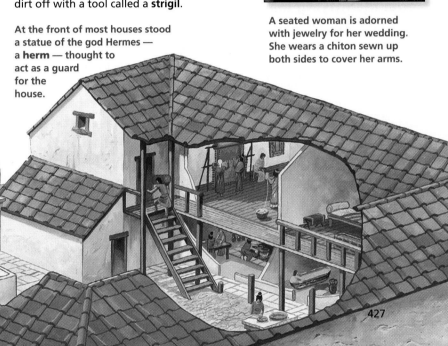

A gold necklace like the one worn by the woman in the vase painting below.

A seated woman is adorned with jewelry for her wedding. She wears a chiton sewn up both sides to cover her arms.

427

Challenge

Create Diagrams

Have students create cut-away diagrams to show special features of part of the school building or their own homes. Have them use labels that give information about key elements in the diagram.

bedroom
living room
kitchen

Wrapping Up

Critical Thinking Questions

Have students use the diagram and the selection to answer these questions.

1. **COMPARE AND CONTRAST** How are ancient Greek homes and modern American homes alike? How are they different? (Sample answer: alike: living rooms on a ground floor and bedrooms above; different: ancient homes arranged around courtyard; separate areas for men and women; smoke hole in kitchen roof)

2. **MAKING GENERALIZATIONS** Why does the article show a photograph of a real gold necklace in addition to the one in the vase painting? (A photo of a real artifact can help readers visualize an item better than a painting can.)

3. **MAKING JUDGMENTS** What information in the text might have benefited from an additional diagram? Why? (Sample answer: public bath; although its function is explained, it is hard to picture it and the tools used in it)

4. **Connecting/Comparing** How is this article about life in ancient Greece similar to the article about the ancient kingdom of Ghana? (Both selections give detailed, nonfiction information about certain aspects of daily life in an ancient culture.)

OBJECTIVES

- Identify the topic, main idea, and details in the selection.
- Identify the main idea and details in several paragraphs from the selection.
- Learn academic language: *topic, main ideas, details.*

Target Skill Trace

Preview; Teach	p. 407CC, p. 410, p. 415; p. 427A
Reteach	p. R12
Review	pp. M32–M33; Theme 2, p. 195; Theme 6, p. 601
See	*Extra Support Handbook,* pp. 152–153; pp. 158–159

Transparency 4–19

Topic, Main Idea, and Details Chart

Topic: Life in the medieval Kingdom of Ghana

Section 1
Main Idea: Ghana's secret gold mines produced gold for use and trade.
Key Details: 1. Gold was common and plentiful in Ghana.
  2. The location of the gold mines was kept secret.
  3. Archaeologists are still searching for the mines.

Section 2
Main Idea: Wangaran miners used dumb bartering to protect their gold.
Key Details: 1. Merchants and miners traded without speaking.
  2. Miners chose death over betraying the location of the mines.
  3. Trade was Ghana's lifeblood, so soldiers protected caravans.

Section 3
Main Idea: Trade caravans carried goods through Ghana and beyond.
Key Details: 1. Camels were essential for desert travel.
  2. Traveling in large groups provided safety and resources.
  3. Caravans traveled during the coolest parts of the day.

Section 4
Main Idea: Daily life in the city differed from life in small villages.
Key Details: 1. City people had expensive belongings and ate exotic food.
  2. Eighty percent of people lived in small farming compounds.
  3. The whole community was one big extended family.

TRANSPARENCY 4-19
TEACHER'S EDITION PAGES 410 AND 427A

Practice Book page 39

Name _____

The Royal Kingdoms of Ghana, Mali, and Songhay
Graphic Organizer Topic, Main Idea, and Details Chart

Topic, Main Idea, and Details Chart

Topic: Life in the medieval Kingdom of Ghana **(2 points)**

Section 1
Main Idea: Ghana's secret gold mines produced gold for use and trade. **(1)**
Key Details: 1. Gold was common and plentiful in Ghana. **(1)**
  2. The location of the gold mines was kept secret. **(1)**
  3. Archaeologists are still searching for the mines. **(1)**

Section 2
Main Idea: Wangaran miners used dumb bartering to protect their gold. **(1)**
Key Details: 1. Merchants and miners traded without speaking. **(1)**
  2. Miners chose death over betraying the location of the mines. **(1)**
  3. Trade was Ghana's lifeblood, so soldiers protected caravans. **(1)**

Section 3
Main Idea: Trade caravans carried goods through Ghana and beyond. **(1)**
Key Details: 1. Camels were essential for desert travel. **(1)**
  2. Traveling in large groups provided safety and resources. **(1)**
  3. Caravans traveled during the coolest parts of the day. **(1)**

Section 4
Main Idea: Daily life in the city differed from life in small villages. **(1)**
Key Details: 1. City people had expensive belongings and ate exotic food. **(1)**
  2. Eighty percent of people lived in small farming compounds. **(1)**
  3. The whole community was one big extended family. **(1)**

TARGET SKILL

COMPREHENSION: Topic, Main Idea, and Details

❶ Teach

Review topic, main ideas, and supporting details in *The Royal Kingdoms of Ghana, Mali, and Songhay.* Remind students that the headings and text helped them figure out the main ideas and supporting details. Complete the Graphic Organizer on **Transparency 4–19** with students. (Sample answers are shown.) Have students refer to the selection and to **Practice Book** page 3￼

Model identifying main idea and details. Ask students to reread the last paragraph on page 421 as you think aloud.

> **Think Aloud** *A main idea is an important point about the topic. In this cas￼ the topic is Ghana. A main idea is often stated in a sentence. The first sentence of this paragraph says* Men and women shared the workload, each taking responsibility for various chores. *The rest of the sentences give detail￼ about what those chores were. In this paragraph, the main idea seems to be wor￼ that men and women did in a Soninke village.*

❷ Guided Practice

Have students identify main ideas and details. Tell partners to reread the first three paragraphs on page 422. Have them record the main idea and details for each paragraph in a chart lik￼ the one below. When they are finished, discuss their answers.

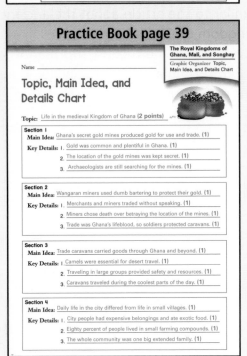

Main Idea and Details on page 422

1. **Main Idea** everyday articles
   Details Men and women shared in making articles that both used; both helped make grinding stones.

2. **Main Idea** village houses
   Details made of sun-dried mud or acacia wood and stone; used for sleeping and storage only

3. **Main Idea** clothing and diet
   Details Farmers wore breeches, tunics, and sandals; women were draped in cloth and wrapped their heads; diet was rice with green peppers, milk, fruit, wild game.

❸ Apply

Assign Practice Book pages 41–42. Also have students apply this skill as they read their **Leveled Readers** for this week. You may also select books from the Leveled Bibliography for this theme (pages 354E–354F).

✔️ **Test Prep** Tell students that whenever there is a nonfiction passage on a test, there will always be questions about topic, main idea, and details. Suggest that as soon as they realize that they are reading a nonfiction passage, they should start looking for these elements.

Leveled Readers and Leveled Practice

Students at all levels apply the comprehension skill as they read their Leveled Readers. See lessons on pages 427O–427R.

● BELOW LEVEL ▲ ON LEVEL ■ ABOVE LEVEL ◆ LANGUAGE SUPPORT

Ancient Baghdad: City at the Crossroads of Trade
by George Capaccio
illustrated by L. R. Galante

Caravan Boy
by Janet Klausner
illustrated by Mou-sien Tseng

The Kingdom of Kush
by Harley Farewell

On the Silk Road: Ancient Bagbdad
by George Capaccio
illustrated by L. R. Galante

Reading Traits

As students develop the ability to identify topic, main idea, and details, they are learning to "read the lines" of a selection. This comprehension skill supports the reading trait **Establishing Comprehension.**

Practice Book page 41

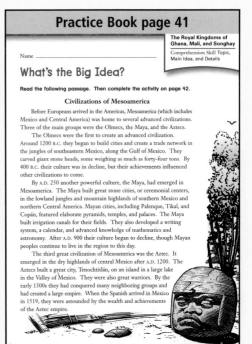

The Royal Kingdoms of Ghana, Mali, and Songhay
Comprehension Skill Topic, Main Idea, and Details

Name _____

What's the Big Idea?

Read the following passage. Then complete the activity on page 42.

Civilizations of Mesoamerica

Before Europeans arrived in the Americas, Mesoamerica (which includes Mexico and Central America) was home to several advanced civilizations. Three of the main groups were the Olmecs, the Maya, and the Aztecs.

The Olmecs were the first to create an advanced civilization. Around 1200 B.C. they began to build cities and create a trade network in the jungles of southeastern Mexico, along the Gulf of Mexico. They carved giant stone heads, some weighing as much as forty-four tons. By 400 B.C. their culture was in decline, but their achievements influenced other civilizations to come.

By A.D. 250 another powerful culture, the Maya, had emerged in Mesoamerica. The Maya built great stone cities, or ceremonial centers, in the lowland jungles and mountain highlands of southern Mexico and northern Central America. Mayan cities, including Palenque, Tikal, and Copán, featured elaborate pyramids, temples, and palaces. The Maya built irrigation canals for their fields. They also developed a writing system, a calendar, and advanced knowledge of mathematics and astronomy. After A.D. 900 their culture began to decline, though Mayan peoples continue to live in the region to this day.

The third great civilization of Mesoamerica was the Aztec. It emerged in the dry highlands of central Mexico after A.D. 1200. The Aztecs built a great city, Tenochtitlán, on an island in a large lake in the Valley of Mexico. They were also great warriors. By the early 1500s they had conquered many neighboring groups and had created a large empire. When the Spanish arrived in Mexico in 1519, they were astounded by the wealth and achievements of the Aztec empire.

Practice Book page 42

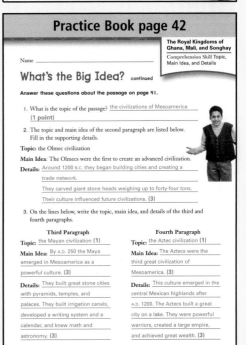

The Royal Kingdoms of Ghana, Mali, and Songhay
Comprehension Skill Topic, Main Idea, and Details

Name _____

What's the Big Idea? continued

Answer these questions about the passage on page 41.

1. What is the topic of the passage? the civilizations of Mesoamerica (1 point)

2. The topic and main idea of the second paragraph are listed below. Fill in the supporting details.

Topic: the Olmec civilization

Main Idea: The Olmecs were the first to create an advanced civilization.

Details: Around 1200 B.C. they began building cities and creating a trade network.

They carved giant stone heads weighing up to forty-four tons.

Their culture influenced future civilizations. (3)

3. On the lines below, write the topic, main idea, and details of the third and fourth paragraphs.

Third Paragraph
Topic: the Mayan civilization (1)

Main Idea: By A.D. 250 the Maya emerged in Mesoamerica as a powerful culture. (3)

Details: They built great stone cities with pyramids, temples, and palaces. They built irrigation canals, developed a writing system and a calendar, and knew math and astronomy. (3)

Fourth Paragraph
Topic: the Aztec civilization (1)

Main Idea: The Aztecs were the third great civilization of Mesoamerica. (3)

Details: This culture emerged in the central Mexican highlands after A.D. 1200. The Aztecs built a great city on a lake. They were powerful warriors, created a large empire, and achieved great wealth. (3)

Monitoring Student Progress

If . . .	Then . . .
students score 13 or below on **Practice Book** page 42,	use the Reteaching lesson on Teacher's Edition page R12.
students have successfully met the lesson objectives,	have them do the Challenge/Extension activities on Teacher's Edition page R13.

STRUCTURAL ANALYSIS

OBJECTIVES

- Read words with unstressed syllables.
- Use the Phonics/Decoding Strategy to decode longer words.
- Learn academic language: *stressed syllables, unstressed syllables.*

Target Skill Trace

Teach	p. 427C
Reteach	p. R18
Review	pp. M34–M35
See	*Handbook for English Language Learners,* p. 155; *Extra Support Handbook,* pp. 150–151; pp. 154–155

Practice Book page 43

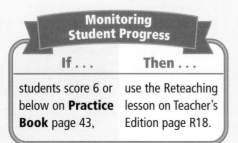

Name _____

The Royal Kingdoms of Ghana, Mali, and Songhay

Structural Analysis
Unstressed Syllables

Recognizing Unstressed Syllables

Read each sentence. Sound out the underlined word several times, placing stress on a different syllable each time. Circle the choice with the correct unstressed and stressed syllables. Unstressed syllables are written in lowercase letters and stressed syllables are written in capital letters.

1. In bartering, the buyer and the seller reach an agreement that is <u>satisfactory</u> to both sides. (1 point)
   SAT•is•fac•to•ry   sat•IS•fac•to•ry   (sat•is•FAC•to•ry)
2. In a caravan, camels are loaded with <u>merchandise</u> and supplies.
   (MER•chan•dise)   mer•CHAN•dise   mer•chan•DISE (1)
3. Royal patrols <u>guaranteed</u> safe passage to all visitors to ancient Ghana.
   GUAR•an•teed   guar•AN•teed   (guar•an•TEED) (1)
4. Smaller towns were <u>surrounded</u> by walls with moats or pits in front of them.
   SUR•round•ed   (sur•ROUND•ed)   sur•round•ED (1)
5. Families in ancient Ghana worked <u>cooperatively</u> on the land.
   CO•op•er•a•tive•ly   (co•OP•er•a•tive•ly)   co•op•er•a•TIVE•ly (1)
6. Village leaders <u>allocated</u> land to each family according to need.
   (AL•lo•cat•ed)   al•LO•cat•ed   al•lo•cat•ED (1)
7. Farmers used dikes and earthen dams for <u>irrigation</u>.
   ir•RI•ga•tion   (ir•ri•GA•tion)   ir•ri•ga•TION (1)
8. The women cooked, ate, worked, and <u>entertained</u> together.
   EN•ter•tained   en•TER•tained   (en•ter•TAINED) (1)

Monitoring Student Progress

If . . .	Then . . .
students score 6 or below on **Practice Book** page 43,	use the Reteaching lesson on Teacher's Edition page R18.

TARGET SKILL

STRUCTURAL ANALYSIS/ VOCABULARY: Unstressed Syllables

❶ Teach

Introduce unstressed syllables. Write *Each party could take their <u>grievance</u> to the local king.*

- Explain that in words with two or more syllables, at least one syllable is stressed, or given more emphasis when spoken, while the other syllable or syllables are unstressed.

- To decode a longer word, suggest that students try emphasizing different syllables.

- Explain that in the word *grievance,* the first syllable is stressed, the second unstressed. The word is *GREE-vuhns,* not *gree-VUHNS.*

Model the Phonics/Decoding Strategy. Write *Miners <u>protected</u> the locations of the mines.* Then model the process of decoding the stressed and unstressed syllables of *protected.*

Think Aloud   *I'll try sounding out this word by emphasizing different syllables:* PRUH-tehk-tihd; pruh-tehk-TIHD; pruh-TEHK-tihd. *My third try sounds like a word I know, and it makes sense in the sentence.*

❷ Guided Practice

Have students identify unstressed syllables. Display the phrases and sentences below. Ask partners to decode the underlined words and figure out their meanings. Have them circle the unstressed syllables in each word and share their work with the class.

inspired a lot of <u>curiosity</u>
miners were <u>secretive</u>
certainly an <u>important</u> city
<u>Ordinary</u> people adorned themselves.

❸ Apply

Assign Practice Book page 43.

PHONICS REVIEW: The /ə/ Sound

OBJECTIVES

- Read words with the schwa sound.
- Apply the Phonics/Decoding Strategy.
- Learn academic language: *schwa sound.*

❶ Teach

Review the /ə/ sound. Tell students that the /ə/ sound is the vowel sound that they hear in many unstressed syllables. Its sound is neither long nor short. Explain these points:

- The letters *a, e, i, o,* and *u* can stand for the schwa sound.
- The letter combinations *ai, eo, ie,* and *ou* can also stand for the schwa sound: *certain, pigeon, patient, jealous.*

Model the Phonics/Decoding Strategy. Write *They possess gold in* <u>abundance</u>. Then model how to decode *abundance.*

Think Aloud *I'll try sounding this word out. It looks as if it might be* ay-BUHN-dans. *That doesn't sound right. I remember that sometimes the letter a can stand for the /ə/ sound. If I try that, I get* uh-BUHN-duhns. *That word means "a large amount." It makes sense here.*

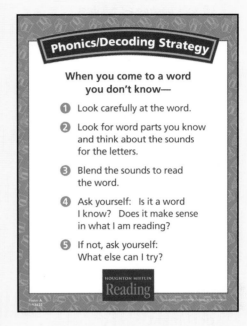

Phonics/Decoding Strategy

When you come to a word you don't know—

❶ Look carefully at the word.

❷ Look for word parts you know and think about the sounds for the letters.

❸ Blend the sounds to read the word.

❹ Ask yourself: Is it a word I know? Does it make sense in what I am reading?

❺ If not, ask yourself: What else can I try?

HOUGHTON MIFFLIN
Reading

❷ Guided Practice

Help students identify the /ə/ sound. Display the sentences below. Have students copy the underlined words and circle the letters that stand for the /ə/ sound in each word. Have them confirm their choice using a dictionary, then pronounce the word and check to see if it makes sense in the sentence. Have students model the correct responses.

1. In attacking the village, the group showed much <u>belligerence</u>.
2. They traded through a <u>system</u> called dumb bartering.
3. Its <u>inhabitants</u> are rich.
4. They <u>possess</u> gold in abundance.

❸ Apply

Have students find words with the /ə/ sound. Ask students to find these words in *The Royal Kingdoms of Ghana, Mali, and Songhay*, decode them, and discuss their meanings.

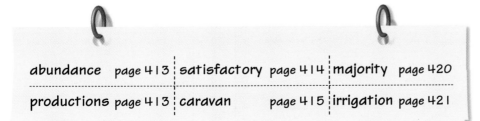

| abundance | page 413 | satisfactory | page 414 | majority | page 420 |
| productions | page 413 | caravan | page 415 | irrigation | page 421 |

SPELLING: Unstressed Syllables

OBJECTIVES

- Write Spelling Words that have unstressed syllables.
- Learn academic language: *stressed syllable, unstressed syllables, schwa sound.*

SPELLING WORDS

Basic

company	crisis
success*	awake
position*	example
problem	ignore
policy	accept*
difficult*	parallel
document	admiral
quality	desire
surprise	garage
physical	ambulance

Review	Challenge
industry	efficient
orphan*	utensil*
president	morale
absent	ethical
attention	potential

Forms of these words appear in the literature.

Extra Support/ Intervention

Basic Word List You may want to use only the left column of Basic Words with students who need extra support.

Challenge

Challenge Word Practice Have students use the Challenge Words to write questions about *The Royal Kingdoms of Ghana, Mali, and Songhay.*

DAY 1 INSTRUCTION

Unstressed Syllables

Pretest Use the Day 5 Test sentences.

Teach Write the words *problem* and *position* on the board.

- Say each word and have students repeat it.
- Draw lines to show the syllabication (*prob | lem, po | si | tion*), and ask the class to identify the stressed syllable in each word. (*problem*— first; *position*—second)
- Point out that the spelling of the vowel sound in unstressed syllables is unclear. Tell students that it is important to pay careful attention to the spelling of any unstressed syllables.
- List the remaining Basic Words. Have students underline the unstressed syllable(s).

Practice/Homework Assign **Practice Book** page 259.

DAY 2 REVIEW & PRACTICE

Reviewing the Principle

Go over unstressed syllables and the schwa sound with students.

Practice/Homework Assign **Practice Book** page 44.

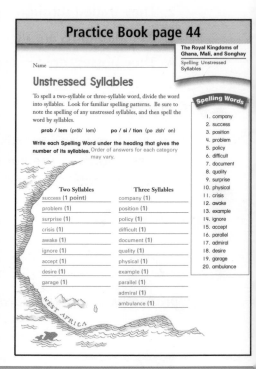

Take-Home Word List

Antonyms

List the Basic Words on the board.

Dictate the following words and ask students to write the Basic Word that is an antonym of each dictated word.

– asleep *(awake)*

– easy *(difficult)*

– failure *(success)*

– refuse *(accept)*

Have students use each Basic Word from the board orally in a sentence. (Sentences will vary.)

Practice/Homework For spelling practice, assign **Practice Book** page 45.

Game: Say "Caravan!"

Have students play as a class or in groups.

- One student in the group is "It" and leaves the room.

- The other players make up a sentence with a spelling word that gives a clue to the word.

- When "It" returns, a player says the sentence but substitutes *caravan* for the spelling word, as in "I 'caravan' your offer of ten dollars," where *caravan* stands for *accept.*

- If "It" guesses the word and spells it correctly, he or she chooses a new "It." If not, that player tries again.

Practice/Homework For proofreading and writing practice, assign **Practice Book** page 46.

Spelling Test

Say each underlined word, read the sentence, and then repeat the word. Have students write only the underlined word.

Basic Words

1. That **company** makes computer games.
2. The **success** of our play thrilled us.
3. Please move the chair to a different **position**.
4. Can you solve the math **problem**?
5. My mother has a strict bedtime **policy**.
6. She played a **difficult** song easily.
7. That **document** is ten pages long.
8. That dress cloth is of fine **quality**.
9. Was the party a **surprise** for the teacher?
10. I am in good **physical** shape from exercising.
11. The house fire caused a financial **crisis**.
12. The baby is sleeping but will **awake** soon.
13. This vase is an **example** of her work.
14. Try to **ignore** his teasing.
15. Please **accept** this gift.
16. She drew **parallel** lines across the chart.
17. The **admiral** led the fleet into the harbor.
18. I **desire** always to be your friend.
19. Is the car in the **garage**?
20. The **ambulance** had a loud siren.

Challenge Words

21. He is an **efficient** teacher.
22. A peeler is a handy kitchen **utensil.**
23. Our **morale** is low this week.
24. Do you think that lying is **ethical**?
25. She is working to her full **potential**.

Practice Book page 45

The Royal Kingdoms of Ghana, Mali, and Songhay

Spelling Spree

Name _____

Phrase Fillers Write the Spelling Word that best completes each phrase.

Spelling Words

1. a government _____ on automobile safety
2. to set a good _____
3. a patient's _____ condition
4. to solve a _____
5. to reach the rank of _____
6. a _____ birthday party
7. a parking _____
8. rushed to the hospital in an _____

1. policy **(1 point)** 5. admiral **(1)**
2. example **(1)** 6. surprise **(1)**
3. physical **(1)** 7. garage **(1)**
4. problem **(1)** 8. ambulance **(1)**

Code Breaker Some Spelling Words have been written in code. Use the code below to figure out each word. Then write the words correctly.

CODE: I S T P W A C D J R H V E L G M Y B
LETTER: a c d e f g i l m n o p q r s t u y

9. GYSSPGG success **(1)** 13. CARHLP ignore **(1)**
10. ISSPVM accept **(1)** 14. VILIDDPD parallel **(1)**
11. TPGCLP desire **(1)** 15. SLCGCG crisis **(1)**
12. VHGCMCHR position **(1)**

1. company
2. success
3. position
4. problem
5. policy
6. difficult
7. document
8. quality
9. surprise
10. physical
11. crisis
12. awake
13. example
14. ignore
15. accept
16. parallel
17. admiral
18. desire
19. garage
20. ambulance

Practice Book page 46

The Royal Kingdoms of Ghana, Mali, and Songhay

Spelling Unstressed Syllables

Proofreading and Writing

Name _____

Proofreading Circle the five misspelled Spelling Words in this travel report. Then write each word correctly.

I write these words because my employers desire a brief *documint* of my recent trading expedition. Our *compeny* of merchants made the desert crossing in good time. We were all *awak* several hours before sunrise each day and did most of our traveling before the sun got too hot. It is a *diffacult* journey, but the sights to be seen at the end of it make it well worthwhile. The cities of the kingdom of Ghana are bustling with many thousands of people. Goods of high *qualty* fill the marketplaces. There are excellent trading opportunities here.

1. document **(1 point)** 4. difficult **(1)**
2. company **(1)** 5. quality **(1)**
3. awake **(1)**

Write a Paragraph of Information From reading the selection, what do you know about daily life in the medieval kingdom of Ghana? What was it like to travel across the desert in a trade caravan?

On a separate piece of paper, write a paragraph about one aspect of life in the Kingdom of Ghana. Use Spelling Words from the list.
Responses will vary. **(5)**

Spelling Words

1. company
2. success
3. position
4. problem
5. policy
6. difficult
7. document
8. quality
9. surprise
10. physical
11. crisis
12. awake
13. example
14. ignore
15. accept
16. parallel
17. admiral
18. desire
19. garage
20. ambulance

- Learn that prefixes and suffixes have entries in the dictionary.
- Use a dictionary to find meanings of words with prefixes and suffixes.
- Learn academic language: *prefixes, suffixes, entry word, base word.*

Target Skill Trace

Teach	p. 427G
Review	pp. M36–M37
Extend	Challenge/Extension Activities, p. R19
See	*Handbook for English Language Learners,* p. 159

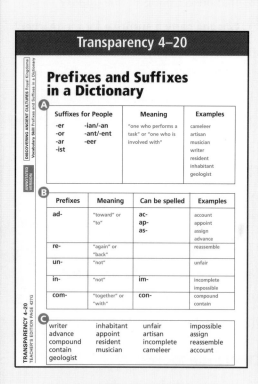

Transparency 4–20

Prefixes and Suffixes in a Dictionary

A

Suffixes for People		Meaning	Examples
-er	-ian/-an	"one who performs a task" or "one who is involved with"	cameleer
-or	-ant/-ent		artisan
-ar	-eer		musician
-ist			writer
			resident
			inhabitant
			geologist

B

Prefixes	Meaning	Can be spelled	Examples
ad-	"toward" or "to"	ac- ap- as-	account appoint assign advance
re-	"again" or "back"		reassemble
un-	"not"		unfair
in-	"not"	im-	incomplete impossible
com-	"together" or "with"	con-	compound contain

C

writer	inhabitant	unfair	impossible
advance	appoint	artisan	assign
compound	resident	incomplete	reassemble
contain	musician	cameleer	account
geologist			

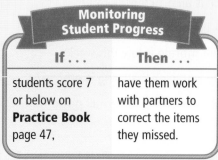

Monitoring Student Progress

If . . .	Then . . .
students score 7 or below on **Practice Book** page 47,	have them work with partners to correct the items they missed.

VOCABULARY: Prefixes and Suffixes in a Dictionary

TARGET SKILL

❶ Teach

Introduce prefixes and suffixes in a dictionary. Dictionaries define prefixes and suffixes. Students can use these definitions to help them understand the meanings of entire words.

- Prefixes and suffixes are listed alphabetically.
- Some prefixes and suffixes may have different spellings.
- A dictionary can show whether a letter pattern *(re)* is a prefix *(reassemble)* or part of the base word *(resident)*.

Display Transparency 4–20. Point out the chart for suffixes Ⓐ, the chart for prefixes Ⓑ, and the list of words at the bottom Ⓒ.

- Help students use a dictionary to find the meaning of the suffixes and summarize these definitions in the second column.
- Have students find the meaning of each prefix.
- Work with students to place each word correctly in the chart.

Model using a suffix to figure out the meaning of a word. Write *Caravan leaders usually hired a full-time cameleer.* Model how to figure out the meaning of *cameleer.*

Think Aloud *I recognize the base word,* camel. *When I look up the suffix -eer in the dictionary, I see it means "someone who is involved with," so a cameleer must be someone who rides or takes care of camels.*

❷ Guided Practice

Give students practice in using prefixes or suffixes. Display these phrases: *some scholars think; archaeologists have found; paternal uncle; returned later.* Have students find the meaning of the prefix or suffix in each underlined word and then figure out the meaning of the word.

❸ Apply

Assign Practice Book page 47.

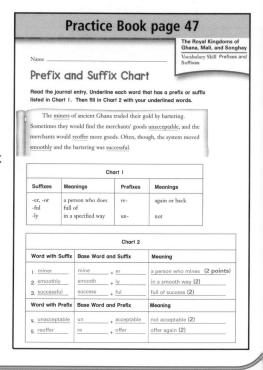

Practice Book page 47

The Royal Kingdoms of Ghana, Mali, and Songhay
Vocabulary Skill Prefixes and Suffixes

Name _____

Prefix and Suffix Chart

Read the journal entry. Underline each word that has a prefix or suffix listed in Chart 1. Then fill in Chart 2 with your underlined words.

The miners of ancient Ghana traded their gold by bartering. Sometimes they would find the merchants' goods unacceptable, and the merchants would reoffer more goods. Often, though, the system moved smoothly and the bartering was successful.

Chart 1

Suffixes	Meanings	Prefixes	Meanings
-er, -or	a person who does	re-	again or back
-ful	full of	un-	not
-ly	in a specified way		

Chart 2

Word with Suffix	Base Word and Suffix		Meaning
1. miner	mine	+ er	a person who mines (2 points)
2. smoothly	smooth	+ ly	in a smooth way (2)
3. successful	success	+ ful	full of success (2)

Word with Prefix	Base Word and Prefix		Meaning
4. unacceptable	un	+ acceptable	not acceptable (2)
5. reoffer	re	+ offer	offer again (2)

STUDY SKILL: Primary and Secondary Sources

OBJECTIVES

- Distinguish between primary and secondary sources.
- Compare and evaluate information from a variety of primary and secondary sources.
- Learn academic language: *primary source, secondary source.*

❶ Teach

Introduce primary sources.

- A primary source is an account of a period or event in history by someone who was there.
- Primary sources may include books, letters, diary entries, newspaper articles, advertisements, and speeches.

Introduce secondary sources.

- A secondary source is an article or book written about a time period or event by someone who was not there.
- Authors of secondary sources get some of their information from primary sources and some from other secondary sources.
- Secondary sources provide summaries and overviews of historical events.

Model comparing and evaluating sources.

Think Aloud *On page 413, I read al-Idrisi's words. Al-Idrisi is a primary source; he saw the townspeople with his own eyes and thought they were all rich. However, I know that as a witness, al-Idrisi's view is limited. A secondary source like the McKissacks' book gives me information taken from many different sources. I learn that most people in Ghana were not wealthy.*

❷ Practice/Apply

Give students practice in comparing and evaluating sources.

- Work with students to create a chart like the one below.
- Have students find a primary and a secondary source about an event related to African history and fill out a similar chart.

Source	Primary or Secondary?	Information
introduction to the selection, p. 412	secondary	Ghana's gold trade
poem, p. 423	primary	Soninke values
"Daily Life in Ancient Greece," pp. 426–427	secondary	how ancient Greeks lived

GRAMMAR: Adverbs

OBJECTIVES

- Identify adverbs that modify verbs and adjectives.
- Write comparative and superlative forms.
- Proofread and correct sentences with grammar and spelling errors.
- Use adjectives and adverbs correctly to improve writing.
- Learn academic language: *adverb, modify, comparative form, superlative form.*

DAY 1 — INSTRUCTION

Kinds of Adverbs

Teach Go over the following:

– An adverb can modify a verb. It tells *how, where, when,* or *to what extent.*

– An adverb can modify an adjective. It tells *how* or *to what extent.*

- Display the example sentences at the top of **Transparency 4–22.** Point out the verb *plodded;* tell students that *slowly* is an adverb that tells *how* the camels *plodded.*

- Identify the adjective *rich;* explain that *very* is an adverb that tells *how* or *to what extent* about *rich.*

- Ask volunteers to underline the adverbs in Sentences 1–8. Have them write either *verb* or *adjective* to indicate which one the adverb modifies, and the verb or adjective modified.

Daily Language Practice
Have students correct Sentences 1 and 2 on **Transparency 4–21.**

DAY 2 — PRACTICE

Independent Work

Practice/Homework Assign **Practice Book** page 48.

Daily Language Practice
Have students correct Sentences 3 and 4 on **Transparency 4–21.**

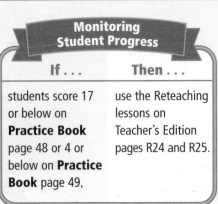

Transparency 4–21

Daily Language Practice

Correct two sentences each day.

1. The ambulince raced quick to the hospital.
   The ambulance raced quickly to the hospital.

2. We always have our car repaired at henderson's Gareage.
   We always have our car repaired at Henderson's Garage.

3. My dogs awack more frequent than I do at night.
   My dogs awake more frequently than I do at night.

4. The school's policey on tardiness is enforced strict.
   The school's policy on tardiness is enforced strictly.

5. This problim was solved more faster than the one last week.
   This problem was solved faster than the one last week.

6. Admiril jones will receive an award today.
   Admiral Jones will receive an award today.

7. The historical document were very interesting to read.
   The historical document was very interesting to read.
   Or
   The historical documents were very interesting to read.

8. Please don't ignour the rules, peter.
   Please don't ignore the rules, Peter.

9. This summer I'm going to work for the johnson Paint Compiny.
   This summer I'm going to work for the Johnson Paint Company.

10. I am proud of my brothers sucess at chess competitions.
    I am proud of my brother's success at chess competitions.

Monitoring Student Progress

If . . .	Then . . .
students score 17 or below on **Practice Book** page 48 or 4 or below on **Practice Book** page 49,	use the Reteaching lessons on Teacher's Edition pages R24 and R25.

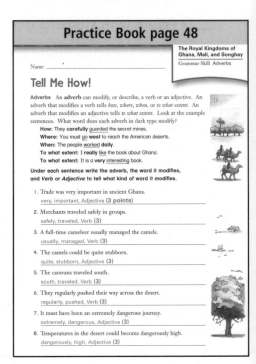

Transparency 4–22

Adverbs that Modify Verbs and Adjectives

Camels carrying trade goods slowly plodded across the desert. Mineral deposits helped ancient Ghana become a very rich kingdom.

1. Camels can be extremely stubborn.   adjective, stubborn

2. They drink thirstily at each oasis.   verb, drink

3. Desert temperatures are too extreme for horses.
   adjective, extreme

4. Temperatures fall rapidly after sunset.   verb, fall

5. They rise steadily after dawn.   verb, rise

6. A camel ride can be a rather uncomfortable experience.
   adjective, uncomfortable

7. We rode north in a camel caravan.   verb, rode

8. Later we returned to camp.   verb, returned

Practice Book page 48

The Royal Kingdoms of Ghana, Mali, and Songhay
Grammar Skill Adverbs

Name _____

Tell Me How!

Adverbs An **adverb** can modify, or describe, a verb or an adjective. An adverb that modifies a verb tells *how, where, when,* or *to what extent.* An adverb that modifies an adjective tells *to what extent.* Look at the example sentences. What word does each adverb in dark type modify?

How: They **carefully** guarded the secret mines.
Where: You must go **west** to reach the American deserts.
When: The people worked **daily**.
To what extent: I really like the book about Ghana.
To what extent: It is a **very** interesting book.

Under each sentence write the adverb, the word it modifies, and *Verb* or *Adjective* to tell what kind of word it modifies.

1. Trade was very important in ancient Ghana.
   very, important, Adjective (3 points)

2. Merchants traveled safely in groups.
   safely, traveled, Verb (3)

3. A full-time cameleer usually managed the camels.
   usually, managed, Verb (3)

4. The camels could be quite stubborn.
   quite, stubborn, Adjective (3)

5. The caravans traveled south.
   south, traveled, Verb (3)

6. They regularly pushed their way across the desert.
   regularly, pushed, Verb (3)

7. It must have been an extremely dangerous journey.
   extremely, dangerous, Adjective (3)

8. Temperatures in the desert could become dangerously high.
   dangerously, high, Adjective (3)

DAY 3 INSTRUCTION

Comparing with Adverbs

Teach Go over these rules:

– Add *-er* to form the comparative and *-est* to form the superlative of many adverbs.

– Use *more* to form the comparative and *most* to form the superlative of most adverbs ending in *-ly.*

Display the sentences at the top of **Transparency 4–23.** Tell students that *fast* is an adverb modifying the verb *fly.* Point out the comparative ending *-er* and the superlative ending *-est.* Then point out the comparative and superlative forms of *frequently,* formed with *more* and *most.*

Ask volunteers to write the correct comparative or superlative form of each adverb in parentheses in Sentences 1–6.

Daily Language Practice
Have students correct Sentences 5 and 6 on **Transparency 4–21.**

Transparency 4–23

Comparing with Adverbs

Hummingbirds fly <u>fast</u>.
Loons fly <u>faster</u>.
Peregrine falcons fly <u>fastest</u> of all.
Sparrows flap their wings <u>more frequently</u> than cuckoos.
Tiny hummingbirds flap their wings <u>most frequently</u> of all.

1. The mother lion rests (long) _____longer_____ than her cubs.

2. The big lion rests the (long) _____longest_____ of all.

3. These lion cubs wrestle (playfully) ____more playfully____ than the ones we saw last week.

4. The cubs near the lake wrestle the (playfully) ____most playfully____ of all.

5. The new park ranger works the (slow) ____slowest____ of all the rangers.

6. She worked (slow) ____slower____ last week than she did this week.

TRANSPARENCY 4–23
TEACHER'S EDITION PAGE 427J
DISCOVERING ANCIENT CULTURES Royal Kingdoms
Grammar Skill Comparing with Adverbs
ANNOTATED VERSION

DAY 4 PRACTICE

Independent Work

Practice/Homework Assign **Practice Book** page 49.

Daily Language Practice
Have students correct Sentences 7 and 8 on **Transparency 4–21.**

Practice Book page 49

The Royal Kingdoms of Ghana, Mali, and Songhay
Grammar Skill Comparing with Adverbs

Name _____

Time to Compare

Comparing with Adverbs Like adjectives, **adverbs** can be used to make comparisons. Use the **comparative** form (*-er*) to compare two things. Use the **superlative** form (*-est*) to compare three or more. Use *more* or *most* with adverbs that end with *-ly.*

Comparative	Superlative
Andrea digs **faster** than Mike.	Tony digs **fastest** of all.
Brian swims **more quickly** than you.	He swims **most quickly** of us all.

Some adverbs have completely different forms of comparison. Study the chart.

Adverb	Comparative	Superlative
well	better	best
badly	worse	worst
little	less	least
much	more	most

Write the comparative or superlative form of the adverb in parentheses ( ) to complete each sentence correctly.

1. I wonder ____more frequently (1 point)____ about the past than I do about the future. (frequently)

2. I'm going to work ____harder (1)____ on my history lesson this week than I did last week. (hard)

3. The archaeologist was the ____most (1)____ interesting speaker of all at the assembly. (much)

4. I was ____less (1)____ interested in the historian's speech than in hers. (little)

5. She went ____deepest (1)____ of all into details about working in the field. (deep)

6. I may think ____more seriously (1)____ now about studying archaeology than before. (seriously)

DAY 5 IMPROVING WRITING

Adjective or Adverb?

Teach Tell students that a good writer uses adverbs, not adjectives, to tell *how much* or *to what extent* about adjectives.

• Model correcting a sentence in which an adjective was used where an adverb should have been used:

– We had a terrible rough ride in the truck.

– *Corrected:* We had a <u>terribly</u> rough ride in the truck.

• Have students proofread a piece of their writing for correct use of adjectives and adverbs.

Practice/Homework Assign **Practice Book** page 50.

Daily Language Practice
Have students correct Sentences 9 and 10 on **Transparency 4–21.**

Practice Book page 50

The Royal Kingdoms of Ghana, Mali, and Songhay
Grammar Skill Adjective or Adverb?

Name _____

Adverbs at Work!

Adjective or Adverb? Good writers are careful to use adverbs, not adjectives, to tell *how much* or *to what extent* about adjectives. Review the examples below.

Incorrect: She plays **real** well.
Correct: She plays **really** well.

Incorrect: The stew was **extreme** delicious.
Correct: The stew was **extremely** delicious.

Brigitte has written a play about an imaginary medieval kingdom. Here is part of the script. Proofread it to change adjectives to adverbs where necessary. Write the correct word above each mistake.

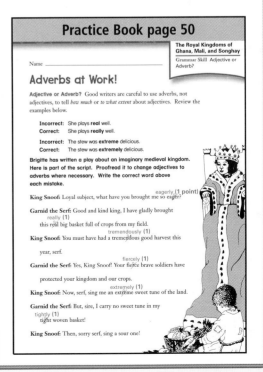

                                                            eagerly (1 point)
King Snoof: Loyal subject, what have you brought me so eager?

Garnid the Serf: Good and kind king, I have gladly brought
                  really (1)
this royal big basket full of crops from my field.

                                           tremendously (1)
King Snoof: You must have had a tremendous good harvest this

year, serf.
                                           fiercely (1)
Garnid the Serf: Yes, King Snoof! Your fierce brave soldiers have

protected your kingdom and our crops.
                                           extremely (1)
King Snoof: Now, serf, sing me an extreme sweet tune of the land.

Garnid the Serf: But, sire, I carry no sweet tune in my
tightly (1)
tight woven basket!

King Snoof: Then, sorry serf, sing a sour one!

WRITING: Comparison-and-Contrast Paragraph

OBJECTIVES

- Identify characteristics of a good comparison-and-contrast paragraph.
- Write a comparison-and-contrast paragraph.
- Combine sentences with adjectives.
- Learn academic language: *comparison-and-contrast paragraph*.

Writing Traits

Sentence Fluency As you teach the lesson on Day 3, remind students that combining sentences will help make their writing sound smoother. Offer these tips:

- Include both long and short sentences.
- Cut out any words that are unnecessary.
- Vary the way sentences begin.

DAY 1 PREWRITING

Introducing the Format

Define a comparison-and-contrast paragraph.

- Comparing means showing how things are alike.
- Contrasting means showing how things are different.
- A comparison-and-contrast paragraph explains how two people, places, or things are both alike and different.

Start students thinking about writing a comparison-and-contrast paragraph.

- Ask students to think about travel today and travel at the time of ancient Ghana.
- Have them list differences between the travel then and now. (Sample answers: camel caravans then; trucks and cars now)
- Have them list ways the two kinds of travel are alike. (Sample answers: Both follow routes; both use rest stops.)
- Have them save their notes.

DAY 2 DRAFTING

Discussing the Model

Display Transparency 4–24. Ask:

- What is the topic of the paragraph? (eastern and western parts of Great Wall)
- Which details compare the two parts? (Both portions keep out Mongol invaders; both built by soldiers, peasants, criminals.)
- Which details contrast the two parts? (western part built from pounded earth; eastern part built of bricks and stone blocks)
- Which does the writer tell first—similarities or differences? (similarities) Which does the writer tell second? (differences)
- What clue words does the writer use? (Sample answers: *Both, As a result*)

Display Transparency 4–25, and discuss the guidelines.

Have students draft a comparison-and-contrast paragraph.

- Have them use their notes from Day 1.
- Assign **Practice Book** page 51 to help students organize their writing.
- Provide support as needed.

Transparency 4–24

A Compare/Contrast Paragraph

Eastern Parts of Great Wall
- built of bricks and blocks of stone
- more durable
- more complicated to build
- skilled stonemasons and brickmasons needed

Both
- built to keep out Mongol invaders
- became part of a continuous Great Wall
- built by criminals, soldiers, and peasants

Western Parts of Great Wall
- built from pounded earth
- simple to build but needed constant repair
- skilled craftsmen not needed
- less durable

The eastern and western parts of China's Great Wall were alike in some ways. Both portions of the wall were built to fend off the Mongol invaders. Also, criminals, peasants, and soldiers were required to work on both parts of the wall. The two portions of the wall were different in some ways too. The western parts of the wall were built mostly from pounded earth. Walls built of pounded earth did not endure weather very well, and often needed repair. Skilled laborers were not needed to build or repair this part of the wall. On the other hand, most of the eastern parts of the wall were built from brick or stone, and were more complicated. The skilled labor of stonemasons and brickmasons was required. As a result, these portions of the wall were more durable than the pounded earth sections.

Transparency 4–25

Guidelines for Writing a Comparison-and-Contrast Paragraph

- Choose two subjects that you can compare and contrast easily.
- Create a Venn diagram to list the likenesses and differences.
- In the topic sentence, clearly state the two subjects that you will compare and contrast.
- Tell details that compare and details that contrast in supporting sentences.
- Group details that compare and details that contrast in a clear manner.
- Use clue words and phrases to help the reader identify likenesses and differences: *on the one hand, on the other hand, both*.

Practice Book page 51

The Royal Kingdoms of Ghana, Mali, and Songhay
Writing Skill A Comparison and Contrast Paragraph

Name _____

Writing a Comparison and Contrast Paragraph

In *The Royal Kingdoms of Ghana, Mali, and Songhay*, the authors compare and contrast the roles played by men and women in Soninke village life. For example, both men and women made baskets and pots, but men served in the military while women harvested and processed crops. One way to explore how things are alike and different is by writing a **comparison and contrast paragraph**. Comparing shows how things are alike, and contrasting shows how they are different.

Use the Venn diagram to help you compare and contrast travel in the days of the camel caravans with travel in modern times.

Travel Then (3 points) — Both (3) — Travel Now (3)

On a separate sheet of paper, write a compare-contrast paragraph about travel today and travel in ancient North Africa. In the opening sentence, clearly state the subject being compared and contrasted. In the supporting sentences, group details that compare and details that contrast in a clear manner. Use clue words such as *both* or *likewise* to help readers identify likenesses, and *on the other hand* or *only* to help them identify differences. (3)

DAY 3 · REVISING

Improving Writing: Combining Sentences

Explain combining sentences with adjectives.

Two or more short, choppy sentences may be combined into one smooth sentence.

Writers often combine sentences with repeated adjectives.

Display Transparency 4–26.

Read aloud Example 1. Have students identify the repeated adjective. (*famous*)

Read aloud Example 2. Discuss how the writing is clearer and more streamlined.

Repeat with Examples 3 and 4.

Have students complete the transparency.

Assign Practice Book page 52.

Have students revise their drafts.

Display **Transparency 4–25** again. Have students use it to revise their paragraphs.

Have partners hold writing conferences.

Ask students to revise any parts of their paragraphs that still need work. Have them look for places to combine sentences.

See Writing Traits on page 427K.

DAY 4 · PROOFREADING

Checking for Errors

Have students proofread for errors in grammar, spelling, punctuation, and usage.

- Students can use the proofreading checklist on **Practice Book** page 273 to help them proofread their comparison-and-contrast paragraphs.

- Students can also use the chart of proofreading marks on **Practice Book** page 274.

DAY 5 · PUBLISHING

Sharing Comparison-and-Contrast Paragraphs

Consider these publishing options.

- Ask students to read their comparison-and-contrast paragraphs or some other piece of writing from the Author's Chair.

- Display students' comparison-and-contrast paragraphs in the classroom or in a class book.

Portfolio Opportunity

Save students' comparison-and-contrast paragraphs as samples of their writing development.

Transparency 4–26

Combining Sentences with Adjectives

Example 1
Wangara had many famous fortresses. It also had gold mines and towns that were also famous.

Example 2
Wangara had many famous fortresses, gold mines, and towns.

Example 3
The Wangaran miners used a special way of trading. It was a silent way of trading.

Example 4
The Wangaran miners used a special, silent way of trading.

Practice:
1. The trip across the desert was long. It was hot. It was difficult. It was dry.

   Answers will vary.

2. The camels were stubborn. The donkeys were stubborn too.

   Answers will vary.

TRANSPARENCY 4–26
TEACHER'S EDITION PAGE 427L

DISCOVERING ANCIENT CULTURES Royal Kingdoms
Writing Skill Improving Your Writing
ANNOTATED VERSION

Practice Book page 52

Name _____

The Royal Kingdoms of Ghana Mali, and Songhay
Writing Skill Improving Your Writing

Combining Sentences with Adjectives

Adjectives describe nouns and pronouns. You can improve your writing by combining repetitive adjectives into a single sentence.

   Ancient Ghanaians had **golden** jewelry. They also had **golden** thread.
   Ancient Ghanaians had **golden** jewelry and thread.

You can also combine several short, choppy sentences with different adjectives into a list of adjectives in one sentence.

   The journey was **long**. The trip was **difficult**, too. It was often **dangerous**.
   The journey across the Sahara was **long**, **difficult**, and **dangerous**.

Revise this paragraph. Combine repetitive adjectives into a single sentence, or combine several short, choppy sentences with different adjectives into a list of adjectives in one sentence.

Men and women played important roles in Soninke village life. Working together, Soninke men and women shared essential tasks. They did daily chores that were essential, too. For example, both made useful baskets. Men and women made pots and utensils that were useful as well. On the other hand, men and women had separate responsibilities. The men hunted, farmed, and served in the military. They used iron to make tools and weapons that were strong. The tools and weapons were durable. They were sharp. The women in the village cooked plain meals. Their dishes were also nutritious.

Men and women played important roles in Soninke village life.
Working together, Soninke men and women shared essential tasks and daily chores. For example, both made useful baskets, pots, and utensils. On the other hand, men and women had separate responsibilities. The men hunted, farmed, and served in the military. They used iron to make tools and weapons that were strong, durable, and sharp. The women in the village cooked plain and nutritious meals.

Monitoring Student Progress

If . . .	Then . . .
students' writing does not follow the guidelines on **Transparency 4–25,**	work with students to improve specific parts of their writing.

Independent Activities

Language Center

VOCABULARY

Words for Leaders

👥 Pairs	🕐 30 minutes
Objective	Find the origins of names for heads of state.
Materials	Activity Master 4-3, 2 copies; dictionary; reference sources

The civilizations discussed in *The Royal Kingdoms of Ghana, Mali, and Songhay* were led by kings. Throughout history, the leaders of countries with different types of governments have had special names.

- Use a dictionary or other reference sources to find the origins of the names for heads of state on Activity Master 4-3.

- Add to the list any other names for heads of state you know.

- Compare your results with your partner's. See who finds the most names and word origins.

GRAMMAR

Adverbs in Fine Form

👤 Singles	🕐 30 minutes
Objective	Identify adverb forms.

A young Ghanaian in a farming village is writing to her city cousin.

- Read the letter.

- Copy the adverbs onto a sheet of paper, labeling each *regular*, *comparative*, or *superlative*.

Dear Cousin,
I would have written you sooner than this, but our work load has been very heavy as we prepare to plant our crops. We must plant them more quickly than we did last year, because the rainy season has started earlier this year. We work hardest during planting season and harvest time. I prefer the harvest, however, because then we feast more grandly than at any other time of year. You must write more often to me!
Love,
Your Village Cousin

VOCABULARY

Vocabulary Game

👥 Pairs	🕐 30 minutes
Objective	Write a story using the Key Vocabulary words.

With a partner, create a story using all of the Key Vocabulary words. Follow these steps.

- One partner begins the story by writing until he or she uses one of the Key Vocabulary words.

- The other partner then writes a continuation of the story, until he or she has used a different Key Vocabulary word.

- Take turns adding story parts, until you have used all the words.

- Try to shape the story so that it has a beginning, middle, and end.

A long caravan was making its way through the Sahara desert.

It was heading for the nearest oasis.

Consider copying and laminating these activities for use in centers.

LISTENING/SPEAKING

Comparing Forms of Information

👥 Pairs	🕐 30 minutes
Objective	Compare and contrast forms of information.
Materials	Activity Master 4-4, 2 copies

Look again at "The Rise of Ghana" (pages 408–409) and "Daily Life in Ancient Greece" (pages 426–427). These articles present information in several ways: text, subheadings, photographs, an illustrated diagram, a timeline, a map, and short and long captions. Work individually, each partner taking a different article, to complete copies of Activity Master 4–4. Answer these questions.

- In what form is the information presented?
- What is the subject matter of the information?
- What is the purpose of the information?

When both of you have filled out your activity master, compare the results. What is similar and what is different about the presentation of information in the two articles?

Form of Information	Subject Matter	Purpose
Text	typical homes and clothes of ancient Greece	to give readers information about certain aspects of daily life in ancient Greece

PHONICS/SPELLING

Words in Hiding

👤 Singles	🕐 30 minutes
Objective	Find and write hidden Spelling Words.

Find the word *manner* hidden in this sentence: *Big dogs make that man nervous.* (Hint: The letters of *manner* are shared between the word *man* and the first three letters of *nervous.*) Now read the following sentences and find the Spelling Word hidden in each one. If necessary, check the Spelling Words on page 259 of your Practice Book.

1. Rebecca, wake your sister!

2. Your ride, sire, is waiting outside.

3. That animal is neither pig nor elephant.

4. A beggar ages faster than a prosperous person.

5. When the sailor saw land from the top of the spar, all else left his mind.

Now write an original sentence for each of the Spelling Words you identified above.

Words in Hiding
1. awake—Rebecca, **wake**
2. desire—**ride**, **sire**
3. ignore—**pig nor** elephant
4. garage— **beggar ages**
5. parallel— **spar, all else**

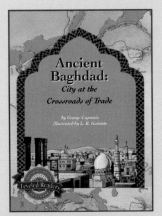

Ancient Baghdad: City at the Crossroads of Trade

Summary This selection tells of the city that was planned and founded in A.D. 762 by Mansur, an Arab king. Situated strategically between the Tigris and Euphrates rivers, Baghdad became a major medieval trading center. Both goods and ideas were exchanged with Asia, Africa, and Europe, both by sea and along the Silk Road and the Incense Road. Mongols destroyed the city in 1258, but it has risen again.

Vocabulary

Introduce the Key Vocabulary and ask students to complete the BLM.

boom a sudden increase in business, *p. 7*

glittering sparkling with light, *p. 7*

exchanged traded one thing for another, *p. 7*

restore bring back to original condition, *p. 11*

sturdier more strongly made or built, *p. 20*

● BELOW LEVEL

Building Background and Vocabulary

Have students share what they know about the Middle East and the city of Baghdad. Tell students that in ancient times, caravans, or groups of traders, followed specific trade routes. Guide students through the text, using some of the vocabulary from the story.

Comprehension Skill: Topic, Main Idea, and Details

Have students read the Strategy Focus on the book flap. Remind students to use the strategy and to think about the topic, main idea, and details as they read the book. (See the Leveled Readers Teacher's Guide for **Vocabulary and Comprehension Practice Masters.**)

Responding

Have partners discuss how to answer the questions on the inside back cover.

Think About the Selection Sample answers:

1. It was built on the Tigris and Euphrates rivers, and boats could sail up and down the rivers, carrying goods.
2. They involved many people and sometimes even thousands of animals.
3. The ships were very sturdy. The sails were shaped like triangles.
4. Answers will vary.

Making Connections Answers will vary.

Building Fluency

Model Point out to students that the heading on page 3 explains what will happen in the following paragraphs.

Practice Within small groups, have one student read aloud a section heading and the paragraphs that follow. Have another student explain why the heading is appropriate.

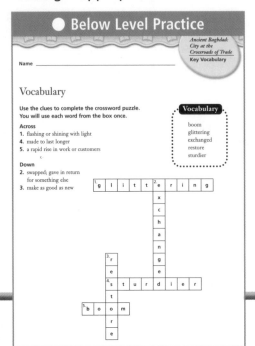

Leveled Readers

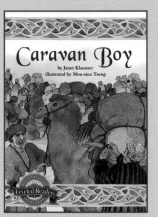

Caravan Boy

Summary *Jamal and Ramzi are animal tenders for the merchant Talib. They are part of a large camel caravan traveling to Herat in Afghanistan, where Talib will trade his goods for the exotic items of the East. When the caravan is attacked, Jamal saves the day and becomes a hero to all, even the gruff Talib.*

Vocabulary

Introduce the Key Vocabulary and ask students to complete the BLM.

fierce hostile, warlike, *p. 5*

caravan* file of vehicles or pack animals traveling together, *p. 6*

threaten intend to hurt, *p. 6*

ruthless cruel, merciless, *p. 7*

laden loaded down, *p. 12*

barter* trade goods without exchanging money, *p. 12*

bazaar marketplace, *p. 12*

obligingly in an accommodating way, *p. 23*

*Forms of these words are Anthology Key Vocabulary words.

Building Background and Vocabulary

Explain that the Silk Road was a very important route connecting Europe and the East. Have students share what they know about caravans. Guide students through the text, using some of the vocabulary from the story.

Comprehension Skill: Topic, Main Idea, and Details

Have students read the Strategy Focus on the book flap. Remind students to use the strategy and to think about the topic, main idea, and details as they read the book. (See the Leveled Readers Teacher's Guide for **Vocabulary and Comprehension Practice Masters.**)

Responding

Have partners discuss how to answer the questions on the inside back cover.

Think About the Selection Sample answers:

1. He's afraid that bandits may attack the caravan.
2. Example: He's responsible for taking care of three camels. He must load and unload them every time the caravan starts and stops.
3. Example: He is proud of himself. Yes, he should be proud, because he was brave.
4. Answers will vary.

Making Connections Answers will vary.

Building Fluency

Model Point out that the word *narrow* on page 4 is hyphenated because it starts on one line and is continued on the next. Explain that a word can be broken up over two lines if it does not fit on one line. Demonstrate that it should be read as one word.

Practice Have students find other examples of words broken up over two lines (pages 5, 9, 12). Ask them to read the divided word as one word, without pausing for the hyphen.

▲ On Level Practice

Caravan Boy
Key Vocabulary

Name _____

Vocabulary

Choose the word from the box that best completes each sentence. Write it on the line.

Vocabulary
bazaar
barter
caravan
fierce
laden
obligingly
ruthless
threaten

1. Ramzi told Jamal about __fierce__ bandits who waited in the mountains to attack the caravans.
2. The camels were heavily __laden__ with olives, oil, and other goods from the Middle East and Europe.
3. Because the route passed through dangerous regions, the traders traveled together in a __caravan__.
4. The bandits were __ruthless__ and showed no mercy toward their captives.
5. Before money was invented, merchants exchanged goods in a system of __barter__.
6. Anxious to please his master, Jamal __obligingly__ baked fresh bread in the morning.
7. The __bazaar__ was a busy place where merchants traded goods and exchanged bits of gossip.
8. Ramzi thought that bandits would not dare to __threaten__ the caravan, but he was wrong.

▲ On Level Practice

Caravan Boy
Comprehension Skill
Topic, Main Idea, and Details

Name _____

Comprehension

Answer the following, using information in the story *Caravan Boy* and your completed Graphic Organizer.

1. What is the main idea on pages 23–24?

Sample answer: Jamal is busy but satisfied at the end of the day.

2. List three details that support that main idea.

Sample answers: Jamal and Ramzi unload their animals and feed and water them; Jamal recites his prayers; he replays his adventure in his mind and falls asleep.

3. Here are some details. Read them and select the main idea to which they relate.
Detail 1: Jamal knew that this day and the days to come would be hard on his shoes.
Detail 2: He knew the trail through the mountains would be steep and stony and narrow.
Detail 3: Though it was only autumn, the morning held a pinch of winter.
Main idea: Possible answer: Jamal recognizes that cold weather and the mountains will make the days to come difficult.

4. Here is a main idea. Review the story and select three details that support it.
Main idea: Jamal went through the routine of loading and unloading the stubborn camel every day.
Detail 1: Possible answer: He tugged at the rope around the camel's neck and spoke firmly.
Detail 2: Possible answer: He placed a heavy woolen blanket over the camel's hump.
Detail 3: Possible answer: He had to remove several bags of merchandise before the camel would stand up.

The Kingdom of Kush

Summary *Scientists have determined that the kingdom of Kush came to an end after years of environmental abuse made the country vulnerable to enemies.*

Vocabulary

Introduce the Key Vocabulary and ask students to complete the BLM.

sophisticated complex, *p. 6*

irrigating watering farmlands by artificial means, *p. 12*

flourished* grew well, *p. 12*

caravans* files of vehicles or pack animals traveling together, *p. 14*

foundries places where metal is molded, *p. 16*

renowned honored, *p. 16*

ornate decorated, *p. 17*

apprenticeship time of learning under a master, *p. 21*

affiliation association, *p. 22*

prosperity financial success, well-being, *p. 23*

*Forms of these words are Anthology Key Vocabulary words.

■ ABOVE LEVEL

Building Background and Vocabulary

Have students share what they know about ancient cultures. Explain that although Kush's neighbor, ancient Egypt, is better known, Kush had a rich and interesting culture of its own. Guide students through the text, using some of the vocabulary from the story.

Comprehension Skill: Topic, Main Idea, and Details

Have students read the Strategy Focus on the book flap. Remind students to use the strategy and to think about the topic, main idea, and details as they read the book. (See the Leveled Readers Teacher's Guide for **Vocabulary and Comprehension Practice Masters.**)

Responding

Have partners discuss how to answer the questions on the inside back cover.

Think About the Selection   Sample answers:

1. Kush was more geographically isolated than Egypt.
2. Its climate was good for farming, and there was plenty of wild game. The land was also rich in iron ore.
3. They were master archers, potters, and ironworkers.
4. Answers will vary.

Making Connections   Answers will vary.

Building Fluency

Model   Read aloud the word *Arnekhamani* on page 10. Explain how to use the pronunciation guide that follows the word.

Practice   Ask small groups to read aloud other words in the story that have pronunciation guides (pages 12, 15, 18). Have them repeat the words until they are able to say them with fluency.

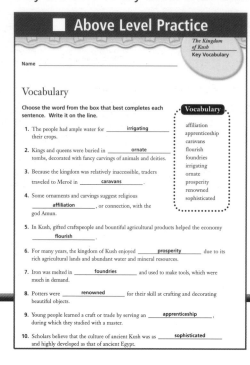

Leveled Readers

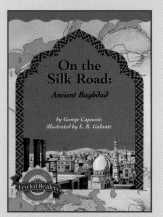

On the Silk Road: Ancient Baghdad

Summary *Built in A.D. 762, Baghdad became the capital of the Arab Empire and the center of trade linking China, India, Central Asia, Africa, Egypt, and Europe. Using land and water routes, the traders of Baghdad exchanged goods and ideas across continents.*

Vocabulary

Introduce the Key Vocabulary and ask students to complete the BLM.

ports towns or cities that have harbors for loading or unloading ships, *p. 3*

traded exchanged one thing for another, *p. 7*

magnificent grand, remarkable, or splendid, *p. 7*

caravans* files of vehicles or pack animals traveling together, *p. 8*

route a road between two places, *p. 12*

incense a substance that is burned to produce a pleasant odor, *p. 15*

*Forms of these words are Anthology Key Vocabulary words.

◆ LANGUAGE SUPPORT

Building Background and Vocabulary

Help students locate Baghdad on a world map. Point out Baghdad's location in relation to China and to Europe. Explain that the city was built in the eighth century and discuss how people might have traveled at that time and place. Distribute the **Build Background Practice Master** and have students complete it in pairs.

Comprehension Skill: Topic, Main Ideas, and Details

Have students read the Strategy Focus on the book flap. Remind students to use the strategy and to look for main ideas and details about the book's topic as they read. (See the Leveled Readers Teacher's Guide for **Build Background, Vocabulary, and Graphic Organizer Masters.**)

Responding

Have partners discuss how to answer the questions on the inside back cover.

Think About the Selection Sample answers:

1. It was a trade route between Chinese cities and Mediterranean ports. Silk was brought from China by caravan.
2. It was between two major rivers; there were seaports to the north and south.
3. Caravans involved many people and animals, and they traveled long distances.
4. Answers will vary.

Making Connections Answers will vary.

Building Fluency

Model Have students follow along in their books as they listen to the recording of page 11 on the audio CD.

Practice Have students read aloud with the recording until they are able to read the text on their own accurately and with expression.

Connecting and Comparing Literature

Check Your Progress

Use these Paired Selections to help students make connections with other theme literature and to wrap up the theme.

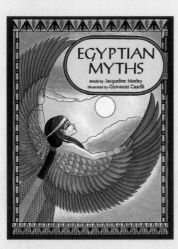

The Lord of the Nile
Genre: Fiction

The pharaoh Zoser and his architect, Imhotep, build a temple to honor the god Khnemu. The god then floods the Nile River to relieve a disastrous drought.

The Great Pyramid
Genre: Nonfiction

Thousands of skilled Egyptian workers build a towering pyramid in Giza to honor their pharaoh Khufu.

Preparing for Tests

Taking Tests: Strategies

Use this material to prepare for tests, to teach strategies, and to practice test formats.

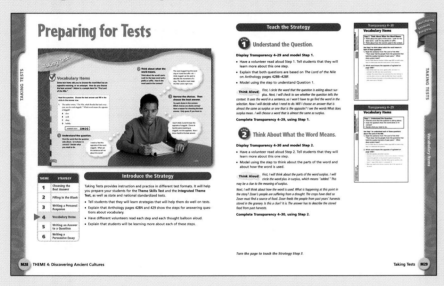

Skill Review

Use these lessons and supporting activities to review tested skills in this theme.

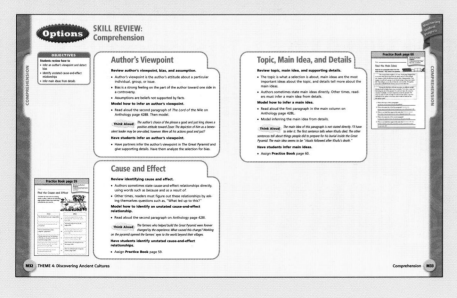

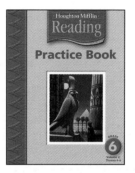

- Independent practice for skills, Level 6.4

- Transparencies
- Strategy Posters
- Blackline Masters

Technology

Audio Selections
The Lord of the Nile

The Great Pyramid

www.eduplace.com
Log on to Education Place for vocabulary support—
e•Glossary
e•WordGame

Theme Connections

Anthology Literature

Activities to help students think critically

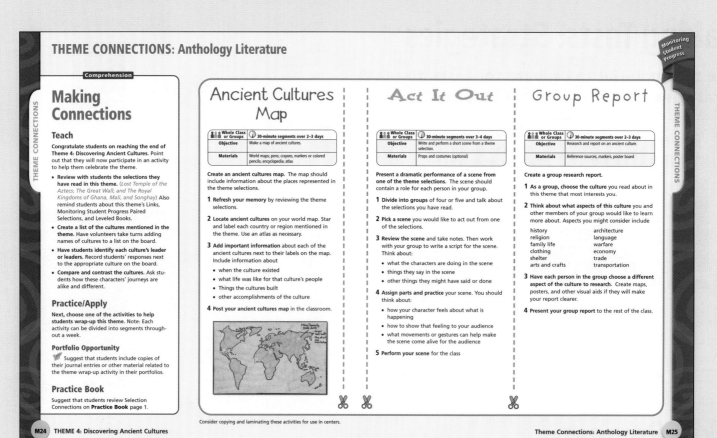

THEME CONNECTIONS: Anthology Literature

Monitoring Student Progress

Comprehension

Making Connections

Teach

Congratulate students on reaching the end of Theme 4: Discovering Ancient Cultures. Point out that they will now participate in an activity to help them celebrate the theme.

- **Review with students** the selections they have read in this theme. (*Lost Temple of the Aztecs; The Great Wall; and The Royal Kingdoms of Ghana, Mali, and Songhay*) Also remind students about this theme's Links, Monitoring Student Progress Paired Selections, and Leveled Books.
- **Create a list** of the cultures mentioned in the theme. Have volunteers take turns adding names of cultures to a list on the board.
- **Have students identify** each culture's leader or leaders. Record students' responses next to the appropriate culture on the board.
- **Compare and contrast** the cultures. Ask students how these characters' journeys are alike and different.

Practice/Apply

Next, choose one of the activities to help students wrap-up this theme. Note: Each activity can be divided into segments throughout a week.

Portfolio Opportunity

Suggest that students include copies of their journal entries or other material related to the theme wrap-up activity in their portfolios.

Practice Book

Suggest that students review Selection Connections on **Practice Book** page 1.

Ancient Cultures Map

👥👥👥 Whole Class or Groups	⏱ 30-minute segments over 2–3 days
Objective	Make a map of ancient cultures.
Materials	World maps; pens; crayons, markers or colored pencils; encyclopedia; atlas

Create an ancient cultures map. The map should include information about the places represented in the theme selections.

1 **Refresh your memory** by reviewing the theme selections.

2 **Locate ancient cultures** on your world map. Star and label each country or region mentioned in the theme. Use an atlas as necessary.

3 **Add important information** about each of the ancient cultures next to their labels on the map. Include information about
- when the culture existed
- what life was like for that culture's people
- Things the cultures built
- other accomplishments of the culture

4 **Post your ancient cultures map** in the classroom.

Act It Out

👥👥👥 Whole Class or Groups	⏱ 30-minute segments over 3–4 days
Objective	Write and perform a short scene from a theme selection.
Materials	Props and costumes (optional)

Present a dramatic performance of a scene from one of the theme selections. The scene should contain a role for each person in your group.

1 **Divide into groups** of four or five and talk about the selections you have read.

2 **Pick a scene** you would like to act out from one of the selections.

3 **Review the scene** and take notes. Then work with your group to write a script for the scene. Think about:
- what the characters are doing in the scene
- things they say in the scene
- other things they might have said or done

4 **Assign parts and practice** your scene. You should think about:
- how your character feels about what is happening
- how to show that feeling to your audience
- what movements or gestures can help make the scene come alive for the audience

5 **Perform your scene** for the class

Group Report

👥👥👥 Whole Class or Groups	⏱ 30-minute segments over 2–3 days
Objective	Research and report on an ancient culture.
Materials	Reference sources, markers, poster board

Create a group research report.

1 **As a group, choose the culture** you read about in this theme that most interests you.

2 **Think about what aspects of this culture** you and other members of your group would like to learn more about. Aspects you might consider include

history	architecture
religion	language
family life	warfare
clothing	economy
shelter	trade
arts and crafts	transportation

3 **Have each person in the group choose a different aspect** of the culture to research. Create maps, posters, and other visual aids if they will make your report clearer.

4 **Present your group report** to the rest of the class.

Consider copying and laminating these activities for use in centers.

THEME CONNECTIONS

M24 **THEME 4: Discovering Ancient Cultures**

Theme Connections: Anthology Literature **M25**

Three Main Selections

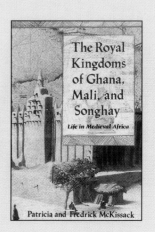

eveled Books

tivities to help students connect and compare

Independent Activities

While you work with small groups, students can choose from a wealth of books to complete these activities.

Leveled Readers . . .

for *Lost Temple of the Aztecs*
The Mighty Maya
A Brave Past
Dream Weaver
Copán: City of the Maya

for *The Great Wall*
The Pyramids of Ancient Egypt
The Pyramids of Giza
A Scribe of Ancient China
The Shape in the Dark: A Story of Hadrian's Wall

for *The Royal Kingdoms of Ghana, Mali, and Songhay*
On the Silk Road: Ancient Baghdad
Ancient Baghdad: City at the Crossroads of Trade
Caravan Boy
The Kingdom of Kush

Leveled Theme Paperbacks
The Librarian Who Measured the Earth
Aida
Between the Dragon and the Eagle

Leveled Bibliography
pages 354E–354F

THEME CONNECTIONS:
Leveled Books

Monitoring Student Progress

THEME CONNECTIONS

Historical Timeline

👤 Singles	⏱ 60 minutes
Objective	Create a timeline of historical events.
Materials	Markers, encyclopedias

Create a timeline that shows some of the events you read about in the books for this theme.

Think about the events in the books and when they happened. Review the books, and note any important dates you come across.

Then draw a timeline on a sheet of paper. Include in chronological order the important events you read about. You might want to include dates for

• when an important leader ruled

• when a monument was started or completed

• when a country was invaded

Draw a picture to go with each event on your timeline. When you have finished, display your timeline in the classroom.

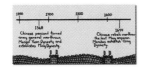

Want Ad

👤 Singles or Pairs	⏱ 30 minutes
Objective	Write a job listing.

The people who lived in ancient societies varied from humble stonemasons and wood carvers to royal emperors and pharaohs. Think about the books you have read for this theme. What were some of the jobs performed by the people you read about?

Choose one of the jobs you read about and write a want ad for it. Your ad might include details about

• the job's duties

• where the job is performed

• what special skills are needed to do the job

Share your want ad with a partner. Then role-play a job interview and interview your partner for the job. Use these questions to guide the interview:

• What interests you about this job?

• Why would you be good at this job?

• How much experience do you have?

End the interview by deciding whether or not to give your partner a job in the ancient world.

Travel Brochures

👤 Singles or Pairs	⏱ 60 minutes
Objective	Create a travel brochure for an ancient culture.
Materials	Crayons or markers; sample travel brochures (optional)

Create travel brochures inviting tourists to visit one of the ancient civilizations you read about in the books for this theme.

Choose the civilization you would most like to visit out of all those you have read about in this theme. Make a list of the reasons why the culture would be interesting to a visitor. Think about

• the people who live there

• amazing buildings or other structures

• unusual and exciting sights

• things a visitor could do

Take a new sheet of paper and fold it in half to make a brochure with a cover and an inside. Draw a picture on the cover that will make people want to visit the culture. Inside your brochure, write the reasons why people should visit. Feel free to illustrate your reasons with more pictures.

Share your brochure with the rest of the class. Discuss how the cultures you chose are different, and talk about what makes each one interesting.

Come Visit the Mayan City of Copán for the Adventure of a Lifetime.

✂ ✂ ✂

Consider copying and laminating these activities for use in centers.

M26 THEME 4: Discovering Ancient Cultures

Theme Connections: Leveled Books M27

welve Leveled Readers

Three Leveled Theme Paperbacks

Daily Lesson Plans

 **Technology**

Lesson Planner CD-ROM allows you to customize the chart below to develop your own lesson plans.

T Skill tested on Theme Skills Test and/or Integrated Theme Test

 50–60 minutes

Connecting and Comparing Literature

CHECK YOUR PROGRESS

 The Lord of the Nile — retold by Jacqueline Morley

 The Great Pyramid

Leveled Readers
• Fluency Practice
• Independent Reading

 40–60 minutes

Preparing for Tests

TAKING TESTS: Strategies

SKILL REVIEW OPTIONS

Comprehension
Structural Analysis
Vocabulary
Spelling
Grammar
Prompts for Writing

DAY 1

 The Lord of the Nile — retold by Jacqueline Morley

Introducing Paired Selections

Key Vocabulary, M9

pharaoh	shrine
vizier	neglect
granaries	decreed

Reading the Selection, M10–M14
The Lord of the Nile

Comprehension Strategy, M10
Summarize **T**

Classroom Management Activities, M6–M7

Leveled Readers
A Brave Past
Dream Weaver
Copán: City of the Maya
The Mighty Maya

Introduce the Strategy, M28
Vocabulary Items

Comprehension, M32–M33
Skill Review Options **T**

Structural Analysis, M34–M35
Skill Review Options **T**

Vocabulary, M36–M37
Skill Review Options **T**

Spelling, M38
The /sh/ Sound **T**

Grammar, M40
Adjectives **T**

Prompts for Writing, M42
Explanation/Eliminating Unnecessary Words

DAY 2

The Lord of the Nile — retold by Jacqueline Morley

Reading the Selection
The Lord of the Nile

Connecting and Comparing
Topic, Main Idea, and Details, M11
Cause and Effect, M13

Stop and Think, M15

Classroom Management Activities, M6–M7

Leveled Readers
The Pyramids of Giza
A Scribe of Ancient China
The Shape in the Dark:
  A Story of Hadrian's Wall
The Pyramids of Ancient Egypt

Step 1: Understand the Question, M29

Comprehension, M32–M33
Skill Review Options **T**

Structural Analysis, M34–M35
Skill Review Options **T**

Vocabulary, M36–M37
Skill Review Options **T**

Spelling, M38
Adding *-ion* or *-ation* **T**

Grammar, M40
Comparing with Adjectives **T**

Prompts for Writing, M42
Paragraph of Information/Elaborating with Adjectives **T**

Target Skills of the Week

Phonics
Comprehension
Vocabulary
Fluency

Monitoring Student Progress

DAILY LESSON PLANS

DAY 3

Key Vocabulary, M16

prospered phenomenal
plateau undertaking
quarries

Reading the Selection, M17–M22
The Great Pyramid

Comprehension Strategy, M20
Summarize **T**

Classroom Management Activities,
M6–M7

Leveled Readers

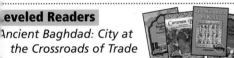

Ancient Baghdad: City at the Crossroads of Trade
Caravan Boy
The Kingdom of Kush
On the Silk Road: Ancient Baghdad

Step 2: Think About What the Word Means, M29

Comprehension, M32–M33
Skill Review Options **T**

Structural Analysis, M34–M35
Skill Review Options **T**

Vocabulary, M36–M37
Skill Review Options **T**

Spelling, M39
Unstressed Syllables **T**

Grammar, M41
Comparing with *good/bad* **T**

Prompts for Writing, M43
Comparison-and-Contrast Paragraph/
Combining Sentences **T**

DAY 4

Reading the Selection
The Great Pyramid

Connecting and Comparing

Noting Details/Compare and Contrast, M19
Author's Viewpoint: Bias and Assumption,
M21

Think and Compare, M23

Theme Connections: Anthology Literature, M24–M25

Classroom Management Activities,
M6–M7

Leveled Readers
Theme Connections: Leveled Books,
M26–M27

Step 3: Narrow the Choices. Then Choose the Best Answer, M30

Comprehension, M32–M33
Skill Review Options **T**

Structural Analysis, M34–M35
Skill Review Options **T**

Vocabulary, M36–M37
Skill Review Options **T**

Spelling, M39
Endings and Suffixes

Grammar, M41
Kinds of Adverbs

Prompts for Writing, M43
News Article/Adding Details

DAY 5

Theme Connections: Anthology Literature, M24–M25

Rereading for Fluency
M13, M19

retold by Jacqueline Morley

Classroom Management Activities,
M6–M7

Leveled Readers
Theme Connections: Leveled Books,
M26–M27

Vocabulary Test Practice, M31

Comprehension, M32–M33
Skill Review Options **T**

Structural Analysis, M34–M35
Skill Review Options **T**

Vocabulary, M36–M37
Skill Review Options **T**

Spelling Test, M39

Grammar, M41
Comparing with Adverbs

Prompts for Writing, M43
Character Sketch **T**/Using Adjectives

Classroom Management

Assign these activities at any time during the week while you work with small groups.

Suggest that students include copies of their work in their portfolios.

Art

Monumental Designs

👤 Singles	🕐 30 minutes
Objective	Write about and draw a modern-day monument.
Materials	Reference sources, Internet, drawing paper, markers

Imhotep created the Temple of Khnemu to honor the Lord of the Nile. Think of a monument you have seen in your community or know of. Write a description of it, including these ideas.

- who or what the monument honors
- how the monument was designed and built
- why you like this monument

Draw a picture of the monument to go along with your report.

Math

Egyptian Number Glyphs

👥 Pairs	🕐 30 minutes
Objective	Write number facts about the Great Pyramid.

The ancient Egyptians used the decimal number system made of the glyphs, or pictures, shown below.

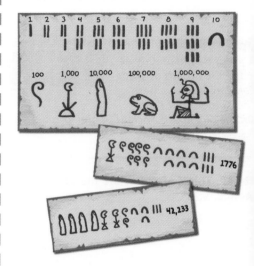

Reading Egyptian numbers is easy. The ones place is to the far right. The tens place is left of the ones. The hundreds place is left of the tens, and so forth. When numbers are stacked, start reading at the top.

- Look for number facts about the Great Pyramid, pages 428G–428L.
- Rewrite the facts using the glyphs from the Egyptian number system.
- Trade your facts with your partner and read them aloud using the chart to interpret the numbers.

Look for more activities in the Classroom Management Kit.

Consider copying and laminating these activities for use in centers.

Social Studies

A Day in the Life

Singles	20 minutes
Objective	Make up a daily schedule for an ancient ruler.

uppose you are a ruler of one of ne ancient countries described in heme 4. Write a schedule for a ypical day. Remember to include his information.

- people you will meet with
- time of each appointment
- places you need to visit
- tasks you need to complete during the day

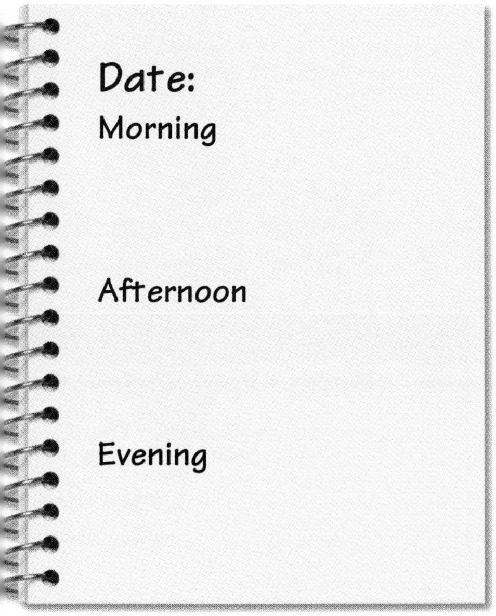

Date:
Morning
Afternoon
Evening

Drama

Ancient Meets Modern

Groups	45 minutes
Objective	Write a script comparing an ancient culture with your own.

What might happen if a citizen of an ancient culture traveled forward in time and spent a day with you in your town? Choose one of the cultures you read about in Theme 4 and write a script in which the citizen of that ancient culture spends a day with you. Discuss how you belive your visitor would react to these things.

- your appearance
- the food you eat
- the modern machines and appliances you use
- the way you spend your free time

Divide writing, editing, and publishing tasks among all group members. On an appropriate occasion, perform your script for the class.

Health

Helpful Products

Singles	20 minutes
Objective	Make a commercial about health products.

Picture Egyptian laborers toiling under the hot sun. Recall Chinese soldiers patrolling the Great Wall in the cold or Ghanaian traders crossing the Sahara during a sandstorm.

- Think of a modern health product that would protect ancient workers as they carried out their duties. (Hint: The health product does not have to be a medicine.)
- Write a commercial for this product, focusing on why ancient workers would have benefited from having it.
- Share your commercial with the class on an appropriate occasion.

Protect your skin from the scorching desert sun. Use Nile Crocodile Lotion, SPF 45!
Nile
Crocodile Lotion
SPF 45

Connecting and Comparing Literature

Theme Wrap-Up

Check Your Progress

Your discovery of ancient cultures has taken you from Tenochtitlán to the western Sudan. Take the time to review how much you've discovered — and discover some more. Now you can revisit the theme by reading and comparing two new selections and practicing your test-taking skills.

Think about what it means to discover an ancient culture by revisiting the McKissacks' letter on pages 356–358. What do you think it would be like to visit an ancient culture?

As you read the two selections that follow, think about what each reveals about ancient Egypt. Compare how well they help you understand that culture. Then think about how these selections compare with the other selections in *Discovering Ancient Cultures*.

428

Read and Compare

The Lord of the Nile

retold by Jacqueline Morley

Discover a myth about how an Egyptian pharaoh brings back the yearly flooding of the Nile River after a long drought.

Try these strategies:
Predict and Infer
Evaluate

The Great Pyramid

Learn about the Great Pyramid of Giza and the pharaoh who ordered its construction.

Try these strategies:
Monitor and Clarify
Summarize

Strategies in Action *Remember to use all your reading strategies while you read.*

428 A

Use Paired Selections: Check Your Progress

Have students read page 428. Discuss these questions:

- Which cultures of the past are explored in the selections in this theme? (the Aztecs, the Chinese, and the peoples of ancient Ghana or northwest Africa)

- Which of these past cultures would you most like to visit if you could? (Answers will vary.)

Have students read page 428A. Ask this question:

- How might *The Lord of the Nile* and *The Great Pyramid* be similar to the other selections in this theme? (Sample answer: They might describe an ancient culture, as in *The Royal Kingdoms of Ghana, Mali, and Songhay,* or tell about a great monument, like *Lost Temple of the Aztecs* and *The Great Wall* do.)

Strategies in Action Remind students to use all of their reading strategies, including the Summarize strategy, as they read the Paired Selections.

M8   THEME 4: Discovering Ancient Cultures

Selection 1

The Lord of the Nile

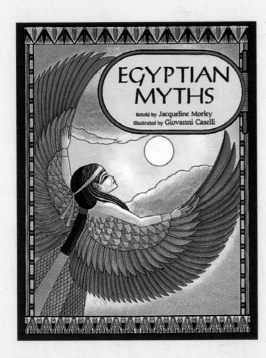

EGYPTIAN MYTHS

Retold by Jacqueline Morley
Illustrated by Giovanni Caselli

retold by Jacqueline Morley

Introducing Vocabulary

Key Vocabulary
These words appear in the selection.

pharaohs kings of ancient Egypt

vizier a high official in a royal government

granaries buildings for storing grain

shrine a sacred or holy site

neglect to ignore or pay no attention to

decreed ordered

e • Glossary
e • WordGame

See Vocabulary notes on pages M10, M12, and M14 for additional words to preview.

Have students locate Key Vocabulary words in the story.

- Have volunteers read aloud each sentence containing a Key Vocabulary word.

Display Transparency 4–27.

- Model how to use context clues to find the meaning of *pharaoh*.
- For each remaining word, ask students to locate context clues and define each Key Vocabulary word.

Practice/Homework Assign **Practice Book** page 53.

Introduce the Graphic Organizer.
Tell students to fill in **Practice Book** page 54 as they read the Paired Selections.

Practice Book page 53

Monitoring Student Progress
Key Vocabulary

Name _____

Pharaoh Words

Next to each word below, write the word from the list that is closest in meaning.

Vocabulary
pharaohs
vizier
granaries
shrine
neglect
decreed

1. ignore neglect (2 points)
2. altar shrine (2)
3. advisor vizier (2)
4. rulers pharaohs (2)
5. commanded decreed (2)
6. storehouses granaries (2)

Now use three words from the box to write a short paragraph about an ancient culture.

Paragraphs will vary, but should include at least three vocabulary words. (3 points)

_____
_____

Practice Book page 54

Monitoring Student Progress
Graphic Organizer
Cause and Effect

Name _____

Cause and Effect Chart

As you read the Paired Selections, fill in the charts below with causes and effects from each selection.
Sample answers are provided. Accept reasonable responses.

The Lord of the Nile

Cause	Effect
Horus sees his people living together in peace and blessing the gods. (2 points)	The god Horus withdraws to the heavens and lets mortals rule Egypt.
Zoser builds himself a fancy tomb but neglects the temple of the Lord of the Nile.	The Nile fails to flood for seven years. (2)
Zoser builds a temple for the Lord of the Nile.	The Nile waters the land again. (2)

The Great Pyramid

Cause	Effect
Khufu declares himself to be the greatest pharaoh ever.	He decides to build the greatest tomb ever. (2 points)
Workers from different villages in Egypt come to Giza to complete the Great Pyramid.	The workers become part of a larger community. (2)
Khufu dies and his body is preserved and buried inside the Great Pyramid. (2)	The Egyptians think that Khufu's ka, or soul, is free.

Reading the Paired Selections

CRITICAL THINKING
Guiding Comprehension

① **STORY STRUCTURE** Who was Imhotep, and what did the pharaoh ask him to do? (Imhotep was the pharaoh Zoser's vizier and a great architect. The pharaoh asked him to build a tomb that would last forever.)

② **CAUSE AND EFFECT** Disaster struck Egypt when the Nile failed to flood and burning winds shriveled the crops. How might this event affect the people of Egypt? (They will have no food; they will go hungry.)

COMPREHENSION STRATEGY
Summarize

Teacher Modeling Remind students that summarizing ideas as they read can help them understand and remember a selection. Read aloud the first paragraph on page 428B. Then model the strategy:

Think Aloud *I would summarize the first paragraph of the selection this way: The Egyptians believed that the pharaohs were gods. They also believed that when the pharaohs died, they would join the other gods in heaven and that without a perfectly preserved body, the soul of the pharaoh would die. So, the Egyptian pharaohs had huge tombs built to preserve their bodies in.*

Vocabulary

pharaohs kings of ancient Egypt

vizier a high official in a royal government

sluggish moving slowly or showing little activity

THE LORD OF THE NILE

retold by Jacqueline Morley   illustrated by Michael Jaroszko

Long ago, when the world was new, the gods lived on earth and were pharaohs in Egypt. By their wise example the gods showed Earth's people how their land should be governed and made them content. The last god to rule on Earth was Horus, the son of Isis. When he saw that his people lived peaceably together and had learned to bless the gods, he withdrew to the heavens and let mortals rule in Egypt. The people of Egypt still believed their pharaohs to be gods and thought that each one, when he died, would join his father Ra, and travel with him in the Boat of the Sun. Before departing, each pharaoh built an "everlasting home" — a tomb in which his body would be preserved forever. The Ancient Egyptians believed that without a perfectly preserved body to live in, the soul would die.

Now, about four thousand six hundred years ago, Zoser, a good and just king, ruled Egypt as pharaoh. He was anxious that his life in the next world should be blessed, but when he looked at the massive brick tombs of former pharaohs he doubted whether even they would

last forever. So h **①** asked his vizier, t great architect Imhotep the Wise to build him a truly god-like tomb that would outlast time itself. Imhotep created tomb of stone, which was made of many slabs of stone set o upon another, making a stairway to the sky. This was the first pyramid, known as the Step Pyramid, and it still stands today.

In the eighteenth year of Zoser's reign, disaster struck Egypt. The Nile, which flooded the land every year, was low and sluggish. Farmers waited anxiously for the river to coat their fields with the rich mud in which the crops grew tall, and to fill the canals that watered them, for rain is hardly known in **②** Egypt. But the flood failed, and when Set sen the burning winds from the desert all growing things shriveled and died.

428B

Challenge
Additional Reading

Students may be interested in reading other books written by Jacqueline Morley. Visit Education Place at **www.eduplace.com** to learn more about this author.

428C

Connecting and Comparing

Topic, Main Idea, and Details

- What is the main idea of the first paragraph on page 428B? (The ancient Egyptians thought their pharaohs were gods and built them tombs to preserve their bodies.)

- What detail from *Lost Temple of the Aztecs* shows that gods were important to the Aztec culture? (Sample answer: The Aztecs welcomed Cortés because they thought he was the returning god, Quetzalcoatl.)

REACHING ALL LEARNERS

Extra Support/Intervention

Selection Preview

pages 428B–428C The pharaoh Zoser builds a god-like tomb for himself. Then a drought strikes. What do you think might be happening?

pages 428D–428E What is happening in the illustrations on these pages?

page 428F How does Zoser get the Nile to rise again?

Reading the Paired Selections **M11**

CRITICAL THINKING
Guiding Comprehension

❸ WRITER'S CRAFT How does the author show that people in Egypt were desperate and frustrated? (She vividly describes how the people behave: *the strong stole from the weak, the old and sick were left to starve,* and *angry crowds beat upon the palace doors.*)

❹ COMPARE AND CONTRAST How did the Temple of Khnemu compare to the pharaoh's tomb? (Sample answer: Khnemu's temple was a humble wooden hut, while Zoser's tomb was an impressive *stairway to the sky.*)

COMPREHENSION STRATEGY
Summarize

Teacher/Student Modeling Have students read page 428D. Work with them to summarize the events that led Zoser to visit the Temple of Khnemu.

Then Zoser fed his people from the granaries that held the surplus harvests of past years. But for seven years the Nile failed to flood, and then when the granaries were opened they yielded only gusts of empty air. People grew desperate; the strong stole from the weak; the old and the sick were left to starve. Angry crowds beat upon the doors of Zoser's palace demanding that he should use his god-like powers to make the river flood.

Zoser was at his wits' end. He had no idea how to make the Nile rise. Then an idea came to him.

"Call Imhotep," he commanded. "There is no man living wiser than he."

Imhotep listened thoughtfully to the pharaoh's agitated questioning, "Where is the birthplace of the Nile? What god or goddess rules there? I must be told, that I may beg this being to send my country life."

"Great Pharaoh," Imhotep replied, "I do not know, but at the Temple of Thoth at Hermopolis there are sacred books in which these secrets may lie hidden. I will go to Hermopolis, and if Thoth guides me I may learn the truth."

Before many days had passed Imhotep returned with an answer, "You must seek the mystery of the Nile in the beginning of all things. In the far south is an island called Abu, which means the City of the Beginning. This

was the first dry land to rise from the waters o[f] Nu. Here Ra stood when he spoke the names of all things. Here lies a cave where the river rests each year and is reborn. Then, with new strength it rushes forth through two caverns t[o] nourish the land of Egypt. The lord of this cav[e] is Khnemu the Nile god. Only he can make th[e] river flood again."

Zoser sailed on the royal barge for many days towards the midday sun. At last he cam[e] to Abu, the birthplace of the Nile, and entered the Temple of Khnemu, which was a humble wooden building with a door made of reeds and a roof of the branches of trees. Zoser bowed before the shrine and piled offerings o[n] the altar of the Lord of the Nile — bread-cake[s] geese, legs of oxen, and all the things that please the gods.

Suddenly, in the darkness of the shrine, a majestic figure with the head of a ram with widespread horns appeared before him. This Being addressed him sternly, "I am Khnemu th[e] Maker who knitted your body together and gave you a heart. I am Nu of the great waters, who was in being at the beginning of time. I am the Lord of the Nile. When I draw back th[e] bolts of the cavern doors and strike the earth with my sandals, the flood pours out upon th[e] land and the people of Egypt are fed and rejoice."

428D

Challenge

Research Ancient Egyptian Gods
Have small groups research one of the Egyptian gods mentioned in the story. Ask the groups to present an oral report about the god they researched.

Vocabulary

granaries buildings for storing grain

agitated disturbed or upset

barge a large, flat-bottomed boat

shrine a sacred or holy site

428**E**

Connecting and Comparing

Cause and Effect

- What did Zoser hope to accomplish by visiting Khnemu, the Lord of the Nile? (Zoser wanted Khnemu to make the river flood again.)

- What did Moctezuma hope to accomplish by sending men to visit Cortés in *Lost Temple of the Aztecs?* (Moctezuma wanted to welcome Cortés, whom he thought was the returning Aztec god, Quetzalcoatl.)

- How were the results different? (Zoser appeased Khnemu, and the Nile flooded and saved the Egyptians. Moctezuma's welcome led to Cortés's conquest of the Aztecs and the destruction of Tenochtitlán.)

TARGET SKILL

Fluency Practice

Rereading for Fluency Suggest that students choose a favorite part of the story to reread to a partner or suggest that they reread page 428D. Encourage them to read expressively.

CRITICAL THINKING
Guiding Comprehension

❺ MAKING INFERENCES What does Zoser think of Khnemu? (Sample answer: He is scared of him but worshipful.)

❻ CAUSE AND EFFECT Why didn't Khnemu make the river flood in Egypt for seven years? (He was angry because Zoser built a beautiful temple for himself, yet allowed the temples of the gods to remain small and rundown.)

❼ NOTING DETAILS What must Zoser do to make the Nile rise again? Do you think this request is fair? (He must build a temple to honor the gods; Answers will vary.)

Summarize Have students use what they wrote on their Graphic Organizers to summarize *The Lord of the Nile*.

❺ Then Zoser asked fearfully, "Lord of the Nile, how has your servant offended you that for seven years you have not sent the flood?"

❻ "Why does Pharaoh build for himself an everlasting home of stone, so splendid that the like of it has never been on Earth before, and yet neglect the gods?" Khnemu replied. "My temple stands on banks of granite, which is called the stone of Abu. And here are gold, silver, copper, lapis lazuli, crystal, and alabaster. Should these things lie untouched in the ground, while the Temple of Khnemu is a mere ❼ hut of reeds? Restore to the gods the honor that is their due and the Nile will rise again."

"It shall be done," said Zoser.

So Imhotep made a temple for Khnemu that outshone all others in the land. Its shrine were filled with statues of gold and silver and its walls were of malachite and lapis lazuli. And the pharaoh decreed that the harvests of the land for many leagues to the north and south of it should belong to the Temple Khnemu forever, so that his altars should neve be bare. Then once more the Nile watered the land and the fields were yellow with ripe grain But, from that time on, no pharaoh forgot that the wealth of Egypt, the comfort of its people and the glory of its kings, were the gift of the Lord of the Nile.

428**F**

English Language Learners

Supporting Comprehension

Explain to students that *lapis lazuli* (LAP-ihs LAZ-uh-lee) is a deep blue stone often used to make jewelry, *alabaster* (AL-uh-bas-tuhr) is a type of fine-grained white rock used by ancient carvers, and *malachite* (MAL-uh-kyt) is a green-black mineral also used to make jewelry. These items all represent great wealth.

Vocabulary

neglect to ignore or pay no attention to

decreed ordered

leagues units of distance, each equal to approximately three miles

Stop and Think

Critical Thinking Questions

MAKING JUDGMENTS Do you think that the pharaoh was wise to give so many things to the temple of Khnemu? Why or why not? (Answers will vary.)

COMPARE AND CONTRAST Compare and contrast Zoser's Step Pyramid and China's Great Wall. How are the structures alike and different? (Both still stand today, and parts of both were built from blocks of stone. However, the Step Pyramid was built to house a ruler's body, while the Great Wall was built to keep out invaders.)

CATEGORIZE AND CLASSIFY Compare *The Lord of the Nile* with *Lost Temple of the Aztecs*. Are both selections myths? Explain your answer. (No; *The Lord of the Nile* is the retelling of a myth, while *Lost Temple of the Aztecs* is based on historical events.)

Strategies in Action Have students model how they used summarize and other strategies to help them understand this selection.

Connecting and Comparing

Compare and Contrast

Remind students that words and descriptions can often reveal an author's bias, or attitude about a subject.

Have students read the key words or descriptions from *The Great Wall* and *The Lord of the Nile* listed on **Practice Book** page 55. Ask them to identify the author's viewpoint in each statement. Have students reread parts of the selections if necessary.

Practice Book page 55

Monitoring Student Progress
Connecting and Comparing
Author's Viewpoint

Name _____

Views of the Past

Read the words or descriptions from *The Great Wall* and *The Lord of the Nile*. Note the author's viewpoint on the lines provided. Then explain your answer. Sample answers are given. Accept reasonable responses.

The Great Wall

Passage	Positive or Negative?	Why?
To defend against their fast-moving enemy, the Chinese used an ingenious system of communications to gather soldiers together for battle. (page 397)	positive (1 point)	the author uses the word "ingenious" to describe the system (1)
Officials and advisors, well-fed and dressed in silk, spent their days quarreling and endlessly vying for the emperor's favor. (page 398)	negative (1)	the author makes the officials and advisors sound pampered and lazy (1)

The Lord of the Nile

Passage	Positive or Negative?	Why?
By their wise example, the gods showed Earth's people how their land should be governed and made them content. (page 428B)	positive (1)	The author refers to the Egyptian gods as "wise." (1)
Now, about four thousand six hundred years ago, Zoser, a good and just king, ruled Egypt as pharaoh. (page 428B)	positive (1)	The author calls Zoser "good and just." (1)

REACHING ALL LEARNERS

Extra Support/Intervention

Review Summaries

Have students review the summaries they made while reading. Ask them how describing what they read in their own words helped them understand the story.

Monitoring Student Progress

If . . .	Then . . .
students had difficulty answering Guiding Comprehension questions,	guide them in reading aloud relevant portions of the text and discussing their answers.

Introducing Vocabulary

Key Vocabulary

These words appear in the selection.

prospered lived very well; succeeded

plateau a flat, raised area of land

quarries deep pits from which stone is dug or cut

phenomenal incredible; amazing

undertaking a task or job

e • Glossary
e • WordGame

See Vocabulary notes on pages M18 and M22 for additional words to preview.

Have students locate Key Vocabulary words in the selection.

- Have volunteers read aloud each sentence containing a Key Vocabulary word.

Display Transparency 4–28.

- Work with students to complete the sentences using Key Vocabulary words.

Practice/Homework Assign **Practice Book** page 56.

Selection 2

The Great Pyramid

The story of the farmers, the god-king, and the most astounding structure ever built.

By Elizabeth Mann

DISCOVERING ANCIENT CULTURES
The Great Pyramid
Monitoring Student Progress Key Vocabulary

ANNOTATED VERSION

Transparency 4–28
Key Vocabulary Words

prospered	plateau	quarries
phenomenal	undertaking	

Paola parked her car and unloaded her gear. She took out her binoculars and examined the high __plateau__ in the distance. For several months, Paola had been studying the ruins of an ancient village on that high, flat piece of land. The people who once lived there had __prospered__ for many years. Then, they fell on hard times and had to leave their village.

When Paola arrived at the ruins, she quickly surveyed the surrounding land. The view was __phenomenal__. From where she stood, she could see two abandoned stone __quarries__ about three miles away from the base of the plateau. Long ago, the villagers had gone there to get their building stones.

Paola had spent a lot of time at the quarries collecting rock samples. Now she was trying to figure out how the stones had been carried to the top of the plateau. However it had been done, Paola believed it must have been a difficult and complicated __undertaking__.

TRANSPARENCY 4–28
TEACHER'S EDITION PAGE M16

Monitoring Student Progress
Key Vocabulary The Great Pyramid

Practice Book page 56

Name _____

Solving Riddles

Solve each riddle with the correct vocabulary word from the box.

Vocabulary

phenomenal   plateau   prospered   quarries   undertaking

1. These are sources of rocks. __quarries__ **(2 points)**
2. Someone might call this a job or project. __undertaking__ **(2)**
3. This word is a short way of saying "made lots of money." __prospered__ **(2)**
4. A mountain with its top half cut off might resemble this. __plateau__ **(2)**
5. Amazing achievements are described using this word. __phenomenal__ **(2)**

Now use two words from the box in a sentence.

6. __Sentences will vary but should include two vocabulary words.__ **(2)**

The Great Pyramid

by Elizabeth Mann, illustrated by Laura Lo Turco

Ancient Egyptians believed their pharaoh was the sky god Horus on Earth, who could watch over his people in the afterlife. They built tombs of stone that they believed would provide a passage to the heavens for the pharaoh and his *ka*, or spirit. About 4,500 years ago, the pharaoh Khufu declared himself both Horus and the sun god Re on Earth. To prepare for the afterlife, Khufu had to build the greatest pyramid of all.

1 Egypt prospered under Khufu and life was luxurious. He led extravagant sailing excursions, hunting expeditions, and fishing trips. Officials, nobles, and priests joined him at his palace for banquets. The guests wore fine linen, scented wigs, and dramatic eye makeup. Their gold jewelry was heavy with precious stones. While musicians and dancers performed tirelessly, servants carried trays heavy with meat and bread and fruit.

The pleasures and duties of a pharaoh's **2** earthly life would only last a few years. His *ka* was expected to exist for eternity, so a pharaoh's most important responsibility was to prepare for the afterlife. For Khufu it was especially important. He had declared himself to be the greatest pharaoh ever. Now he had to build the greatest tomb ever.

428**G**

1 **DRAWING CONCLUSIONS** What kind of life did the pharaoh Khufu lead? (Sample answer: easy and full of luxury)

2 **CAUSE AND EFFECT** Why did Khufu believe he had to build the greatest tomb ever? (He had declared himself to be the greatest pharaoh ever.)

Continue the Graphic Organizer.

Remind students to fill in their Cause and Effect Graphic Organizers as they read *The Great Pyramid*.

Extra Support/Intervention

Selection Preview

page 428G The pharaoh Khufu wants to build a great tomb for himself. Why is preparing for his death so important to him?

pages 428H–428I What are the people in these two illustrations doing?

pages 428J–428L What steps do the workers follow to build the pyramid?

Guiding Comprehension

❸ NOTING DETAILS What details tell readers that the laborers were proud to work on the pharaoh's pyramid? (The workers chose names for their gangs and painted them proudly on the stone blocks.)

❹ AUTHOR'S VIEWPOINT Do you think the author thinks the building of the Great Pyramid had a positive effect on Egyptian society? Why or why not? (Sample answer: Yes; she writes that it brought together people from different villages in Egypt and gave them a sense of being part of a greater community.)

He chose the location carefully. It had to be on high ground, above the flood waters. Like all Egyptian graves, it had to be in the Western Desert, close to where the Land of the Dead was believed to be. To set himself apart, Khufu wanted a site where no pharaoh had been buried before.

The Giza Plateau was all of these things, and more.

The plateau is solid limestone, firm enough to support the tremendous weight of a 50-story, 13-acre pyramid. There is so much limestone that quarries on the plateau could provide most of the stone blocks needed to build the pyramid. It was a practical location, and, with cliffs soaring 100 feet up from the valley, a very impressive one.

Khufu alerted his governors that he would need laborers. Every summer thousands and thousands of farmers would come to work for him while the Nile flooded their fields.

Once the workers arrived at Giza, bread had to be provided for them. They needed shelter and clothing. They needed tools, sharpened and in good repair. And they needed to be organized so that they did not get in each other's way on the construction site. It was a phenomenal undertaking. Work gangs were assembled, each with an overseer. The workers chose names for their gangs like "Enduring Gang" and "Beloved of Khufu." They painted them proudly in red on the stone blocks.

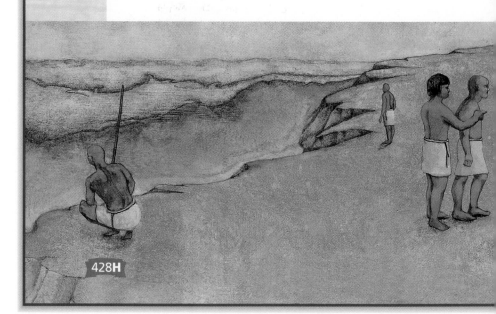

428H

Vocabulary

plateau a flat, raised area of land

quarries deep pits from which stone is dug or cut

phenomenal incredible; amazing

undertaking a task or job

overseer a person who watches over and directs workers

Stone from quarries hundreds of miles away came by boat to a man-made harbor near the Giza Plateau. Using only primitive tools, Egyptian stonemasons shaped blocks so skillfully that a knife couldn't slide between them.

Quarries all over Egypt echoed with the sound of mallets as massive blocks were carved out of the surrounding stone. From Fayyum came dark, greenish-black basalt for the temple floors. From Aswan came granite, so heavy that a single block weighed 40 tons. And from Tura came the fine white limestone to cover the outside of the pyramid.

The Great Pyramid had a tremendous effect on Egyptians who lived 4,500 years ago. Egyptians were farmers. Their lives had always centered on their fields and livestock, their villages and local gods. But those who left their homes every year and gathered at the Giza Plateau became part of a bigger world, a bigger society. They were loyal, not just to their village, but to the great work they were doing. By contributing to the afterlife of their pharaoh, they were insuring prosperity for all of Egypt. When they returned to their villages, they brought with them the sense of belonging to a larger community.

For some, the change in their lives was even greater. Many skilled workers did not return to their fields. They stayed at Giza with their families and worked year round for the pharaoh. Freed from the hard labor of farming, they developed remarkable talents as artists, boat builders, goldsmiths, and stonemasons.

❹

428**I**

Connecting and Comparing

Compare and Contrast

- The people of ancient Egypt and the people of ancient Ghana felt like they were part of strong communities. What details from *The Great Pyramid* and *The Royal Kingdoms of Ghana, Mali, and Songhay* are evidence of this? (Sample answers: Egyptians were loyal to the great work they were doing, and they felt they were ensuring prosperity for all of Egypt. In Ghana, there were no orphans or homeless people because everyone was part of a large family.)

- How were the Egyptian laborers working on Khufu's pyramid treated differently from the Chinese laborers working on the Great Wall? (The Egyptian laborers were treated well, while the Chinese workers suffered many hardships.)

TARGET SKILL

🎯 Fluency Practice

Rereading for Fluency Have students choose a favorite part of the selection to reread to a partner or suggest that they reread the final two paragraphs on page 428I. Remind students how to read with expression.

Guiding Comprehension

5 **TEXT ORGANIZATION** How is the text organization on these pages different from the rest of the selection? (Details about the building of the Great Pyramid are provided in information boxes inside the illustration.)

6 **NOTING DETAILS** How did the stone blocks reach the higher layers of the pyramid? (A ramp was built around the pyramid, and blocks were dragged up on wooden sleds.)

COMPREHENSION STRATEGY

Summarize

Student Modeling Have students pause and restate in their own words the information box at the top of page 428J. If necessary, use this prompt: What is the main idea of the information box?

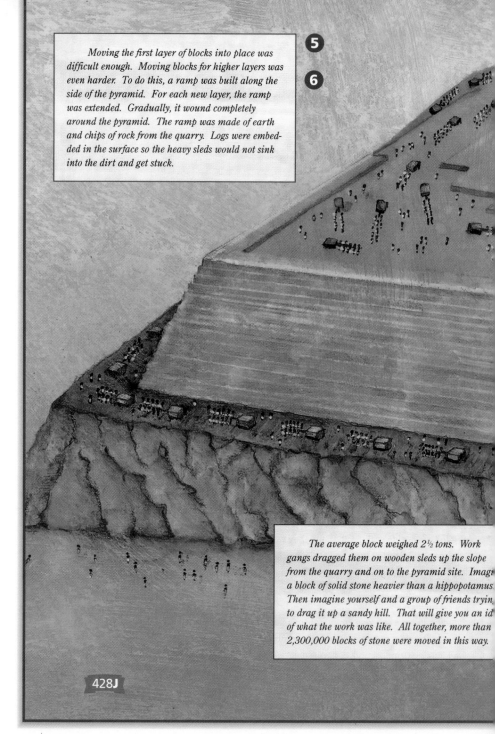

5
6

Moving the first layer of blocks into place was difficult enough. Moving blocks for higher layers was even harder. To do this, a ramp was built along the side of the pyramid. For each new layer, the ramp was extended. Gradually, it wound completely around the pyramid. The ramp was made of earth and chips of rock from the quarry. Logs were embedded in the surface so the heavy sleds would not sink into the dirt and get stuck.

The average block weighed 2½ tons. Work gangs dragged them on wooden sleds up the slope from the quarry and on to the pyramid site. Imagi a block of solid stone heavier than a hippopotamus. Then imagine yourself and a group of friends tryin to drag it up a sandy hill. That will give you an id' of what the work was like. All together, more than 2,300,000 blocks of stone were moved in this way.

428J

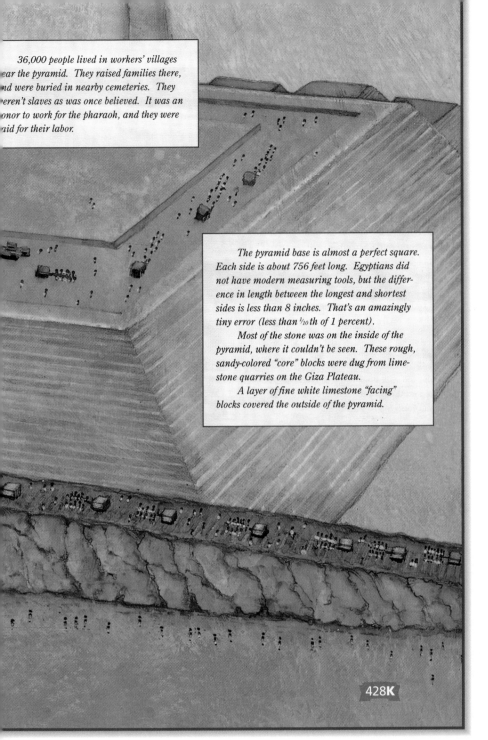

36,000 people lived in workers' villages near the pyramid. They raised families there, and were buried in nearby cemeteries. They weren't slaves as was once believed. It was an honor to work for the pharaoh, and they were paid for their labor.

The pyramid base is almost a perfect square. Each side is about 756 feet long. Egyptians did not have modern measuring tools, but the difference in length between the longest and shortest sides is less than 8 inches. That's an amazingly tiny error (less than ¹⁄₁₀ th of 1 percent).

Most of the stone was on the inside of the pyramid, where it couldn't be seen. These rough, sandy-colored "core" blocks were dug from limestone quarries on the Giza Plateau.

A layer of fine white limestone "facing" blocks covered the outside of the pyramid.

428**K**

Connecting and Comparing

Author's Viewpoint: Bias and Assumption

- What phrase on page 428K shows that the author admires and respects the pyramid builders' workmanship? (The author refers to the difference in the lengths of the pyramid's sides as *an amazingly tiny error*.)

- Which descriptions in *Lost Temple of the Aztecs* show that the author admires the ancient city of Tenochtitlán? (Sample answer: *The first Europeans who saw Tenochtitlán found the city so beautiful, they thought it must be enchanted. The Great Temple stood at the heart of this remarkable city.*)

- Compare the way the author of *The Great Pyramid* feels about the ancient Egyptian government with the way the author of *The Great Wall* feels about the leaders of the Ming dynasty. (Sample answer: The author of *The Great Pyramid* has a positive view of the pharaoh Khufu, while the author of *The Great Wall* does not think well of the leaders of the Ming dynasty.)

English Language Learners

Language Development

Explain to students that the word *wound* can mean "an injury" and is pronounced *woond*. However, the word *wound* as it is used on page 428J means "circled or wrapped" and is pronounced *wownd*.

Guiding Comprehension

7 NOTING DETAILS How did Khufu's burial chamber differ from those of earlier pharaohs? Why was it done differently? (Instead of being buried in a chamber beneath the pyramid, Khufu was buried high in the middle of the pyramid; to show that he was on the same level as the sun)

COMPREHENSION STRATEGY

Summarize

Student Modeling Have students sum up in their own words what happened after Khufu died. If necessary, use this prompt: What happened to Khufu's body?

Finish the Graphic Organizer. Have students share and discuss their completed Graphic Organizers.

The final block was the pyramid-shaped capstone. It was placed on the top and coated with gold. Then, from the top down, workers polished the white Tura limestone "facing" blocks until they gleamed.

Khufu had planned to be buried like earlier pharaohs, in a chamber beneath his pyramid. When he became Re on earth, he changed his mind. He built a second burial chamber, and then a third and final burial chamber, high in the middle of the pyramid. It was a way of showing that he was on the same level as the sun.

To prevent tomb robbers from getting in, the passageway to the burial chamber was blocked with huge slabs of granite and the pyramid entrance was concealed with "facing" blocks.

burial chamber

passageway

7

In the twenty-third year of his reign, the pharaoh Khufu died. Mourners stood along the Nile, striking sti together and weeping as the funeral boat passed by. Priests waited at the valley temple to receive the body of their king. The painstaking job of mummification begar After 70 days, the body was ready for burial.

The coffin containing Khufu's mummy was lowered into the granite sarcophagus deep within the pyramid. heavy lid was closed. Khufu's body was sealed inside th Great Pyramid. His *ka* was free.

428L

Vocabulary

mummification the process of drying and preserving the dead

sarcophagus a large stone coffin

Think and Compare

The Lord of the Nile

EGYPTIAN MYTH

retold by Jacqueline Morley

The Great Pyramid

1. Compare the pharaoh Zoser with the pharaoh Khufu. How are the two rulers alike? How are they different?

2. How does the construction of The Great Pyramid affect the farmers of ancient Egypt? Describe their lives before and after construction begins.

3. Compare the construction of The Great Pyramid with that of The Great Wall. How are the reasons for their being built different?

4. Compare the two wrap-up selections. How are the myth and the nonfiction selection different? How are they alike in providing information?

5. Which ancient culture in this theme would you like to learn more about? Why?

Strategies in Action Explain which reading strategies you found most useful while reading this theme and why.

Informing

Write a Travel Brochure

Write a paragraph for a travel brochure about one of the ancient cultures in the theme. Tell readers about the culture and its history.

Tips

- Explain how the people lived and how they were governed.
- Include a map with possible destinations.

428M

Discuss or Write Have students discuss or write their answers. Sample answers are provided; accept reasonable responses.

1. Both Zoser and Khufu were concerned with building tombs that would last forever. They are different because Zoser faced problems as a leader, such as the long drought, but Khufu led an extravagant life with few problems.

2. Before construction, most farmers viewed themselves as simple villagers. After construction began, farmers working on the pyramid at Giza started to see themselves as part of a larger community. Some gave up farming altogether in order to become craftspeople.

3. The Great Pyramid was built as a final resting place for the pharaoh Khufu. The Great Wall was built to keep Mongol invaders out of China.

4. In the myth, Zoser learned the importance of honoring the gods by visiting the god Khnemu. In the nonfiction selection, no one interacted with gods. The selection described the construction of the Great Pyramid instead. Both provided information about ancient Egyptian culture and beliefs.

5. Answers will vary.

Strategies in Action Have students take turns modeling how and where they used Summarize and other reading strategies.

Extra Support/ Intervention	English Language Learners

Review Summarizing

Have students tell when they paused to summarize while reading *The Great Pyramid*. Then ask them how restating important ideas helped them understand the selection.

Language Development

Beginning/Preproduction Work with students to create a word web of words that describe ancient Egyptian culture as depicted in the two selections they have just read.

Early Production and Speech Emergence Ask students to give examples of words or phrases they would use in their travel brochures to describe the ancient culture of their choice.

Intermediate and Advanced Fluency Have partners discuss the governments of their chosen cultures, comparing and contrasting the ways the ordinary people of those times were treated by their rulers.

Monitoring Student Progress

If . . .	Then . . .
students had difficulty answering Guiding Comprehension questions,	guide them in reading aloud relevant portions of the text and discussing their answers.

Reading the Paired Selections **M23**

THEME CONNECTIONS

Comprehension

Making Connections

Teach

Congratulate students on reaching the end of Theme 4: Discovering Ancient Cultures. Point out that they will now participate in an activity to help them celebrate the theme.

- **Review with students the selections they have read in this theme.** (*Lost Temple of the Aztecs; The Great Wall; and The Royal Kingdoms of Ghana, Mali, and Songhay*) Also remind students about this theme's Links, Monitoring Student Progress Paired Selections, and Leveled Books.

- **Create a list of the cultures mentioned in the theme.** Have volunteers take turns adding names of cultures to a list on the board.

- **Have students identify each culture's leader or leaders.** Record students' responses next to the appropriate culture on the board.

- **Compare and contrast the cultures.** Ask students how these characters' journeys are alike and different.

Practice/Apply

Next, choose one of the activities to help students wrap-up this theme. Note: Each activity can be divided into segments throughout a week.

Portfolio Opportunity

Suggest that students include copies of their journal entries or other material related to the theme wrap-up activity in their portfolios.

Practice Book

Suggest that students review Selection Connections on **Practice Book** page 1.

Ancient Cultures Map

👥👥 Whole Class or Groups	🕐 30-minute segments over 2–3 days
Objective	Make a map of ancient cultures.
Materials	World maps; pens; crayons, markers or colored pencils; encyclopedia; atlas

Create an ancient cultures map. The map should include information about the places represented in the theme selections.

1 Refresh your memory by reviewing the theme selections.

2 Locate ancient cultures on your world map. Star and label each country or region mentioned in the theme. Use an atlas as necessary.

3 Add important information about each of the ancient cultures next to their labels on the map. Include information about

- when the culture existed
- what life was like for that culture's people
- Things the cultures built
- other accomplishments of the culture

4 Post your ancient cultures map in the classroom.

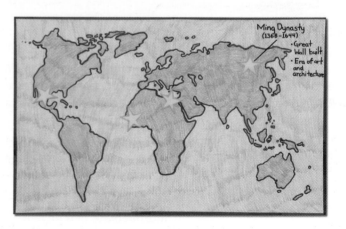

Consider copying and laminating these activities for use in centers.

Act It Out

![Whole Class or Groups] Whole Class or Groups	⏱ 30-minute segments over 3–4 days
Objective	Write and perform a short scene from a theme selection.
Materials	Props and costumes (optional)

Present a dramatic performance of a scene from one of the theme selections. The scene should contain a role for each person in your group.

1 Divide into groups of four or five and talk about the selections you have read.

2 Pick a scene you would like to act out from one of the selections.

3 Review the scene and take notes. Then work with your group to write a script for the scene. Think about:

- what the characters are doing in the scene
- things they say in the scene
- other things they might have said or done

4 Assign parts and practice your scene. You should think about:

- how your character feels about what is happening
- how to show that feeling to your audience
- what movements or gestures can help make the scene come alive for the audience

5 Perform your scene for the class

Group Report

![Whole Class or Groups] Whole Class or Groups	⏱ 30-minute segments over 2–3 days
Objective	Research and report on an ancient culture.
Materials	Reference sources, markers, poster board

Create a group research report.

1 As a group, choose the culture you read about in this theme that most interests you.

2 Think about what aspects of this culture you and other members of your group would like to learn more about. Aspects you might consider include

history	architecture
religion	language
family life	warfare
clothing	economy
shelter	trade
arts and crafts	transportation

3 Have each person in the group choose a different aspect of the culture to research. Create maps, posters, and other visual aids if they will make your report clearer.

4 Present your group report to the rest of the class.

Independent Activities

THEME CONNECTIONS:
Leveled Books

While you work with small groups, students can choose from a wealth of books to complete these activities.

Historical Timeline

👤 Singles	🕐 60 minutes
Objective	Create a timeline of historical events.
Materials	Markers, encyclopedias

Create a timeline that shows some of the events you read about in the books for this theme.

Think about the events in the books and when they happened. Review the books, and note any important dates you come across.

Then draw a timeline on a sheet of paper. Include in chronological order the important events you read about. You might want to include dates for

- when an important leader ruled
- when a monument was started or completed
- when a country was invaded

Draw a picture to go with each event on your timeline. When you have finished, display your timeline in the classroom.

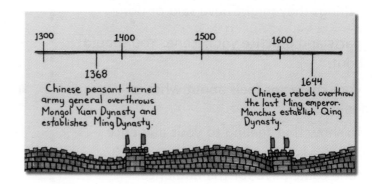

Consider copying and laminating these activities for use in centers.

Want Ad

👥 **Singles or Pairs**	🕐 **30 minutes**
Objective	Write a job listing.

The people who lived in ancient societies varied from humble stonemasons and wood carvers to royal emperors and pharaohs. Think about the books you have read for this theme. What were some of the jobs performed by the people you read about?

Choose one of the jobs you read about and write a want ad for it. Your ad might include details about

- the job's duties
- where the job is performed
- what special skills are needed to do the job

Share your want ad with a partner. Then role-play a job interview and interview your partner for the job. Use these questions to guide the interview:

- What interests you about this job?
- Why would you be good at this job?
- How much experience do you have?

End the interview by deciding whether or not to give your partner a job in the ancient world.

Travel Brochures

👥 **Singles or Pairs**	🕐 **60 minutes**
Objective	Create a travel brochure for an ancient culture.
Materials	Crayons or markers; sample travel brochures (optional)

Create travel brochures inviting tourists to visit one of the ancient civilizations you read about in the books for this theme.

Choose the civilization you would most like to visit out of all those you have read about in this theme. Make a list of the reasons why the culture would be interesting to a visitor. Think about

- the people who live there
- amazing buildings or other structures
- unusual and exciting sights
- things a visitor could do

Take a new sheet of paper and fold it in half to make a brochure with a cover and an inside. Draw a picture on the cover that will make people want to visit the culture. Inside your brochure, write the reasons why people should visit. Feel free to illustrate your reasons with more pictures.

Share your brochure with the rest of the class. Discuss how the cultures you chose are different, and talk about what makes each one interesting.

Come Visit the Mayan City of Copán for the Adventure of a Lifetime.

Preparing for Tests

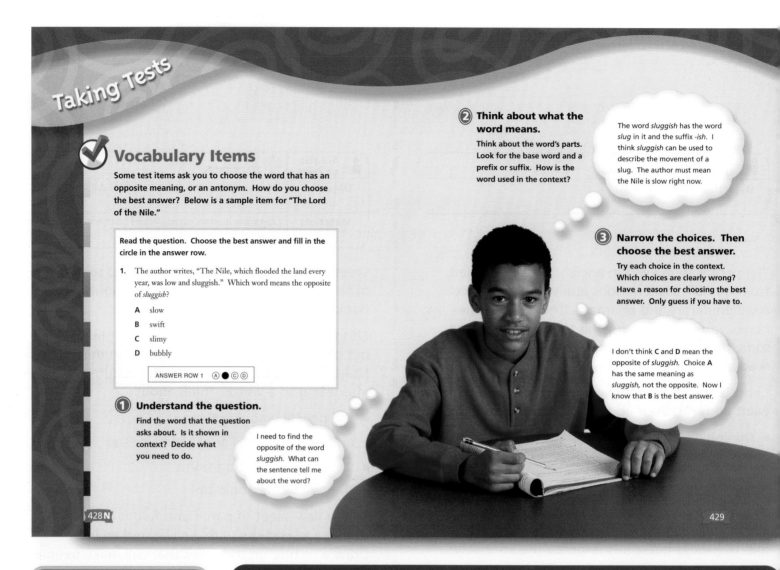

Taking Tests

✓ Vocabulary Items

Some test items ask you to choose the word that has an opposite meaning, or an antonym. How do you choose the best answer? Below is a sample item for "The Lord of the Nile."

Read the question. Choose the best answer and fill in the circle in the answer row.

1. The author writes, "The Nile, which flooded the land every year, was low and sluggish." Which word means the opposite of *sluggish*?

   A   slow
   B   swift
   C   slimy
   D   bubbly

   ANSWER ROW 1 Ⓐ ● Ⓒ Ⓓ

① Understand the question.
Find the word that the question asks about. Is it shown in context? Decide what you need to do.

I need to find the opposite of the word sluggish. What can the sentence tell me about the word?

② Think about what the word means.
Think about the word's parts. Look for the base word and a prefix or suffix. How is the word used in the context?

The word sluggish has the word slug in it and the suffix -ish. I think sluggish can be used to describe the movement of a slug. The author must mean the Nile is slow right now.

③ Narrow the choices. Then choose the best answer.
Try each choice in the context. Which choices are clearly wrong? Have a reason for choosing the best answer. Only guess if you have to.

I don't think C and D mean the opposite of sluggish. Choice A has the same meaning as sluggish, not the opposite. Now I know that B is the best answer.

428N   429

THEME	STRATEGY
1	Choosing the Best Answer
2	Filling in the Blank
3	Writing a Personal Response
▶ 4	Vocabulary Items
5	Writing an Answer to a Question
6	Writing a Persuasive Essay

Introduce the Strategy

Taking Tests provides instruction and practice in different test formats. It will help you prepare your students for the **Theme Skills Test** and the **Integrated Theme Test,** as well as state and national standardized tests.

- Tell students that they will learn strategies that will help them do well on tests.
- Explain that Anthology pages 428N and 429 show the steps for answering questions about vocabulary.
- Have different volunteers read each step and each thought balloon aloud.
- Explain that students will be learning more about each of these steps.

Teach the Strategy

 Understand the Question.

Display Transparency 4–29 and model Step 1.

Have a volunteer read aloud Step 1. Tell students that they will learn more about this one step.

Explain that both questions are based on *The Lord of the Nile* on Anthology pages 428B–428F.

Model using the step to understand Question 1.

Think Aloud *First, I circle the word that the question is asking about:* surplus. *Next, I will check to see whether the question tells the context. It uses the word in a sentence, so I won't have to go find the word in the selection. Now I will decide what I need to do. Will I choose an answer that is almost the same as* surplus *or one that is the opposite? I see the words* What does surplus mean. *I will choose a word that is almost the same as* surplus.

Complete Transparency 4–29, using Step 1.

 Think About What the Word Means.

Display Transparency 4–30 and model Step 2.

• Have a volunteer read aloud Step 2. Tell students that they will learn more about this one step.

• Model using the step to think about the parts of the word and about how the word is used.

Think Aloud *First, I will think about the parts of the word* surplus. *I will circle the word* plus *in* surplus, *which means "added." This may be a clue to the meaning of* surplus.

Next, I will think about how the word is used. What is happening at this point in the story? Zoser's people are suffering from a drought. The crops have died so Zoser must find a source of food. Zoser feeds the people from past years' harvests stored in the granary. Is this a clue? It is. The answer has to describe the stored food from past harvests.

Complete Transparency 4–30, using Step 2.

Turn the page to teach the Strategy Step 3.

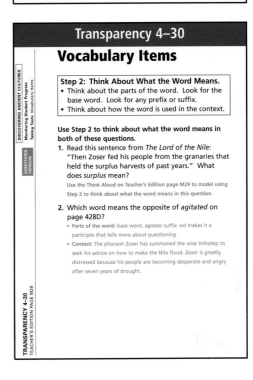

Transparency 4–29

Vocabulary Items

DISCOVERING ANCIENT CULTURES
Monitoring Student Progress
Taking Tests Vocabulary Items

ANNOTATED VERSION

Step 1: Understand the Question.
• Find the word that the question is asking about.
• Does the question show the word alone or in context?
• Decide what you need to do.

Use Step 1 to understand each of these questions about *The Lord of the Nile.*
1. Read this sentence from *The Lord of the Nile:* "Then Zoser fed his people from the granaries that held the surplus harvests of past years." What does *surplus* mean?
   Use the Think Aloud on Teacher's Edition page M29 to model using Step 1 to understand this question.

2. Which word means the opposite of *agitated* on page 428D?
   • Word the question asks about: *agitated*
   • Context: I will need to find the context in the selection: "Imhotep listened thoughtfully to the pharaoh's agitated questioning, 'Where is the birthplace of the Nile? What god or goddess rules there?'" (page 428D, column 1, paragraph 4)
   • What you need to do: choose an answer that is the opposite of the word

TRANSPARENCY 4–29
TEACHER'S EDITION PAGE M29

Transparency 4–30

Vocabulary Items

DISCOVERING ANCIENT CULTURES
Monitoring Student Progress
Taking Tests Vocabulary Items

ANNOTATED VERSION

Step 2: Think About What the Word Means.
• Think about the parts of the word. Look for the base word. Look for any prefix or suffix.
• Think about how the word is used in the context.

Use Step 2 to think about what the word means in both of these questions.
1. Read this sentence from *The Lord of the Nile:* "Then Zoser fed his people from the granaries that held the surplus harvests of past years." What does *surplus* mean?
   Use the Think Aloud on Teacher's Edition page M29 to model using Step 2 to think about what the word means in this question.

2. Which word means the opposite of *agitated* on page 428D?
   • Parts of the word: base word, *agitate;* suffix -ed makes it a participle that tells more about *questioning*
   • Context: The pharaoh Zoser has summoned the wise Imhotep to seek his advice on how to make the Nile flood. Zoser is greatly distressed because his people are becoming desperate and angry after seven years of drought.

TRANSPARENCY 4–30
TEACHER'S EDITION PAGE M29

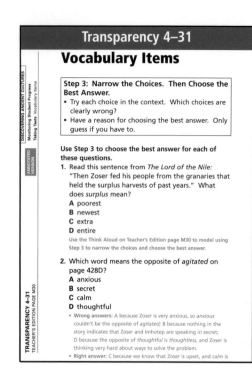

 STEP 3 Narrow the Choices.
Then Choose the Best Answer.

Display Transparency 4–31 and model Step 3.

- Have a volunteer read aloud Step 3. Tell students that they will learn more about this one step.

- Emphasize that many words have more than one meaning and that the best answer will fit the meaning of the word in the selection.

- Model how to narrow the answer choices and then choose the best answer for Question 1.

Think Aloud *I will start by narrowing the choices. I will try A in the sentence: "Then Zoser fed his people from the granaries that held the <u>poorest</u> harvests of past years." I know A is wrong, because people would not store their poorest crops. The stored harvests are from past years, so B is a wrong answer.*

Two choices are left, C and D. I can guess, but I would rather be sure I am choosing the best answer. People would use part of their harvest each year rather than store the entire harvest, so D must be wrong. C must be right. Let me make sure. Any food stored from past harvests would be extra food. Yes, C is the best answer.

Complete Transparency 4–31, using Step 3.

English Language Learners

If English language learners don't know the answer to a vocabulary question right away, tell them to skip it and come back to it later. After they have answered all the other questions in that section of the test, they should try answering the vocabulary questions that they skipped. Offer these steps.

- Sound out the word. Is it familiar? Do you remember hearing it before?

- Find the sentence in the test passage where the word is used. Look carefully at the words that come before and after the word. Try to understand what the author is trying to say.

- Eliminate answer choices that are clearly wrong. If you can eliminate at least two answer choices, it is usually worth guessing.

Apply the Steps

Vocabulary Test Practice

Remind students to mark answers carefully.

- Make sure that you mark your answer in the correct place. Be especially careful if you have to mark your answer at the bottom of a page or on a separate answer sheet.

- Be very careful to fill in the answer bubble completely.

- When you change an answer, be sure to erase it completely.

Discuss how to check answers.

- Take a short break before checking answers. Stretch, stare out the window, or close your eyes and relax for a minute.

- Focus on the questions that gave you trouble. Don't check answers that you feel confident about.

- When you check an answer, try using a different strategy to find the answer than you did the first time.

Assign Practice Book pages 57 and 58.

- Provide students with practice answering multiple-choice vocabulary questions about *The Great Pyramid* on Anthology pages 428G–428L.

- Point out the answer rows at the bottom of each **Practice Book** page.

- Emphasize that students should use all three steps to answer each question.

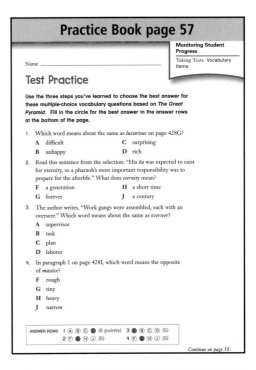

Practice Book page 57

Monitoring Student Progress
Taking Tests Vocabulary Items

Name _____

Test Practice

Use the three steps you've learned to choose the best answer for these multiple-choice vocabulary questions based on *The Great Pyramid*. Fill in the circle for the best answer in the answer rows at the bottom of the page.

1. Which word means about the same as *luxurious* on page 428G?
   A difficult
   B unhappy
   C surprising
   D rich

2. Read this sentence from the selection: "His *ka* was expected to exist for eternity, so a pharaoh's most important responsibility was to prepare for the afterlife." What does *eternity* mean?
   F a generation
   G forever
   H a short time
   J a century

3. The author writes, "Work gangs were assembled, each with an overseer." Which word means about the same as *overseer*?
   A supervisor
   B task
   C plan
   D laborer

4. In paragraph 1 on page 428I, which word means the opposite of *massive*?
   F rough
   G tiny
   H heavy
   J narrow

ANSWER ROWS 1 Ⓐ Ⓑ Ⓒ ● (5 points)   3 Ⓐ Ⓑ Ⓒ Ⓓ (5)
             2 Ⓕ ● Ⓗ Ⓙ (5)   4 Ⓕ ● Ⓗ Ⓙ (5)

Continue on page 58.

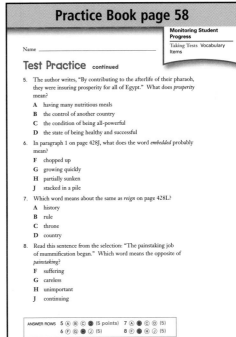

Practice Book page 58

Monitoring Student Progress
Taking Tests Vocabulary Items

Name _____

Test Practice continued

5. The author writes, "By contributing to the afterlife of their pharaoh, they were insuring prosperity for all of Egypt." What does *prosperity* mean?
   A having many nutritious meals
   B the control of another country
   C the condition of being all-powerful
   D the state of being healthy and successful

6. In paragraph 1 on page 428J, what does the word *embedded* probably mean?
   F chopped up
   G growing quickly
   H partially sunken
   J stacked in a pile

7. Which word means about the same as *reign* on page 428L?
   A history
   B rule
   C throne
   D country

8. Read this sentence from the selection: "The painstaking job of mummification began." Which word means the opposite of *painstaking*?
   F suffering
   G careless
   H unimportant
   J continuing

ANSWER ROWS 5 Ⓐ Ⓑ Ⓒ ● (5 points)   7 Ⓐ ● Ⓒ Ⓓ (5)
             6 Ⓕ Ⓖ ● Ⓙ (5)   8 Ⓕ ● Ⓗ Ⓙ (5)

Additional Resources

Teacher's Assessment Handbook

Suggests more strategies for preparing students for standardized tests

OBJECTIVES

Students review how to
- infer an author's viewpoint and detect bias
- identify unstated cause-and-effect relationships
- infer main ideas from details

COMPREHENSION

Author's Viewpoint

Review author's viewpoint, bias, and assumption.

- Author's viewpoint is the author's attitude about a particular individual, group, or issue.
- Bias is a strong feeling on the part of the author toward one side in a controversy.
- Assumptions are beliefs not supported by facts.

Model how to infer an author's viewpoint.

- Read aloud the second paragraph of *The Lord of the Nile* on Anthology page 428B. Then model.

Think Aloud *The author's choice of the phrase* a good and just king *shows a positive attitude toward Zoser. The depiction of him as a benevolent leader may be one-sided, however. Were all his actions good and just?*

Have students infer an author's viewpoint.

- Have partners infer the author's viewpoint in *The Great Pyramid* and give supporting details. Have them analyze the selection for bias.

Practice Book page 59

Name _____

Monitoring Student Progress

Comprehension Skill Cause and Effect

Find the Cause and Effect

Complete the chart with the missing cause or effect. Refer to the Anthology page numbers listed if you need help remembering story events.

Cause		Effect
The Nile floods every year. (page 428B)	▶	The flood waters fill the canals and leave rich mud in the nearby fields. (2)
One year, the Nile does not flood. (2 points)	▶	All growing things shrivel and die. (page 428B)
The lack of food makes people desperate. (page 428D)	▶	The strong steal from the weak, and the old and sick are left to starve. (2)
Imhotep does not know the birthplace of the Nile nor the god or goddess who rules there. (page 428D)	▶	Imhotep goes to the Temple of Thoth to find an answer. (2)
Zoser learns that at the birthplace of the Nile is a god who can make the river flood again. (2)	▶	Zoser travels to the birthplace of the Nile. (page 428D)
Khnemu tells Zoser that he has neglected the gods. (2)	▶	Zoser has Imhotep build a temple for Khnemu. (page 428F)

Cause and Effect

Review identifying cause and effect.

- Authors sometimes state cause-and-effect relationships directly, using words such as *because* and *as a result of*.
- Other times, readers must figure out these relationships by asking themselves questions such as, "What led up to this?"

Model how to identify an unstated cause-and-effect relationship.

- Read aloud the second paragraph on Anthology page 428I.

Think Aloud *The farmers who helped build the Great Pyramid were forever changed by the experience. What caused this change? Working on the pyramid opened the farmers' eyes to the world beyond their villages.*

Have students identify unstated cause-and-effect relationships.

- Assign **Practice Book** page 59.

Topic, Main Idea, and Details

Review topic, main idea, and supporting details.

- The topic is what a selection is about, main ideas are the most important ideas about the topic, and details tell more about the main ideas.

- Authors sometimes state main ideas directly. Other times, readers must infer a main idea from details.

Model how to infer a main idea.

- Read aloud the first paragraph in the main column on Anthology page 428L.

- Model inferring the main idea from details.

Think Aloud *The main idea of this paragraph is not stated directly. I'll have to infer it. The first sentence tells when Khufu died. The other sentences tell about things people did to prepare for his burial inside the Great Pyramid. The main idea seems to be "rituals followed after Khufu's death."*

Have students infer main ideas.

- Assign **Practice Book** page 60.

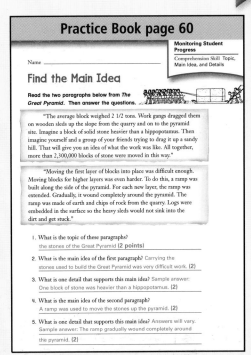

Practice Book page 60

Monitoring Student Progress

Comprehension Skill Topic, Main Idea, and Details

Name _____

Find the Main Idea

Read the two paragraphs below from *The Great Pyramid.* Then answer the questions.

"The average block weighed 2 1/2 tons. Work gangs dragged them on wooden sleds up the slope from the quarry and on to the pyramid site. Imagine a block of solid stone heavier than a hippopotamus. Then imagine yourself and a group of your friends trying to drag it up a sandy hill. That will give you an idea of what the work was like. All together, more than 2,300,000 blocks of stone were moved in this way."

"Moving the first layer of blocks into place was difficult enough. Moving blocks for higher layers was even harder. To do this, a ramp was built along the side of the pyramid. For each new layer, the ramp was extended. Gradually, it wound completely around the pyramid. The ramp was made of earth and chips of rock from the quarry. Logs were embedded in the surface so the heavy sleds would not sink into the dirt and get stuck."

1. What is the topic of these paragraphs?
   the stones of the Great Pyramid **(2 points)**

2. What is the main idea of the first paragraph? Carrying the stones used to build the Great Pyramid was very difficult work. **(2)**

3. What is one detail that supports this main idea? Sample answer: One block of stone was heavier than a hippopotamus. **(2)**

4. What is the main idea of the second paragraph?
   A ramp was used to move the stones up the pyramid. **(2)**

5. What is one detail that supports this main idea? Answers will vary. Sample answer: The ramp gradually wound completely around the pyramid. **(2)**

SKILL REVIEW:
Structural Analysis/Vocabulary

OBJECTIVES

Students review how to
- decode words with *-ure, -ic,* and *-al*
- decode words with *-ion* and *-ation*
- identify unstressed syllables

More Suffixes

Review the suffixes *-ic, -al,* and *-ure.*

- A suffix is added to the end of a base word and changes its meaning.
- The suffixes *-ic* and *-al* mean "characterized by."
- The suffix *-ure* means "the act or condition of."

Model how to decode a word with *-ure.*

- Display *under <u>pressure</u>*. Model how to decode *pressure*.

 **Think Aloud** *I see the suffix* -ure *and the base word* press. Pressure *must mean "the act or condition of being pressed."*

Have partners decode words.

- Display *historic, failure, periodic, betrayal, departure, musical.*
- Have partners take turns decoding the words.

Suffixes *-ion* and *-ation*

Review the suffixes *-ion* and *-ation.*

- The suffixes *-ion* and *-ation* can mean "action or process" or "state or condition."
- The suffixes *-ion* and *-ation* are often used to form nouns from verbs.

Model how to decode a word with *-ion.*

- Display *<u>combination</u> of causes*. Model decoding *combination*.

Think Aloud *I see the suffix* -ion, *a clue that the word is a noun. I also recognize the verb* combine, *meaning "to join." This word must be a noun that means "the condition of being joined." That makes sense.*

Have students decode words.

- Display *civilization, reflection, irrigation, construction.*
- Have students decode each word and tell its meaning.

Unstressed Syllables

Review unstressed syllables.

- Unstressed syllables have less emphasis than stressed syllables when spoken.
- In words with more than one syllable, at least one syllable is unstressed.
- To decode longer words, try emphasizing different syllables.

Model how to decode stressed and unstressed syllables.

- Display this phrase: *dramatic* *makeup*.
- Model decoding *dramatic*.

Think Aloud *I'll try sounding out the word by emphasizing different syllables:* DRUH-mat-ihk, druh-mat-IHK, druh-MAT-ihk. *That last one sounds right and makes sense in the phrase.*

Have students decode words.

- Assign **Practice Book** page 61.

Options

SKILL REVIEW:
Vocabulary

OBJECTIVES

Students review how to

- choose the correct definition for a multiple-meaning word
- use synonyms correctly
- use prefixes and suffixes to determine meaning

Multiple-Meaning Words

Review multiple-meaning words.

- Some words have more than one meaning.
- The correct meaning can often be figured out from the context.

Model how to figure out the correct meaning of a word.

- Display these sentences: *The ground was covered with small rocks. Blowing sand had ground away the cliff.*
- Model using context to figure out each meaning of *ground*.

Think Aloud   *In the first sentence, the writer talks about a surface that has rocks on it. The word* ground *must be a noun that means "the surface of the earth." In the second sentence, the writer talks about an action that can wear away a cliff. Here* ground *must be a verb: the past tense of* grind.

Have partners use context to determine meaning.

- Assign **Practice Book** page 62.

Synonyms

Review synonyms.

- Synonyms are words with the same or nearly the same meaning.
- Keep in mind shades of meaning when choosing synonyms.
- Look up synonyms in a dictionary to confirm their meanings.

Model how to choose a correct synonym.

- Display this sentence: *The Civil War reenactment was a series of pretend battles.*
- Display these synonyms for *pretend: play, make-believe, mock, imaginary.*
- Try each one in place of *pretend*, discussing shades of meaning and demonstrating that *mock* is the best substitute.

Have students choose synonyms.

- Display these synonyms: *fight, argument, scuffle, battle, clash.*
- Have partners discuss their shades of meaning and use each synonym correctly in a sentence.

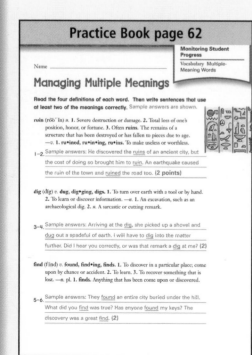

Practice Book page 62

Dictionary: Prefixes and Suffixes

Review how to use prefixes and suffixes.

- Prefixes and suffixes are listed alphabetically in a dictionary, with their meanings.

- Some prefixes and suffixes may have various spellings.

- A dictionary can show whether a letter pattern (*de*) is a prefix (*destruct*) or part of the base word (*dessert*).

Model how to use a prefix to figure out a meaning.

- Display this sentence: *The blast <u>dislodged</u> the stones.*

- Model how to figure out the meaning of *dislodged*.

Think Aloud *I see a prefix,* dis-. *Looking it up in a dictionary, I find that* dis- *means "not." The base word is* lodge, *meaning "to become embedded."* Dislodged *must mean the opposite of this, so the stones must have come out of somewhere, such as a wall.*

Have students use prefixes and suffixes.

- Display *magnification, predawn, grateful, disrepair, reelect, operator.*

- Have students use prefixes and suffixes to help them figure out each word's meaning.

Options — SKILL REVIEW: Spelling

SPELLING

OBJECTIVES

Students review
- words that have the /sh/ sound
- verbs and the nouns formed by adding the suffix *-ion* or *-ation* to the verbs
- words that have unstressed syllables
- words with endings and suffixes

SPELLING WORDS

Basic

ancient	edition
pressure	mission
connect	combination
cooperate	position
problem	physical
shallow	musician
partial	construct
connection	admire
cooperation	difficult
ambulance	surprise
official	establish
cushion	construction
combine	admiration
success	accept
example	crisis

Challenge

expedition	negotiate
diminish	morale
beneficial	insulation
insulate	potential
utensil	negotiation

DAY 1 — THE /sh/ SOUND

Pretest Use the Day 5 sentences.

Review words that have the /sh/ sound.

- Display *polish, station, session,* and *glacier.* Read each word aloud, emphasizing /sh/.
- Point out the *sh, ti, ss,* and *ci* spellings for /sh/.

Have students identify words with different spellings of /sh/.

- Have students make a four-column chart with the headings *sh, ti, ss,* and *ci.*
- Display these words: *cushion, edition, establish, ancient, musician, pressure, shallow, partial, mission,* and *official.*
- Have students write each word in the appropriate column.
- Repeat with the Challenge Words *expedition, diminish,* and *beneficial.*

Practice/Homework Assign **Practice Book** page 259.

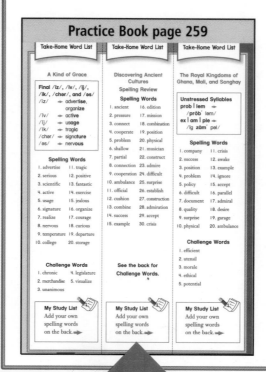

Practice Book page 259

DAY 2 — ADDING *-ion* OR *-ation*

Review verbs and the nouns formed by adding the suffix *-ion* or *-ation* to the verbs.

- Display *examine* and *examination.* Read each word aloud.
- Point out that the final *e* was dropped from the verb *examine* and the suffix *-ation* was added to make the noun *examination.*

Have students match verbs with nouns formed by adding *-ion* or *-ation* to them.

- Display *connect, construct, admire, cooperate,* and *combine* in one column and *cooperation, admiration, construction, combination,* and *connection* in another.
- Have students pair verbs with the related nouns formed by adding *-ion* or *-ation* to them.
- Then have students list what was done to each verb to create the related noun.

Practice/Homework Assign **Practice Book** page 63.

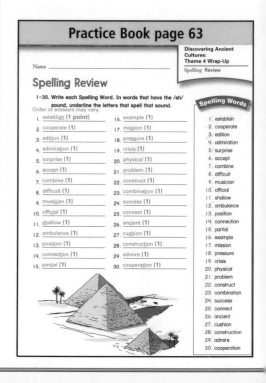

Practice Book page 63

Take-Home Word List

M38 THEME 4: Ancient Cultures

anasase

DAY 3 — UNSTRESSED SYLLABLES

Review words that have unstressed syllables.

Display *awake* and *parallel*. Say each word.

Divide both words into syllables. Have students identify the stressed syllable in each word. (*wake; par*)

Circle the unstressed syllable in *awake* (*a*) and the two unstressed syllables in *parallel* (*al, lel*). Point out that the spellings of the vowel sounds in these syllables are unclear and must be remembered.

Have students identify unstressed syllables.

Display *position, problem, success, surprise, physical, example, ambulance, accept, difficult,* and *crisis*.

Have partners read each word, identify the unstressed syllables, and tell what letter(s) spell the vowel sounds.

Practice/Homework Assign **Practice Book** page 64.

Practice Book page 64

Discovering Ancient Cultures:
Theme 4 Wrap-Up
Spelling Review

Name _____

Spelling Spree

Spelling Words
1. ambulance
2. physical
3. admire
4. difficult
5. musician
6. edition
7. surprise
8. accept
9. problem
10. ancient
11. partial
12. success
13. combine
14. cushion
15. shallow

Headline Help Write the Spelling Word that means the opposite of the underlined word in each headline. Begin each word with a capital letter.

1. Solution Surfaces at Archaeological Dig Site Problem **(1 point)**
2. Thousand-Year-Old Artifacts Found in Deep Pit Shallow **(1)**
3. Protecting the Great Wall from Vandals Proves Easy Difficult **(1)**
4. Experts Reject Award for Preserving Historic City Accept **(1)**
5. Modern Aztec Stone Discovered in Mexico Ancient **(1)**
6. Workers Uncover Total Remains of Mummy Partial **(1)**
7. Mental Fitness Helps Dig Workers Handle Desert Heat Physical **(1)**
8. Archaeologists Meet with Failure on African Dig Success **(1)**

Tongue Twisters Write the Spelling Word that completes each tongue twister.

9. Milly the muddled musician **(1)** made many mistakes.
10. Cousin Carl can't combine **(1)** cucumbers and carrots.
11. Adrian will always admire **(1)** Aunt Alice's albums.
12. Sarah spilled soup when startled by Sam's silly surprise **(1)**.
13. Ed's early edition **(1)** of the encyclopedia was expensive.
14. A calico cat is curled up on the couch cushion **(1)**.
15. Amber asked for an ambulance **(1)** after the accident.

DAY 4 — ENDINGS/SUFFIXES

Review words with endings and suffixes.

- Display *blaming* and *entirely*.
- Point out the suffix *-ing* and the ending *-ly*.
- Show that *e* was dropped when *-ing* was added to *blame*.

Have students identify endings and suffixes.

- Display *advanced, adorable, excitement, amusement, scarcely, graceful, heaving,* and *forgiveness*.
- Have students write each word and then write the base word and suffix that make it up.
- Then have students circle each base word from which a final *e* was dropped when the ending or suffix was added.

Practice/Homework Assign **Practice Book** page 65.

Practice Book page 65

Discovering Ancient Cultures:
Theme 4 Wrap-Up
Spelling Review

Name _____

Proofreading and Writing

Spelling Words
1. crisis
2. example
3. position
4. cooperate
5. cooperation
6. admiration
7. combination
8. connection
9. connect
10. construction
11. construct
12. mission
13. pressure
14. establish
15. official

Proofreading Circle the six misspelled Spelling Words in this report. Then write each word correctly.

It can be exciting to *establish* facts about an ancient culture. Often it is necessary to set up an *oficial* camp. The exact *position* of the camp can be based on old records. One useful activity is to *construck* a model of a building that may have existed. Another is to study an *exsample* of the tools the people used. A *combonation* of study and exploration is needed.

1. establish **(1 point)**
2. official **(1)**
3. position **(1)**
4. construct **(1)**
5. example **(1)**
6. combination **(1)**

Write the Spelling Words that best complete this log entry.

August 16

I am filled with 7. admiration **(1)** for my fine crew. With their help and 8. cooperation **(1)**, we are able to resolve each new 9. crisis **(1)** quickly. We are working under some 10. pressure **(1)**, but we are coping. Our goal, or 11. mission **(1)**, is to study the methods of 12. construction **(1)** used to build an old temple. I hope to find a 13. connection **(1)** between the temple and the buildings in the north. If I can prove that the styles 14. connect **(1)** with one another, it will be a great discovery. Now, if the weather would only 15. cooperate **(1)**!

_____ **Write a News Report** On a separate sheet of paper, write a news report. **Use the Spelling Review Words.** Responses will vary. **(5)**

DAY 5 — TEST

Say the underlined word, read the sentence, say the word again. Students write the underlined words.

Basic Words

1. We will dig a **shallow** hole and **construct** the fountain.
2. He is **difficult** to **surprise**.
3. The **official** ignored the town's **problem**.
4. Which **musician** do you **admire**?
5. I have great **admiration** for the **ancient** Egyptians.
6. Don't **pressure** us to **accept** her offer.
7. You cannot ride in the **ambulance** in that **position**.
8. Raylene's effort to **establish** a new club was a **partial** success.
9. Sharing tools is an **example** of **cooperation**.
10. Nikki will have **success** with the new **edition** of her cookbook.
11. The performers must **combine** their **physical** talents.
12. The **mission** calls for a **combination** of courage and intelligence.
13. Everyone must **cooperate** on a **construction** site.
14. Do not put a **cushion** over an electrical **connection**.
15. I'll **connect** the phone in case of **crisis**.

Challenge Words

16. It will be **beneficial** to **negotiate**.
17. Better **insulation** would warm the office and improve **morale**.
18. Bring that **utensil** on the **expedition**.
19. A **potential** disaster can be averted if you **insulate** the cabin.
20. The chances for **negotiation** **diminish** with each passing hour.

SPELLING

Spelling M39

SKILL REVIEW: Grammar

OBJECTIVES

Students review how to

- identify adjectives, demonstrative adjectives, and the articles *a, an,* and *the*
- correctly capitalize and use proper adjectives
- identify and write comparative and superlative forms of adjectives
- identify and write comparative and superlative forms of *good* and *bad*
- identify adverbs that modify verbs and adjectives
- identify and write comparative and superlative forms of adverbs

---

DAY 1 — ADJECTIVES

Review kinds of adjectives and proper adjectives.

- An adjective modifies, or describes, a noun or a pronoun. It can tell what kind, which one, or how many: <u>rich</u> mud, <u>these</u> crops, <u>six</u> years.

- *A, an,* and *the* are special adjectives called articles. *A* and *an* refer to any item in a group; *the* refers to a specific item or items: <u>a</u> pyramid, <u>an</u> early flood, <u>the</u> pharaoh.

- Demonstrative adjectives tell which one. *This* and *these* point out items nearby; *that* and *those* point out items farther away. *This* and *that* refer to one item; *these* and *those* refer to more than one.

- A proper adjective is an adjective formed from a proper noun: <u>Egyptian</u> pyramids.

- Proper adjectives are always capitalized.

Have students identify kinds of adjectives, including proper adjectives.

- Assign **Practice Book** page 66.

Practice Book page 66

Name _____

Monitoring Student Progress
Grammar Adjectives

Finding Adjectives

Identify the adjectives in each sentence. Draw one line under each descriptive adjective. Draw two lines under each demonstrative adjective. Circle each article. Draw a box around each proper adjective.

1. Zoser was an Egyptian ruler. (1 point)
2. He wanted happiness in the afterlife. (1)
3. An architect designed an unusual structure. (1)
4. This pyramid would become the royal tomb. (1)
5. A terrible drought occurred at that time. (1)
6. The Nile is a long African river. (1)
7. It brings rich silt and abundant water to thirsty fields. (1)
8. For seven years the Nile did not flood. (1)
9. Zoser traveled to a faraway shrine. (1)
10. After that visit, the Nile watered the dry lands. (1)

DAY 2 — COMPARING WITH ADJECTIVE

Review comparing with adjectives

- Use the comparative form of an adjective to compare two things: *The Nile is a <u>longer</u> river than the Mississippi.*

- Add *-er* to most adjectives to compare two things: *long—longer.*

- Use *more* with long adjectives to compare two things: *important—<u>more</u> important.*

- Use the superlative form to compare three or more: *The Nile is the <u>longest</u> river in Africa.*

- Add *-est* to most adjectives to compare three or more things: *long—longest.*

- Use *most* with long adjectives to compare three or more things: *important—<u>most</u> important.*

Have students use comparative forms of adjectives.

- Assign **Practice Book** page 67.

Practice Book page 67

Name _____

Monitoring Student Progress
Grammar Comparing with Adjectives

Comparing with Adjectives

Complete each sentence with the correct form of the adjective in parentheses. Remember to use *more* or *most* with long adjectives.

1. The Step Pyramid is ___older (1 point)___ than the pyramid of Khufu. (old)
2. The pyramid of Khufu is called the ___greatest (1)___ of all the pyramids. (great)
3. Life in Egypt was ___more luxurious (1)___ in the time of Khufu than it was in the time of Zoser. (luxurious)
4. Preparing for the afterlife was a pharaoh's ___most important (1)___ responsibility. (important)
5. Khufu considered himself to be the ___most distinguished (1)___ ruler in the history of Egypt. (distinguished)
6. He was determined to build the ___grandest (1)___ pyramid of all. (grand)
7. The Giza Plateau seemed a ___more favorable (1)___ location than the area where the Step Pyramid had been built. (favorable)
8. The Egyptian villagers who worked on the Great Pyramid felt that they were part of a ___larger (1)___ community. (large)

DAY 3 — COMPARING WITH *good/bad*

Review comparing with *good* and *bad*.

The adjectives *good* and *bad* have irregular comparative and superlative forms.

Use *better* to compare two things and *best* to compare three or more.

Use *worse* to compare two things and *worst* to compare three or more.

Identify comparative forms of *good* and *bad*.

Display these sentences: *I am a good stonemason. He is a better stonemason than I am. You are the best stonemason in the work gang.*

Point out the comparative and superlative forms of *good*.

Display these sentences: *He has a bad blister on his hand. You have a worse blister than he has. I have the worst blister of all.*

Point out the comparative and superlative forms of *bad*.

Have students write comparative forms of *good* and *bad*.

Display these incomplete sentences: *He has a ____ ladder than I have. Our overseer has the ____ ladder of all.*

Have students complete the sentences with comparative and superlative forms of *good*.

Then have students complete them using the comparative and superlative forms of *bad*.

DAY 4 — KINDS OF ADVERBS

Review adverbs that modify verbs and adjectives.

- An adverb can modify a verb. It tells how, where, when, or to what extent.
- An adverb can modify an adjective. It tells how or to what extent.

Identify adverbs.

- Display these sentences: *The royal barge moved slowly toward Abu. Zoser entered a very dark shrine.*
- Circle the adverbs *slowly* and *very*.
- Point out that *slowly* tells how about the verb *moved* and *very* tells to what extent about the adjective *dark*.

Have students identify adverbs.

- Display these sentences: *Khnemu was an eternally powerful deity. He sternly reproved Zoser.*
- Have students identify the adverb in each sentence and tell which adverb modifies a verb (*sternly*) and which modifies an adjective (*eternally*).

DAY 5 — COMPARING WITH ADVERBS

Review comparing with adverbs.

- Add *-er* to form the comparative and *-est* to form the superlative of many adverbs.
- Use *more* to form the comparative and *most* to form the superlative of most adverbs ending in *-ly*.

Identify adverbs used to compare.

- Display these sentences: *Our crew rows faster than your crew. Pharaoh's crew rows fastest of all. We practice more frequently than you do. Pharaoh's crew practices most frequently of all.*
- Identify *faster* and *more frequently* as adverb forms used to compare two actions.
- Identify *fastest* and *most frequently* as adverb forms used to compare more than two.

Have students write comparative forms of adverbs.

- Have students write sentences about work done on a project they helped with or observed. Ask them to use at least one adverb that compares two actions and one adverb that compares more than two actions.

SKILL REVIEW:
Prompts for Writing

WRITING

OBJECTIVES

Students review how to
- write an explanation
- write a paragraph of information
- write a comparison-and-contrast paragraph
- write a news article
- write a problem-solution composition

Explanation

👤 **Singles**	🕐 **30 minutes**
Objective	Write an explanation.

Lost Temple of the Aztecs and other selections in this theme explain some of the impressive structures built by ancient civilizations. Have you ever been curious about how something was built or was done? Written explanations help us understand events and processes. They also help answer our questions and satisfy our curiosity about things in the world. Locate a portion of one of the selections that mentions a topic you find interesting. Write an explanation that

- answers a question about who or what something is, how something works, or why something happens or happened
- presents details in logical groups
- contains additional information obtained from reference resources, if needed

Remember to delete unnecessary or repeated words.

Question
Detail
Detail
Detail

Paragraph of Information

👤 **Singles**	🕐 **30 minutes**
Objective	Write an informational paragraph.

Selections such as *The Great Wall* present facts in groups, such as how the wall was built, why it was built, what different sections of the wall now exist, and so on. Choose an event from one of the selections in this theme and write an informational paragraph about it. Make sure that your paragraph

- presents the main idea in a topic sentence
- presents facts that tell more about the main idea
- leaves out opinions
- leaves out details that are not about the main idea

Remember to add adjectives to create clearer, more vivid pictures in the mind of your reader.

Consider copying and laminating these activities for use in centers.

Comparison-and-Contrast Paragraph

👤 Singles	🕐 30 minutes
Objective	Write a comparison-and-contrast paragraph.

China's Great Wall and Egypt's Great Pyramid have fascinated people for many centuries. One way to remember more about these structures, or other interesting topics, is to note how they are similar and how they are different. Write a comparison-and-contrast paragraph about two of the ancient structures featured in this theme. To help organize your thoughts before you write, create a Venn diagram similar to the one shown below. Remember to

- explore how the two things are similar, by making comparisons, and how they are different, by showing contrasts

- use clue words to signal to the reader that you are comparing or contrasting

Remember to combine short, choppy sentences into longer, smoother sentences.

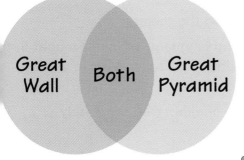

News Article

👤 Singles	🕐 30 minutes
Objective	Write a news article.

When a great new building project is finally finished, a news article often will announce or report on its opening ceremonies. Such an article helps the people who cannot be there to learn the details of the event. Choose an event from the theme to write a news article about. Remember to include detailed information about

- what the event is
- who is involved in the event
- when the event takes place
- where the event takes place
- why and how it happens or happened

Include an attention-getting headline.

Remember to add specific details to make your writing clearer and more interesting.

Problem-Solution Composition

👤 Singles	🕐 30 minutes
Objective	Write a problem-solution composition.

Think of a problem that had to be solved in one of the selections you read in this theme. Write a composition that states the problem and describes its solution. Remember that

- the composition should be two or three paragraphs long

- an introductory sentence should tell whom or what you are writing about

- the problem should be stated in the first paragraph

- the solution, along with details that lead to the solution, should be described in the second paragraph

- your composition should end with a concluding sentence

Remember to use vivid adjectives to make your descriptions more accurate.

WRITING

Assessing Student Progress

Preparing for Testing

Throughout the theme your students have had opportunities to read and think critically, connect and compare, and practice and apply new and reviewed skills and reading strategies.

Monitoring Student Progress

For Theme 4, *Discovering Ancient Cultures,* students have read the paired selections—*The Lord of the Nile* and *The Great Pyramid*—and made connections between these and other selections in the theme. They have practiced strategies for vocabulary items, and they have reviewed all the tested skills taught in this theme, as well as some tested skills taught in earlier themes. Your students are now ready to have their progress formally assessed in both theme assessments and standardized tests.

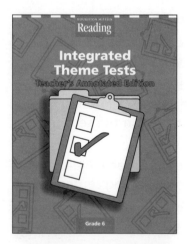

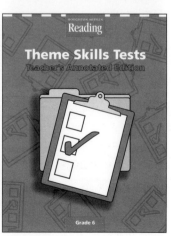

Testing Options

The **Integrated Theme Test** and the **Theme Skills Test** are formal group assessments used to evaluate student performance on theme objectives. In addition to administering one or both of these tests, you may wish to assess students' oral reading fluency

Integrated Theme Test

- Assesses students' progress as readers and writers in a format that reflects instruction
- Integrates reading and writing skills: comprehension strategies and skills, high-frequency words, spelling, grammar, and writing
- Includes authentic literary passages to test students' reading skills in context

Theme Skills Test

- May be used as a pretest or administered following the theme
- Assesses students' mastery of discrete reading and language arts skills taught in the theme: comprehension skills, high-frequency words, spelling, grammar, writing, and information and study skills
- Consists of individual skill subtests, which can be administered separately

Fluency Assessment

ral reading fluency provides a useful way to measure students' development of pid automatic word recognition. Students who are on level in Grade 6 should be le to read, accurately and with expression, an appropriate level text at the proximate rates shown in the table below.

Early Grade 6	Mid-Grade 6	Late Grade 6
106–132 words correct per minute	118–143 words correct per minute	128–151 words correct per minute

You can use the **Leveled Reading Passages Assessment Kit** to assess fluency or a **Leveled Reader** from this theme at the appropriate level for each student.

For some students you may check their oral fluency rate three times during the year. If students are working below level, you might want to check their fluency rate more often. Students can also check their own fluency by timing themselves reading easier text.

Consider decoding and comprehension, as well as reading rate, when evaluating students' reading development.

For information on how to select appropriate text, administer fluency checks, and interpret results, see the **Teacher's Assessment Handbook** pages 25–28.

Use Multiple Measures

addition to the tests mentioned on page M44, multiple measures might include e following:

Observation Checklist from this theme

Their research report writing from the Reading-Writing Workshop

Other writing, projects, or artwork

One or more items selected by the student

udent progress is best evaluated through multiple measures. Multiple measures of sessment can be collected in a portfolio. The portfolio provides a record of student ogress over time and can be useful when conferencing with the student, parents, other educators.

rn the page to continue.

Technology

Managing Assessment

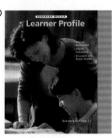

The Learner Profile® CD-ROM lets you record, manage, and report your assessment of student progress electronically.

You can

- record student progress on objectives in Theme 4.

- add or import additional objectives, including your state standards, and track your students' progress against these.

- record and manage results from the **Integrated Theme Test** and the **Theme Skills Test** for Theme 4, as well as results from other reading assessments.

- organize information about student progress and generate a variety of student assessment reports.

- use *Learner Profile To Go®* to record student progress throughout the day on a handheld computer device and then upload the information to a desktop computer.

Using Assessment to Plan Instruction

You can use the results of theme assessments to determine individual students' need for additional skill instruction and to modify instruction during the next theme. For more detail, see the test manuals or the **Teacher's Assessment Handbook**.

This chart shows Theme 4 resources for differentiating additional instruction. As you look ahead to Theme 5, you can plan to use the corresponding Theme 5 resources.

Differentiating Instruction

Assessment Shows	Use These Resources	
Difficulty with Comprehension **Emphasize** Oral comprehension, strategy development, story comprehension, vocabulary development	• **Get Set for Reading CD-ROM** • Reteaching: Comprehension, *Teacher's Edition,* pp. R8; R10; R12 • Selection Summaries in *Teacher's Resource Blackline Masters,* pp. 33–35	• *Extra Support Handbook,* pp. 132–133 138–139; 142–143, 148–149; 152–153, 158–159 • Below Level **Leveled Readers**
Difficulty with Word Skills Structural Analysis Phonics Vocabulary **Emphasize** Word skills, phonics, reading for fluency, phonemic awareness	• **Get Set For Reading CD-ROM** • Reteaching: Structural Analysis, *Teacher's Edition,* pp. R14; R16; R18 • *Extra Support Handbook,* pp. 130–131, 134–135; 140–141, 144–145; 150–151, 154–155	• *Handbook for English Language Learners,* pp. 134–135, 136, 138–140, 142; 144–145, 146, 148–150, 152; 154–155, 156, 158–160, 162 • **Lexia Quick Phonics Assessment CD-ROM** • **Lexia Phonics CD-ROM: Intermediate Intervention**
Difficulty with Fluency **Emphasize** Reading and rereading of independent level text, vocabulary development	• Leveled Bibliography, *Teacher's Edition,* pp. 354E–354F • Below Level **Theme Paperback** • Below Level **Leveled Readers**	• Leveled Readers: Below Level lesson, *Teacher's Edition,* pp. 383O; 407O; 427O
Difficulty with Writing **Emphasize** Complete sentences, combining sentences, choosing exact words	• *Handbook for English Language Learners,* pp. 143; 153; 163 • Reteaching: Grammar Skills, *Teacher's Edition,* pp. R20–R25	• Improving Writing, *Teacher's Edition,* pp. 383J, 383L; 387E; 407J, 407L; 427J 427L
Overall High Performance **Emphasize** Independent reading and writing, vocabulary development, critical thinking	• Challenge/Extension Activities: Comprehension, *Teacher's Edition,* pp. R9; R11; R13 • Challenge/Extension Activities: Vocabulary, *Teacher's Edition,* pp. R15; R17; R19 • Reading Assignment Cards, *Teacher's Resource Blackline Masters,* pp. 73–78	• Above Level **Theme Paperback** • Above Level **Leveled Readers** • Leveled Readers: Above Level lesson, *Teacher's Edition,* pp. 383Q; 407Q; 427Q • Challenge Activity Masters, *Challenge Handbook,* CH4–1 to CH4–6

Literature

MYTHS

1 **Background and Genre Vocabulary**

2 **Main Selections**

3 **Write a Myth**

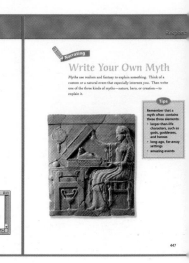

Instructional Support

Planning and Practice

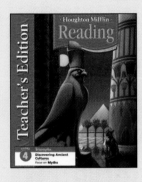

- Planning and classroom management
- Reading instruction
- Skill lessons
- Materials for reaching all learners

- Independent practice for skills, Level 6.2

- Transparencies
- Strategy Posters
- Blackline Masters

Technology

Audio Selections

Arachne the Spinner

Guitar Solo

How Music Was Fetched Out of Heaven

www.eduplace.com

Log on to Education Place for vocabulary support—

- **e•Glossary**
- **e•WordGame**

Leveled Books for Reaching All Learners

Leveled Readers and Leveled Practice

- Independent reading for building fluency

- Topic, comprehension strategy, and comprehension skill linked to selections

- Lessons in Teacher's Edition, pages 447O–447R

- Leveled practice for every book

Technology

Leveled Readers
Audio available

● BELOW LEVEL

THE QUEST FOR
Medusa's Head

retold by
Stephanie Cohen
illustrated by
Craig Spearing

▲ ON LEVEL

THE SUN'S
STRENGTH
An Ancient Chinese Myth

retold by Jiang Qingling
illustrated by Kristen Sorra

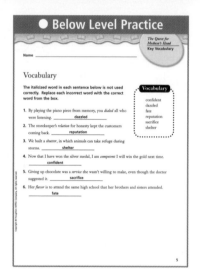

● Below Level Practice

The Quest for Medusa's Head
Key Vocabulary

Name

Vocabulary

The italicized word in each sentence below is not used correctly. Replace each incorrect word with the correct word from the box.

Vocabulary
confident
dazzled
fate
reputation
sacrifice
shelter

1. By playing the piano piece from memory, you *dialed* all who were listening. _____ dazzled

2. The storekeeper's *relation* for honesty kept the customers coming back. _____ reputation

3. We built a *shutter*, in which animals can take refuge during storms. _____ shelter

4. Now that I have won the silver medal, I am *competent* I will win the gold next time. _____ confident

5. Giving up chocolate was a *service* she wasn't willing to make, even though the doctor suggested it. _____ sacrifice

6. Her *flavor* is to attend the same high school that her brothers and sisters attended. _____ fate

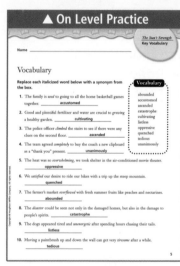

▲ On Level Practice

The Sun's Strength
Key Vocabulary

Name

Vocabulary

Replace each italicized word below with a synonym from the box.

Vocabulary
abounded
accustomed
ascended
catastrophe
cultivating
listless
oppressive
quenched
tedious
unanimously

1. The family is *used* to going to all the home basketball games together. _____ accustomed

2. Good and plentiful fertilizer and water are crucial to *growing* a healthy garden. _____ cultivating

3. The police officer *climbed* the stairs to see if there were any clues on the second floor. _____ ascended

4. The team agreed *completely* to buy the coach a new clipboard as a "thank you" present. _____ unanimously

5. The heat was so *overwhelming*, we took shelter in the air-conditioned movie theater. _____ oppressive

6. We *satisfied* our desire to ride our bikes with a trip up the steep mountain. _____ quenched

7. The farmer's market *overflowed* with fresh summer fruits like peaches and nectarines. _____ abounded

8. The *disaster* could be seen not only in the damaged homes, but also in the damage to people's spirits. _____ catastrophe

9. The dogs appeared tired and *unenergetic* after spending hours chasing their tails. _____ listless

10. Moving a paintbrush up and down the wall can get very *tiresome* after a while. _____ tedious

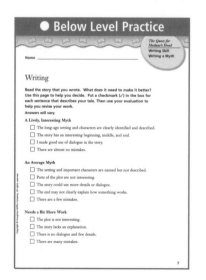

● Below Level Practice

The Quest for Medusa's Head
Writing Skill
Writing a Myth

Name

Writing

Read the story that you wrote. What does it need to make it better? Use this page to help you decide. Put a checkmark (✓) in the box for each sentence that describes your tale. Then use your evaluation to help you revise your work.
Answers will vary.

A Lively, Interesting Myth
- ☐ The long-ago setting and characters are clearly identified and described.
- ☐ The story has an interesting beginning, middle, and end.
- ☐ I made good use of dialogue in the story.
- ☐ There are almost no mistakes.

An Average Myth
- ☐ The setting and important characters are named but not described.
- ☐ Parts of the plot are not interesting.
- ☐ The story could use more details or dialogue.
- ☐ The end may not clearly explain how something works.
- ☐ There are a few mistakes.

Needs a Bit More Work
- ☐ The plot is not interesting.
- ☐ The story lacks an explanation.
- ☐ There is no dialogue and few details.
- ☐ There are many mistakes.

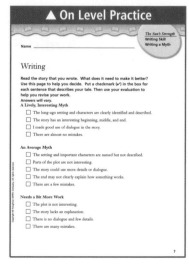

▲ On Level Practice

The Sun's Strength
Writing Skill
Writing a Myth

Name

Writing

Read the story that you wrote. What does it need to make it better? Use this page to help you decide. Put a checkmark (✓) in the box for each sentence that describes your tale. Then use your evaluation to help you revise your work.
Answers will vary.

A Lively, Interesting Myth
- ☐ The long-ago setting and characters are clearly identified and described.
- ☐ The story has an interesting beginning, middle, and end.
- ☐ I made good use of dialogue in the story.
- ☐ There are almost no mistakes.

An Average Myth
- ☐ The setting and important characters are named but not described.
- ☐ Parts of the plot are not interesting.
- ☐ The story could use more details or dialogue.
- ☐ The end may not clearly explain how something works.
- ☐ There are a few mistakes.

Needs a Bit More Work
- ☐ The plot is not interesting.
- ☐ The story lacks an explanation.
- ☐ There is no dialogue and few details.
- ☐ There are many mistakes.

ABOVE LEVEL

ODIN'S WISDOM

adapted by Marta Mordwitt
illustrated by Val Paul Taylor

Leveled Readers

Above Level Practice

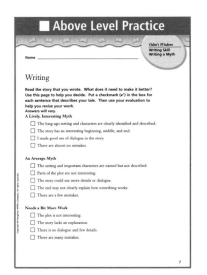

LANGUAGE SUPPORT

Perseus and Medusa

Leveled Readers

retold by Stephanie Cohen
illustrated by Craig Spearing

Language Support Practice

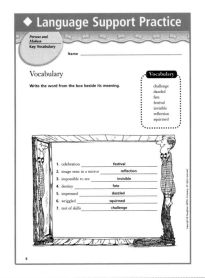

Suggestions for Independent Reading

- Recommended trade books for independent reading in the genre

D'Aulaires' Book of Greek Myths

(Doubleday)
by Ingri and Edgar D'Aulaire

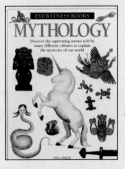

Mythology

(Dorling Kindersley)
by Neil Philip

Mythical Birds & Beasts from Many Lands

(Dutton)
retold by Margaret Mayo

Celtic Myths

(Bedrick)
by Sam MacBratney

Daily Lesson Plans

Technology

Lesson Planner CD-ROM allows you to customize the chart below to develop your own lesson plans.

Reading
Comprehension

50–60 minutes

Leveled Readers
- Fluency Practice
- Independent Reading

DAY 1

Teacher Read Aloud, 429K–429L
"Chinook Wind Wrestles Cold Wind"

Building Background, 430

Genre Vocabulary, 431

| ancient | characteristics | myth | relationship |
| behavior | hero | nature | task |

Reading the Selection, 432–436
Arachne the Spinner

Comprehension Skill, 432
Understanding Myths

Comprehension Strategy, 432
Predict/Infer

Leveled Readers
The Quest for Medusa's Head
The Sun's Strength,
  An Ancient Chinese Myth
Odin's Wisdom
Perseus and Medusa

Lessons and Leveled Practice, 447O–447R

DAY 2

Reading the Selections, 437–445
Guitar Solo; How Music Was Fetched Out of Heaven

Comprehension Check, 445

Responding, 446
Think About the Selections

Comprehension Strategy, 438
Predict/Infer

Leveled Readers
The Quest for Medusa's Head
The Sun's Strength,
  An Ancient Chinese Myth
Odin's Wisdom
Perseus and Medusa

Lessons and Leveled Practice, 447O–447R

Word Work
Phonics/Decoding
Vocabulary
Spelling

20–30 minutes

Phonics/Decoding Longer Words, 433
Phonics/Decoding Strategy

Vocabulary, 432–436
Selection Vocabulary

Spelling, 447E
Consonant Changes

Structural Analysis, 447C
Prefixes and Suffixes

Vocabulary, 437–445
Selection Vocabulary

Spelling, 447E
Consonant Changes Review and Practice

Writing and Oral Language
Writing
Grammar
Listening/Speaking/Viewing

20–30 minutes

Writing, 447, 447K
Prewriting a Myth

Grammar, 447I
Using the Right Word

Daily Language Practice
1. The democratic system of politicks comes from ancient greece. (politics; Greece.)
2. In his excellent introducshun to greek myths, the author moved easy from one topic to another. (introduction; Greek; easily)

Listening/Speaking/Viewing, 429K–429L, 436
Teacher Read Aloud, Stop and Think

Writing, 447K
Drafting a Myth

Grammar, 447I
Using the Right Word Practice

Daily Language Practice
3. When she looked at the equations the mathem tishun felt confidently. (equations,; mathematicia confident)
4. Did the clinician work quick to diduce the caus of the infection. (quickly; deduce; infection?)

Listening/Speaking/Viewing, 445–446
Wrapping Up, Responding

Target Skills of the Week

Phonics	Prefixes and Suffixes
Comprehension	Predict/Infer, Understanding Myths
Vocabulary	Words from Myths
Fluency	Leveled Readers

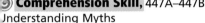

DAY 3

Rereading the Selections

Rereading for Genre, 439
Fantasy

Responding, 446
Preparing for Literature Discussion

Comprehension Skill, 447A–447B
Understanding Myths

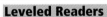

Leveled Readers
The Quest for Medusa's Head
The Sun's Strength,
  An Ancient Chinese Myth
Odin's Wisdom
Perseus and Medusa
Lessons and Leveled Practice, 447O–447R

Phonics Review, 447D
Variant Consonant Pronunciations

Vocabulary, 447G
Words from Myths

Spelling, 447F
Vocabulary: Word Part *poli*; Consonant Changes Practice

Writing, 447L
Revising a Myth
Using Dialogue

Grammar, 447J
Using *good* and *well*

Daily Language Practice
5. Did the french or the spanish politishun give the best answer? (French; Spanish; politician; better)
6. Did your practisce session go good? (practice; well)

DAY 4

Rereading the Selections

Rereading for Writer's Craft, 443
Similes

Responding, 446
Literature Discussion

Comprehension Skill, 435
Visualizing

Leveled Readers
The Quest for Medusa's Head
The Sun's Strength,
  An Ancient Chinese Myth
Odin's Wisdom
Perseus and Medusa
Lessons and Leveled Practice, 447O–447R

Structural Analysis, 447M
Language Center: Word Parts Challenge

Vocabulary, 447M
Language Center: Building Vocabulary

Spelling, 447F
Consonant Changes Game, Proofreading

Writing, 447L
Proofreading a Myth

Grammar, 447J
Using *good* and *well* Practice

Daily Language Practice
7. The electrishion did not feel good at the end of the day. (electrician; well)
8. My mothers' suggestions are always very praktical. (mother's; practical)

Listening/Speaking/Viewing, 446
Literature Discussion

DAY 5

Rereading for Fluency, 443

Responding, 446
Internet Activity

Information and Study Skills, 447H
Finding Media Resources

Leveled Readers
The Quest for Medusa's Head
The Sun's Strength,
  An Ancient Chinese Myth
Odin's Wisdom
Perseus and Medusa
Lessons and Leveled Practice, 447O–447R

Phonics, 447N
Language Center: Race to the Sun

Vocabulary, 447M
Language Center: Vocabulary Game

Spelling, 447F
Test: Consonant Changes

Writing, 447L
Publishing a Myth

Grammar, 447J
Using Forms of *good* and *bad*

Daily Language Practice
9. We saw two performers, and the magishun was the best one. (magician; better)
10. He performs magick tricks while he tells storys. (magic; stories)

Listening/Speaking/Viewing, 447N
Language Center: Retell an Oral History

Managing Flexible Groups

Leveled Instruction and Leveled Practice

	DAY 1	**DAY 2**
WHOLE CLASS	• Teacher Read Aloud (TE pp. 429K–429L) • Building Background, Introducing Vocabulary (TE pp. 430–431, 433) • Comprehension Strategy: Introduce (TE p. 432) • Comprehension Skill: Introduce (TE p. 432) • Purpose Setting (TE p. 433) **After reading** *Arachne the Spinner* • Stop and Think (TE p. 436)	• Building Background (TE pp. 437, 441) • Comprehension Strategy: Reinforce (TE p. 438) **After reading** *Guitar Solo, How Music Was Fetched Out of Heaven* • Wrapping Up (TE p. 445) • Comprehension Check (Practice Book p. 71) • Responding: Think About the Selections (TE p. 446)
SMALL GROUPS		
Extra Support	**TEACHER-LED** • Preview *Arachne the Spinner* (TE pp. 432–436). • Support reading with Extra Support/Intervention notes (TE pp. 433, 434, 435, 436, 437, 438, 441, 442, 444).	**Partner or Individual Work** • Reread *Arachne the Spinner* (TE pp. 432–436). • Preview, read *Guitar Solo, How Music Was Fetched Out of Heaven* (TE pp. 437–445). • Comprehension Check (Practice Book p. 71)
Challenge	**Individual Work** • Extend reading with Challenge notes (TE pp. 439, 445). • See Independent Activities below and Classroom Management (TE pp. 429I–429J).	**Individual Work** • See Independent Activities below and Classroom Management (TE pp. 429I–429J).
English Language Learners	**TEACHER-LED** • Preview vocabulary and *Arachne the Spinner* to Stop and Think (TE pp. 431–436). • Support reading with English Language Learners notes (TE pp. 430, 442, 443).	**TEACHER-LED** • Review *Arachne the Spinner* (TE pp. 432–436). ✔ • Preview, read *Guitar Solo, How Music Was Fetched Out of Heaven* (TE pp. 437–445). • Begin Comprehension Check together (Practice Book p. 71).

Independent Activities

- Journals: selection notes, questions
- Complete, review Practice Book (pp. 69–73) and Leveled Readers Practice Blackline Masters (TE pp. 447O–447R).
- Leveled Readers (TE pp. 447O–447R) or Suggestions for Independent Reading (TE p. 429D)
- Responding activities (TE pp. 446–447)
- Language Center activities (TE pp. 447M–447N)

✔ Opportunity to informally assess oral reading rate

DAY 3

- Rereading: Lesson on Genre (TE p. 439)
- Comprehension Skill: Main lesson (TE pp. 447A–447B)
- Responding: Preparing for Literature Discussion (TE p. 446, Practice Book p. 72)

DAY 4

- Rereading: Lesson on Writer's Craft (TE p. 443)
- Rereading: Comprehension Skill lesson (TE p. 435)
- Responding: Literature Discussion (TE p. 446)

DAY 5

- Responding: Select from Activities (TE pp. 446-447)
- Information and Study Skills (TE p. 447H)

TEACHER-LED

Review Comprehension Check (Practice Book p. 71).

Preview Leveled Reader: Below Level (TE p. 447O), or read book from Suggestions for Independent Reading (TE p. 429D) ✔

Partner or Individual Work

- Complete Leveled Reader: Below Level (TE p. 447O), or read book from Suggestions for Independent Reading (TE p. 429D).

TEACHER-LED

- Read or reread book from Suggestions for Independent Reading (TE p. 429D). ✔

TEACHER-LED

- Preview Leveled Reader: Above Level (TE p. 447Q), or read book from Suggestions for Independent Reading (TE p. 429D). ✔

Individual Work

- Complete Leveled Reader: Above Level (TE p. 447Q), or read book from Suggestions for Independent Reading (TE p. 429D).

TEACHER-LED

- Read or reread book from Suggestions for Independent Reading (TE p. 429D). ✔

Partner or Individual Work

- Complete Comprehension Check (Practice Book p. 71).
- Begin Leveled Reader: Language Support (TE p. 447R), or read book from Suggestions for Independent Reading (TE p. 429D).

TEACHER-LED

- Complete Leveled Reader: Language Support (TE p. 447R), or continue book from Suggestions for Independent Reading (TE p. 429D). ✔

Partner or Individual Work

- Read or reread book from Suggestions for Independent Reading (TE p. 429D).

- **Fluency Practice:** Reread *Arachne the Spinner, Guitar Solo, How Music Was Fetched Out of Heaven.* ✔
- Activities relating to *Arachne the Spinner, Guitar Solo, How Music Was Fetched Out of Heaven* at Education Place® www.eduplace.com

Turn the page for more independent activities.

Managing Flexible Groups 429H

Classroom Management

Independent Activities

Assign these activities while you work with small groups.

Differentiated Instruction

- **Leveled Readers** Below Level, On Level, Above Level, Language Support

- Lessons and Leveled Practice, pp. 447O–447R

Audio CD

Independent Activities

- Language Center, pp. 447M–447N

Language Arts

Animal Myths

👥 Pairs	🕐 30 minutes
Objective	Tell an animal myth.
Materials	Reference sources with pictures of animals and insects.

Many myths explain how certain animals came to be and why they behave as they do. The myth, "Arachne the Spinner," for example, explains how spiders came to be. With a partner, write your own myth explaining how an animal or insect came into being or why it behaves as it does.

- Agree on an animal or insect you would like to write about. Look at pictures in reference books, if need be.

- Jot down notes about the animal's appearance and behavior that you might mention in your myth.

- Share research, writing, illustrating, and editing tasks with your partner.

- Give your myth a title and publish it in your class's reading center.

Science

Web Weavers

👤 Singles	🕐 60 minutes
Objective	Research and write about spiders
Materials	Reference sources, Internet, drawing paper, pencil, ruler

Become an arachnologist, or spider expert.

- Find information about spiders and how they make their webs.

- Draw a large spider web, leaving space between the strands of the web.

- Write spider facts in these spaces all around the web.

- Display your web to inform your classmates about spiders.

Look for more activities in the **Classroom Management Kit.**

Consider copying and laminating these activities for use in centers.

Social Studies

Who's Who Among the Gods and Goddesses?

👥👥👥 Groups	🕐 45 minutes
Objective	Make a book about Greek gods and goddesses.
Materials	Books of Greek myths, drawing paper, colored pencils, stapler

thene and Arachne weave pictures f the gods and goddesses who live n Mount Olympus. Create a book hat tells about the twelve deities alled the Olympians. Work with a roup.

Find the names of these gods and goddesses and divide them equally among group members.

Research the Olympians you are assigned, then write and illustrate a description of each, giving a separate page for each god or goddess.

Bind the pages into a book. Design a cover and place your book in a classroom reading area.

Art

Magic Words

👤 Singles	🕐 20 minutes
Objective	Invent magic words and draw a wish-come-true.
Materials	Large pieces of drawing paper, markers

Wouldn't it be nice to say a magic word like Faran did in *Guitar Solo* and have something happen to make your life easier?

- Make up your own magic words. Look at the examples in *Guitar Solo* for ideas.
- Write the words at the bottom of a piece of drawing paper. Then draw a picture above them showing what will happen when you say these words.
- Share your pictures with classmates and try pronouncing the magic words together.

Dee dee delly booperdog

Writing

Gifts from the Moon

👤 Singles	🕐 30 minutes
Objective	Write a sequel to a myth.
Materials	Anthology pp. 441–445

The Aztec god Quetzalcoatl was said to have brought the gift of music back from the sun to make the world a happier place. Write a sequel to this myth.

- Reread *How Music Was Fetched Out of Heaven* and jot down details you might use.
- In your sequel, send Quetzalcoatl to the moon to bring back a gift that will make the world a healthier place.
- Tell what Quetzalcoatl has to do to get to the Moon and what obstacles he has to overcome in order to bring back his gift.
- Describe how the world changes upon Quetzalcoatl's return.
- Share your myth and compare your ideas with a classmate's.

Listening Comprehension

• Listen to identify elements of myths.

Building Background

Tell students that they will read three myths from ancient cultures in this section. They will learn elements of myths and try writing a myth of their own. Explain that you will begin by reading aloud a Native American myth called "Chinook Wind Wrestles Cold Wind." Explain that this myth tells a story about a set of stars in the sky.

Fluency Modeling

Explain that as you read aloud, you will be modeling fluent oral reading. Ask students to listen carefully to your phrasing and your expression, or tone of voice and emphasis.

COMPREHENSION SKILL

Understanding Myths

Discuss with students how myths are different from other stories. (Myths were told in ancient times by people in many cultures. They have larger-than-life characters and tell about natural phenomena.)

Purpose Setting Read the selection aloud, asking students to note the different elements of myths as they listen. Then use the Guiding Comprehension questions to assess students' understanding. Reread the myth for clarification as needed.

Teacher Read Aloud

Chinook Wind Wrestles Cold Wind

by Jean Guard Monroe and Ray A. Williamson

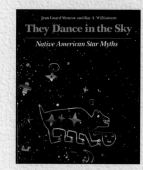

Once there was an old grandfather who always caught many salmon in Big River. His grandson Chinook Wind was very proud of him. They always had plenty to eat and some to give away to more unfortunate fishermen's families.

This began to change, however, when Chinook Wind left to visit relatives in a faraway camp. That was when Cold Wind decided he should take over.

Cold Wind wanted salmon too. But because he was lazy, he always came to Big River too late for good fishing. He would go down to the river to fish and see Chinook Wind's grandfather going home with plenty of salmon. Cold Wind usually caught nothing and this made him angry. He decided simply to take a salmon from Old Grandfather.

Of course, if he had been less impatient, he would not have had to steal the salmon. Old Grandfather was such a generous soul that he would gladly have given Cold Wind a share. But greedy people are seldom patient or courteous.

Every day, Cold Wind got up later and later. Every day he went down to fish too late to catch anything. Every day he stole a salmon from Old Grandfather. Oh, how bold he got!

❶ One day, Chinook Wind returned from his journey. When he heard how Cold Wind had been taking salmon from Old Grandfather, he grew angry and decided to teach him a lesson.

Chinook Wind hid in Old Grandfather's tipi and waited patiently until he came home from fishing. That day Old Grandfather returned whistling merrily, for he had caught more fish than usual. Everyone in the village would feast that night.

As usual, Cold Wind came roaring up to the tipi demanding salmon. This time, however, Chinook Wind boldly stepped out. "You cannot take any more of my grandfather's salmon!" he exclaimed.

"You cannot stop me, you scrawny boy," said Cold Wind. "I will wrestle you for Old Grandfather's salmon."

"All right," said Chinook Wind. "That is why I am come—to do whatever I have to do to protect the tribe and my grandfather."

And so the two wrestled. Chinook Wind fought hard and won the match. Because Chinook Wind won, Cold Wind can never again take salmon away from Old Grandfather. To this day Chinook Wind is stronger than Cold Wind.

If you look closely at the sky, you can see Chinook Wind and his brothers in their canoe close to Old Grandfather's salmon. Cold Wind and his brothers are in a canoe far behind. Cold Wind can never get Old Grandfather's last salmon.

CRITICAL THINKING

Guiding Comprehension

❶ UNDERSTANDING MYTHS How are Chinook Wind and Cold Wind larger-than-life characters? (Sample answer: They are forces of nature, winds, that have been given the qualities of people. Chinook Wind is good and helps the tribe, while Cold Wind steals salmon from the tribe.)

❷ UNDERSTANDING MYTHS How does Chinook Wind's victory over Cold Wind help explain changes in nature? (It explains why one type of wind, Chinook Wind, blows stronger than another type of wind, Cold Wind.)

❸ UNDERSTANDING MYTHS What other natural phenomenon does this myth explain? (It explains the positions of certain star constellations.)

Discussion Options

Personal Response Ask students what qualities they liked or disliked about the mythical characters Chinook Wind and Cold Wind, and why.

⭐ **Connecting/Comparing** Have students discuss how this myth is similar to and different from another myth, folktale, or fairy tale they have read.

 English Language Learners

Supporting Comprehension

Point out that different cultures may have different names for the same stars and constellations. Explain that the constellation that some Native Americans called Chinook Wind Brothers is also called Orion's sword in other western cultures, and the Cold Wind's Canoe constellation is also called Orion's Belt. Invite students to tell names of stars and constellations they know.

Building Background

Key Concept: Myths

Connecting to the Genre Point out that myths originated as stories that were handed down orally from generation to generation. Explain that because they were part of this oral tradition, myths changed over time, and many versions of each tale now exist. Discuss myths that students might have heard or read.

- Have a volunteer read aloud the text on page 431.

- Have students brainstorm ideas for things that might be explained by a myth. List their responses on the board in these categories: sky, earth, sea, and human behavior.

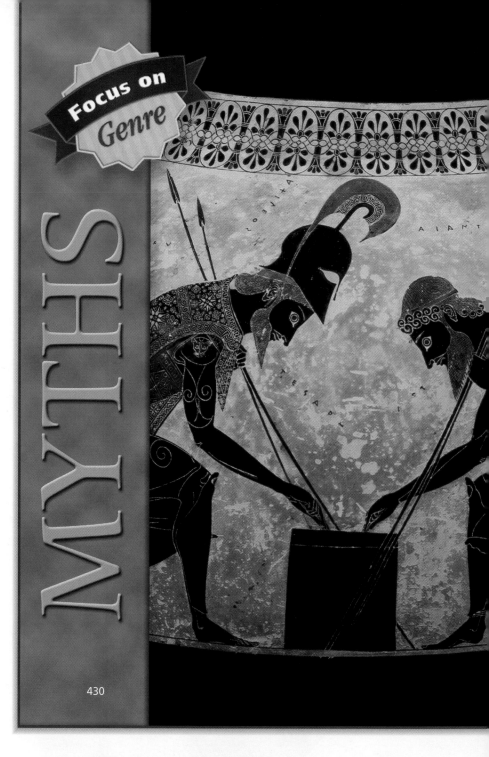

Focus on Genre

MYTHS

430

REACHING ALL LEARNERS

English Language Learners

Supporting Comprehension

Beginning/Preproduction Have students listen as you read aloud the introduction on page 431. Have them draw a hero carrying out a difficult task or an aspect of the natural world that might need an explanation.

Early Production and Speech Emergence Have students brainstorm difficulties that might challenge a hero. Organize students into small groups, and have them pantomime a hero confronting a problem.

Intermediate and Advanced Fluency Have partners read the titles and study the illustrations for each myth on pages 432–445. Then have them write predictions about what belief, practice, or aspect of nature may be explained by each myth.

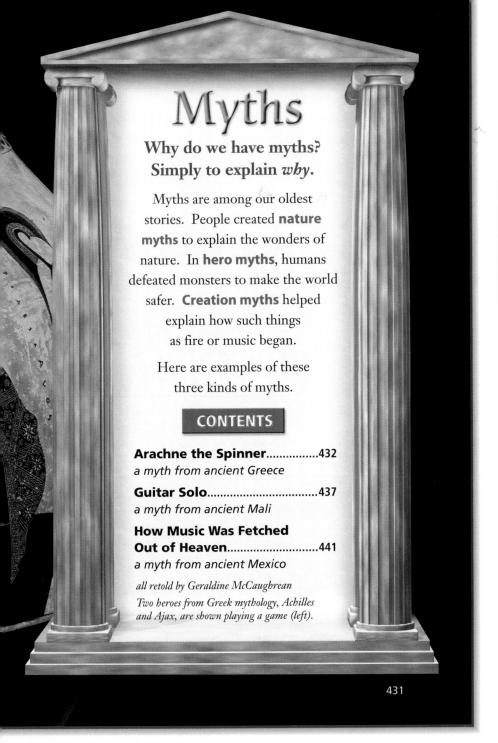

Myths

Why do we have myths?
Simply to explain *why*.

Myths are among our oldest stories. People created **nature myths** to explain the wonders of nature. In **hero myths**, humans defeated monsters to make the world safer. **Creation myths** helped explain how such things as fire or music began.

Here are examples of these three kinds of myths.

CONTENTS

all retold by Geraldine McCaughrean

Two heroes from Greek mythology, Achilles and Ajax, are shown playing a game (left).

431

Introducing Vocabulary

Genre Vocabulary
These words support the Key Concept.

ancient of or relating to times long past

behavior the way in which a person acts; conduct

characteristics features or qualities that distinguish a person or thing

hero in mythology and legend, a person of great courage and strength who is celebrated for his or her bold deeds

myth a traditional story dealing with ancestors, heroes, or supernatural beings, that usually explains a belief, practice, or natural occurrence

nature the physical world and the events that occur in it

relationship a connection or tie between persons or beings

task a difficult job or undertaking

 e • Glossary
e • WordGame

See Vocabulary notes on pages 432, 438, 440, 442, and 444 for additional words to preview.

I Wonder Why

Since early times, people have tried to explain what they heard and saw around them. Today, we hear daily news reports about knowledge that scientists have gained through their study of the world. People living in ancient cultures did not have the benefit of modern scientific knowledge to explain what they saw around them. Instead, they created oral tales about the relationships among gods, goddesses, and mortals. These tales reveal the ancient storytellers' observations about people, the behavior of animals, and events in nature.

Even though the gods and goddesses were dieties, many of them had human characteristics. Often, their behavior was ruled by emotions such as love, hate, jealousy, or the desire for vengeance. Sometimes mythological heroes performed difficult tasks with superhuman skill.

These stories, called myths, were handed down orally from generation to generation. Because of this oral tradition, myths changed over time, and many versions of each one now exist. To make them easier to remember and tell aloud, myths often use repetition, or stock phrases such as, "Once upon a time when the world was new."

Practice Book page 69

Focus on Myths
Genre Vocabulary

Name _____

A Mighty Myth

Use the words in the box to complete the paragraph about the Greek hero Heracles, who is also known as Hercules.

Vocabulary

ancient
behavior
characteristics
hero
myths
nature
relationship
tasks

Some of the world's most exciting tales originated in <u>ancient</u> **(1 point)** Greece. Perhaps the most famous of these Greek <u>myths</u> **(1)** is the story of Heracles, a mighty <u>hero</u> **(1)**. Heracles was the son of Zeus, the ruler of the gods. Many other gods were jealous of Heracles' close <u>relationship</u> **(1)** with Zeus. Hera, queen of the gods, hated Heracles and created many difficult <u>tasks</u> **(1)** for him to perform.

During his life, Heracles had to battle unique monsters—each with deadly <u>characteristics</u> **(1)**. The monster Hydra and the watchdog, Cerberus, had many heads, and the ferocious birds near Lake Stymphalus shot arrowlike feathers at people. Heracles defeated them all and then fought the forces of <u>nature</u> **(1)**. He cleaned the stables of King Augeas by making two rivers flow through them, and he climbed the tree of life to capture the golden apples guarded by the Hesperides. Heracles' brave deeds and fearless <u>behavior</u> **(1)** have made him one of Greece's most legendary heroes.

Display Transparency F4–1.

- Model how to use context clues to find the meaning of the word *ancient*.

- Have students use context clues to figure out the remaining Genre Vocabulary words. Have volunteers explain how they figured out each word.

- Ask students to use these words as they discuss myths.

Practice/Homework Assign **Practice Book** page 69.

Introducing Vocabulary 431

COMPREHENSION STRATEGY
Predict/Infer

Teacher Modeling Remind students that they can make predictions by thinking about the title, the illustrations, and what they already know. Have volunteers read aloud the first three paragraphs on page 432. Then model the strategy.

Think Aloud *Arachne says that she* can weave better than the gods. *This sounds boastful. I know that in myths people often get into trouble with the gods. I predict that Arachne's boastfulness will get her into trouble. I will keep reading to find out if my prediction is correct.*

Remind students to use other strategies as they read.

COMPREHENSION SKILL
Understanding Myths

Introduce the Graphic Organizer. Tell students that an Understanding Myths Chart can help them sort out and summarize the important information in a myth. Explain that as they read, they will complete the chart on **Practice Book** page 70.

- Display **Transparency F4–2.**
- Model filling in the first box. Monitor students' work, as needed.

Vocabulary

tapestries heavy, woven fabrics

bodkin an exclamation; a small sharp instrument for making holes in fabric or leather

---

Focus on Genre **MYTHS**

As you read this nature myth from ancient Greece, think about why Athene was so angry. How could Arachne have changed the outcome of the contest?

GREEK MYTHS

Arachne the Spinner

Retold by Geraldine McCaughrean
Illustrated by Emma Chichester Clark

Once, when all cloths and clothes were woven by hand, there was a weaver called Arachne more skillful than all the rest. Her tapestries were so lovely that people paid a fortune to buy them. Tailors and weavers came from miles around just to watch Arachne at work on her loom. Her shuttle flew to and fro, and her fingers plucked the strands as if she were making music rather than cloth.

"The gods certainly gave you an amazing talent," said her friends.

"Gods? Bodkins! There's nothing the gods could teach me about weaving. I can weave better than any god or goddess."

432

Transparency F4–2

Understanding Myths Chart

Myth: Arachne the Spinner	Myth: Guitar Solo
Characters Arachne, Athene, Arachne's friends	**Characters** Zin, Faran, Faran's mother, the fish, two hippopotami, other animals, village people
Setting long ago in ancient Greece	**Setting** Mali, the "place where six rivers join"
Problem or Challenge Can Arachne beat Athene in a weaving competition?	**Problem or Challenge** Can Faran overcome Zin, the bully, to protect his crops?
Outcome Athene punishes Arachne for her pride and for making fun of the gods by turning Arachne into a spider.	**Outcome** Faran defeats Zin by calling the two hippopotami. Then he wisely gets rid of magic.
Realistic Elements Sample answers: weaving as a profession, weaving equipment, weaving shop	**Realistic Elements** Sample answers: riverside setting, fishing from a canoe, meanness of the bully Zin, Faran's fear of starvation
Fantasy Elements Sample answers: old woman turning into a goddess, the goddess's powers, turning Arachne into a spider	**Fantasy Elements** Sample answers: dancing fish, guitar strings with magical powers, use of magic words

THEME 4 Focus on Myths
Graphic Organizer Understanding Myths Chart

ANNOTATED VERSION

TRANSPARENCY F4–2
TEACHER'S EDITION PAGES 432 AND 447A

Practice Book page 70

Focus on Myths
Graphic Organizer
Understanding Myths

Name _____

Understanding Myths Chart

Arachne the Spinner	Guitar Solo
Characters Arachne, Athene, Arachne's friends **(1 point)**	**Characters** Zin, Faran, Faran's mother, the fish, two hippopotami, other animals, village people **(1)**
Setting long ago in ancient Greece **(1)**	**Setting** in Mali, the "place where six rivers join" **(1)**
Problem or Challenge Can Arachne beat Athene in a weaving competition? **(1)**	**Problem or Challenge** Can Faran overcome Zin, the bully, to protect his crops? **(1)**
Outcome Athene punishes Arachne for her pride and for making fun of the gods by turning her into a spider. **(1)**	**Outcome** Faran defeats Zin by calling the two hippopotami. Then he wisely gets rid of magic. **(1)**
Realistic Elements Sample answers: weaving as a profession, weaving equipment, weaving shop **(1)**	**Realistic Elements** Sample answers: riverside setting, fishing from a canoe, meanness of the bully Zin, Faran's fear of starvation **(1)**
Fantasy Elements Sample answers: old woman turning into a goddess, the goddess's powers, turning Arachne into a spider **(1)**	**Fantasy Elements** Sample answers: dancing fish, guitar strings with magical powers, use of magic words **(1)**

Her friends turned rather pale. "Better not let the goddess Athene hear you say that."

"Don't care who hears it. I'm the best there is," said Arachne.

An old lady sitting behind her examined the yarns Arachne had spun that morning, feeling their delightful texture between finger and thumb. "So if there were a competition between you and the goddess Athene, you think you would win?" she said.

"She wouldn't stand a chance," said Arachne. "Not against me."

All of a sudden the old lady's gray hair began to float like smoke about her head and turn to golden light. A swish of wind blew her old coat into shreds and revealed a robe of dazzling white. She grew taller and taller until she stood head and shoulders above the crowd. There was no mistaking the beautiful gray-eyed goddess, Athene.

1

2

433

Building Background

- Tell students that Athene was the Greek goddess of wisdom and the arts. Explain that like many myths, this one portrays a conflict between gods and mortals.

- Have a volunteer read the short introduction and the title on page 432.

- Ask, What problem do you think the Greek gods and the mortals will have to work out?

Purpose Setting

- Have students read to find out more about the problem that gods and mortals will have to work out.

- Ask students to predict what aspect of the natural world *Arachne the Spinner* explains.

Journal ▶ Students can write about other myths they know that explain an aspect of the natural world.

STRATEGY REVIEW

Phonics/Decoding

Remind students to use the Phonics/Decoding Strategy as they read.

Extra Support/Intervention

Selection Preview

pages 432–433 Arachne boasts that she is a better weaver than anyone else, even the gods. The goddess Athene overhears Arachne and challenges her to a contest. Who do you think will win? Why do you think so?

pages 434–435 Sitting side by side, Arachne and Athene weave beautiful tapestries. Arachne pictures the gods behaving foolishly. Is it wise for Arachne to be so proud and self-important? Why or why not?

pages 435–436 Athene shows Arachne and her friends that making fun of the gods has serious consequences. Arachne will never be the same again. What do you think happens to her?

Guiding Comprehension

1 **MAKING INFERENCES** What words can you use to describe Arachne? (*talented, proud, self-satisfied, arrogant*)

2 **TOPIC, MAIN IDEA, AND DETAILS** What does Arachne say that would support the theory that she is boastful? (Sample answer: *"She wouldn't stand a chance," said Arachne. "Not against me."*)

3 **NOTING DETAILS** Why is Athena angry about Arachne's tapestry? (It makes fun of the gods.)

4 **MAKING INFERENCES** To what is Athena referring when she hangs Arachne in the tree and says, *"Weave your tapestries forever!"*? (Arachne is now a spider, and she will weave a spider's web.)

"Let it be so!" declared Athene. "A contest between you and me."

Arachne's friends fell on their faces in awe. But Arachne simply threaded another shuttle. And although her face was rather pale and her hands did tremble a little, she smiled and said, "A contest then. To see who is the best weaver in the world."

To and fro went the shuttles, faster than birds building a nest.

Athene wove a picture of Mount Olympus. All the gods were there: heroic, handsome, generous, clever, and kind. She wove all the creatures of creation onto her loom. And when she wove a kitten, the crowd sighed, "Aaaah!" When she wove a horse, they wanted to reach out and stroke it.

Alongside her sat Arachne, also weaving a picture of the gods.

But it was a comical picture. It showed all the silly things the gods had ever done: dressing up, squabbling, lazing about, and bragging. In fact she made them look just as foolish as ordinary folk.

But oh! when she pictured a butterfly sitting on a blade of grass, it looked as if it would fly away at any moment. When she wove a lion, the crowd shrieked and ran away in fright. Her sea shimmered and her corn waved, and her finished tapestry was more beautiful than nature itself.

Athene laid down her shuttle and came to look at Arachne's weaving. The crowd held its breath.

434

English Language Learners

Supporting Comprehension

Help students understand story dialogue.

- Explain that sometimes written dialogue uses incomplete sentences because the author is trying to make it sound the way people actually talk.

- Have students locate sentence fragments on page 432. (*"Better not let the goddess Athene hear you say that"; "Don't care who hears it"; "Not against me."*)

"You are the better weaver," said the goddess. "Your skill is matchless. Even I don't have your magic."

Arachne preened herself and grinned with smug satisfaction. "Didn't I tell you as much?"

"But your pride is even greater than your skill," said Athene. "And your irreverence is past all forgiving." She pointed at Arachne's tapestry. "Make fun of the gods, would you? Well, for that I'll make such an example of you that no one will ever make the same mistake again!"

She took the shuttle out of Arachne's hands and pushed it into her mouth. Then, just as Athene had changed from an old woman into her true shape, she transformed Arachne.

Arachne's arms stuck to her sides, and left only her long, clever fingers straining and scrabbling. Her body shrank down to a black blob no bigger than an ink blot: an end of thread still curled out of its mouth. Athene used the thread to hang Arachne up on a tree, and left her dangling there.

"Weave your tapestries forever!" said the goddess. "And however wonderful they are, people will only shudder at the sight of them and pull them to shreds."

435

Visualizing

Review

- Remind students that visualizing helps readers use the author's words to create a picture in their mind.
- Explain that story details and vivid language often help create these pictures.

Practice

- Point out that the author of *Arachne the Spinner* uses vivid language to describe a weaving contest between Arachne and the goddess Athene.
- Read aloud the last five paragraphs on page 434.
- Have students close their eyes and picture the weaving contest as they listen.
- Ask, How would you describe Athena's tapestry? What did Arachne's weaving look like?
- Discuss the differences between the two tapestries.

Apply

- Have students close their eyes and listen as you read the next-to-last paragraph on page 435 aloud.
- Then have students draw a three-panel storyboard showing Arachne's transformation.

Extra Support/Intervention

Selection Review (pages 432–436)

Before students who need extra support join the whole class for Stop and Think on page 436, have them

- review their prediction/purpose
- complete the chart for *Arachne the Spinner* on **Practice Book** page 70
- summarize the myth

Stop and Think

Critical Thinking Questions

1. DRAWING CONCLUSIONS What lesson does the myth *Arachne the Spinner* teach? (Sample answers: Don't be boastful and conceited; Don't think you are better than the gods.)

2. MAKING INFERENCES What human attitude toward spiders' webs does the myth point out? (dislike them; want to remove them)

3. STORY STRUCTURE At what point in this story does it becomes obvious that this tale is a myth? (when the old lady turns into the beautiful goddess Athene)

Strategies in Action

Have students take turns modeling Predict/Infer and other strategies they used while reading.

Monitoring Student Progress

If . . .	Then . . .
students have successfully completed the Extra Support activities on page 435,	have them read the next selection cooperatively or independently.

It all came true. For Arachne had been turned into the first spider, doomed forever to spin webs in the corners of rooms, in bushes, in dark, unswept places. And though cobwebs are as lovely a piece of weaving as you'll ever see, just look how people hurry to sweep them away.

436

English Language Learners

Supporting Comprehension

- Have students list words that describe Arachne and Athene in a T-chart like the one shown.
- Then help students identify the qualities that make one a mortal and one a god.

Arachne	Athene
skillful weaver	uses magic
proud	beautiful
boastful	taller than mortals
self-satisfied	powerful
	angry

MYTHS

The Songhay people, who live by the upper Niger River in the African country of Mali, still tell this hero myth today. What makes this myth especially appealing?

Guitar Solo

by Geraldine McCaughrean
Illustrated by Bee Willey

In a place where six rivers join like the strings of a guitar, lived Zin the Nasty, Zin the Mean, Zin-Kibaru, the water spirit. Even above the noise of rushing water rose the sound of his magic guitar, and whenever he played it, the creatures of the river fell under his power. He summoned them to dance for him and to fetch him food and drink. In the daytime, the countryside rocked to the sound of Zin's partying.

But come nighttime, there was worse in store for Zin's neighbor, Faran. At night, Zin played his guitar in Faran's field, hidden by darkness and the tall plants. Faran was not rich. In

⑤

437

Extra Support/Intervention

Selection Preview

Pages 437–438 When Zin, the water spirit, plays his magic guitar, the creatures of the river fall under his power, dancing and bringing him food and drink. At night, millions of fish hear Zin's music and slither up the riverbank, ruining the crops of Zin's neighbor, Faran. How do you think Faran will solve this problem?

Pages 439–440 Faran challenges Zin to a fight for the magic guitar. Zin agrees and the two neighbors wrestle all night. From what you know about Zin already, do you think this fight will be easy to win? Why or why not?

Building Background

- Point out that this myth is told by the Songhay people in the African country of Mali. Have students locate the setting for this myth (the country of Mali and the Niger River) on the map on page 409.

- Remind students that characters in myths can be supernatural beings.

- Have a volunteer read the short introduction, the title, and the first paragraph on page 437.

- Ask, In what ways does Zin-Kibaru, the water spirit, seem like a supernatural being?

Purpose Setting

- Ask students to read to find out about why *Guitar Solo* is considered a hero myth.

- Have students identify the hero and the villain in this story.

Journal ▶ Students can use the opening sentences of *Arachne the Spinner* and *Guitar Solo* as models and compose opening sentences for a myth of their own.

CRITICAL THINKING
Guiding Comprehension

5 **NOTING DETAILS** Do you think the reference to *Zin the Nasty, Zin the Mean, Zin-Kibaru, the water spirit* is to one character or to three different characters? Why do you think so? (one character, because later in the paragraph the character is referred to as *Zin* or *he*)

6 **MAKING INFERENCES** Is Faran portrayed as strong and resourceful in the beginning of the story? (Sample answer: no, because he just complains about his problem and seems to rely on his mother for ideas for solving it)

COMPREHENSION STRATEGY
Predict/Infer

Teacher/Student Modeling Help students model using the Predict/Infer strategy to make predictions about what happens next. Use this prompt:

- What will Faran do to solve his problem with Zin, the water spirit?

Vocabulary

mesmerized hypnotized, in a trance

spiteful hateful

maize corn

all the world he only had a field, a fishing rod, a canoe, and his mother. So when Zin began to play, Faran clapped his hands to his head and groaned, "Oh no! Not again!"

Out of the rivers came a million mesmerized fish, slithering up the bank, walking on their tails, glimmering silver. They trampled Faran's green shoots, gobbled his tall leaves, picked his ripe crop to carry home for Zin-Kibaru. Like a flock of crows they stripped his field, and no amount of shooing would drive them away. Not while Zin played his spiteful, magic guitar.

"We shall starve!" complained Faran to his mother.

 "Well, boy," she said, "there's a saying I seem to recall: When the fish eat your food, it's time to eat the fish."

438

Extra Support/Intervention

Strategy Modeling: Predict/Infer

Use this example to model the strategy.

At the bottom of page 438, Faran's mother gives him some advice to help him solve his problem: When the fish eat your food, it's time to eat the fish. *I can infer that she is suggesting that he should take strong action to make the fish stop ruining the crops. I think she believes he should try to catch these fish.*

So Faran took his rod and his canoe and went fishing. All day he fished, but Zin's magic simply kept the fish away, and Faran caught nothing. All night he fished, too, and never a bite: the fish were too busy gathering the maize in his field.

"Nothing, nothing, nothing," said Faran in disgust, as he arrived home with his rod over his shoulder.

"Nothing?" said his mother seeing the bulging fishing basket.

"Well, nothing but two hippopotami," said Faran, "and we can't eat them, so I'd better let them go."

The hippopotami got out of Faran's basket and trotted away. And Faran went to where the rivers meet and grabbed Zin-Kibaru by the shirt. "I'll fight you for that guitar of yours!"

Now Zin was an ugly brute and got most of his fun from tormenting Faran and the fish. But he also loved to wrestle. "I'll fight you, boy," he said, "and if you win, you get my guitar. But if I win, I get your canoe. Agreed?"

"If I don't stop your magic, I shan't need no canoe," said Faran, "because I'll be starved right down to a skeleton, me and Mama both."

So, that was one night the magic guitar did not play in Faran's field — because Faran and Zin were wrestling.

All the animals watched. At first they cheered Zin: he had told them to. But soon they fell silent, a circle of glittering eyes.

All night Faran fought, because so much depended on it. "Can't lose my canoe!" he thought, each time he grew tired. "Must stop that music!" he thought, each time he hit the ground. "Must win, for Mama's sake!" he thought, each time Zin bit or kicked or scratched him.

And by morning it really seemed as if Faran might win.

"Come on, Faran!" whispered a monkey and a duck.

"COME ON, FARAN!" roared his mother.

Then Zin cheated.

He used a magic word.

"Zongballyhoshbuckericket!" he said, and Faran fell to the ground like spilled water. He could not move. Zin danced around him, hands clasped

439

Fantasy

Review

- Remind students that fantasy contains imaginary, dreamlike, or supernatural elements.

- Explain that fantasy in literature must make sense even though it is describing something imaginary. For example, it would not be logical for Zin, the water spirit, to drown.

Practice

- Read aloud the first paragraph on page 438, which begins *Out of the rivers* . . .

- Have students identify the imaginary, dreamlike, or supernatural elements and write them on a chart, as shown below.

- Discuss any questions that students have.

Elements of Fantasy

Page 438

- one million fish
- walking on tails
- fish glimmering silver
- trampled new shoots in garden
- ate tall plants
- picked ripe crop for Zin
- nothing could make them go when music was playing

Apply

- Have partners identify the elements of fantasy on pages 439–440.

- Have students record their information on a similar chart to the one above.

Challenge

Character Pairs in Literature

Have students compare and contrast Zin, the bully, and Faran, the hero.

- Have students brainstorm characteristics of each character.

- Remind them to consider what each character does, what he says, and what is said about him.

- Have students use a graphic organizer, such as a Venn diagram, to sort out their thoughts.

- Then have them write two paragraphs explaining the similarities and differences between these characters.

Reading the Selection

CRITICAL THINKING

Guiding Comprehension

7 MAKING INFERENCES Why does Faran change the strings on the guitar so it has no special powers? (Sample answer: liked having friends instead of using magic to control people and animals.)

8 DRAWING CONCLUSIONS Who is the real hero of this myth—Faran or his mother? Use details from the selection to support your answer. (Sample answers: Faran, because he challenged Zin to a wrestling match and wrestled all night along; Mother, because she gave Faran many suggestions, including calling the hippopotami)

9 MAKING INFERENCES How does the theme of this myth apply to life today? (There are still bullies who must be outsmarted.)

above his head — "I win! I win! I win!" — then laughed and laughed till he had to sit down.

"Oh, Mama!" sobbed Faran. "I'm sorry! I did my best, but I don't know no magic words to knock this bully down!"

"Oh yes, you do!" called his mama. "Don't you recall? You found them in your fishing basket one day!"

Then Faran remembered. The perfect magic words. And he used them. "Hippopotami? HELP!" Just like magic, the first hippopotamus Faran had caught came and sat down — just where Zin was sitting. I mean right on the spot where Zin was sitting. I mean right on top of Zin. And then his hippopotamus mate came and sat on his lap. And that, it was generally agreed, was when Faran won the fight. Zin was crushed.

7 So nowadays Faran floats half-asleep in his canoe, fishing or playing a small guitar. He has changed the strings, of course, so as to have no magic **8** power over the creatures of the six rivers. But he does have plenty of friends to help him tend his maize and mend his roof and dance with his mother. **9** And what more can a boy ask than that?

440

Vocabulary

plowshare a plow's blade

This is a very ancient creation myth of Quetzalcoatl (keht-zahl-COH-atl), the feathered serpent, the Lord of Spirit, in what is now Mexico. As you read, think about how Quetzalcoatl got his musicians and whether you approve or disapprove of what he did.

How Music Was Fetched Out of Heaven

*by Geraldine McCaughrean
Illustrated by Bee Willey*

Once the world suffered in Silence. Not that it was a quiet place, nor peaceful, for there was always the groan of the wind, the crash of the sea, the grumble of lava in the throats of volcanoes, and the grate of man's plowshare through the stony ground. Babies could be heard crying at night, and women in the daytime, because of the hardness of life and the great unfriendliness of Silence.

441

Building Background

- Have a volunteer read the introduction at the top of page 441. Explain that the feathered serpent, Quetzalcoatl (keht-SAHL-koh-AHT-uhl), is featured in many myths from Mexico.

- Ask students to use the title and the introduction to predict what this creation myth explains.

- Ask, What would the world be like without music?

Purpose Setting

- Have students read to find out how this myth explains the beginning of music.

- Have students think about the meaning of the phrase *the sound of Nothingness* as they read this myth.

Journal ► Have students write in their journals about other creation myths that they know.

Extra Support/Intervention

Selection Preview

Pages 441–442 Tezcatlipoca (tehs-kah-tlee-POH-kah) and Quetzalcoatl (keht-SAHL-koh-AHT-uhl) plan to bring music to Earth. How do you think they will bring it down from heaven?

Pages 443–445 Quetzalcoatl asks the musicians of the Sun to come to Earth, but the Sun makes them afraid. Use details in the illustration to explain how you think this problem is solved.

CRITICAL THINKING
Guiding Comprehension

10 **MAKING INFERENCES** Why did the author use the word *fetched* instead of *brought* in the title? (*Fetched* suggests a stronger action.)

11 **WRITER'S CRAFT** Why does the author use similes such as *his body heavy as clay*? (to create a visual image of the characters)

12 **MAKING INFERENCES** What words would you use to describe the Sun? (Sample answer: *angry, stingy, and mean*)

13 **WRITER'S CRAFT** What images of Quetzalcoatl and the Sun do the author's choice of words convey? (Sample answers: Quetzalcoatl: skillful leader, welcoming; Sun: self-assured, conceited)

COMPREHENSION STRATEGY
Predict/Infer

Student Modeling Have students model the strategy. Use this prompt:

• Why does Tezcatlipoca feel that the world needs music?

Vocabulary

preening cleaning or smoothing feathers with a beak

livid full of anger

thrummed tapped rhythmically

monumental immense

11 Tezcatlipoca, his body heavy as clay and his heart heavy as lead (for he was the Lord of Matter), spoke to Quetzalcoatl, feathery Lord of Spirit. He spoke from out of the four quarters of the Earth, from the north, south, easterly and westerly depths of the iron-hard ground. "The world needs music, Quetzalcoatl! In the thorny glades and on the bald seashore, in the square comfortless houses of the poor and in the dreams of the sleeping, there should be music, there ought to be song. Go to Heaven, Quetzalcoatl, and fetch it down!"

"How would I get there? Heaven is higher than wings will carry me."

"String a bridge out of cables of wind, and nail it with stars: a bridge to the Sun. At the feet of the Sun, sitting on the steps of his throne, you will find four musicians. Fetch them down here. For I am so sad in this Silence, and the People are sad, hearing the sound of Nothingness ringing in their ears."

"I will do as you say," said Quetzalcoatl, preening his green feathers in readiness for the journey. "But will they come, I ask myself. Will the musicians of the Sun want to come?"

442

 Extra Support/ Intervention

English Language Learners

Pronunciation

Help students pronounce the names of these ancient gods: Tezcatlipoca (tehs-kah-tlee-POH-kah) and Quetzalcoatl (keht-SAHL-koh-AHT-uhl).

Language Development

Help students understand word endings that are used in comparisons.

• Adjectives ending in *–er* compare two things, such as *higher than all Creation.*

• Adjectives ending in *–est* compare three or more things and mean "the best" or "the most," such as *the four mightiest winds.*

442 **THEME 4: Focus on Myths**

He whistled up the winds like hounds. Like hounds they came bounding over the bending treetops, over the red places where dust rose up in twisting columns, and over the sea, whipping the waters into mountainous waves. Baying and howling, they carried Quetzalcoatl higher and higher — higher than all Creation — so high that he could glimpse the Sun ahead of him. Then the four mightiest winds braided themselves into a cable, and the cable swung out across the void of Heaven: a bridge planked with cloud and nailed with stars.

"Look out, here comes Quetzalcoatl," said the Sun, glowering, lowering, his red-rimmed eyes livid. Circling him in a cheerful dance, four musicians played and sang. One, dressed in white and shaking bells, was singing lullabies; one, dressed in red, was singing songs of war and passion as he beat on a drum; one, in sky-blue robes fleecy with cloud, sang the ballads of Heaven, the stories of the gods; one, in yellow, played on a golden flute.

This place was too hot for tears, too bright for shadows. In fact the shadows had all fled downward and clung fast to men. And yet all this sweet music had not served to make the Sun generous. "If you don't want to have to leave here and go down where it's dark, dank, dreary and dangerous, keep silent, my dears. Keep silent, keep secret and don't answer when Quetzalcoatl calls," he warned his musicians. **12**

Across the bridge rang Quetzalcoatl's voice. "O singers! O marvelous makers of music. Come to me. The Lord of the World is calling!" The voice of Quetzalcoatl was masterful and inviting, but the Sun had made the musicians afraid. They kept silent, crouching low, pretending not to hear. Again and again Quetzalcoatl called them, but still they did not stir, and the Sun smiled smugly and thrummed his fingers on the sunny spokes of his chair back. He did not intend to give up his musicians, no matter who needed them. **13**

So Quetzalcoatl withdrew to the rain-fringed horizon and, harnessing his four winds to the black thunder, had them drag the clouds closer, circling the Sun's citadel. When he triggered the lightning and loosed the thunderclaps, the noise was monumental. The Sun thought he was under siege.

Thunder clashed against the Sun with the noise of a great brass cymbal, and the musicians, their hands over their ears, ran this way and that looking for

443

English Language Learners

Language Development

Help students understand the figurative language in this myth. Discuss the meaning of these phrases:

- *The shadows had all fled downward and clung fast to men.* (third paragraph, page 443)
- *their footprints were everywhere. . .* (last paragraph, page 445)
- *that had previously been. . .cobwebbed with silence* (last paragraph, page 445)

Similes

Teach

- A simile is a comparison between two things that are not alike.
- A simile uses the signal words *like* or *as*.
- The comparisons in a simile help to create images about a character or a situation.

Practice/Apply

- Write this simile from page 445 on the board: *The Sun shook and trembled with rage like a struck gong.*
- Ask, What two things are compared? (Sun shaking with rage and a vibrating gong)
- Ask, In what way does this simile help you understand the Sun's anger? (creates a picture in your mind that shows how intense his feeling was)
- Have partners reread the first full paragraph on pages 442 and on 445.
- Have them identify similes describing these characters: Tezcatlipoca, the crooner of lullabies, and the singer of battle-songs.
- Discuss the comparison in each simile with the whole class.

 Fluency Practice

Rereading for Fluency Have students choose a favorite part of the story to reread to a partner, or suggest that they read the second and third paragraphs on page 443. Encourage students to read expressively.

CRITICAL THINKING

Guiding Comprehension

14 **CAUSE AND EFFECT** What resulted from the thunderstorm that Quetzalcoatl unleashed on the Sun? (The musicians left the Sun and came to Earth.)

15 **MAKING JUDGMENTS** Do you agree with Tezcatlipoca, who says that *the world needs music?* Why or why not? (Sample answers: yes, because music makes our lives seem less difficult and more friendly; no, because music is a gift rather than something we have to have)

444

Extra Support/Intervention

Selection Review (pages 441–445)

Before students join the whole class for Wrapping Up on page 445, have them

- review their predictions/purpose
- summarize the elements of a myth

Vocabulary

mourner a person who grieves

cadences phrases of music

help. "Come out to me, little makers of miracles," said Quetzalcoatl in a loud but gentle voice. *BANG* went the thunder, and all Heaven shook.

The crooner of lullabies fluttered down like a sheet blown from a bed. The singer of battle-songs spilled himself like blood along the floor of Heaven and covered his head with his arms. The singer of ballads, in his fright, quite forgot his histories of Heaven, and the flautist dropped his golden flute. Quetzalcoatl caught it.

As the musicians leapt from their fiery nest, he opened his arms and welcomed them into his embrace, stroking their heads in his lap. "Save us, Lord of Creation! The Sun is under siege!"

"Come, dear friends. Come where you are needed most."

The Sun shook and trembled with rage like a struck gong, but he knew he had been defeated, had lost his musicians to Quetzalcoatl. **14**

At first the musicians were dismayed by the sadness and silence of the Earth. But no sooner did they begin to play than the babies in their cribs stopped squalling. Pregnant women laid a hand on their big stomachs and sighed with contentment. The man laboring in the field cupped a hand to his ear and shook himself, so that his shadow of sadness fell away in the noonday. Children started to hum. Young men and women got up to dance, and in dancing fell in love. Even the mourner at the graveside, hearing sweet flute music, stopped crying.

Quetzalcoatl himself swayed his snaky hips and lifted his hands in dance at the gate of Tezcatlipoca, and Tezcatlipoca came out of doors. Matter and Spirit whirled together in a dance so fast: had you been there, you would have thought you were seeing only one.

And suddenly every bird in the sky opened its beak and sang, and the stream moved by with a musical ripple. The sleeping child dreamed music and woke up singing. From that day onward, life was all music — rhythms and refrains, falling cadences and fluting calls. No one saw just where the Sun's **15** musicians settled or made their homes, but their footprints were everywhere and their bright colors were found in corners that had previously been gray and cobwebbed with silence. The flowers turned up bright faces of red and yellow and white and blue, as if they could hear singing. Even the winds ceased to howl and roar and groan, and learned love songs.

445

Wrapping Up

Critical Thinking Questions

1. **STORY STRUCTURE** Describe the elements of a myth. (Sample answer: larger-than-life characters; long-ago, far-away settings; conflict between gods and humans or among gods; explain nature or human behavior)

2. **MAKING INFERENCES** What practical advice do the messages in these myths offer us? (Sample answers: Be patient; good behavior is rewarded.)

3. **MAKING GENERALIZATIONS** Make a generalization about myths that summarizes why people created them. (Sample answer: Myths were first told by early people as a way to explain what they saw in the world.)

4. **MAKING INFERENCES** Think of a contemporary hero story. This could be a story in a book, a movie, or on television. Describe the elements of a myth this story includes. (Sample answer: *Superman;* includes larger-than-life characters; involves people's efforts to fight evil)

Strategies in Action

Have students model how and where they used the Predict/Infer strategy.

Comprehension Check

Use **Practice Book** page 71 to assess students' comprehension of the selection.

REACHING ALL LEARNERS

Challenge

Mythology of Ancient Mexico

Have students compare and contrast Quetzalcoatl and Tezcatlipoca.

Have students research Quetzalcoatl and Tezcatlipoca using nonfiction resources such as the encyclopedia or library books.

Have them use a graphic organizer, such as a Venn diagram, to present their findings.

Practice Book page 71

Focus on Myths
Comprehension Check

Name _____

What Really Happened?

Read these sentences about the three myths that you have just read. Write T if the sentence is true and F if it is false. If the statement is false, correct it on the line below the sentence.

1. __T__ Zin's magic guitar controls the fish, who ruin Faran's crops. (2 points)

2. __F__ Zin, the river spirit, played his magic guitar only at night.
Zin, the water spirit, played his magic guitar in the daytime and at night. (2)

3. __F__ Faran did not change the strings on Zin's guitar.
Faran changed the strings on Zin's guitar so he did not have magic power. (2)

4. __T__ Athene changed Arachne into a spider because she made fun of the gods. (2)

5. __F__ Arachne wove a picture showing all the gods as handsome, heroic, generous, clever, and kind.
Arachne wove a picture showing the gods as foolish as ordinary people. (2)

6. __T__ Athene agreed that Arachne was a better weaver. (2)

7. __F__ Before music came to Earth, there were no noises at all.
Before music came to Earth, there were only noises that weren't nice. (2)

8. __T__ When Quetzalcoatl triggered the lightning and thunder, the Sun thought he was under siege. (2)

9. __T__ Before the musicians came to Earth, they circled the Sun in a cheerful dance, playing and singing. (2)

Monitoring Student Progress

If . . .	Then . . .
students score 13 or below on **Practice Book** page 71,	have partners review the story for details that support the correct answer.

Responding

Think About the Selections

Discuss or Write

1. **COMPARE AND CONTRAST** Sample answers: Common elements: larger-than-life characters; long-ago or imaginary settings; conflicts; Human characters: Arachne: talented, boastful; Faran: not greedy for power

2. **COMPARE AND CONTRAST** *Arachne the Spinner:* Athene turns Arachne into a spider. *Guitar Solo:* Faran beats Zin and solves his problem.

3. **DRAWING CONCLUSIONS** Answers will vary.

4. **MAKING JUDGMENTS** Sample answers: no, because he stole them; yes, because he brought them where they were needed

5. **DRAWING CONCLUSIONS** make myths seem special; help explain things; Athene could not have created the first spider and Quetzalcoatl could not have brought music to Earth without special powers.

Literature Discussion

To help students prepare for discussion, assign **Practice Book** page 72. Students may also refer to **Practice Book** page 71.

1. **COMPARE AND CONTRAST** *Arachne the Spinner* and *Guitar Solo* both include a competition. How are the competitions the same and different? (Sample answers: Same: someone gets a harsh punishment; Different: The weaving contest is about skill, while the wrestling match deals with strength and wit.)

2. **COMPARE AND CONTRAST** What characteristics of the gods in these myths make them seem superhuman? (Sample answers: special powers; areas of influence, for example, Athene, wisdom, and Quetzalcoatl, spirit)

Think About the MYTHS

1. Compare the three myths. What common elements do they share? How are the human characters in each myth portrayed differently?

2. In "Arachne the Spinner" and "Guitar Solo," humans compete against a god and a spirit. What is different about the way the competitions end?

3. Who is your favorite character in the myths? Why?

4. Do you think the way Quetzalcoatl brought the musicians down from the Sun was right? Why or why not?

5. How important is having larger-than-life characters in telling myths? Give examples from two of the myths.

Send an E-Postcard

If you want to tell a friend that you've been reading myths, send an e-postcard. You'll find one at Education Place. **www.eduplace.com/kids**

446

Practice Book page 72

Focus on Myths
Literature Discussion

Name _____

Describe Mythical Characters

Every myth must have at least one superhuman character. Compare and contrast two superhuman characters from the myths in this section.

Sample answer: Athene and Zin both possess special powers and have power over mortals. Athene changes from an old lady into a beautiful goddess. Later she turns Arachne into a spider. Zin uses a magic word to paralyze Faran. Athene and Zin have differences, too. Athene is taller than mortals, beautiful, and wise. Zin is described as an *ugly brute* who gets *most of his fun from tormenting Faran and the fish.* **(10 points)**

Illustrate one of the characters you described.

(5 points)

Narrating

Write Your Own Myth

Myths use realism and fantasy to explain something. Think of a custom or a natural event that especially interests you. Then write one of the three kinds of myths—nature, hero, or creation—to explain it.

Tips

Remember that a myth often contains these three elements:
- larger-than-life characters, such as gods, goddesses, and heroes
- long-ago, far-away settings
- amazing events

447

Write a Myth

Have students read and briefly discuss the writing assignment on page 447 of the Anthology. Before students begin their own myths, present the writing lesson on pages 447K–447L.

Extra Support/Intervention

Prewriting

Help students plan their myth by creating a story map. Discuss these story elements and have students record their ideas on a chart, as shown.

Story Elements	Story Ideas
Setting	
Characters	
Conflict	
Solution	
Conclusion	

Monitoring Student Progress

End-of-Selection Assessment

Student Self-Assessment Have students assess their reading and writing with questions such as these:

- Which parts of the selections were difficult to read? Why?

- Which strategies helped me understand the stories?

- Would I recommend these stories to my friends? Why or why not?

Reading the Selection **447**

- Identify story elements of the myth genre.
- Discuss the use of realism and fantasy in particular myths.

Target Skill Trace

Preview; Teach   p. 429K, p. 432, p. 447A

Transparency F4–2

Understanding Myths Chart

Myth: Arachne the Spinner	Myth: Guitar Solo
Characters Arachne, Athene, Arachne's friends	**Characters** Zin, Faran, Faran's mother, the fish, two hippopotami, other animals, village people
Setting long ago in ancient Greece	**Setting** Mali, the "place where six rivers join"
Problem or Challenge Can Arachne beat Athene in a weaving competition?	**Problem or Challenge** Can Faran overcome Zin, the bully, to protect his crops?
Outcome Athene punishes Arachne for her pride and for making fun of the gods by turning Arachne into a spider.	**Outcome** Faran defeats Zin by calling the two hippopotami. Then he wisely gets rid of magic.
Realistic Elements Sample answers: weaving as a profession, weaving equipment, weaving shop	**Realistic Elements** Sample answers: riverside setting, fishing from a canoe, meanness of the bully Zin, Faran's fear of starvation
Fantasy Elements Sample answers: old woman turning into a goddess, the goddess's powers, turning Arachne into a spider	**Fantasy Elements** Sample answers: dancing fish, guitar strings with magical powers, use of magic words

---

Practice Book page 70

Focus on Myths
Graphic Organizer
Understanding Myths

Name _____

Understanding Myths Chart

Arachne the Spinner	*Guitar Solo*
Characters Arachne, Athene, Arachne's friends (1 point)	**Characters** Zin, Faran, Faran's mother, the fish, two hippopotami, other animals, village people (1)
Setting long ago in ancient Greece (1)	**Setting** in Mali, the "place where six rivers join" (1)
Problem or Challenge Can Arachne beat Athene in a weaving competition? (1)	**Problem or Challenge** Can Faran overcome Zin, the bully, to protect his crops? (1)
Outcome Athene punishes Arachne for her pride and for making fun of the gods by turning her into a spider. (1)	**Outcome** Faran defeats Zin by calling the two hippopotami. Then he wisely gets rid of magic. (1)
Realistic Elements Sample answers: weaving as a profession, weaving equipment, weaving shop (1)	**Realistic Elements** Sample answers: riverside setting, fishing from a canoe, meanness of the bully Zin, Faran's fear of starvation (1)
Fantasy Elements Sample answers: old woman turning into a goddess, the goddess's powers, turning Arachne into a spider (1)	**Fantasy Elements** Sample answers: dancing fish, guitar strings with magical powers, use of magic words (1)

COMPREHENSION: Understanding Myths

❶ Teach

Review the characteristics of a myth. Display **Transparency F4–2.** Explain these points.

- Myths include both ordinary human characters and characters with special, superhuman powers.
- Myths often combine realistic events with fantasy events.
- Myths are often set in a faraway place in the distant past.
- The characters in the myth often face a problem or challenge.
- The solution to this problem often teaches a lesson or explains how something came to be.

Explain different types of myths. Discuss these types but explain that some myths can fit into more than one category.

- Some myths teach a lesson about how people ought to behave
- Some myths explain how something in nature first came into being.
- Some myths explain how a particular human skill or tradition first came into being.

Model identifying fantasy and realism in a myth. Have students reread *Arachne the Spinner* on Anthology pages 432–436. Then think aloud.

> **Think Aloud**   *I know that myths bring together realistic and fantasy elements. I can see that at the beginning, the business of weaving and the presence of tailors and weavers seem true to real life. I am sure this kind of thing happened in ordinary life in ancient Greece. Also, Arachne's boasting sounds like plain old human pridefulness. However, when the old woman's gray hair unravels like smoke and turns into golden light, I've found something that I'm sure I wouldn't encounter in reality. This must be the first fantasy element.*

❷ Guided Practice

Have student discuss elements of a myth. In small groups, have students reread and discuss *Guitar Solo* on pages 437–440.

- Have them use **Practice Book** page 70 to identify the story elements and explain how these elements fit the genre of myth.
- Ask them to discuss what lessons might be learned from *Guitar Solo*. (Don't give in to bullies; fight fair rather than using tricks)
- Then talk about their findings in class.

Apply

Assign Practice Book page 73. In addition, students can apply the skill as they read their Leveled Readers for this week. You may also suggest books from the Books for Independent Reading on the Lesson Overview (page 429D).

✓ Test Prep Tell students that reading tests will sometimes ask them to identify the genre of a passage they have read. Emphasize that students can identify a myth by looking for an ancient setting in a distant land, a combination of realism and fantasy, and superhuman creatures such as gods.

Leveled Readers

Students at all levels apply the comprehension skill as they read their Leveled Readers. See the lessons on pages 447O–447R.

● BELOW LEVEL ▲ ON LEVEL ■ ABOVE LEVEL ◆ LANGUAGE SUPPORT

Reading Traits

Teaching students to think about genre is one way of encouraging them to "read between the lines" of a selection. This comprehension skill supports the reading trait **Decoding Conventions**.

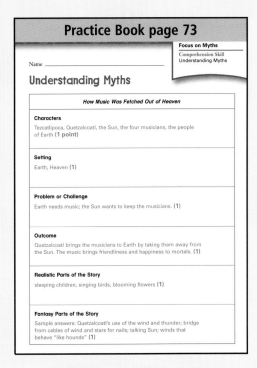

Practice Book page 73

Focus on Myths
Comprehension Skill
Understanding Myths

Name _____

Understanding Myths

How Music Was Fetched Out of Heaven
Characters
Tezcatlipoca, Quetzalcoatl, the Sun, the four musicians, the people of Earth **(1 point)**
Setting
Earth, Heaven **(1)**
Problem or Challenge
Earth needs music; the Sun wants to keep the musicians. **(1)**
Outcome
Quetzalcoatl brings the musicians to Earth by taking them away from the Sun. The music brings friendliness and happiness to mortals. **(1)**
Realistic Parts of the Story
sleeping children, singing birds, blooming flowers **(1)**
Fantasy Parts of the Story
Sample answers: Quetzalcoatl's use of the wind and thunder; bridge from cables of wind and stars for nails; talking Sun; winds that behave "like hounds" **(1)**

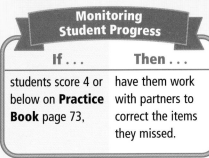

Monitoring Student Progress

If . . .	Then . . .
students score 4 or below on **Practice Book** page 73,	have them work with partners to correct the items they missed.

STRUCTURAL ANALYSIS/ VOCABULARY: Prefixes and Suffixes

❶ Teach

Discuss using prefixes to read words. Write *doomed forever to spin webs in dark, <u>unswept</u> places.*

- Have a volunteer circle the prefix in the underlined word. (*un-*)
- Ask students to use their knowledge of the prefix *un-* to figure out the meaning of *unswept*. ("not swept")
- Discuss other prefixes and words that use each prefix. (Sample answers: *re-, reapply; de-, destructive; in-, inhabit*)

Discuss using suffixes to read words. Write *Even the <u>mourner</u> at the graveside stopped crying.*

- Have a volunteer circle the suffix in the underlined word. (*-er*)
- Ask students to use their knowledge of the suffix *-er* to figure out the meaning of *mourner*. ("one who mourns")
- Discuss other suffixes and words that use each suffix. (Sample answers: *-less, hopeless; -ful, hopeful; -ous, fabulous*)

Model the Phonics/Decoding Strategy. Write:"*O <u>marvelous</u> makers of music.*" Then model the strategy.

Think Aloud *I see that the underlined word contains the adjective suffix -ous. If I remove the suffix, I see the base word* marvel, *which means "to be filled with amazement." The adjective* marvelous *might mean "causing amazement." That makes sense in the sentence.*

❷ Guided Practice

Have students practice using prefixes and suffixes. Display these phrases, and ask partners to circle each prefix or suffix, and underline each base word. Then have them decode the words and determine their meanings. Discuss their work.

<u>monumental</u> noise   <u>remake</u> her web
<u>mountainous</u> waves   grew <u>impatient</u>
<u>mesmerize</u> fish   a skilled <u>guitarist</u>
<u>musical</u> ripple   the <u>unfriendly</u> silence

❸ Apply

Assign Practice Book page 74.

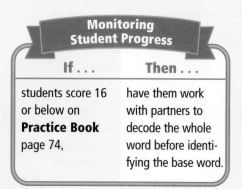

Practice Book page 74

Focus on Myths
Structural Analysis
Prefixes and Suffixes

Name _____

Fishing for Words

Read the base words below. Add a prefix or a suffix to change each base word into another familiar word. Then write one sentence using the word you made.
Sample answers are shown.

Prefixes	Suffixes
re-	-or
un-	-ist
in-	-ation
im-	-ize
com-	-eer
	-ure

1. phrase
   I tried to *rephrase* the question so he would
   understand it. **(2 points)**
2. tangle
   We *untangled* the kite from the bushes. **(2)**
3. rocket
   The *rocketeers* launched their model rockets at the same time. **(2)**
4. mature
   An oak tree goes through a long process of *maturation*. **(2)**
5. present
   We made a *presentation* to the whole school in the auditorium. **(2)**
6. audit
   An *auditor* might review the budget of a business or a government. **(2)**
7. violin
   The audience applauded for the *violinist*. **(2)**
8. coherent
   He talked so fast that his words were *incoherent*. **(2)**
9. standard
   A factory might *standardize* the size of the nuts and bolts they use. **(2)**
10. passion
    I felt *compassion* for the lost kittens. **(2)**
11. fail
    My *failure* to complete my homework caused problems at school. **(2)**

Monitoring Student Progress

If . . .	Then . . .
students score 16 or below on **Practice Book** page 74,	have them work with partners to decode the whole word before identifying the base word.

PHONICS REVIEW: Variant Consonant Pronunciations

❶ Teach

Review different sounds for the letter c. Discuss these points.

- It usually stands for /k/ at the end of a word, as in *toxic*, as well as before consonants and the vowels *a*, *o*, and *u*: *crack, cat, cot*.

- It usually stands for /s/ before *e*, *i*, or *y*: *cereal, circus, cycle*.

- It can stand for /sh/ before the suffix *-ian*: *electrician*.

Review other consonants that stand for more than one sound. Discuss these points:

- The letter *t* can stand for the /sh/ sound: *pollution*.

- The letter *s* can stand for the /z/ sound, as in *music*, or the /zh/ sound, as in *confusion*.

- The letter *b* is sometimes silent: *climb*.

- The letters *wh* can stand for the /w/ sound, as in *which*, or the /h/ sound, as in *whole*.

Model the Phonics/Decoding Strategy. Write *Life was all music—rhythms and refrains, falling* <u>cadences</u> *and fluting calls.* Model how to decode *cadences*.

Think Aloud *The word is in plural form. The first letter is c. Since the next letter is a, I think this c has the /k/ sound. I can pronounce the next three letters ayd. The letter n is next, then another c. This c is followed by the letter e, so I think it has the /s/ sound. When I blend the sounds together, I get KAYD-ns-ehz.*

❷ Guided Practice

Help students practice decoding consonants. Display the following sentences. Have partners decode each underlined word. Have them circle each *t, s, b, wh,* and *c* and underline key letters that helped them figure out the correct pronunciation of each.

1. The men <u>whispered</u> as they entered the <u>tomb</u>.

2. I will make a <u>decision</u> if you can't <u>choose</u>.

3. The townspeople <u>rejoiced</u> in <u>celebration</u>.

❸ Apply

Have students find words with consonants that stand for different sounds. Tell students to find these words in *Focus on Myths*, decode them, and discuss their meanings: *competition*, page 433; *musicians*, 441; *citadel*, page 443; *embrace*, page 444.

- Read words with variant consonant pronunciations.
- Use the Phonics/Decoding Strategy to decode longer words.

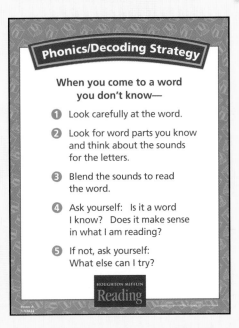

Phonics/Decoding Strategy

When you come to a word you don't know—

❶ Look carefully at the word.

❷ Look for word parts you know and think about the sounds for the letters.

❸ Blend the sounds to read the word.

❹ Ask yourself: Is it a word I know? Does it make sense in what I am reading?

❺ If not, ask yourself: What else can I try?

HOUGHTON MIFFLIN
Reading

SPELLING: Consonant Changes

OBJECTIVE

- Write pairs of related Spelling Words in which the spelling of a final *c* is retained, even though its pronunciation changes, when a suffix is added.

SPELLING WORDS

Basic

electric	mathematics
electrician	mathematician
magic*	deduction
magician	deduce
practical	politics
practice	politician
clinic	reduction
clinician	reduce
introduction	tactics
introduce	tactician

Review†   **Challenge**

Review†	Challenge
ache	statistics
fashionable	statistician
prefer	cosmetics
scarce	cosmetician
loyal	

* *Forms of these words appear in the literature.*

† *Because this lesson presents this spelling principle for the first time, the Review Words do not contain the lesson's patterns.*

Extra Support/ Intervention

Basic Word List You may want to use only the left column of Basic Words with students who need extra support.

Challenge

Challenge Word Practice Have students write help-wanted ads, using the Challenge Words.

The Sound of *c*

Pretest Use the Day 5 Test sentences.

Teach Write *electric* and *electrician*.

- Ask these questions:

  What is the meaning of each word? (*electric*: relating to electricity; *electrician*: one who works with electrical equipment) Note both words have to do with electricity.

  How is the final *c* pronounced? (*electric*: /k/; *electrician*: /sh/)

- Write *introduction* and *introduce*. Have students note that the *c* is pronounced /k/ in *introduction* and /s/ in *introduce*.

- Explain that words related in meaning are also often related in spelling even though the sound of one or more letters changes.

- Write the rest of the Basic Words, reviewing the meaning, spelling, and pronunciation of final *c* in each word.

Practice/Homework Assign **Practice Book** page 269.

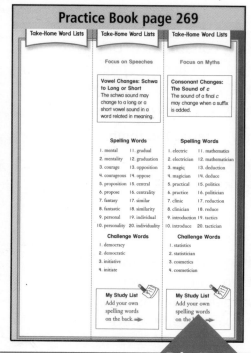

Practice Book page 269

Reviewing the Principle

Go over the spelling principle that a final *c* spelling in one word is often retained in another word related in meaning even though the pronunciation may change.

Practice/Homework Assign **Practice Book** page 75.

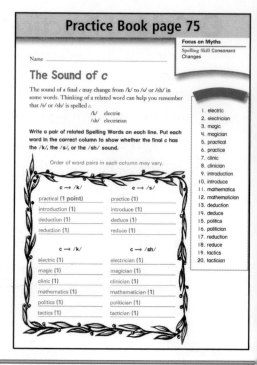

Practice Book page 75

Take-Home Word List

DAY 3 VOCABULARY

Word Part *poli*

Draw a word web, writing *poli* in the center circle. In two satellite circles, write *politics* and *politician*.

Explain that *poli* is a Greek word part that means "city" or "government." Discuss how the meaning of *poli* is incorporated into *politics* and *politician*. (*Politics* is the art or science of government; a *politician* is someone who runs for or holds an office in government.)

Ask students to suggest other words with *poli*. Add the words to the word web. Discuss how the meaning of *poli* is reflected in the meaning of each word. If necessary, provide these examples: *police, polite, policy, metropolis, metropolitan,* and *acropolis*.

Write the remaining Basic Words. Have students use each one orally in a sentence. (Sentences will vary.)

Practice/Homework For spelling practice, assign **Practice Book** page 76.

Practice Book page 76

Name _____

Spelling Spree

Focus on Myths
Spelling Skill Consonant Changes

Spelling Words

Find the Pair Write the pair of related Spelling Words that completes each statement.

1. If this electric (1 point) _____ socket won't work, I'll have to call an electrician (1) _____

2. I'd like to introduce (1) _____ the person who wrote the introduction (1) _____ to my new book.

3. I like to follow politics (1) _____, but I don't like every politician (1) _____.

4. This magician (1) _____ performs the most amazing magic (1) _____ tricks that fool us every time.

5. If your aches and pains do not lessen soon, you should visit a clinic (1) _____ to see a clinician (1) _____.

Syllable Scramble Rearrange the syllables in each item to write a Spelling Word. There is one extra syllable in each item.

e c lec p tric   ducc

11. duc fil de tion   deduction (1)
12. duce ment re   reduce (1)
13. cian ti dis tac   tactician (1)
14. tice re prac   practice (1)
15. mat dre ics e math   mathematics (1)

1. electric
2. electrician
3. magic
4. magician
5. practical
6. practice
7. clinic
8. clinician
9. introduction
10. introduce
11. mathematics
12. mathematician
13. deduction
14. deduce
15. politics
16. politician
17. reduction
18. reduce
19. tactics
20. tactician

DAY 4 PROOFREADING

Game: Spelling Rummy

Have students work in pairs to make 4 cards for each of these letters: *a, d, e, g, i, l, m, n, p, r, s, t,* and *u*. Make 10 cards for *c*.

- The dealer shuffles the cards, deals 7 cards to each player, and stacks the other cards face-down.
- If possible, Player 1 lays down cards, face-up, that spell a Spelling Word. If not, Player 1 draws a card and discards one card face-up.
- Player 2 can either put down a word, pick up the discarded card, or draw a card. If a discarded card is picked up, it must be used to spell a word on that turn.
- A player can pick up a card that was discarded on a previous turn, but the player must also pick up all of the discarded cards that were laid on top of the desired card.
- The first player to spell two Spelling Words wins.

Practice/Homework For proofreading and writing practice, assign **Practice Book** page 77.

Practice Book page 77

Name _____

Proofreading and Writing

Focus on Myths
Spelling Skill The Sound of c

Spelling Words

Proofreading Circle the six misspelled Spelling Words in the following myth. Then write each word correctly. Order of answers may vary.

There once was a mathematishian who loved music. He was always listening to his electric radio. His friends would ask him, "Why don't you become a musician?"

He would reply, "It takes too much practiss. Besides, I can't afford any reduktion in pay."

Then one day he had an idea—he would use new tactix. He would deduse a way to turn numbers into musical notes. He also wanted his idea to be practikal so that it would it help other people learn and understand music more easily. Eventually, he devised a system of eighth notes, quarter notes, half notes, and so on. Now he could do math and music at the same time!

1. mathematician (1 point)   4. tactics (1)
2. practice (1)   5. deduce (1)
3. reduction (1)   6. practical (1)

1. electric
2. electrician
3. magic
4. magician
5. practical
6. practice
7. clinic
8. clinician
9. introduction
10. introduce
11. mathematics
12. mathematician
13. deduction
14. deduce
15. politics
16. politician
17. reduction
18. reduce
19. tactics
20. tactician

Write an Opinion Scientific research has replaced the need for myths to explain natural occurrences. What has been gained as a result? What has been lost? Did myths offer people something special that cannot be part of scientific explanations?

On a separate sheet of paper, write a paragraph that expresses your thoughts about the replacement of myths by scientific explanations. Try to use Spelling Words from the list.
Responses will vary. (4 points)

DAY 5 ASSESSMENT

Spelling Test

Say each underlined word, read the sentence, and then repeat the word. Have students write only the underlined word.

Basic Words

1. He rode in an **electric** golf cart.
2. An **electrician** fixed the wiring.
3. The elf waved a **magic** wand.
4. A **magician** explained tricks.
5. Be **practical** and save money.
6. Try to **practice** every day.
7. I went to a **clinic** for a flu shot.
8. Tanya is a **clinician** in a lab.
9. I read the book's **introduction**.
10. Please **introduce** me to his dad.
11. My best subject is **mathematics**.
12. The **mathematician** solved the equation.
13. The officer made a **deduction**.
14. Can you **deduce** the answer?
15. Avery wants to study **politics**.
16. The **politician** ran for mayor.
17. I asked for a **reduction** in price.
18. We want to **reduce** litter.
19. If our **tactics** work, we'll win.
20. The **tactician** made plans.

Challenge Words

21. The **statistics** about car accidents are frightening.
22. The **statistician** analyzed the data.
23. My aunt wears many **cosmetics**.
24. The **cosmetician** sold lipstick.

OBJECTIVES

- Learn that some English words come from ancient myths.
- Find the meanings of English words derived from myths.

English Language Learners

You might discuss words from myths in students' first language.

Practice Book page 78

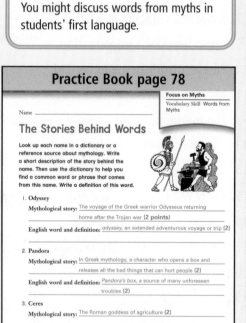

Name _____

Focus on Myths
Vocabulary Skill Words from Myths

The Stories Behind Words

Look up each name in a dictionary or a reference source about mythology. Write a short description of the story behind the name. Then use the dictionary to help you find a common word or phrase that comes from this name. Write a definition of this word.

1. Odyssey
   Mythological story: The voyage of the Greek warrior Odysseus returning home after the Trojan war **(2 points)**

   English word and definition: *odyssey*, an extended adventurous voyage or trip **(2)**

2. Pandora
   Mythological story: In Greek mythology, a character who opens a box and releases all the bad things that can hurt people **(2)**

   English word and definition: *Pandora's box*, a source of many unforeseen troubles **(2)**

3. Ceres
   Mythological story: The Roman goddess of agriculture **(2)**

   English word and definition: *cereal*, food made from the seeds of wheat, rice, or corn **(2)**

4. Titan
   Mythological story: a family of giants in Greek mythology **(2)**

   English word and definition: *titanic*, having great size, strength, or importance **(2)**

Monitoring Student Progress

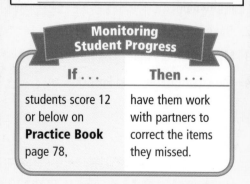

If . . .	Then . . .
students score 12 or below on **Practice Book** page 78,	have them work with partners to correct the items they missed.

VOCABULARY: Words from Myths

❶ Teach

Introduce words from myths. Discuss with students the character of Arachne from *Arachne the Spinner* on pages 432–436.

- Write *Arachne* on the board.
- Ask students what Athene turned Arachne into at the end of the myth. (a spider)
- Then write the word *arachnid* on the board, read it aloud, and explain that this is the name for the class of creatures that spiders belong to.
- Explain that the English word *arachnid* came from the Greek word *arachne*, meaning "spider." Explain that many other English words come from characters, places, and things found in myths.

Discuss other examples of words from myths. Write each of the following words on the board, ask a volunteer to look up its definition, and then explain the word's origin.

- *Herculean* demanding great strength or courage; from the Greek hero Hercules, known for his strength
- *narcissistic* excessively in love with or admiring of oneself; from the Greek character Narcissus who falls in love with his own reflection
- *martial* of, relating to, or suitable to war; from the Roman god of war, Mars

❷ Guided Practice

Have students practice using words from myths. Display the sentences shown below. Have partners rewrite the sentences, changing the underlined phrase with a mythological name to the English word derived from it. Have volunteers share their work.

1. You will need the strength <u>of Hercules</u> to move that rock. You will need <u>Herculean</u> strength to move that rock.

2. You are <u>as vain as Narcissus</u> if you think you are the best looking actor. *You are <u>narcissistic</u> if you think you are the best looking actor.*

3. He was trained in the arts <u>of the Roman god Mars</u>. He was trained in the <u>martial</u> arts.

❸ Apply

Assign Practice Book page 78.

STUDY SKILL: Finding Media Resources

OBJECTIVES

- Learn about audio and video productions of myths.
- Use the library to find such resources.

❶ Teach

Discuss myths available in audio and video formats.

- Tell students that myths have been adapted for different media.

- Explain that some are available on video, featuring real actors or animated characters. Myths have also been recorded on audiotape.

- Ask students to give examples of video or audio productions of myths that they've seen or heard. Write examples on the board.

- Explain that many libraries stock these media.

Display Transparency F4–3, and discuss locating media resources at the library.

- Tell students that they can use an electronic catalogue to locate media resources. They may search by title or by key words.

- Display the top of the transparency. Point out the title of the myth (*Hercules*) used in the search and the chart showing the results of the search. Explain that to find out where these items are kept in the library, the user clicks on its listing.

- Display the bottom half of the transparency. Point out the key words used in this search (*Myths and Legends*) and the chart showing the results of the search.

- Display the list at the bottom of the transparency. Mention that these key words may be helpful when searching for myths.

❷ Practice/Apply

Have students locate media resources at the library.

- Assign small groups to find examples of audio and video productions of myths at the library. Encourage them to search the catalogue by the titles of myths as well as by key words.

- Have students share their results in class, giving specific information about the audios and videos they have found, such as the names of actors or readers, whether a work is animated, and its length in hours and minutes.

- If there is time, view a video or listen to an audiotape.

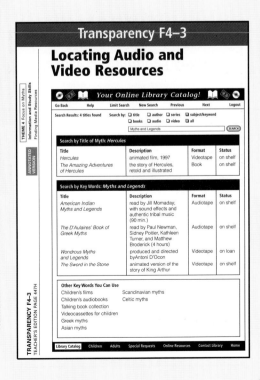

Transparency F4–3

Locating Audio and Video Resources

Information and Study Skills   **447H**

GRAMMAR: Adjectives and Adverbs

OBJECTIVES

- Use adjectives following linking verbs.
- Complete sentences, using *good* and *well* correctly.
- Proofread and correct sentences for incorrect use of forms of *good* and *bad*.
- Proofread and correct sentences with grammar, spelling, capitalization, and punctuation errors.

Using the Right Word

Teach Remind students that forms of *be* and verbs such as *look, feel, taste, smell, seem,* and *become* can be linking verbs.

- Display **Transparency F4–5**. Read aloud the first pair of examples. Point out that *felt* is a linking verb because *soft* describes the subject, *tapestries*. When a word describes a noun or pronoun, the adjective form is used.

- Point out that *softly* describes *walked*. When a word describes a verb, the adverb form is used.

- Repeat with the other sentences. (linking verbs/adjectives: *was/foolish, appeared/angry*; action verbs/adverbs: *behaved/foolishly, spoke/angrily*)

- Have students complete Sentences 1–7.

Daily Language Practice
Have students correct Sentences 1 and 2 on **Transparency F4–4**.

Independent Work

Practice/Homework Assign **Practice Book** page 79.

Daily Language Practice
Have students correct Sentences 3 and 4 on **Transparency F4–4**.

Transparency F4–4
Daily Language Practice

1. The democratic system of politicks comes from ancient greece.
   The democratic system of politics comes from ancient Greece.

2. In his excellent introducshun to greek myths, the author moved easy from one topic to another.
   In his excellent introduction to Greek myths, the author moved easily from one topic to another.

3. When she looked at the equations the mathematishun felt confidently.
   When she looked at the equations, the mathematician felt confident.

4. Did the clinician work quick to diduce the cause of the infection.
   Did the clinician work quickly to deduce the cause of the infection?

5. Did the french or the spanish politishun give the best answer?
   Did the French or the Spanish politician give the better answer?

6. Did your practise session go good?
   Did your practice session go well?

7. The electricion did not feel good at the end of the day.
   The electrician did not feel well at the end of the day.

8. My mothers' suggestions are always very praktical.
   My mother's suggestions are always very practical.

9. We saw two performers, and the magishun was the best one.
   We saw two performers, and the magician was the better one.

10. He performs magick tricks while he tells storys.
    He performs magic tricks while he tells stories.

Transparency F4–5
Using Adjectives with Linking Verbs

> Arachne's tapestries felt soft.
> The goddess walked softly.
> Arachne was foolish.
> Arachne behaved foolishly.
> Athene appeared angry.
> Athene spoke angrily.

1. Tezcatlipoca felt _____ sad . (sad, sadly)

2. Babies cried _____ loudly at night. (loud, loudly)

3. The winds howled _____ wildly over the tree-tops. (wild, wildly)

4. Four musicians danced _____ cheerfully around the Sun. (cheerful, cheerfully)

5. Their music sounded _____ sweet , but the Sun was still angry. (sweet, sweetly)

6. The musicians leapt _____ gratefully into the arms of Quetzalcoatl. (grateful, gratefully)

7. At last the people of the Earth were _____ joyful . (joyful, joyfully)

Practice Book page 79

Focus on Myths
Grammar Skill Using the Right Word

Name _____

Roman Gods

Using the Right Word Use an adjective, not an adverb, following a linking verb to describe a subject. Use an adverb, not an adjective, to modify an action verb.

> **Adjective:** Some Roman gods were kind.
> **Adverb:** Not all Roman gods behaved admirably.

Write the word in parentheses that completes each sentence correctly. Then write *adjective* or *adverb* to identify how the word is used.

1. The Roman god Saturn was _____ mighty (1 point) (mighty, mightily) adjective (1)

2. His children acted more _____ aggressively (1) than he did. (aggressive, aggressively) adverb (1)

3. They plotted _____ secretly (1) against Saturn and overthrew him. (secret, secretly) adverb (1)

4. Jupiter, the strongest son, became the most _____ powerful (1) and ruled the universe. (powerful, powerfully) adjective (1)

5. Jupiter ruled more _____ forcefully (1) than Saturn. (forceful, forcefully) adverb (1)

THEME 4: Focus on Myths

DAY 3 — INSTRUCTION

Using *good* and *well*

Teach Display **Transparency F4–6**. Read aloud the three example sentences.

Explain that *good* is an adjective and *well* is an adverb unless *well* refers to someone's health.

For each sentence, ask students to identify the word that *good* or *well* modifies and its part of speech. (*storyteller,* noun; *tells,* verb; *Anton,* noun)

Point out that the verb *feel* in the third sentence is a linking verb that links the adjective *well* with the subject *Anton.*

Have volunteers complete Sentences 1–6 and explain their choices.

Daily Language Practice

Have students correct Sentences 5 and 6 on **Transparency F4–4**.

Transparency F4–6

Using *good* and *well*

> Anton is a <u>good</u> storyteller.
> He tells stories very <u>well</u>.
> Anton doesn't feel <u>well</u> today.

1. The weaver Arachne was so ___good___ at her craft that she challenged Athene to a contest.

2. Arachne felt too ___good___ about her picture.

3. Zin played the guitar very ___well___.

4. Faran fought ___well___, but he thought he didn't know any magic words.

5. Tezcatlipoca wanted to make life ___good___ for the people on Earth.

6. The music must have made even sick people feel ___well___.

THEME 4 Focus on Myths
Grammar Skill Using good and well
ANNOTATED VERSION
TRANSPARENCY F4–6
TEACHER'S EDITION PAGE 447J

DAY 4 — PRACTICE

Independent Work

Practice/Homework Assign **Practice Book** page 80.

Daily Language Practice

Have students correct Sentences 7 and 8 on **Transparency F4–4**.

Practice Book page 80

Focus on Myths
Grammar Skill Using good and well

Name _____

A Touch of Gold

Using *good* and *well* Remember that *good* is an adjective and *well* is an adverb, unless *well* refers to health.

Write the word in parentheses that completes each sentence correctly.

1. In ancient Greece, rich King Midas lived very ___well (1 point)___, but he desired even more riches. (good, well)

2. His wish that everything he touch change to gold would not turn out ___well (1)___. (good, well)

3. The centaur that granted the wish warned Midas that the results would not be ___good (1)___. (good, well)

4. At first Midas thought his new power was very ___good (1)___. (good, well)

5. When Midas turned his food to gold, he began to wonder if his choice was so ___good (1)___ after all. (good, well)

6. When he turned his daughter into gold, he knew his life would never be ___good (1)___ again. (good, well)

7. Midas realized that greed was not ___good (1)___ and caused much unhappiness. (good, well)

8. Midas learned his lesson ___well (1)___. (good, well)

9. Midas wanted his life to be ___good (1)___ again. (good, well)

10. He knew that he had not behaved ___well (1)___. (good, well)

DAY 5 — IMPROVING WRITING

Using Forms of *good* and *bad*

Teach Write the following sentences to review the use of forms of *good* and *bad*.

> Arachne's tapestry was <u>better</u> than Athene's.
>
> Zin-Kibaru was the <u>best</u> guitar player in the land.
>
> Zin's wrestling was <u>worse</u> than Faran's.
>
> Arachne's pride was her <u>worst</u> quality.

- Point out that students can use forms of *good* and *bad* in their writing to describe positive and negative events and actions.

- Have students proofread a piece of their own writing for correct forms of *good* and *bad*.

Practice/Homework Assign **Practice Book** page 81.

Daily Language Practice

Have students correct Sentences 9 and 10 on **Transparency F4–4**.

Practice Book page 81

Focus on Myths
Grammar Skill Using Forms of good and bad

Name _____

The Menehune

Using Forms of *good* and *bad* Use the forms of irregular adjectives *good* and *bad* correctly. Use *better* and *worse* to compare two things. Use *best* and *worst* to compare more than two.

Proofread the following summary. Use proofreading marks to correct three missing or incorrect end marks, three errors in capitalization, one missing comma, and five incorrect forms of *good* or *bad*.

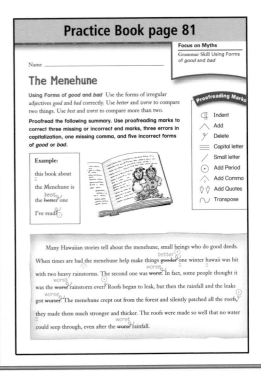

Proofreading Marks

⊓ Indent
∧ Add
⟍ Delete
≡ Capital letter
/ Small letter
⊙ Add Period
∧ Add Comma
∨∨ Add Quotes
∼ Transpose

Example:

this book about
the Menehune is
~~better~~ *best*
the ~~better~~ one
I've read ⊙

Many Hawaiian stories tell about the menehune, small beings who do good deeds. When times are bad the menehune help make things ~~gooder~~ *better* one winter hawaii was hit with two heavy rainstorms. The second was ~~worst~~ *worse*. In fact, some people thought it was the ~~worse~~ *worst* rainstorm ever? Roofs began to leak, but then the rainfall and the leaks got ~~worser~~ *worse*. The menehune crept out from the forest and silently patched all the roofs, they made them much stronger and thicker. The roofs were made so well that no water could seep through, even after the ~~worse~~ *worst* rainfall.

WRITING: Myth

OBJECTIVES

- Plan a myth using elements of the genre.
- Write a myth.
- Use dialogue effectively.

DAY 1 PREWRITING

Introducing the Format

Review the characteristics of a myth.

- Myths include ordinary characters and characters with special, superhuman powers.
- Myths often combine realistic events with fantasy events.
- Myths are often set in the distant past in faraway countries.
- The characters often face a problem.
- The solution often teaches a lesson or explains how something came to be.

Start students thinking about writing their own myth. Ask:

- Will your myth teach a lesson? Will it explain how something came to be?
- What will be the setting?
- Who will be your characters? What special powers will your characters have?
- What will be the problem or challenge?
- What will be the solution?

Have students brainstorm and list ideas for their myth.

- Tell them to save their notes.

Transparency F4–7

Guidelines for Writing a Myth

- Create interesting characters. Use details to show their appearance, how they act, and what they say. Some might have intriguing powers.
- Keep the action moving. Use strong verbs to portray what the characters do.
- Don't give away the outcome too soon. Keep readers in suspense!
- Give details that highlight the elements of realism and fantasy in the myth.
- Begin sentences in different ways. Let your voice sparkle.

THEME 4: Focus on Myths · Writing Skill Guidelines for Writing a Myth

ANNOTATED VERSION

TRANSPARENCY F4–7
TEACHER'S EDITION PAGES 447K AND 447L

DAY 2 DRAFTING

Discussing the Model

Have students refer to Anthology pages 432–445. Ask:

- Which myths teach a lesson? (*Arachne the Spinner, Guitar Solo*)
- Which myths explain how something in nature first came into being? (*Arachne the Spinner, Guitar Solo*)
- Which myth explains how a particular human skill first came into being? (*How Music Was Fetched Out of Heaven*)

Display Transparency F4–7, and discuss the guidelines.

Help students brainstorm ideas for a myth.

- Discuss possible settings. List these suggestions: an underground city; an ancient kingdom; a world of animals with no people.
- Discuss possible plots. List these suggestions: why the sky is blue; how people learned to laugh; why people need to sleep.

Have students draft a myth.

- Have them use their notes from Day 1.
- Assign **Practice Book** page 82 to help students organize their writing.

Practice Book page 82

Focus on Myths
Writing Skill Writing a Myth

Name _____

Elements of a Myth

Characters	(5 points)
Setting	(5)
Plot: Problem	(5)
Plot: Events	(5)
Plot: Outcome	(5)

Writing Traits

Voice As students start to write their myths on Day 2, encourage them to use words and phrases that show how they feel. Discuss these examples.

Without Voice Alix had done a bad thing.

With Voice It was a terrible, thoughtless, wicked act. Alix should have felt ashamed of herself. But she didn't.

DAY 3 — REVISING

Improving Writing: Using Dialogue

Discuss using dialogue.

Dialogue can help tell a story by showing what characters are like.

Characters can show personality traits such as shyness, boldness, cheerfulness, or grumpiness through their words.

Dialogue can also tell what happens in a story. Characters can comment on events, helping readers understand the plot.

Display Transparency F4–8.

Use the examples at the top of the transparency to review capitalization and punctuation of dialogue.

Work with students to complete the exercises at the bottom of the transparency.

Assign Practice Book page 83.

Have students revise their drafts.

Display **Transparency F4–7** again. Have students use it to revise their myths.

Tell partners to hold writing conferences.

Ask students to further revise their myths. Have them add some dialogue.

Transparency F4–8

Using Dialogue in Myths

- "Do you want to know why rivers freeze in winter?" asked Dave.
- "I can tell a story," said Dave, "about why the river freezes."
- "Listen to my story," said Dave. "You'll understand why the river freezes."

Read the paragraph. Rewrite the numbered sentences as dialogue.

Lia listened as Dave began his story. (1) He said that long ago, the river flowed all winter long. It never froze. Then Dave described how one day the river claimed it could flow faster than the wind could fly. (2) The wind, Dave explained, was jealous and proud of how fast it was. Without a word, it froze the river, and flew back and forth across it for months. (3) Lia said she didn't think that was possible. (4) Ever since, Dave declared, the wind freezes the river once a year to prove who is faster.

Sample answers are shown.

1. "Long ago, the river flowed all winter long," he said. "It never froze."

2. "The wind," Dave explained, "was jealous and proud of how fast it was. Without a word, it froze the river, and flew back and forth across it for months."

3. "I didn't think that was possible," Lia said.

4. "Ever since," Dave declared, "the wind freezes the river once a year to prove who is faster."

THEME 4 Focus on Myths
Writing Skill Improving Your Writing
ANNOTATED VERSION
TRANSPARENCY F4–8
TEACHER'S EDITION PAGES 447K AND 447L

DAY 4 — PROOFREADING

Checking for Errors

Have students proofread for errors in grammar, spelling, punctuation, or usage.

- Students can use the proofreading checklist on **Practice Book** page 273 to help them proofread their myths.

- Students can also use the chart of proofreading marks on **Practice Book** page 274.

Practice Book page 83

Name _____

Focus on Myths
Writing Skill
Improving Your Writing

Using Dialogue

Read the paragraph. Then rewrite the underlined sentences as dialogue. Add details, and show the voice of the speaker.

Long ago the giraffe had a very short neck. The clouds passing overhead taunted him. (1) They said that the giraffe could not get near them. The leaves on the trees laughed when he tried to reach them for a tasty meal. (2) The leaves told him to go away and graze somewhere else. This made the giraffe feel discouraged. (3) He said that he was tired of being short. Then he got a splendid idea. (4) He told himself that he would visit the wise owl and ask how to grow taller.

The wise owl listened to his question. (5) Then he explained that if the giraffe wanted to grow taller, he needed to stretch out his neck. The giraffe should stick his head in the fork of a tree and find someone to pull his tail.

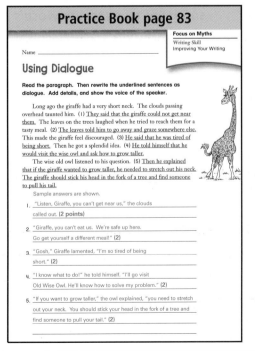

Sample answers are shown.

1. "Listen, Giraffe, you can't get near us," the clouds called out. **(2 points)**

2. "Giraffe, you can't eat us. We're safe up here. Go get yourself a different meal!" **(2)**

3. "Gosh," Giraffe lamented, "I'm so tired of being short." **(2)**

4. "I know what to do!" he told himself. "I'll go visit Old Wise Owl. He'll know how to solve my problem." **(2)**

5. "If you want to grow taller," the owl explained, "you need to stretch out your neck. You should stick your head in the fork of a tree and find someone to pull your tail." **(2)**

DAY 5 — PUBLISHING

Sharing Myths

Consider these publishing options.

- Ask students to read their myth or some other piece of writing from the Author's Chair.

- Encourage students to make their myths into a class book called Modern Myths.

Portfolio Opportunity

Save students' myths as samples of their writing development.

Monitoring Student Progress

If . . .	Then . . .
students' writing does not follow the guidelines on **Transparency F4–7**,	work with students to improve specific parts of their writing.

Language Center

VOCABULARY
Building Vocabulary

👤👤👤 Groups	🕐 20 minutes
Objective	Brainstorm synonyms of *see*.
Materials	Thesaurus, dictionary

The winds carried Quetzalcoatl so he could *glimpse* the Sun. *Glimpse* is another word for *see*. Make a word web that includes words for "ways to *see*."

- Brainstorm as many words for "ways to see" that you can think of. (One group member should act as recorder.)

- Then check a thesaurus for more ideas.

- Discuss the positive, neutral, or negative connotations of each word. (A word's connotation is a meaning it suggests in addition to its literal, exact meaning.)

- Share your web with other groups and add new words.

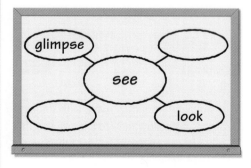

VOCABULARY
Myth Riddles

👤👤👤 Groups	🕐 30 minutes
Objective	Create riddles from mythological words.
Materials	Activity Master 4–5, dictionary, reference sources

Make up riddles about words derived from myths.

- Work in small groups. Cut out the word cards on Activity Master 4–5.

- Divide the word cards among group members. Use a dictionary to find the common meaning of the word as well as the mythological meaning.

- Shuffle the word cards.

- One student selects a word and gives clues to the word's identity based on its mythological origin and common meaning. For example, the clues for *atlas* could be *I am the giant who held the world on his shoulders and a book full of maps.*

- The student who correctly identifies the word has the next turn.

SPELLING/PHONICS
Race to the Sun

👤👤👤 Groups	🕐 20 minutes
Objective	Play a spelling game.
Materials	Activity Master 4–6, index cards, number cube

Play a spelling game with two or three other students. Be the first person to reach the sun and find the musicians, as Quetzalcoatl did in *How Music Was Fetched Out of Heaven*.

- Use the game board found on Activity Master 4–6. Use different coins as markers.

- Together write each Spelling Word from **Practice Book** page 269 on an index card and place the cards in a stack face-down near the game board.

- When it is your turn, have the player on your left choose a card and say the word. If you spell the word correctly, roll the number cube and move that many spaces. If you spell the word incorrectly, stay where you are.

- The first person to reach the sun wins the game.

Consider copying and laminating these activities for use in centers.

LISTENING/SPEAKING

Retell an Oral History

👥 **Pairs**	🕐 **30 minutes**
Objective	Listen to and retell an oral history.

Myths are ancient stories that have been preserved by being passed down orally from generation to generation before being finally written down. For families, oral histories are a way to preserve important events and experiences. In order not to lose or confuse details in an oral history, it is necessary to listen carefully when the story is told.

- Read the listening tips below.

- Think of a family tradition or memorable personal experience you think is worth telling about.

- Tell your story and listen to your partner's story.

- Then try to retell your partner's story using his or her own words and storytelling style.

Listening to Oral Histories
- Try to create a mental picture of the people, places, and events described.
- When the storyteller is finished, ask questions you have about the story.
- Take notes about the most important parts of the story.

STRUCTURAL ANALYSIS

Prefix and Suffix Game

👥 **Pairs**	🕐 **30 minutes**
Objective	Play a game to identify prefixes and suffixes.
Materials	Index cards, paper bag, dictionary

Look for familiar prefixes and suffixes to help you decode words. Work with a partner.

- Write each of these words on an index card: *uncertain, delightful, foolish, impatient, matchless, mourner, massive, unfriendly, impoliteness, motivation, unselfish, replacement, unmanageable, lifeless, insincerely*

- Give a point value from 1 to 4 points to each word and write it on the back of the card. Place the cards in a bag.

- Take turns removing a card. Read the word, identify the prefix and/or suffix, and tell how the word parts help you define the word.

- If you are correct, add the points to your score. If you are incorrect, return the card.

- Keep playing until all of the words have been identified.

foolish

massive

Leveled Readers

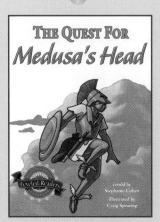

The Quest for Medusa's Head

Summary *An evil Greek king sends Perseus on a quest to bring back Medusa's head. The king plans to persuade Perseus's mother to marry him while her son is away on this impossible mission. But with the help of Hermes and Athena, Perseus manages to slay Medusa. Returning home with her head, Perseus rescues his mother from the king and goes on to fulfill his fate.*

Vocabulary

Introduce the Key Vocabulary and ask students to complete the BLM.

fate destiny, future, *p. 3*

shelter take in, harbor, *p. 5*

dazzled amazed, impressed, *p. 6*

reputation estimation in which a person is held, *p. 6*

confident self-assured, *p. 8*

sacrifice offering, *p. 14*

Building Background and Vocabulary

Have students share what they know about Greek myths and the Greek gods Zeus, Athena, and Hermes. Explain that ancient myths, like those surrounding these gods, served to explain things people didn't understand. Guide students through the text, using some of the vocabulary from the story.

Writing Skill: Writing a Myth

Have students read the Strategy Focus on the book flap. Remind students to use the strategy and to think about the elements of myths as they read the book. (See the Leveled Readers Teacher's Guide for **Vocabulary and Comprehension Practice Masters.**)

Responding

Have partners discuss how to answer the questions on the inside back cover.

Think About the Selection Sample answers:

1. The king fears that his grandson will someday kill him.
2. The fisherman discovers Perseus and his mother and offers to take care of them.
3. Anyone who looks at her is turned to stone.
4. Answers will vary.

Making Connections Answers will vary.

Building Fluency

Model Read aloud the last paragraph on page 4, emphasizing the exclamation. Explain that sentences that end with an exclamation point should be read with great emotion.

Practice Have students look for other sentences in the story that end with exclamation points (pages 7, 10, 15, etc.). Ask them to read the sentences aloud until they are able to read them with feeling.

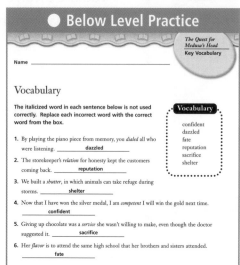

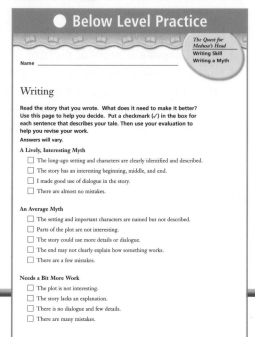

Leveled Readers

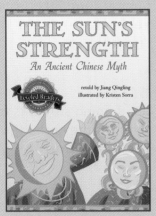

The Sun's Strength

Summary *When the ten suns decide to rise and shine as a group rather than one at a time—as had been their previous practice—life changes drastically. People and animals grow parched and lethargic. Crops wilt, and rivers dry up. But the ten suns enjoy their new routine so much that they refuse to go back to rising one at a time. Finally, a marksman shoots nine of the suns out of the sky, and life returns to normal.*

Vocabulary

Introduce the Key Vocabulary and ask students to complete the BLM.

quenched satisfied, *p. 3*

abounded flourished, *p. 3*

ascended climbed, rose, *p. 4*

tedious boring, dull, *p. 4*

unanimously in complete agreement, *p. 6*

listless lacking energy, *p. 8*

accustomed used to, *p. 9*

cultivating preparing the land for growing crops, *p. 9*

oppressive overwhelming, *p. 10*

catastrophe disaster, *p. 11*

▲ ON LEVEL

Building Background and Vocabulary

Tell students that myths serve to explain things people don't understand, such as the changing seasons and lightning and thunder. Ask students why the rising sun might have inspired a myth. Guide students through the text, using some of the vocabulary from the story.

Writing Skill: Writing a Myth

Have students read the Strategy Focus on the book flap. Remind students to use the strategy and to think about the elements of myths as they read the book. (See the Leveled Readers Teacher's Guide for **Vocabulary and Comprehension Practice Masters.**)

Responding

Have partners discuss how to answer the questions on the inside back cover.

Think About the Selection Sample answers:

1. They are bored with their routine, and lonely sitting in the sky by themselves.
2. People, animals, and plants become scorched and parched.
3. He tells Hou Yi that he must leave one sun in the sky so that there will be warmth and light.
4. Answers will vary.

Making Connections Answers will vary.

Building Fluency

Model Read aloud the first paragraph on page 3. Point out to students the list of things the emperor's subjects had (i.e., *fresh food*, etc.). Demonstrate how lists of words separated by commas should be read.

Practice Ask students to find and read aloud other examples of lists in the story (pages 4, 7, 10), until they read them with fluidity.

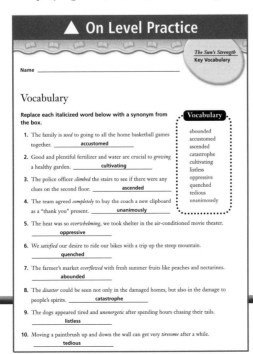

LEVELED READERS

Odin's Wisdom

Summary *Odin is the all-powerful Scandinavian god who is on an eternal quest for greater wisdom. He gives up an eye to drink from the well of knowledge. He lives in a tree for three days to learn the secrets of life. He works in a field of wheat for three months and disguises himself as a snake in order to drink the Mead of Poetry. Finally, he triumphs over the wisest giant, Vafthrudnir, in a battle of wits.*

Vocabulary

Introduce the Key Vocabulary and ask students to complete the BLM.

deities divinities, gods, *p. 3*

pitiless hard, unfeeling, *p. 4*

vengeful merciless, *p. 4*

wondrous amazing, *p. 5*

intoxicating invigorating, stimulating, *p. 6*

magnitude scale, size, *p. 7*

deciphered decoded, interpreted, *p. 9*

entreaties appeals, pleas, *p. 12*

assured guaranteed, *p. 16*

Building Background and Vocabulary

Share that myths serve to explain things people don't understand, and usually contain characters such as powerful gods or talking animals. Guide students through the text, using some of the vocabulary from the story.

Writing Skill: Writing a Myth

Have students read the Strategy Focus on the book flap. Remind students to use the strategy and to think about the elements of myths as they read the book. (See the Leveled Readers Teacher's Guide for **Vocabulary and Comprehension Practice Masters.**)

Responding

Have partners discuss how to answer the questions on the inside back cover.

Think About the Selection Sample answers:

1. He has many different roles and many different personality traits.

2. The Runes are mysterious written symbols that can grant magic powers over nature and explain the meaning of life.

3. He believes that anyone who can use words in beautiful and imaginative ways will have mastery over life.

4. Answers will vary.

Making Connections Answers will vary.

Building Fluency

Model Read aloud page 4. Point out to students the adjectives used to describe Odin (*muscular, fierce, vengeful*).

Practice Have small groups of students find other adjectives in the story that describe Odin (pages 7, 13, 14). Then ask them to say other words they would use to describe Odin, based on what they read.

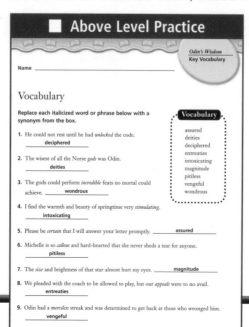

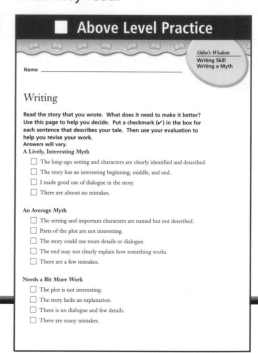

Leveled Readers

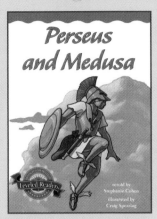

Perseus and Medusa

Summary *A cruel king, told he will be killed by his grandson, casts his daughter and grandson into the sea. Rescued, Perseus grows up in another kingdom. Aided by two gods, he captures the head of the monster Medusa, and saves his mother from marrying another cruel king. Then he accidentally kills his grandfather, thus fulfilling his fate.*

Vocabulary

Introduce the Key Vocabulary and ask students to complete the BLM.

fate result, destiny, *p. 3*

dazzled astonished, *p. 6*

challenge something to test a person's skills, *p. 7*

reflection image formed by reflected light, as in a mirror, *p. 8*

invisible impossible to see, *p. 8*

squirmed twisted about in a wiggling motion, *p. 13*

festival an occasion for feasting or performing, *p. 16*

◆ LANGUAGE SUPPORT

Building Background and Vocabulary

Explain that myths are stories in which the characters include heroes, strange creatures, and gods. Invite students to tell about any myths they know. Distribute the **Build Background Practice Master** and have students complete it in pairs. (See the Leveled Readers Teacher's Guide for **Build Background** and **Vocabulary Masters.**)

Reading Strategy: Predict

Have students read the Strategy Focus on the book flap. Remind students to use the strategy to make predictions as they read the book.

Responding

Have partners discuss how to answer the questions on the inside back cover.

Think About the Selection Sample answers:

1. He is told that he will be killed by Perseus, his grandson.
2. First, he locks up his daughter to keep her from having a child. When she has a child, he puts her and the baby into a chest and throws it in the ocean.
3. He uses Athena's shield as a mirror so that he can see Medusa without looking directly at her.
4. Answers will vary.

Making Connections Answers will vary.

Building Fluency

Model Read aloud page 7 as students follow along in their books. Point out that the king and Perseus are talking to each other.

Practice Have small groups take the roles of Perseus, the king, and the narrator, and act out the scene on page 7. Suggest that students rehearse several times before performing for the class.

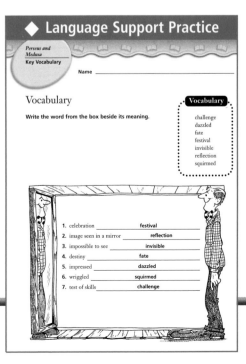

◆ Language Support Practice

Perseus and Medusa
Build Background

Name _____

Build Background

Myths are stories in which the characters include heroes, strange mythological creatures, and gods. Think of a myth you know, or make up one of your own. Fill in the chart below to describe the elements of the story. Answers will vary.

Setting: _____
Hero: _____
Enemy or foe: _____
_____
_____

The hero's challenge: _____
_____

Difficulties the hero overcomes to meet the challenge: _____
_____

The hero's reward: _____

◆ Language Support Practice

Perseus and Medusa
Key Vocabulary

Name _____

Vocabulary

Write the word from the box beside its meaning.

Vocabulary
challenge
dazzled
fate
festival
invisible
reflection
squirmed

1. celebration ___ festival
2. image seen in a mirror ___ reflection
3. impossible to see ___ invisible
4. destiny ___ fate
5. impressed ___ dazzled
6. wriggled ___ squirmed
7. test of skills ___ challenge

447R

Resources for Theme 4

Contents

Leveled Theme Paperbacks

The Librarian Who Measured the Earth

Summary *This illustrated biography combines fact and fiction to present the work of Eratosthenes of ancient Greece, the librarian and geographer who calculated the circumference of the earth.*

Vocabulary

ecstatic, p. 18: joyful, delighted

scholar, p. 18: a learned person

inspire, p. 21: to stimulate someone to be creative

axis, p. 30: the imaginary straight line around which the earth rotates

circumference, p. 32: the length of the boundary of a circle

surveyor, p. 42: a person who measures angles and distances along the earth's surface

Preparing to Read

Building Background Read aloud the author's note on page 3; briefly discuss why the author chose to write about Eratosthenes and why Eratosthenes's story might be interesting to people today. Remind students to use their reading strategies as they read the book.

Developing Vocabulary Most technical terms are defined within the text. Preview with students the meanings of the Vocabulary words listed at the left for each segment of the book, pages 4–27 and pages 28–47.

Previewing the Text

The Librarian Who Measured the Earth may be read in its entirety or broken into two reading segments, pages 4–27 and pages 28–47. Students may preview each segment by looking over the pictures and making predictions about the content.

Supporting the Reading

pages 4–27

- Why does Eratosthenes earn the nickname Pentathlos? (It is the name for an athlete who competes in five different events. It means "all-rounder," which fits Eratosthenes because he is a questioner, list maker, and writer in many subject areas.)

- What is Alexandria, Egypt, famous for in Eratosthenes's time? (It has a great museum and library where the most intelligent thinkers of the time make discoveries and inventions. There are seven hundred thousand scrolls containing all the knowledge of the day.)

- How has the meaning of museum changed over time? (In ancient Greece, museum meant "place of the Muses." A museum was a place for artists and scientists to be inspired by the Muses, the nine daughters of the god Zeus. Now a museum is mainly a place for people to learn from exhibits.)

THEME PAPERBACKS

irect students to the following terms and have them tell whether the
uthor has provided specific definitions or indirect or nontext clues
bout their meanings: *cistern* (page 6), *styluses* (page 10), *lyre* (page 12),
hronology (page 16), *promenades* (page 21), *papyrus* (page 24).

es 28–47

y Eratosthenes's time, people knew that the earth was not a cylinder
ut a sphere. What is the difference? (A cylinder is like a column; a sphere
a ball.)

Vhy does Eratosthenes write a geography book? (He has many questions
bout the earth, and the answers are in scrolls that cover math, people, and
istory. As a librarian and an organizer of ideas, he wants to compile all the
nformation in a single scroll.)

Vhat pieces of information must Eratosthenes gather in order to figure
ut the circumference of the earth? (He needs to find the distance of one
rc from Earth and the inside angle of that arc in order to determine the num-
er of arcs in 360 degrees and their total distance.)

n her author's note, Kathryn Lasky says that she has tried to *responsi-*
ly imagine the story of Eratosthenes. Do you think she has succeeded?
xplain. (Answers will vary. Students should acknowledge the author's
esearch as they discuss the challenge of describing someone about whom
here is little factual information.)

esponding

e students summarize the major events in Eratosthenes's story. Then
them to point out details in the diagrams and illustrations that help
m figure out the technical explanations of angles, shadows, and meas-
ments.

Language Development

Have students make drawings captioned
with the geometric terms used in this
book: *circumference, inside angle,
degree, arc.*

Leveled Theme Paperbacks

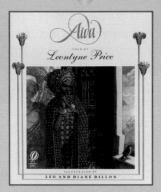

Aïda

Summary *This is a retelling of the tragic love story told in the opera* Aïda *by Giuseppe Verdi.* Aïda *is an Ethiopian princess enslaved by the Egyptians. She must choose between her love for an Egyptian army captain and loyalty to her native land.*

Vocabulary

handmaiden, p. 4: a woman servant

confided, p. 6: shared a secret with

decree, p. 8: an order from a ruler or person in charge

vanity, p. 12: excessive pride

betray, p. 14: to give aid or information to an enemy

vault, p. 26: an underground burial chamber

▲ ON LEVEL

Preparing to Read

Building Background Tell students that this is a story version of a famous opera set in an ancient time when Egypt and Ethiopia were at war. Use a map to point out both countries. Also read aloud the Storyteller's Note at the end of the book, identifying author Leontyne Price as a world-famous opera star. Remind students to use their reading strategies as they read the book.

Developing Vocabulary The context will offer meanings for most terms. Preview with students the meanings of the Vocabulary words listed at the left for the two suggested segments of the book, pages 2–13 and pages 14–29.

Previewing the Text

Aïda may be read in its entirety or broken into two reading segments, pages 2–13 and pages 14–29. Students may preview the illustrations to predict likely events. Suggest that students jot down characters' names while reading to help them keep track of relationships.

Supporting the Reading

pages 2–13

- Why does the author begin the story by comparing Aïda to a sunrise and starlight touching a flower? (The author wants to show the difference between Aïda and the atmosphere of fear and danger in Ethiopia.)

- Why does Amneris first suspect that Radames and Aïda are in love, and how does she know for sure? (Princess Amneris first grows suspicious when she sees Radames's eyes light up at Aïda's arrival. Amneris later tests Aïda by telling her first that Radames is dead and then that he is alive. Aïda's sorrowful and then joyful reactions confirm Amneris's suspicions.)

- What is a consecration song, described on page 10? (It is a religious song that the priestesses chant to grant holy power to Radames as he leads the army against the Ethiopians.)

- Why doesn't Aïda tell her captors that she is the daughter of King Amonasro? (She might be punished, since her father is Egypt's enemy.)

ges 14–29

How does each character react to the Pharaoh's announcement of Radames's reward, and why? (Radames acts as if he is grateful, but he really is horrified that he will be forced to marry Amneris because he had hoped to marry Aïda. Aïda weeps in her father's arms because she has just lost the man she loves. Amneris looks scornfully at her rival and marches proudly to the palace with Radames because she feels triumphant.)

What does Amneris mean when she screams "Traitor!" on page 22? (She means that Radames has committed treason. He has betrayed Egypt, the country he is pledged to defend. He has been disloyal by revealing a military secret to Aïda and her father.)

What are the most important events that happen after Radames is sentenced to death? (Radames is sealed into a deep vault and hears Aïda's voice. She has returned to die with him. While Amneris prays for forgiveness and for heavenly rest for Radames, Aïda and Radames die peacefully in each other's arms.)

Does this book make you want to see the opera Aïda performed? Why or why not? (Answers will vary. As they offer support for their opinions, students should reflect on the drama, intense emotions, suspense, and other story features they might also find in a performance.)

esponding

ve students tell how they used the Monitor/Clarify strategy to keep ck of characters' motives and actions. Encourage students to share ir reactions to the story and the illustrations. Then have them summa- e the plot.

English Language Learners

Supporting Comprehension

Focus on figurative expressions incorporating the word *heart;* students may be able to add to the list of these expressions from the story: *heart was torn, heart has been broken, heart was filled with sorrow, longed with all her heart and soul, first in my heart, deep in her heart, room in my heart.*

Between the Dragon and the Eagle

Summary *This work of historical fiction, set in a.d. 100, follows a bolt of blue silk as it travels from its creation in Changan to its final destination in Rome. The story provides a look at the belief systems and values of different ancient cultures.*

Vocabulary

barbarians, p. 10: foreign peoples who were considered uncivilized or primitive

meditation, p. 39: a mental exercise centering on deep thought

province, p. 69: a self-governed area of a country or empire

quay, p. 120: a wharf where ships are loaded or unloaded

reverence, p. 123: deep respect or honor

exquisite, p. 144: beautifully made or designed

transcended, p. 151: rose above or surpassed

■ ABOVE LEVEL

Preparing to Read

Building Background Briefly discuss where students get their clothing and where it was made. Ask them to think about how goods traveled from one part of the world to another long ago, and explain that this book tells how a bolt of blue silk, made in China in a.d. 100, traveled to Rome. Remind students to use their reading strategies as they read this book.

Developing Vocabulary Context clues will provide support for most unfamiliar words. Preview with students the meanings of the Vocabulary words listed at the left for each segment of the book: pages 12–59, pages 62–105, and pages 108–151.

Previewing the Text

Between the Dragon and the Eagle may be read in its entirety or in three segments: pages 12–59, pages 62–105, and pages 108–151. Invite students to look at the maps that appear throughout the book and read the author's preface. Encourage students to make predictions about what will happen in the story.

Supporting the Reading

pages 12–59

- How does the author show that the bolt of blue silk is very special? (It is the first thing to catch Han Tzu's attention in the shop; the look and feel of the fabric are described in detail; and the weaver tells how memory gives it its beauty.)

- What events lead to Han Tzu's great anger at Wei Chien? (When Wei Chien's nephew, Wei Po, is accused of being a thief, Han Tzu stands up for him. Later, Han Tzu finds that Wei Po's thievery could ruin the expedition, Han Tzu's reputation, and his livelihood.)

- On page 42, what language does the author use to describe the scene after the sandstorm? (Han Tzu's lips are *cracked,* and he uses water to rinse the sand from his mouth; the sand is a *smooth blanket* marked by *long overlapping ripples.*)

Why do you think memory, especially of his family, is so important to Han Tzu? (Answers will vary.)

ges 62–105

How does the author show that traders are viewed differently in Merv han in Changan? (Merv is a center of trading, and Vardanes and his culture value trading. Trading is not valued in Changan. Family is also very important to the Merv traders.)

What memory haunts Rabel Dushara? (On an earlier trip down the Euphrates, Rabel led a caravan that lost half its members to fever, and Rabel till feels somewhat responsible.)

Do you think the author believes that any one culture along the Silk Road is better than another? How can you tell? (The author treats all cultures equally; he tries to show that there are virtuous people and troublesome people in all cultures.)

ges 108–151

What hopes does Firmus carry along with the blue silk? (Firmus hopes to go to Rome, out-trade Claudius, turn a great profit, and help his grandfather's business.)

Why does Tullia say that only Lydia can tell Firmus the name of the silk dealer in Rome? (Because Tullia respects her daughter and her late husband's family, she leaves it up to Lydia to decide whether to give Firmus information.)

Who finally possesses the blue silk? What will it be used for? (Julia, a young woman from a wealthy Roman family, procures the silk and hopes to use it for her wedding dress.)

esponding

students to use the Evaluate strategy to think about how the author ows the values of the many cultures in the book. Then have students re their reactions to the book. Finally, ask them to summarize the ok.

nus Students can choose one of the cultures described in the book d do further research on the role trade has played in that culture.

THEME PAPERBACKS

Author's Viewpoint/Bias and Assumption

OBJECTIVES

- Analyze author's viewpoint.
- Identify bias and assumption.

Target Skill Trace

- Author's Viewpoint/Bias and Assumption, pp. 383A–383B

Teach

Ask students if they can give you examples of cartoons or comic strips that include "good guys" and "bad guys." Ask these questions about their examples:

- *What is the purpose of the cartoon? Does it inform or entertain?*
- *Does the cartoon explain why the characters are in conflict?*
- *What facts or opinions are expressed by the characters?*

Explain that in nonfiction as well as fiction, readers are exposed to an author's viewpoint, or the author's attitude towards a subject.

Direct students to page 363. Use a Think Aloud to model identifying an author's viewpoint.

Think Aloud *The author states that the Aztec empire was once the most powerful empire in North America. On page 365, I read facts about the city that support this statement. I also read that the Aztecs' conquered enemies brought them gifts. My impression is that the author's purpose is to inform and that the author has a positive, yet balanced, attitude towards the Aztecs.*

Practice

Tell students that they will examine the author's viewpoint on the meeting between the Aztecs and the

- Author's purpose for writing
- Evidence included or left out
- Illustrations used
- Language used
- Facts and opinions about people and events

Spanish conqueror Cortés. Display the list below. Tell students to refer to this list to determine the author's viewpoint about the meeting.

page 372 *What does the author describe in this part of the story?* (the meeting between Cortés and the Aztecs) *Does the author try to persuade you to feel something about this meeting?* (yes, sympathy for the Aztecs and that Cortés was dangerous) *Do readers know why Moctezuma is willing to greet Cortés?* (Yes, he thought that Cortés might be Quetzalcoatl.)

page 373 *Who looks more powerful in this illustration?* (the soldiers)

page 374 *How are the words that the author uses to describe the Aztecs different from the words used to describe Cortés and his men?* (Aztecs: descriptive and full of feeling; Cortés: abrupt and violent)

page 375 *Does the caption for this picture contain facts that support the author's statement that the Aztecs had a great empire?* (yes)

Elicit from students that this author shows a positive viewpoint toward the Aztecs.

Apply

As they read their **Leveled Readers** for the week, have students keep track of the author's viewpoint. Remind them to analyze the author's attitude as they read.

Monitoring Student Progress

If . . .	Then . . .
students need more practice with author's viewpoint/bias and assumption	have students try to determine the author's viewpoint in other stories from this theme.

HALLENGE/EXTENSION: Author's iewpoint/Bias and Assumption

Independent Activities

Persuasive Texts

ind examples of texts that persuade people to do or oin something. Try looking in school newspapers, lyers posted in the community, or newspaper articles bout health or fitness. At an appropriate time, read loud examples you found to your classmates.

Create an Advertisement

Advertisements are generally biased in favor of the products they promote. Write and illustrate a travel ompany's ad for a special vacation. Draw a picture or ut out pictures from other sources, and then write a

headline and caption that will persuade tourists to "buy" the vacation. Remember to use appealing and inviting words.

CHALLENGE

Finding the Author's Point of View

Review the story *The View from Saturday*. Determine he author's viewpoint on (1) the value of saving turtles nd (2) the character, Nadia. Write a sentence that tates each viewpoint. Then list a few examples of the acts or opinions, language, and illustrations that sup- ort your conclusions. When you have completed the ctivity, compare your conclusions with those of your lassmates.

RETEACHING: Comprehension Skills

Cause and Effect

OBJECTIVES

- Identify cause-and-effect relationships when no clue word is stated.
- Identify cause-and-effect relationships in a nonfiction text.

Target Skill Trace

- Cause and Effect, pp. 407A–407B

Teach

On the board, write the following sentences: *The flooding continued during the night. Morning traffic was slow, and many schools and businesses opened late.*

Ask students, *Do you think morning traffic was slow because of the flood?* Explain that why something happens is the *cause*. The *effect* is what happened as a *result*. Ask: *What happened because of the flood?*

Use a Think Aloud to model finding a cause-and-effect relationship.

Think Aloud *I know that some cause-and-effect relationships are signalled by clue words such as* so, *because,* and *when.* *I can restate the sentences using one of these words to decide if events have a cause-and-effect relationship. For example, "Because the flooding continued during the night, morning traffic was slow and many schools and businesses opened late" makes me quite sure that the events are related.*

Explain that to find cause and effect, students should ask themselves why something happens, or what led up to an event. Also point out that a cause may be stated in one sentence or paragraph, and the effect may be stated either before or later on in the text.

Practice

Help students identify the following cause-and-effect relationships from the selection *The Great Wall:*

page 393 *What group was threatening China?* (the Mongols) *Why did the Chinese build the Great Wall?* (The Mongols were invading China.) *What was the effect of building the Great Wall?* (The Chinese kept the Mongols out of China.)

page 393 *Why were tens of thousands of workers needed to build the Great Wall?* Help students make inferences that the Great Wall was a huge undertaking: (from preceding phrases on the page) *in the western part of the country, in the eastern mountains,* and *progress was slow.*

page 398 *What was the cause of the peasants' rebellion?* (They were overtaxed.) *What was the effect on the Ming government?* (The government was overthrown.)

Apply

As they read their **Leveled Readers** for the week, have students look for cause-and-effect relationships. Remind them to identify what happens and why it happens.

Monitoring Student Progress

If . . .	Then . . .
students need more practice with cause and effect,	repeat the Practice activity using another story they have recently read.

CHALLENGE/EXTENSION: Cause and Effect

Model Peer Mediation

Work in small groups, and within the group, divide into pairs. Pairs of students should think of a disagreement that might occur between students. For example, students might disagree about whether someone played a game fairly or about whether someone spoke out of turn. Discuss the possible causes and effects of the disagreement. Have one partner explain to the group the cause of the disagreement. Then have the other partner tell the effects of the disagreement. Finally, have the members of the group discuss how the disagreement could be resolved.

CHALLENGE

Causes and Effects of Current Events

You will need newspapers and magazines and an article that explains the causes and effects of a news event to do this activity. Look for articles on the environment, political elections, or scientific discoveries.

After you have chosen and read an article, cut out the article and paste it on a piece of paper.

Then list below the article two or more causes and effects that you identified in the article.

"What If" Questions

Working in pairs, identify four events that happen during the school day, such as lunch period, math center, or band practice. Then write four questions about the events, beginning each question with the words "What if;" for example, "What if we had no lunch period?" Notice that the question describes a cause. The answer to the question would, therefore, be an effect. Ask your questions of other student pairs.

RETEACHING: Comprehension Skills

Topic, Main Idea, and Details

> ### OBJECTIVES
> - Identify topic, main idea, and details.
> - Use details to make inferences about main ideas.
>
> ### Target Skill Trace
> - Topic, Main Idea, and Details, pp. 427A–427B

Teach

Tell students that identifying the topic and main idea of a selection or a part of a selection can help them summarize what it is about. Direct students to page 413. Read aloud the first paragraph.

Use a Think Aloud to model how to define a topic and how to use details to make inferences about main ideas.

Think Aloud *The topic is the subject, or what the selection is about. I should be able to identify the topic with a noun or phrase. The topic of this selection is "ancient Ghana." The main idea is the main point that the author makes. In some texts, I can use the details, or specific information the author gives, to help me find the main idea. In this paragraph, I read the details that people wore gold jewelry and cloth and that the king's gold hitching post weighed close to forty pounds. When I put these details together to find what ideas they have in common, I can infer that the main idea of this paragraph is that "ancient Ghana had a lot of gold."*

Practice

Direct students to reread the second paragraph on page 416 through the last paragraph on page 417. Explain that you want to find the main idea and supporting details in this section of the text.

Display the following chart.

Ask students, *What are most of the facts and details in this section about?* (camels) Ask students to name specific details about camels. Fill in the chart with their responses.

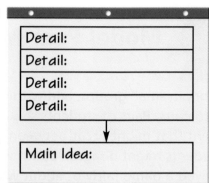

Explain that students can use the details they listed to figure out what point the author wants to make. Ask, *What is the main idea of this section of the text?* (Camels made trading caravans possible.)

Direct students to page 420. Point out the subtitle "Daily Life," and explain that this is the topic of this section of the text.

Read aloud the first two paragraphs on page 421. Ask, *What are the details in this section about?* (farming, land use, farming skills, farming crops) Fill in a second chart with details about farming from the text. Then ask, *What is the main idea of these paragraphs?* (People in ancient Ghana were accomplished farmers.)

Apply

As they read their **Leveled Readers** for the week, have students keep track of the topic, main ideas, and details. Remind students to use details to identify main ideas.

> ### Monitoring Student Progress
>
> | If . . . | Then . . . |
> | --- | --- |
> | students need more practice with topic, main idea, and details, | suggest that they identify the main idea of other stories they read. |

COMPREHENSION

CHALLENGE/EXTENSION:
Topic, Main Idea, and Details

Listening for Main Idea and Details

Working in pairs, revisit a story such as *Amelia Earhart, Lost Temple of the Aztecs,* or another nonfiction story you have recently read. Have your partner read aloud one or two paragraphs of the text. Then identify the main idea of the paragraphs and the details that support the main idea. Repeat the activity with other paragraphs from the text you and your partner have chosen. Listen carefully as each partner reads.

CHALLENGE

Write a Research Paper

Choose a research topic such as, "Ancient Cultures of Central America." Use information from this theme and library materials to write your paper. State the main idea of your paper in the first paragraph, and include details about your main idea in the paragraphs that follow.

Plan a Letter

Working in small groups, plan a letter to a business or organization about a topic that concerns you. For example, you might want to write to a local pizza store, asking if students could have a special discount when they buy pizza. Have one member of your group write a word or phrase that defines the topic of the letter, a second student write a sentence that states the main idea of the letter, and the remaining students list details that support the main idea. Repeat the activity by asking a different student to begin by writing a topic.

RETEACHING: Structural Analysis/Vocabulary Skills

More Suffixes

OBJECTIVES

- Decode words with suffixes *-ic*, *-al*, and *-ure*.
- Identify the meanings of words with suffixes *-ic*, *-al*, and *-ure*.

Target Skill Trace

- Suffixes *-al*, *-ic*, *-ure*, p. 383C

Teach

Review that suffixes are word parts added to the ends of words. They add to the meaning of the word. The suffix *-ic* means "relating to." The suffix *-al* also means "relating to." The suffix *-ure* means "action or process."

Write this sentence on the board and model decoding the underlined word: *The Aztecs built a majestic city with great temples and statues.*

Think Aloud *When I see the word* majestic, *I notice the suffix* -ic. *I know that the suffix means* "relating to," *so that is part of the word's meaning. The first part of the word reminds me of* "majesty," *so I think that the whole word must mean* "relating to majesty" *or* "something powerful and splendid."

Practice

Remind students that the following tips can help them decode words with suffixes:

- A suffix always appears after the base word.
- A suffix is usually a syllable.
- A suffix has the same pronunciation in different words.

Write these sentences on the board. Ask students to circle the words with *-al*, *-ic*, and *-ure* and define them.

> The cultural center sponsored an art show.
>
> The firefighters made a heroic effort to save the school.
>
> The crop failure hurt farmers throughout the state.

Apply

Write these words on a chart or on the board and have students write their meanings. Have pairs work together to write a sentence for each word.

historical	apologetic
enclosure	natural
realistic	gigantic
departure	continual

Monitoring Student Progress

If . . .	Then . . .
students need more practice reading words with suffixes *-al*, *-ic*, and *-ure*,	suggest that they look for other words in the selection with the suffixes *-al*, *-ic*, and *-ure*.

HALLENGE/EXTENSION: Vocabulary

Vocabulary Expansion

Independent Activity The selection is about events that take place in Mexico, where Spanish is spoken. English grows by borrowing words from other languages. List words borrowed from Mexican Spanish *(burrito, cafeteria, canyon, chocolate, macho, serape, stampede, taco)* and give their meanings.

CHALLENGE

Multiple-Meaning Words

Small Group Activity Form small groups. Look at the list of words below and provide as many different meanings for each word as you can. There are at least two meanings for each word; the group with the most meanings for each word wins. Groups may compare lists and discuss the meanings they found.

long	land	rich	power
sign	gift	safe	gold

Partner Activity Partners should brainstorm and write at least two meanings for the following words: *fork, course, right, warm.* Each partner should write a sentence for one of the meanings. Then review your sentences together to be sure that they represent different meanings.

RETEACHING: Structural Analysis/Vocabulary Skills

Adding *-ion, -ation*

OBJECTIVES
- Decode words with suffixes *-ion* and *-ation*.
- Identify the meanings of words with suffixes *-ion* and *-ation*.

Target Skill Trace
- Suffixes *-ion, -ation,* p. 407C

The man used an expression I didn't know.

Through her determination, the girl set a school record for swimming.

There will be a continuation of this course after spring break.

The student submitted his revision of the story after receiving a classmate's feedback.

Teach

Review that suffixes are word parts added to the ends of words that change the meaning of the word. Both the suffix *-ion* and the suffix *-ation* mean "action or process of."

Write this sentence on the board, and model decoding the underlined word.

> People grew tired of the <u>corruption</u> in the Ming court.

Think Aloud *When I see the word* corruption, *I notice the suffix* -ion. *I know that the suffix means "action or process of," so that is part of the word's meaning. The first part of the word is "corrupt" so I think that the whole word must mean "the action or process of being corrupt;" in other words, dishonesty and wickedness.*

Practice

Write these sentences on the board. Ask students to circle the words with *-ion* and *-ation* and explain their meanings.

Apply

Write these words on the board, and have students write their meanings. Ask students to write each word in a sentence and share their sentences with the group.

permission	destination
creation	negotiation
discoloration	selection

Monitoring Student Progress

If . . .	Then . . .
students need more practice with reading words with suffixes *-ion* and *-ation,*	suggest that they look for other words in the selection with the suffixes *-ion* and *-ation.*

CHALLENGE/EXTENSION:
Vocabulary

✎ Synonyms

Working with a partner, think of synonyms for the underlined words and rewrite the sentences using the synonyms.

The wall was built along the <u>crests</u> of tall hills.
Many workers didn't survive the <u>harsh</u> conditions.
People grew <u>angry</u> at the expense.
Officials were always <u>vying</u> for the emperor's favor.

Discuss how the synonyms change the meanings of the original sentences.

Small Group Activity

Read down the word list, taking turns to list a synonym for each word: *preventing, fear, swift, work, survive, expensive, strong, seize.* Compare your lists and discuss the shades of meaning among the synonyms you found. Add as many other words and synonyms to the list as you can.

 ## Vocabulary Expansion

Independent Activity The selection discusses the government of ancient China. Brainstorm words relating to government, such as *democracy, politics, voting, tax, mayor, senator,* and *president.* Record the words you brainstormed in a word web.

RETEACHING: Structural Analysis/Vocabulary Skills

RETEACHING

Unstressed Syllables

OBJECTIVE

- Read words with unstressed syllables.

Target Skill Trace

- Unstressed Syllables, p. 427C

Teach

Review that in words with two or more syllables, at least one syllable is stressed, or given emphasis. The others are unstressed. Many unstressed syllables are pronounced with the schwa sound (ə).

Write this sentence on the board and model pronouncing the underlined word.

> A hundred camels were loaded with <u>merchandise</u> and supplies.

Think Aloud *To sound out this word, I divide it into syllables. It could be* mur CHAN dise, *but that doesn't sound familiar.* MUR chun dise *sounds better. And I recognize it—it means something to sell and buy.*

Practice

Write the following sentences on the board and ask students to pronounce the underlined words and give their meanings.

> An Arabic <u>commentator</u> described the city of Wangara.
>
> Traders announce their <u>presence</u> by beating on a drum.
>
> The Wangaran miners were <u>secretive</u>.
>
> Traders brought items to market by <u>caravans</u>.
>
> Royal patrols <u>guaranteed</u> safe passages to all visitors.
>
> Ghana's farmers had <u>adequate</u> food to share with visitors.

Apply

Write these words on the board and have students copy and decode them: *kingdom, utensils, official, majority, allocated, population*. Ask students to circle the unstressed syllable or syllables in each word.

Monitoring Student Progress

If . . .	Then . . .
students need more practice reading words with unstressed syllables,	provide them with examples of two- and three-syllable words and ask them to decode the words.

Vocabulary Expansion

Partner Activity The selection tells how the people dressed. Working with a partner, look up the words *breeches, tunics,* and *sandals* and find other names for garments.

Create a basic guide to clothing, contrasting items from ancient times with modern fashions.

Include background information that explains why certain articles of clothing are suited to a particular time and place.

CHALLENGE

Prefixes and Suffixes

Small Group Activity Form small groups and make sure you have dictionaries. Take turns looking up the following words to find the prefix or suffix of each and its meaning: *advance, consist, include, writer, assume, resident, archaeologist, complex, merchant, assign, improve, doctor, dentist, complete, appear.*

Organize the words in categories, according to each word's prefix or suffix and its meaning. Add other words to each category or write a paragraph using words from two or more catagories.

Adjectives

OBJECTIVES

- Identify adjectives.
- Use adjectives in sentences.

Target Skill Trace

- Adjectives, pp. 383I, 383K

Teach

Ask students to describe the city or town in which they live. Record their responses on the chalkboard. Underline the adjectives that students use. Explain that the underlined words in the sentences are adjectives. Remind students that adjectives are words that describe nouns and pronouns. Then read aloud the following sentences. Have students listen carefully and identify the adjectives. Ask them to name the noun that each adjective describes.

- *The Aztecs once ruled a <u>powerful</u> empire.* (empire)
- *They built a city in the middle of a <u>large</u> lake.* (lake)
- *They built <u>towering</u> temples.* (temples)
- *They carved <u>elaborate</u> sculptures.* (sculptures)
- *They enjoyed <u>rich</u>, <u>spicy</u> foods.* (foods)

Practice

Use the story to model how to identify adjectives. Have students look at the paragraph on page 365 that begins, "Five hundred years ago . . ." Model how to find adjectives in the paragraph.

Think Aloud *As I read this paragraph, I look for adjectives that tell me more about the Aztec city. I see the words* sparkling *and* blue *before the word* lake. *These words must be adjectives because they tell what the lake looked like. The words* spotless *and* white *describe the buildings, so they must be adjectives, too. What other adjectives can I identify? The words* lush *and* green *describe the gardens. The word* Long *tells*

about the causeways. The word snowcapped *describes the mountains. All these adjectives help paint a vivid picture of what the Aztec city was like.*

Ask students to look at page 365 and identify the adjectives in these sentences.

One <u>fateful</u> day in 1519, an <u>unusual</u> group of visitors approached Tenochtitlán.

They came with <u>strange</u>, <u>wild-eyed</u> beasts and they carried <u>heavy</u> weapons that clanked and gleamed in the sun.

Ask students to look for other sentences in the selection that contain adjectives.

Summarize by asking students: *What is an adjective?* (An adjective is a word that describes a noun or a pronoun.) Have students use adjectives to describe the day's weather.

Apply

As they read their **Leveled Readers** for the week, have students write a description based on one of the illustrations from the selection. Remind them to use adjectives to help bring their description to life.

Monitoring Student Progress

If . . .	Then . . .
students need more practice with adjectives,	use the Practice or Apply activity with another story from this theme.

Proper Adjectives

OBJECTIVES

- Identify proper adjectives and use them in sentences.
- Distinguish proper adjectives from proper nouns.

Target Skill Trace

- Proper Adjectives, pp. 383I, 383J

Teach

Ask students to name some of their favorite foods from other countries, such as <u>Spanish</u> rice, <u>Italian</u> sausage, <u>Mexican</u> salsa, <u>Jamaican</u> chicken, or <u>French</u> bread. Record responses on the chalkboard and underline the proper adjective in each.

Point out to students that the underlined words are proper adjectives. Explain that like other adjectives, proper adjectives describe nouns and pronouns. However, since proper adjectives are formed from proper nouns, they are always capitalized.

Write the following sentences on a chart or chalkboard and have students identify the proper adjectives.

The Aztecs were a group of <u>Native American</u> people who lived in Mexico.

The <u>Toltec</u> people had built an empire in Mexico before the Aztecs.

In 1519, the <u>Spanish</u> explorer Cortés arrived in the <u>Aztec</u> empire.

The <u>European</u> explorer and his men seemed very strange to the Aztecs.

Today some <u>United States</u> citizens are descendants of the Aztecs.

Practice

Ask a student to read aloud the sentence on page 365 that begins, *This was where the Aztecs worshipped their gods. . .* Then model how to distinguish proper adjectives from proper nouns.

Think Aloud *I notice that the word* Aztec *is used twice in this sentence. The beginning of the sentence tells me: This is where the Aztecs worshipped their gods . . . The*

word Aztec *is capitalized, but it does not describe another word. It must be used as a proper noun here.* Aztec *is also used at the end of the sentence:* where the Aztec ruler Moctezuma received important guests. *The word is capitalized again, but this time it describes the noun* ruler. *In this case,* Aztec *must be a proper adjective.*

Have students read the following sentences from the story and tell if the underlined words are proper nouns or proper adjectives.

> Page 365 *The first <u>Europeans</u> who saw Tenochtitlán found the city so beautiful, they thought it must be enchanted.* (proper noun)

> Page 370 *Today the eagle on a cactus is part of the <u>Mexican</u> flag.* (proper adjective)

> Page 371 *The <u>Aztec</u> calendar was shown as a round disk, since the <u>Aztecs</u> saw time as being like a wheel, endlessly turning.* (proper adjective, proper noun)

Review by asking student volunteers to use a proper adjective in a sentence. Then ask: *How are proper adjectives different from proper nouns?* (Proper nouns are names. Proper adjectives describe nouns and pronouns.)

Apply

Ask students to make a list of important facts from the story. Ask them to use at least three proper adjectives in their lists. Then have students exchange papers and identify the proper adjectives in each other's work.

Monitoring Student Progress

If . . .	Then . . .
students need more practice with proper adjectives,	use the Practice or Apply activity with another story about an ancient culture.

Comparing with Adjectives

OBJECTIVES

- Identify adjectives that compare.
- Use adjectives to make a comparison.

Target Skill Trace

- Comparing with Adjectives, pp. 407I, 407J

Teach

Write the following sentences on the chalkboard and invite volunteers to complete them by adding the name of a building.

> _____ is a <u>tall</u> building.
>
> _____ is a <u>taller</u> building.
>
> _____ is the <u>tallest</u> building I have ever seen.

Point out the words *tall, taller,* and *tallest* in the sentences. Review that these words are adjectives. Remind students that the endings *-er* and *-est* are often added to form adjectives that compare. Explain that some adjectives that compare are irregular in form, such as *better, best* and *less, least.*

Display the following sentences. Have students choose the adjective that best completes each sentence.

> The Nile River is (long, <u>longer</u>, longest) than the Mississippi River.
>
> Mount Everest is the (high, higher, <u>highest</u>) mountain in the world.
>
> Lake Michigan is a (<u>large</u>, larger, largest) lake.

Practice

Have students look at the second paragraph on page 397. Using a Think Aloud, model how to identify adjectives that compare.

Think Aloud *The second sentence in this paragraph tells me that a smoky fire was built on top of the nearest signal tower. The word* nearest *is an adjective that tells more about the signal tower. The ending* -est *lets me know that all the signal towers are being compared. So the signal tower on which the fire was built was closer than any other signal tower around.*

Have students look in the story to find adjectives that compare. Direct their attention to the following sentences.

> Page 398 *Once again lacking <u>strong</u> leadership, the Mongols were growing <u>weaker</u>.*
>
> Page 398 *The combined Manchu and Chinese forces were far <u>stronger</u> than the Mongols.*
>
> Page 400 *In 1644 the Great Wall was <u>longer</u>, <u>stronger</u>, and <u>better</u> guarded than it had ever been before . . .*

Review by asking students to name some adjectives that compare two things and some adjectives that compare more than two things.

Apply

Have students use adjectives that compare to write a description of three structures or land formations. Have students exchange papers and underline adjectives that compare in each other's writing.

Monitoring Student Progress

If . . .	Then . . .
students need more practice comparing with adjectives,	use the Practice or Apply activity with another story from this theme.

Comparing with *more* and *most*

Teach

Write the following sentences on the board and read them with students.

> Our classroom has <u>many</u> seats.
>
> The library has <u>more</u> seats than our classroom.
>
> The lunchroom has the <u>most</u> seats of all.

Underline the words *many, more,* and *most* in the sentences. Review that two of these words are adjectives that compare. The adjective *more* compares two things. The adjective *most* compares more than two.

Read aloud the following sentences. Have students listen carefully and identify which adjective best completes each sentence.

The Great Wall is the _____ recognized structure in China. (most)

There were _____ Chinese soldiers than Mongol warriors. (more)

People in the Ming government had the _____ power of all. (most)

Practice

Have students reread the last paragraph on page 401. Then model how to identify an adjective that compares.

Think Aloud *This paragraph tells me that the Great Wall has emerged as the most famous and enduring creation of the Ming dynasty. The adjective* most *is used here, so I know the Great Wall is not being compared to just one other creation. It is being compared to all creations of the Ming dynasty. This helps me understand the importance of the Great Wall.*

Ask students to find the comparing adjectives in the following sentences and to explain what is being compared.

> Page 398 *The Qing emperors ruled the land on both sides of the Great Wall. The Mongols were not a threat. The wall no longer marked a border, and it wasn't needed for defense. The wall was more useful before the Qing emperors ruled the land than after they came to power.* (before and after the Qing emperors came to power)

> Page 400 *In 1644 the Great Wall was longer, stronger, and better guarded than it had ever been before, but for the Manchus it was as though it didn't exist at all. In 1644, the wall was the most awesome structure in all of China.* (all structures in China)

Review by having students tell the difference between the adjectives *more* and *most*. (The adjective *more* is used to compare two things. The adjective *most* compares more than two.)

Apply

Have students use the adjectives *more* and *most* in a written review of *The Great Wall*. Ask volunteers to read aloud their reviews. Have classmates exchange papers to check that the adjectives are used correctly.

Monitoring Student Progress

If . . .	Then . . .
students need more practice comparing with *more* and *most,*	use the Practice or Apply activity with another nonfiction story they have read.

RETEACHING: Grammar Skills

Adverbs That Modify Verbs and Adjectives

OBJECTIVES

- Identify adverbs that modify verbs and adjectives.
- Use adverbs that modify verbs and adjectives in sentences.

Target Skill Trace

- Adverbs That Modify Verbs and Adjectives, pp. 427I, 427J

Teach

Have students describe a recent visit to a store. What kind of store did they visit? When did they go? What did they buy? Write sentences on the chalkboard that reflect their responses. Include adverbs in the sentences, such as: *Keith visited an unusually large music store; He listened to a deafeningly loud CD.*

Remind students that adverbs are used to tell more about verbs or adjectives. Ask volunteers to identify the adverbs in the sentences on the chalkboard. Then have them name the word in each sentence that the adverb modifies. Ask if that word is a verb or an adjective.

Then display the following sentences. Have students underline the adverb, identify the word it modifies, and name whether the modified word is a verb or an adjective.

Wangaran miners were <u>extremely</u> cautious. (cautious: adjective)

The traders beat a drum <u>loudly</u> to announce their presence. (beat: verb)

Then the miners <u>carefully</u> crept from their hiding places. (crept: verb)

They put out a <u>surprisingly</u> accurate amount of gold. (accurate: adjective)

Practice

Write this sentence on the board:

Camels can endure exceptionally high temperatures.

Then model how to identify adverbs.

Think Aloud *I notice that this sentence includes the words* exceptionally high temperatures. *The ending -ly tells me that exceptionally is probably an adverb. I ask myself, What word does exceptionally describe? As I read the sentence again, I can see that exceptionally describes how high the temperatures are. The word* high *is an adjective. Exceptionally is an adverb that describes the adjective* high.

Have students find the adverbs in these passages, identify the words they modify, and name whether the modified word is a verb or an adjective.

Page 417 <u>Famously</u> stubborn, camels cannot be handled by just anybody . . . (famously; modifies the adjective stubborn)

Page 418 <u>Occasionally</u> they must have been greeted by a lizard . . . (occasionally; modifies the verb must have been greeted)

Summarize by asking students to name some common adverbs. Then ask, *What kinds of words can adverbs modify?* (verbs and adjectives)

Apply

Have students scan the subtitles in the selection. Ask them to write a summary of one subtitled section. Have them include adverbs in their summary. Students can exchange papers and identify the adverbs that their classmates used.

Monitoring Student Progress

If . . .	Then . . .
students need more practice with adverbs that modify verbs and adjectives,	use the Practice or Apply activity with another story from this theme.

Comparing with Adverbs

OBJECTIVES

- Identify adverbs that compare.
- Use adverbs that compare in sentences.

Target Skill Trace

- Comparing with Adverbs, pp. 427I, 427J

Teach

Ask students to complete the following sentences and to choose the sentence that best describes their nonfiction reading.

I read all nonfiction carefully.
I read (selection title) more carefully than (selection title).
(Selection title) had to be read most carefully.

Point out that the adverb *more carefully* makes a comparison between two actions. The adverb *most carefully* makes a comparison between more than two actions.

Explain that the words *more* and *most* are usually added to adverbs that end in *-ly* to form adverbs that compare. With some adverbs such as *soon* or *fast*, the endings *-er* and *-est* are added; for example, *sooner, soonest; faster, fastest.*

Display the following sentences. Have students name the comparing adverb that best completes each sentence.

Ancient Ghana grew rich (sooner, soonest) than some other parts of Africa.

Of all the areas, goods were taken (more quickly, most quickly) to large cities.

Caravans took the western route (more often, most often) than other routes.

Practice

Have students look at the third paragraph on page 416. Model how to recognize irregular forms of adverbs.

Think Aloud *This paragraph tells me that* camels can endure the dry heat better than any other beast of burden. *The adverb* better *compares how two things endure the heat: camels and other beasts of burden. It's important for me to know that some adverbs have irregular forms when used to compare; for example,* better, best *and* worse, worst.

Ask students to name the comparative forms of the underlined adverbs in these sentences from the selection.

Page 414 *"Through years of experience, both sides had a general idea of what would be acceptable, so the system generally moved quickly and smoothly."* (more generally, most generally; more quickly, most quickly; more smoothly, most smoothly)

Page 421 *"Eighty percent of the population lived outside the towns, in small farming compounds, where a man and his sons' and daughters' families worked cooperatively."* (more cooperatively, most cooperatively)

Review by asking: *How do you form most adverbs that compare?* (Add the words *more* and *most* to adverbs that end in *-ly*; add the ending *-er* or *-est*.)

Apply

Have students write a paragraph comparing daily life in the royal kingdoms with their own daily life. Tell them to include in their writing adverbs that compare. Invite students to read their comparisons aloud. Ask listeners to identify the adverbs.

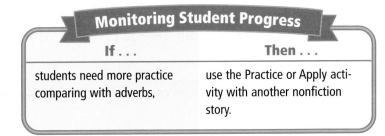

Monitoring Student Progress

If . . .	Then . . .
students need more practice comparing with adverbs,	use the Practice or Apply activity with another nonfiction story.

Name_____

Mystery Word Challenge

Write a word from the Word Bank to complete each sentence.

1. On February 21, 1978, workmen in Mexico City made a _____ discovery, a stone disk depicting the Aztec moon goddess Coyolxauhqui.

   _ _ _ _ _ _ _ _ _

adorned	empire	momentous
causeways	intricate	sites
conquered	metropolis	tributes

2. The flat, round stone was covered with _____ carvings.

   _ _ _ _ _ _ _ _ _

3. It showed Coyolxauhqui _____ with an elaborate headdress.

   _ _ _ _ _ _ _

4. Professor Matos Moctezuma had excavated Aztec archaeological _____.

   _ _ _ _ _

5. Mexico City is built where the Aztec _____ of Tenochtitlán had stood.

   _ _ _ _ _ _ _ _ _ _

6. Long _____ had connected that island city with the mainland.

   _ _ _ _ _ _ _ _ _

7. Tenochtitlán had been the capital city of the Aztec _____.

   _ _ _ _ _ _

8. The mighty Aztecs had _____ nearly all of the surrounding peoples.

   _ _ _ _ _ _ _ _ _

9. The Aztecs required these people to pay them heavy _____ and other gifts.

   _ _ _ _ _ _ _ _

Unscramble the boxed letters to find the mystery word.

Through his mother's __ __ __ __ __ __ __ __ __, Professor Eduardo Matos Moctezuma's family tree led back to Moctezuma.

Theme 4: **Discovering Ancient Cultures**

6. causeways
7. empire
8. conquered

1. momentous
2. intricate
3. adorned

Name _____

Vocabulary Challenge

Cut out the word cards.

craftsmen	insurmountable
domain	laborers
durable	massive
dynasty	nomadic
excluding	steppe
extravagance	stonemasons
grueling	terrain
ingenious	unity

Theme 4: **Discovering Ancient Cultures**

Consider copying and laminating game pieces for use in centers.

Name_____

Leader Name Challenge

Use a dictionary to find the meaning and origin of each of these names
for leaders.

Head of State	Meaning	Origin
Czar and czarina		
Dictator		
Emir		
Emperor and empress		
Monarch		
President		
Queen		
Sultan		

Theme 4: **Discovering Ancient Cultures**

Name _____

Comparing Forms
of Information

Complete the chart with information from the selection.

Form of Information	Subject Matter	Purpose
Text		
Subheadings		
Photographs		
Illustrated diagram		
Timeline		
Map		
Short captions		
Long captions		

Theme 4: **Discovering Ancient Cultures**

Focus on Myths

Language Center, p. 447M
Activity Master 4–5

Myth Riddles

Write the common meaning and the mythological meaning of each word.

mercurial
Common: _____

Mythological: _____

titanic
Common: _____

Mythological: _____

oracle
Common: _____

Mythological: _____

labyrinth
Common: _____

Mythological: _____

tripod
Common: _____

Mythological: _____

Olympian
Common: _____

Mythological: _____

odyssey
Common: _____

Mythological: _____

siren
Common: _____

Mythological: _____

nectar
Common: _____

Mythological: _____

atlas
Common: _____

Mythological: _____

medusa
Common: _____

Mythological: _____

cupid
Common: _____

Mythological: _____

Theme 4: **Discovering Ancient Cultures**

Name _____

Race to the Sun

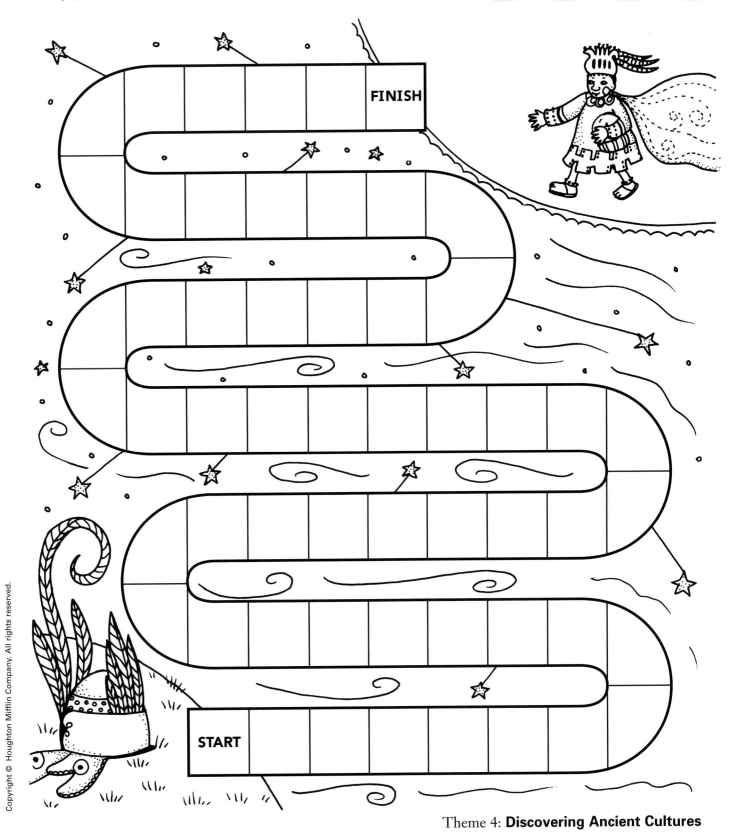

FINISH

START

Theme 4: **Discovering Ancient Cultures**

Consider copying and laminating this page for use in centers.

Writer _____ Listener _____

Writing Conference
What Should I Say?

In a writing conference, a writer reads a draft to a partner or a small group. A listener can help the writer by discussing the draft and asking questions such as these.

If you're thinking . . .

- How does the writer know that?
- Some facts aren't important.
- This part is hard to understand.

You could say . . .

- Where did you find this information?
- Does your reader really need to know this?
- Can you give facts to make this part clearer?

More Questions a Listener Might Ask

Read these questions before you listen. Take notes on the other side of this paper. Then discuss your thoughts with the writer.

1. What do you like about the writer's research report?

2. What topic is the writer telling about? Retell the information that you heard.

3. What facts did you find most interesting?

4. Are there places where the writer needs to tell more? or tell less? Give examples.

Theme 4: **Discovering Ancient Cultures**

TECHNOLOGY RESOURCES

erican Melody
ox 270
rd, CT 06437
20-5557
.americanmelody.com

io Bookshelf
rescott Hill Road
port, ME 04849
34-1713
.audiobookshelf.com

er & Taylor
Business Center Drive
urgh, PA 15205
75-2600
.btal.com

Audio/Random House
ohn Road
minster, MD 21157
33-3000

Kids Productions
Dywer Ave.
n, TX 78704
477-7811
.bigkidsvideo.com

ks on Tape
ox 25122
Ana, CA 92799
41-5525
.booksontape.com

derbund Company
rtha's Way
atha, IA 52233
.broderbund.com

nic Archives
inema Center
ord, CT 06404
66-1920
.filmicarchives.com

at White Dog Picture
mpany
on Lane
NH 03824
97-7641
.greatwhitedog.com

HarperAudio
10 E. 53rd St.
New York, NY 10022
800-242-7737
www.harperaudio.com

Houghton Mifflin Company
222 Berkeley St.
Boston, MA 02116
800-225-3362

Informed Democracy
P.O. Box 67
Santa Cruz, CA 95063
800-827-0949

JEF Films
143 Hickory Hill Circle
Osterville, MA 02655
508-428-7198

Kimbo Educational
P.O. Box 477
Long Branch, NJ 07740
800-631-2187
www.kimboed.com

Library Video Co.
P.O. Box 580
Wynnewood, PA 19096
800-843-3620
www.libraryvideo.com

Listening Library
P.O. Box 25122
Santa Ana, CA 92799
800-541-5525
www.listeninglibrary.com

Live Oak Media
P.O. Box 652
Pine Plains, NY 12567
800-788-1121
www.liveoakmedia.com

Media Basics
Lighthouse Square
P.O. Box 449
Guilford, CT 06437
800-542-2505
www.mediabasicsvideo.com

Microsoft Corp.
One Microsoft Way
Redmond, WA 98052
800-426-9400
www.microsoft.com

**National Geographic
School Publishing**
P.O. Box 10597
Des Moines, IA 50340
800-368-2728
www.nationalgeographic.com

New Kid Home Video
P.O. Box 10443
Beverly Hills, CA 90213
800-309-2392
www.NewKidhomevideo.com

Puffin Books
345 Hudson Street
New York, NY 10014
800-233-7364

**Rainbow Educational
Media**
4540 Preslyn Drive
Raleigh, NC 27616
800-331-4047
www.rainbowedumedia.com

Recorded Books
270 Skipjack Road
Prince Frederick, MD 20678
800-638-1304
www.recordedbooks.com

Sony Wonder
Dist. by Professional Media Service
19122 S. Vermont Ave.
Gardena, CA 90248
800-223-7672
www.sonywonder.com

Spoken Arts
195 South White Rock Road
Holmes, NY 12531
800-326-4090
www.spokenartsmedia.com

SRA Media
220 E. Danieldale Rd.
DeSoto, TX 75115
800-843-8855
www.sra4kids.com

SVE & Churchill Media
6677 North Northwest Highway
Chicago, IL 60631
800-829-1900
www.svemedia.com

Tom Snyder Productions
80 Coolidge Hill Road
Watertown, MA 02472
800-342-0236
www.tomsnyder.com

Troll Communications
100 Corporate Drive
Mahwah, NJ 07430
800-526-5289
www.troll.com

Weston Woods
143 Main St.
Norwalk, CT 06851-1318
800-243-5020
www.scholastic.com/westonwoods

PRONUNCIATION GUIDE

In this book some unfamiliar or hard-to-pronounce words are followed by respellings to help you say the words correctly. Use the key below to find examples of various sounds and their respellings. Note that in the respelled word, the syllable in capital letters is the one receiving the most stress.

Dictionary letter or mark		Respelled as	Example	Respelled word
ă	(pat)	a	basket	BAS-kiht
ā	(pay)	ay	came	kaym
âr	(care)	air	share	shair
ä	(father)	ah	barter	BAHR-tur
ch	(church)	ch	channel	CHAN-uhl
ĕ	(pet)	eh	test	tehst
ē	(bee)	ee	heap	heep
g	(gag)	g	goulash	GOO-lahsh
ĭ	(pit)	ih	liver	LIHV-ur
ī	(pie, by)	y	alive	uh-LYV
		eye	island	EYE-luhnd
îr	(hear)	eer	year	yeer
j	(judge)	j	germ	jurm
k	(kick, cat, pique)	k	liquid	LIHK-wihd
ŏ	(pot)	ah	otter	AHT-ur
ō	(toe)	oh	solo	SOH-loh
ô	(caught, paw)	aw	always	AWL-wayz
ôr	(for)	or	normal	NOR-muhl
oi	(noise)	oy	boiling	BOYL-ihng
ŏŏ	(took)	u	pull, wool	pul, wul
ōō	(boot)	oo	bruise	brooz
ou	(out)	ow	pound	pownd
s	(sauce)	s	center	SEHN-tur
sh	(ship, dish)	sh	chagrin	shuh-GRIHN
ŭ	(cut)	uh	flood	fluhd
ûr	(urge, term, firm, word, heard)	ur	earth	urth
			bird	burd
z	(zebra, xylem)	z	cows	kowz
zh	(vision, pleasure, garage)	zh	decision	dih-SIHZH-uhn
ə	(about)	uh	around	uh-ROWND
	(item)	uh	broken	BROH-kuhn
	(edible)	uh	pencil	PEHN-suhl
	(gallop)	uh	connect	kuh-NEHKT
	(circus)	uh	focus	FOH-kuhs
ər	(butter)	ur	liter	LEE-tur

Glossary

This glossary contains meanings and pronunciations for some of the words in this book. The Full Pronunciation Key shows how to pronounce each consonant and vowel in a special spelling. At the bottom of the glossary pages is a shortened form of the full key.

Full Pronunciation Key

Consonant Sounds

b	**bib**, ca**bb**age	kw	**ch**oir, **qu**ick	t	**t**ight, stopp**ed**
ch	**ch**urch, sti**tch**	l	**l**id, need**le**, ta**ll**	th	**b**a**th**, **th**in
d	**d**ee**d**, mai**l**ed, pu**ddle**	m	a**m**, **m**an, du**mb**	th	ba**th**e, **th**is
		n	**n**o, su**dd**en	v	ca**ve**, **v**alve, **v**ine
f	**f**ast, **f**i**f**e, o**ff**, **ph**rase, rough	ng	thi**ng**, i**nk**	w	**w**ith, **w**olf
g	**g**a**g**, **g**et, fin**g**er	p	**p**o**p**, ha**pp**y	y	**y**es, **y**olk, on**i**on
h	**h**at, **wh**o	r	**r**oar, **rh**yme	z	ro**s**e, **s**i**z**e, **x**ylophone, **z**ebra
hw	**wh**ich, **wh**ere	s	mi**ss**, **s**auce, **sc**ene, **s**ee	zh	gara**g**e, plea**s**ure, vi**s**ion
j	**j**u**dg**e, **g**em	sh	**d**i**sh**, **sh**ip, **s**ugar, ti**ss**ue		
k	**c**at, **k**i**ck**, s**ch**ool				

Vowel Sounds

ă	p**a**t, l**au**gh	ŏ	h**o**rrible, p**o**t	ŭ	c**u**t, fl**oo**d, r**ou**gh, s**o**me
ā	**a**pe, **ai**d, p**ay**	ō	g**o**, r**o**w, t**oe**, th**ough**	û	c**i**rcle, f**u**r, h**ea**rd, t**e**rm, t**u**rn, **u**rge, w**o**rd
â	**a**ir, c**a**re, w**ea**r	ô	**a**ll, c**au**ght, f**o**r, p**aw**		
ä	f**a**ther, k**o**ala, y**a**rd	oi	b**oy**, n**oi**se, **oi**l		
ĕ	p**e**t, pl**ea**sure, **a**ny	ou	c**ow**, **ou**t	yōō	c**u**re
ē	b**e**, b**ee**, **ea**sy, p**ia**no	ŏŏ	f**u**ll, b**oo**k, w**o**lf	yōō	**a**b**u**se, **u**se
ĭ	**i**f, p**i**t, b**u**sy	ōō	b**oo**t, r**u**de, fr**ui**t, fl**ew**	ə	**a**go, sil**e**nt, penc**i**l, lem**o**n, circ**u**s
ī	r**i**de, b**y**, p**ie**, h**igh**				
î	d**ea**r, d**ee**r, f**ie**rce, m**e**re				

Stress Marks

Primary Stress ´: bi·ol·o·gy [bī **ŏl**´ ə jē]
Secondary Stress ʹ: bi·o·log·i·cal [bī´ ə **lŏj**´ ĭ kəl]

Pronunciation key and definitions © 1998 by Houghton Mifflin Company. Adapted and reprinted by permission from *The American Heritage Children's Dictionary.*

A

a·ban·doned (ə **băn**´ dənd) *adj.* Permanently left behind; deserted. *A colony of squirrels is living in the abandoned house.*

ab·stract (ăb **străkt**´, **ăb**´ străkt´) *adj.* Not representing a recognizable image. *People enjoy abstract art for its colors and forms.*

ac·ces·si·ble (ăk **sĕs**´ ə bəl) *adj.* Affordable; easy to get. *The silver bowls are very expensive, but the stainless steel ones are accessible to most customers.*

ac·com·plish (ə **kŏm**´ plĭsh) *v.* To succeed in doing something. *Her education will help her accomplish great things.*

ac·count·ant (ə **koun**´ tant) *n.* Someone trained to keep the financial records of a business. *The accountant figured out how much money the company owed in taxes.*

ac·count·ing (ə **koun**´ ĭng) *n.* A detailed narrative; a record of events. *For several days, the newspaper gave a detailed accounting of destruction from the hurricane.*

a·dorn (ə **dôrn**´) *v.* To decorate. *The Hawaiians adorned their visitors with garlands of beautiful flowers.*

aer·o·nau·tics (âr´ ə **nô**´ tĭks) *n.* The design and construction of aircraft. *The person in charge of our rocket experiments has vast knowledge of aeronautics.*

af·ter·deck (**ăf**´ tər dĕk´) *n.* The part of a ship's deck near the rear. *The passengers stood on the afterdeck, watching the island disappear.*

a·nal·y·sis (ə **năl**´ ĭ sĭs) *n., pl.* **analyses** (ə **năl**´ ĭ sēs) The separation of a substance into its parts in order to study each part. *A high-powered microscope was used for an analysis of the virus.*

ap·pli·cant (**ăp**´ lĭ kənt) *n.* A person who requests employment or acceptance. *There were six applicants for the shipping clerk job.*

as·cent (ə **sĕnt**´) *n.* An upward climb. *The ascent to the mountain's summit took two days.*

as·tro·naut (**ăs**´ trə nôt´) *n.* A person trained to fly in a spacecraft. *Sally Ride was the first American female astronaut in space.*

at·ten·tion (ə **tĕn**´ shən) *n.* Close or careful observing or listening. *The tour guide asked the group to give her their full attention.*

a·vi·a·tion (ā´ vē ā´ shən, ăv´ ē ā´ shən) *n.* The operation of aircraft. *The history of aviation goes back to the days of hot air balloons.*

awk·ward (**ôk**´ wərd) *adj.* Uncomfortable. *Roger felt awkward when he realized that everyone else had worn nice clothes to the party.*

astronaut

aviation
French speakers in the nineteenth century created a word for the operation of aircraft from the Latin word *avis*, which means "bird."

B

bartering
Our modern meaning for the word *barter* comes from the old French word *barater*, which means both "to exchange" and "to deceive."

bar·ter·ing (**bär**´ tər ĭng) *n.* The trading of goods without the exchange of money. *By clever bartering, the milkmaid got two geese in exchange for the butter.*

be·lay (bĭ **lā**´) *v.* To secure by means of a rope, in mountain climbing. *To protect themselves, the mountain climbers will belay as they climb.* —*adj.* Secured by a rope. *He waited in the belay position while the others caught up with him.*

brag (brăg) *v.* To boast. *Nella bragged that she was the best basketball player in her class.*

brisk·ly (**brĭsk**´ lē) *adv.* Quickly, energetically. *The pilot strode briskly through the airport to the plane.*

bulk·head (**bŭlk**´ hĕd´) *n.* One of the walls that divides the cabin of a ship into compartments. *A sailing chart was pinned on the bulkhead by the cabin door.*

buoy (bōō´ ē, boi) *n.* An anchored float, often with a bell or light, used on a lake or ocean to mark safe passage or to warn of danger. *Swimmers are told not to swim beyond the harbor buoy.*

buoy

C

can·vas (**kăn**´ vəs) *n.* The stiff, heavy fabric on which an artist paints. *Before painting, Emma stretched the canvas tightly over a wooden frame.*

car·a·bi·ner (kăr´ ə **bē**´ nər) *n.* In mountain climbing, an oval ring that attaches to a piton. *The carabiners allow ropes to run freely through them.*

car·a·van (**kăr**´ ə văn´) *n.* A file of vehicles or pack animals traveling together. *Twenty camels led the caravan of spice traders across the desert.*

cause·way (**kôz**´ wā´) *n.* A raised roadway across water or marshland. *The farmers built causeways crossing the fields that flooded in the spring.*

cer·ti·fy (**sûr**´ tə fī´) *v., pl.* **certifies** Official recognition of a particular skill or function. *Medical technicians are certified to provide help in an emergency.*

cheap (chēp) *adj.* Costing very little. *Because she had very little money, Randi bought a cheap rubber ball instead of a real baseball.*

com·mon room (**kŏm**´ ən rōōm) *n.* A large room where people gather to eat or share other activities. *The storyteller drew a crowd in the common room after dinner.*

D

com·mute (kə **myōōt**´) *v.* To travel back and forth regularly. *My aunt and uncle commute from Gilroy to Sunnyvale every day.*

con·cep·tu·al (kən **sĕp**´ chōō əl) *adj.* Having to do with ideas. *A conceptual artist uses a variety of media to communicate an idea.*

con·di·tion·ing (kən **dĭsh**´ ə nĭng) *adj.* Contributing to the process of becoming physically fit. *The track coach stressed the importance of conditioning drills.*

con·quered (**kŏng**´ kərd) *adj.* Defeated in battle. *The conquered peoples gave up their treasures to their victorious enemy.*

con·sol·ing (kən **sōl**´ ĭng) *adj.* Comforting. *Marcia's father gave her a consoling hug after she wrecked her bike.*

con·ver·sa·tion (kŏn´ vər **sā**´ shən) *n.* A spoken sharing of thoughts between two or more people. *Cho knows so much about sports that our conversations are always interesting.*

crafts·man (**krăfts**´ mən) *n., pl.* **craftsmen** A skilled worker. *The work of colonial craftsmen is highly valued today.*

crus·ta·cean (krŭ **stā**´ shən) *n.* One of a large group of hard-shelled animals that have jointed parts and live mostly in the water. *The lobster is a well-known crustacean.*

day·dream (**dā**´ drēm´) *v.* To think in a dreamy way, often about things one wishes would come true. *Because Cho was daydreaming, he did not hear my question.*

de·ci·sion (dĭ **sĭzh**´ ən) *n.* A choice that involves judgment. *Alex's decision was to quit the team.*

dem·on·strate (**dĕm**´ ən strāt´) *v.* To show clearly. *Mike demonstrates that he has what it takes to become a great pitcher.*

de·pot (**dē**´ pō, **dĕp**´ ō) *n.* A railroad station. *Brent arrived at the depot just as the train from Baltimore was pulling in.*

der·e·lict (**dĕr**´ ə lĭkt´) *n.* A piece of property, usually a ship at sea, that has been deserted by its owner. *A derelict was blown in by the storm and smashed on the rocks.*

des·o·late (**dĕs**´ ə lĭt, **dĕz**´ ə lĭt) *adj.* Having few or no inhabitants; deserted. *The car ran out of gas on a desolate stretch of highway.*

des·per·ate (**dĕs**´ pər ĭt) *adj.* Feeling full of despair, hopeless. *The girl made a desperate plea for someone to save the cat.*

de·ter·mi·na·tion (dĭ tûr´ mə **nā**´ shən) *n.* The firm intention to accomplish a goal. *The combination of talent and determination enabled Alf to win a medal.*

depot

Glossary continued

dip·lo·mat (**dĭp´** lə măt´) *n.* One who is appointed to represent his or her government in its relations with other governments. *Rachel's mother was sent as a diplomat to Brazil.*

dis·ap·pear·ance (dĭs´ ə **pîr´** əns) *n.* The state of having vanished. *Lydia was saddened by the disappearance of her pet mouse.*

dis·count (**dĭs´** kount, dĭs **kount´**) *v.* To doubt the truth of something or regard it as a wild exaggeration. *Reference books discount myths about dragons and sea serpents.*

dis·cour·aged (dĭ **skûr´** ĭjd, dĭ **skûr´** ĭjd) *adj.* Disheartened; in a low mood because of a disappointment. *Having never won a baseball game, Nathan felt very discouraged.*

do·main (dō **mān´**) *n.* The territory ruled by a government. *Spain was included in the domain of ancient Rome.*

du·ra·ble (**dŏŏr´** ə bəl, **dyŏŏr´** ə bəl) *adj.* Sturdy and long-lasting. *Stone fences are more durable than wooden fences.*

dy·nas·ty (**dī´** nə stē) *n., pl.* **dynasties** A line of rulers from one family. *China's ancient Ming dynasty held power for about 300 years.*

erosion

E

em·pire (**ĕm´** pīr) *n.* A large area made up of many territories under one government. *The ancient Roman empire once included parts of Great Britain.*

en·cour·age (ĕn **kûr´** ĭj, ĕn **kûr´** ĭj) *v.* To give support or confidence. *Effective coaches encourage their players during a game.*

en·deav·or (ĕn **dĕv´** ər) *v.* To attempt. *She endeavored to keep her balance on the rocking deck of the ship.*

en·dur·ance (ĕn **dŏŏr´** əns, ĕn **dyŏŏr´** əns) *n.* The ability to keep going without giving in to stress or tiredness. *A marathon runner must have exceptional endurance.*

en·gi·neer (ĕn´ jə **nîr´**) *n.* A person specially trained to design and build machines and systems. *The engineers designed a complex landing system for the spacecraft.*

en·tan·gled (ĕn **tăng´** gəld) *adj.* Twisted together. *The kitten's paws became entangled in the yarn.*

en·tou·rage (ŏn´ tŏŏ **räzh´**) *n.* A group of followers. *The queen's entourage included both servants and people of high rank.*

e·ro·sion (ĭ **rō´** zhən) *n.* All the natural processes that wear away earth and rock. *The erosion of the hillside was caused by heavy rains and wind.*

F

ev·i·dence (**ĕv´** ĭ dəns) *n.* The data used to draw a conclusion. *Scientists studying dinosaurs look at the evidence found in prehistoric bones.*

ex·ca·va·tion (ĕk´ skə **vā´** shən) *n.* The process of finding something by digging for it. *A later excavation of the site turned up more fossils.*

ex·clude (ĭk **sklŏŏd´**) *v.* To keep someone or something out. *The boys angered the girls by excluding them from the basketball game.*

ex·hi·bi·tion (ĕk´ sə **bĭsh´** ən) *n.* A show of an artist's work. *A traveling exhibition of Winslow Homer's work has come to our museum.*

ex·press (ĭk **sprĕs´**) *v.* To put into words; to communicate. *Toddlers express their feelings through words, noises, and actions.*

ex·tinct (ĭk **stĭngkt´**) *adj.* No longer living on the earth; having died out. *The passenger pigeon became extinct at the beginning of the twentieth century.*

ex·trav·a·gance (ĭk **străv´** ə gəns) *n.* Careless, wasteful spending on luxuries. *Luke's extravagance put him deeply into debt.*

fa·tigue (fə **tēg´**) *n.* Extreme tiredness. *Her fatigue was so great she wanted to sleep for days.*

fig·u·rine (fĭg´ yə **rēn´**) *n.* A small molded or sculpted figure. *China figurines of children and dogs were lined up on the windowsill.*

flour·ish·ing (**flûr´** ĭsh ĭng, **flŭr´** ĭsh ĭng) *adj.* Growing energetically. *After the railroad was built, Greensville became a flourishing community.*

foot·hold (**fŏŏt´** hōld´) *n.* A place that gives firm support for a foot while climbing. *The crumbling ledge could not provide a safe foothold.*

fos·sil (**fŏs´** əl) *n.* The hardened skeleton or other remains of a creature of prehistoric times. *Dinosaur fossils have been found in many parts of the world.*

frus·tra·tion (frŭ **strā´** shən) *n.* The discouragement and irritation that comes from not being able to achieve one's goal. *She felt frustration at not being able to solve the math problem.*

func·tion (**fŭngk´** shən) *v.* To fill a particular purpose or role. *The knife functioned as a screwdriver to take the screws out of the clock.*

excavation
For ancient Latin speakers, *excavare* meant to hollow something out. Thus, an excavation is the hollowing out of a space by digging. The English word *cave* is from the same Latin verb.

flourishing
The Latin verb *florere*, meaning "to flower," is the origin of both *flourish* and *flower*.

fossil
Our word *fossil* came from the Latin adjective *fossilis*, meaning "dug up."

G

humble
Humble has its origins in the Latin word *humus*, meaning "ground."

ge·lat·i·nous (jə **lăt´** n əs) *adj.* Like gelatin; thick and slow to flow. *Tapioca pudding has a lumpy, gelatinous texture.*

ge·ol·o·gist (jē **ŏl´** ə jĭst) *n.* A scientist who studies the earth's crust and the rocks it is made of. *Rocks can tell geologists a lot about how the earth changed in a particular place.*

goods (gŏŏdz) *n.* Items for sale. *The small store sold fabric, boots, farm tools, and other useful goods.*

gov·ern·ment (**gŭv´** ərn mənt) *n.* The body or organization that manages a nation. *Our government sent representatives to Australia to discuss trade regulations.*

H

hatch·et (**hăch´** ĭt) *n.* A small, short-handled ax, to be used with only one hand. *A hatchet is useful for cutting firewood.*

hearth (härth) *n.* The floor of a fireplace, which usually extends into a room. *Julia sat by the wide brick hearth and warmed her hands.*

hov·er (**hŭv´** ər, **hŏv´** ər) *v.* To remain close by. *Helicopters hovered above the freeways so reporters could check the traffic conditions.*

hatchet

hum·ble (**hŭm´** bəl) *adj.* Not rich or important. *The humble workers could not afford luxury items.*

hy·per·re·al·ist·ic (hī´ pər rē´ ə **lĭs´** tĭk) *adj.* Extremely real-looking. *Many hyperrealistic paintings look exactly like photographs.*

hy·poth·e·sis (hī **pŏth´** ĭ sĭs´) *n., pl.* **hypotheses** (hī **pŏth´** ĭ sēz´) A scientific suggestion based on what is known so far. *Ideas remain hypotheses until evidence proves that they are true.*

I

ice ax (īs ăks) *n.* An ax used by mountain climbers to cut into the ice. *Jennifer hacked at the cliff with her ice ax.*

im·pro·vise (**ĭm´** prə vīz´) *v.* To make something from available materials. *When it began to rain, the hikers improvised a tent out of plastic garbage bags.*

in·quir·y (ĭn **kwîr´** ē, ĭn´ kwə rē) *n., pl.* **inquiries** A request for information. *The park ranger received many inquiries about campsites.*

in·spi·ra·tion (ĭn´ spə **rā´** shən) *n.* A positive example that encourages others to attempt to reach their goals. *Her success in college is an inspiration to her younger sisters.*

L

in·ter·fer·ing (ĭn´ tər **fîr´** ĭng) *adj.* Intruding in the business of other people; meddling. *Kara did not ask why her brother was crying, because she didn't want to seem to be interfering.*

in·ter·pret (ĭn **tûr´** prĭt) *v.* To determine or explain the meaning of something. *She interpreted the lab data to draw conclusions about the experiment.*

in·tri·cate (**ĭn´** trĭ kĭt) *adj.* Complicated; made up of many details. *The bracelet has an intricate design.*

J

jour·nal (**jûr´** nəl) *n.* A personal record of events; a diary. *Angela wrote about her vacation in her journal.*

K

kay·ak (**kī´** ăk´) *n.* A lightweight canoe, propelled by a double-bladed paddle, with a small opening for one or two people. *The girls paddled the kayak across the bay.*

kin·dling (**kĭnd´** lĭng) *n.* Small pieces of wood or other material used for starting fires. *A big log won't catch fire unless kindling is burning below it.*

lab·o·ra·to·ry (**lăb´** rə tôr´ ē, **lăb´** rə tôr´ ē) *n., pl.* **laboratories** A room or building equipped for scientific research or experiments. *She works in a laboratory where blood cells are analyzed.*

la·bor·er (**lā´** bər ər) *n.* A worker who does tasks that do not require special skills. *The managers of the mines hired many laborers.*

ledg·er (**lĕj´** ər) *n.* A book in which financial records are kept. *The ledgers show how much the business has paid its employees.*

M

main·land (**mān´** lănd´, **mān´** lənd) *n.* The large land mass of a country or continent that does not include its islands. *Hawaiians refer to the rest of the United States as the mainland.*

make·shift (**māk´** shĭft´) *adj.* Used as a substitute for something. *The pioneer mother used a bureau drawer as a makeshift crib for the new baby.*

man·age (**măn´** ĭj) *v.* To succeed in doing something with difficulty. *Rolf managed to finish the race even though he turned his ankle near the end.*

kayak

ma·neu·ver (mə nōō´ vėr, mə nyōō´ vər) n. A controlled change in the movement or direction of a vehicle. *Beginning drivers practice maneuvers for getting into tight parking spaces.*

meticulous
Perhaps Latin speakers of long ago lived in fear of making mistakes, for this adjective comes from the Latin word *meticulosus*, meaning "fearful."

metropolis
The ancient Greeks combined their words for *mother* and *city* to form *metropolis*, a word they used to describe the first settlement in a colony.

navigation, navigator
The Latin word *navis*, meaning "ship," and the word *agere*, meaning "to drive," were combined to form the Latin verb *navigare*, "to navigate."

mas·sive (măs´ ĭv) adj. Large and solid. *Redwoods are massive trees.*

me·nag·er·ie (mə năj´ ə rē, mə năzh´ ə rē) n. A collection of wild animals. *The veterinarian attended to a menagerie of wounded animals at the wildlife shelter.*

me·thod·i·cal·ly (mə thŏd´ ĭ ka lē, mə thŏd´ ĭk lē) adv. In a careful, orderly way. *She methodically searched through her books for the facts she needed.*

me·tic·u·lous (mĭ tĭk´ yə ləs) adj. Extremely careful and exact. *His meticulous lettering made the poster easy to read.*

me·trop·o·lis (mĭ trŏp´ ə lĭs) n. A major city; a center of culture. *Being a transportation center has made Chicago a great metropolis.*

mon·i·tor (mŏn´ ĭ tər) v. To supervise; to keep watch over. *The fire chief monitored the rescue operation.*

N

nav·i·ga·tion (năv´ ĭ gā´ shən) n. The practice of planning and controlling the course of a craft. *The captain's skill at navigation brought the ship safely through the storm.*

nav·i·ga·tor (năv´ ĭ gā´ tər) n. Someone who plans, records, and controls the course of a ship or plane. *The navigator plotted a course across the Pacific Ocean.*

no·mad·ic (nō măd´ ĭk) adj. Moving from place to place. *Nomadic shepherds often move their sheep to new grazing lands.*

no·tice (nō´ tĭs) v. To become aware of. *People will notice the colorful balloons tied to the stair railing.*

O

o·a·sis (ō ā´ sĭs) n., pl. **oases** (ō ā´ sēz) A green spot in a desert, where water can be found. *The travelers rested at the oasis and watered their camels at its spring.*

ob·sta·cle (ŏb´ stə kəl) n. Something that makes it difficult to continue. *His sister's loud music and his lack of privacy were obstacles to serious studying.*

o·cean·og·ra·pher (ō´ shə nŏg´ rə fər) n. A scientist who specializes in the study of the sea. *Both oceanographers are interested in undersea volcanoes.*

ă rat / ā pay / â care / ä father / ĕ pet / ē be / ĭ pit / ī pie / î fierce / ŏ pot / ō go / ô paw, for / oi oil / ōō book

650

---

op·ti·cal·ly (ŏp´ tĭk ə lē, ŏp´ tĭk lē) adv. Having to do with vision. *As I stared at the painting, the colors blended optically into a vivid swirl.*

o·ver·come (ō´ vər kŭm´) v. To conquer. *She has overcome her fear of heights.*

P

pains·tak·ing (pānz´ tā´ kĭng) adj. Requiring great and careful effort. *Repairing watches is painstaking work.*

pa·le·on·tol·o·gist (pā´ lē ŏn tŏl´ ə jĭst) n. A scientist who studies prehistoric life. *A paleontologist compares the bones of dinosaurs to those of modern animals.*

pal·ette (păl´ ĭt) n. A board on which an artist mixes colors. *Austin squeezed dabs of white and blue paint onto his palette.*

per·mis·sion (pər mĭsh´ ən) n. Necessary approval to do something. *The travelers need official permission to cross the border.*

per·mit·ted (pər mĭt´ əd) adj. Allowed. *Swimming is permitted from sunrise to sunset at Howe's Beach. —n. A person who is allowed to do something. Only permitteds can go past the gate.*

phase (fāz) n. One of the changes in appearance that the moon or a planet goes through each month. *The moon looks like a half circle in one of its phases.*

palette

palette
In Old French, *pale* was the word for a shovel or spade. A palette, then, was a small shovel.

phys·ics (fĭz´ ĭks) n. The science of matter and energy and of how they relate to one another. *You can use simple physics to predict how soon a falling object will hit the ground.*

pi·ton (pē´ tŏn´) n. A metal spike, used in mountain climbing, with an eye or ring at one end. *The mountain climber's standard gear includes pitons.*

pix·el (pĭk´ səl, pĭk sĕl´) n. One of the tiny elements that make up an image on a TV or computer screen. *In computer drawing programs, widths of lines are measured in pixels.*

por·trait (pôr´ trĭt, pôr´ trāt) n. A drawing, painting, or photograph of a person. *A portrait of the first mayor of Centervale hangs in the lobby of the town hall.*

port (pôrt) n. The left side of a ship as one faces forward. *A small rowboat pulled up on the port side of the ship.*

pre·vi·ous (prē´ vē əs) adj. Occurring before something else in time or order. *The professor had explained the rule in a previous lecture.*

pri·mar·y (prī´ mĕr´ ē, prī´ mə rē) adj. Main; basic. *The club's primary purpose is to welcome new students.*

pixel
The word *pixel* was created around 1969 by combining the word *pix* (short for *pictures*) and the first syllable of the word *elements*.

---

pro·vi·sions (prə vizh´ ənz) n. Necessary supplies, especially food. *The hikers had enough provisions for only one more day of camping.*

Q

quill

qual·i·fi·ca·tion (kwŏl´ ə fĭ kā´ shən) n. A skill or other trait that suits a person for a particular job or activity. *What qualifications are needed to join the Peace Corps?*

quill (kwĭl) n. One of a collection of sharp, hollow spines on the back of a porcupine. *It isn't true that porcupines can shoot their quills at their attackers.*

rover
The Middle English verb *roven* meant "to shoot arrows at a mark." From this origin came the English verb *rove*, meaning "to roam or wander."

R

rat·line (răt´ lĭn) n. One of the small ropes, fastened horizontally to ropes supporting a ship's mast, which together form a ladder. *A large seabird perched on one of the ratlines of the ship.*

ref·u·gee (rĕf´ yōō jē´) n. A person who flees his or her home in order to escape harm. *Many refugees escaped from Cuba in small boats.*

rel·e·gate (rĕl´ ĭ gāt´) v. To put in a less important place. *Her least favorite clothes were relegated to the back of the closet.*

re·lieve (rĭ lēv´) v. To aid, to help. *A cool washcloth might relieve the pain of your headache.*

re·set·tling (rē´ sĕt´ əl ĭng) n. The process of moving to a new place. *I have been watching the raccoon family's recent resettling in the tree next door.*

rig·ging (rĭg´ ĭng) n. The system of ropes, chains, and other gear used to control a ship's sails. *A good sailor had to be able to climb the rigging like a rat.*

rock·et·ry (rŏk´ ĭ trē) n. The science of designing, building, and flying rockets. *His knowledge of rocketry led to a job in the NASA space program.*

rov·er (rō´ vər) n. A vehicle designed to explore the surface of a planet. *The rover rolled down the ramp of the spacecraft and onto the Martian soil.*

run·way (rŭn´ wā´) n. A strip of level ground where airplanes take off and land. *The plane sped down the runway and rose into the air.*

S

sea·soned (sē´ zənd) adj. Experienced. *After four months at sea, Mario felt like a seasoned sailor.*

ă rat / ā pay / â care / ä father / ĕ pet / ē be / ĭ pit / ī pie / î fierce / ŏ pot / ō go / ô paw, for / oi oil / ōō book

652

---

sen·sor (sĕn´ sər, sĕn´ sôr) n. A sensitive device that responds to changes in the environment. *The toy's electronic sensors kept it from bumping into the wall.*

ses·sion (sĕsh´ ən) n. A gathering held for a special purpose. *The cheerleaders hold their practice sessions after school.*

shel·ter (shĕl´ tər) n. A place that provides protection from the weather. *They found a cave to use for a shelter.*

sim·u·late (sĭm´ yə lāt´) v. To pretend in an imitation of something. *The computer program lets users simulate driving on a real highway.*

site (sīt) n. The place where things were, are, or will be located. *Diggers have turned up old pottery at several sites.*

slith·er·ing (slĭth´ ər ĭng) n. A sliding, slipping movement. *The rustling noise was made by the slithering of a snake. —adj. Slipping and sliding. A slithering movement in the grass caught his attention.*

sod (sŏd) n. A chunk of grassy soil held together by matted roots. *Pioneers sometimes built their houses out of sod where trees were scarce.*

spar·kling (spär´ klĭng) adj. Giving off flashes of light. *Sparkling fireflies darted across the dark lawn.*

spec·i·men (spĕs´ ə mən) n. A sample taken for scientific study. *The specimens of pond water were full of tiny creatures.*

sprint (sprĭnt) n. A short race run at top speed. *Runners don't have to pace themselves when they run sprints.*

squad (skwŏd) n. A small group of people organized for an activity. *Antonio hopes to become a member of the football squad.*

steppe (stĕp) n. A vast dry, grassy plain. *Very little rain falls on a steppe.*

ster·e·o·scop·ic (stĕr´ ē ə skŏp´ ĭk, stĭr´ ē ə skŏp´ ĭk) adj. Seeing objects in three dimensions. *Human beings have stereoscopic vision.*

stoop (stōōp) n. A small porch, staircase, or platform leading to the entrance of a house or building. *Our family sits on the stoop of our building on warm nights.*

sub·mers·i·ble (səb mûr´ sə bəl) n. A craft that operates underwater. *The submersible carried a camera into the depths of the ocean.*

sub·tle (sŭt´ l) adj. Not obvious; hard to detect. *The waiter's gesture was so subtle that none of the diners noticed it.*

su·pe·ri·or (sōō pîr´ ē ər) n. One who has higher rank and more authority. *The worker took orders from his superiors.*

slithering
A shift in pronunciation over the centuries turned the Old English word *slidrian* ("to slide" or "to slip") into *slither.*

sparkling
In the thirteenth century, to say that something was sparkling was to say that it gave off sparks.

specimen
The word *specimen* comes from the Latin word *specere*, which means "to look at."

squad
A Latin slang word for "square" may have inspired the medieval Italians to use the word *squadra* to refer to a group of soldiers marching in square formation.

Glossary   **G3**

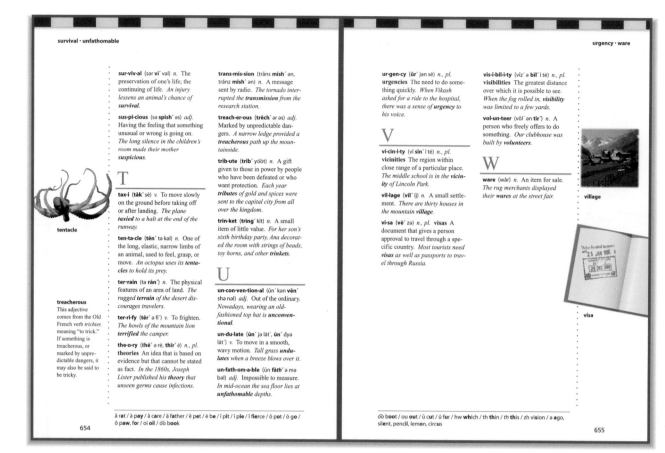

sur·viv·al (sər **vī**´ vəl) *n.* The preservation of one's life; the continuing of life. *An injury lessens an animal's chance of **survival**.*

sus·pi·cious (sə **spish**´ əs) *adj.* Having the feeling that something unusual or wrong is going on. *The long silence in the children's room made their mother **suspicious**.*

T

tax·i (**tăk**´ sē) *v.* To move slowly on the ground before taking off or after landing. *The plane **taxied** to a halt at the end of the runway.*

tentacle

ten·ta·cle (**tĕn**´ tə kəl) *n.* One of the long, elastic, narrow limbs of an animal, used to feel, grasp, or move. *An octopus uses its **tentacles** to hold its prey.*

ter·rain (tə **rān**´) *n.* The physical features of an area of land. *The rugged **terrain** of the desert discourages travelers.*

ter·ri·fy (**tĕr**´ ə fī´) *v.* To frighten. *The howls of the mountain lion **terrified** the camper.*

the·o·ry (**thē**´ ə rē, **thîr**´ ē) *n., pl.* **theories** An idea that is based on evidence but that cannot be stated as fact. *In the 1860s, Joseph Lister published his **theory** that unseen germs cause infections.*

trans·mis·sion (trăns **mish**´ ən, trănz **mish**´ ən) *n.* A message sent by radio. *The tornado interrupted the **transmission** from the research station.*

treach·er·ous (**trĕch**´ ər əs) *adj.* Marked by unpredictable dangers. *A narrow ledge provided a **treacherous** path up the mountainside.*

treacherous
This adjective comes from the Old French verb *trichier,* meaning "to trick." If something is treacherous, or marked by unpredictable dangers, it may also be said to be tricky.

trib·ute (**trĭb**´ yōōt) *n.* A gift given to those in power by people who have been defeated or who want protection. *Each year **tributes** of gold and spices were sent to the capital city from all over the kingdom.*

trin·ket (**tring**´ kĭt) *n.* A small item of little value. *For her son's sixth birthday party, Ana decorated the room with strings of beads, toy horns, and other **trinkets**.*

U

un·con·ven·tion·al (ŭn´ kən **vĕn**´ shə nəl) *adj.* Out of the ordinary. *Nowadays, wearing an old-fashioned top hat is **unconventional**.*

un·du·late (**ŭn**´ jə lāt´, **ŭn**´ dyə lāt´) *v.* To move in a smooth, wavy motion. *Tall grass **undulates** when a breeze blows over it.*

un·fath·om·a·ble (ŭn **făth**´ ə mə bəl) *adj.* Impossible to measure. *In mid-ocean the sea floor lies at **unfathomable** depths.*

ă rat / ā pay / â care / ä father / ĕ pet / ē be / ĭ pit / ī pie / î fierce / ŏ pot / ō go / ô paw, for / oi oil / ŏŏ book

ur·gen·cy (**ûr**´ jən sē) *n., pl.* **urgencies** The need to do something quickly. *When Vikash asked for a ride to the hospital, there was a sense of **urgency** to his voice.*

V

vi·cin·i·ty (vĭ **sĭn**´ ĭ tē) *n., pl.* **vicinities** The region within close range of a particular place. *The middle school is in the **vicinity** of Lincoln Park.*

vil·lage (**vĭl**´ ĭj) *n.* A small settlement. *There are thirty houses in the mountain **village**.*

vi·sa (**vē**´ zə) *n., pl.* **visas** A document that gives a person approval to travel through a specific country. *Most tourists need **visas** as well as passports to travel through Russia.*

vis·i·bil·i·ty (vĭz´ ə **bĭl**´ ĭ tē) *n., pl.* **visibilities** The greatest distance over which it is possible to see. *When the fog rolled in, **visibility** was limited to a few yards.*

vol·un·teer (vŏl´ ən **tîr**´) *n.* A person who freely offers to do something. *Our clubhouse was built by **volunteers**.*

W

ware (wâr) *n.* An item for sale. *The rug merchants displayed their **wares** at the street fair.*

village

visa

ōō boot / ou out / ŭ cut / û fur / hw which / th thin / *th* this / zh vision / ə ago, silent, pencil, lemon, circus

Acknowledgments

Main Literature Selections

Selection from *The Adventures of Sojourner: The Mission to Mars That Thrilled the World,* by Susi Trautmann Wunsch. Copyright © 1998 by Susi Trautmann Wunsch. Reprinted by permission of the publisher, Mikaya Press Inc.

Selection from *Amelia Earhart: First Lady of Flight,* by Jan Parr. Copyright © 1997 by Jan Parr. Reprinted by permission of Franklin Watts, a division of Grolier Publishing.

Selection from *Beneath Blue Waters: Meetings with Remarkable Deep-Sea Creatures,* by Deborah Kovacs and Kate Madin, principal photographs by Larry Madin. Copyright © 1996 by Deborah Kovacs and Kate Madin. Reprinted by permission of Viking Children's Books, a division of Penguin Putnam Inc.

Selections from *The Buried City of Pompeii,* a Hyperion/Madison Press Book by Shelley Tanaka, diagrams by Jack McMaster. Copyright © 1997 by Madison Press Limited. Reprinted by permission of Madison Press Limited.

"The Challenge" from *Local News,* by Gary Soto. Copyright © 1993 by Gary Soto. Reprinted with permission of Harcourt Inc.

Selection from *Chuck Close Up Close,* by Jan Greenberg and Sandra Jordan. Copyright © 1998 by Jan Greenberg and Sandra Jordan. Reprinted by permission of Dorling Kindersley Publishing, Inc.

Selection from *Climb or Die,* by Edward Myers. Copyright © 1996 by Edward Myers. Reprinted by permission of Hyperion Books for Children.

Selection from *Dinosaur Ghosts: The Mystery of Coelophysis,* by J. Lynett Gillette, illustrated by Doug Henderson. Text copyright © 1997 by J. Lynett Gillette. Illustrations copyright © 1997 by Douglas Henderson. Reprinted by permission of Dial Books for Young Readers, a division of Penguin Putnam Inc.

Excerpt from *Eugenie Clark: Adventures of a Shark Scientist,* by Ellen R. Butts and Joyce R. Schwartz. Copyright © 2000 by Ellen R. Butts and Joyce R. Schwartz. Reprinted by permission of Linnet Book, an imprint of The Shoe String Press, Inc., North Haven, CT.

"Franklin R. Chang-Diaz" from *Standing Tall: The Stories of Ten Hispanic Americans,* by Argentina Palacios. Copyright © 1994 by Argentina Palacios. Reproduced by permission of Scholastic Inc.

The Girl Who Married the Moon: Tales from Native North America. Text copyright © 1994 by Joseph Bruchac and Gayle Ross. Published by BridgeWater Books, an imprint and trademark of Troll Communications, LLC. Reprinted by permission of Troll Communications LLC.

Selection from *The Great Pyramid,* by Elizabeth Mann, illustrations by Laura Lo Turco. Copyright © Mikaya Press. Reprinted by permission of Mikaya Press.

Selection from *The Great Wall,* by Elizabeth Mann, with illustrations by Alan Witschonke. Copyright © 1997 Mikaya Press. Original illustrations copyright © by Alan Witschonke. Reprinted by permission of Mikaya Press Inc.

Selection from *Hatchet,* by Gary Paulsen. Jacket painting by Neil Waldman. Copyright © 1987 by Gary Paulsen. Jacket copyright © 1987 by Bradbury Press. Reprinted by permission of Simon & Schuster Books for Young Readers, an imprint of Simon & Schuster Children's Publishing Division.

Selection from *The Ink-Keeper's Apprentice,* by Allen Say. Text copyright © 1979 by Allen Say. Reprinted by permission of Houghton Mifflin Company. All rights reserved.

"Jerry Pinkney: My Story," published in the book *Talking with Artists* © 1992, compiled and edited by Pat Cummings, published by Bradbury Press, a division of Macmillan Publishing Company. Copyright © 1992 by Jerry Pinkney. Reprinted by permission of the author and the Sheldon Fogelman Agency, Inc. The watercolor painting "Boy with a Wagon" by Jerry Pinkney. Copyright © 1946 by Jerry Pinkney. Reprinted by permission of the author and the Sheldon Fogelman Agency, Inc. The illustration from *Black Cowboy, Wild Horses: A True Story,* by Julius Lester, illustrated by Jerry Pinkney. Illustration copyright © 1998 by Jerry Pinkney. Reprinted by permission of Dial Books for Young Readers, a division of Penguin Young Readers Group, a member of Penguin Group (USA) Inc. The illustration from *Aesop's Fables,* illustrated by Jerry Pinkney, published by Sea Star Books, a division of North-South Books Inc. Copyright © 2000 by Jerry Pinkney. Reprinted by permission of the publisher. Cover and one-page spread from *The Adventures of Spider,* by Joyce Cooper Arkhurst, illustrated by Jerry Pinkney. Text copyright © 1964 by Joyce Cooper Arkhurst. Illustration copyright © 1964 by Barker/Black Studio, Inc. Reprinted by permission of Little, Brown and Company, (Inc.). All rights reserved.

Selection from *A Kind of Grace,* by Jackie Joyner-Kersee. Copyright © 1997 by Jackie Joyner-Kersee. Reprinted by permission of Warner Books Inc.

Selection from *Last Summer with Maizon,* by Jacqueline Woodson. Copyright © 1990 by Jacqueline Woodson. Reprinted by permission of Random House Children's Books, a division of Random House Inc.

"The Lord of the Nile" from *Egyptian Myths,* by Jacqueline Morley, published by Peter Bedrick Books. Copyright © 1999 by Jacqueline Morley. Reprinted by permission of The McGraw-Hill Companies.

Selection from *Lost Temple of the Aztecs,* by Shelley Tanaka, illustrated by Greg Ruhl. Copyright © 1998 by The Madison Press Ltd. Illustrations © by Greg Ruhl. Reprinted by permission of Hyperion Books for Children.

"The Night of the Pomegranate" from *Some of the Kinder Planets,* by Tim Wynne-Jones, published by Orchard Books, an imprint of Scholastic Inc. Copyright © 1993 by Tim Wynne-Jones. Reprinted by permission of Scholastic Inc., and Groundwood Books/Douglas & McIntyre Ltd., Toronto, Canada.

"Out There" from *Rogue Wave and Other Red-Blooded Sea Stories,* by Theodore Taylor. Copyright © 1996 by Theodore Taylor. Reprinted by permission of Harcourt Inc.

Passage to Freedom, by Ken Mochizuki, illustrated by Dom Lee. Text copyright © 1997 by Ken Mochizuki. Illustrations copyright © 1997 by Dom Lee. Reprinted by permission of Lee & Low Books, Inc.

Selection from *Rosa Parks: My Story,* by Rosa Parks with Jim Haskins. Copyright © 1992 by Rosa Parks. Published by arrangement with Dial Books for Young Readers, a member of Penguin Putnam Inc.

Selection from *The Royal Kingdoms of Ghana, Mali, and Songhay,* by Patricia and Fredrick McKissack. Copyright © 1994 by Patricia and Fredrick McKissack. Reprinted by permission of Henry Holt and Company, LLC.

Selection from *The True Confessions of Charlotte Doyle,* by Avi. Copyright © 1990 by Avi. Reprinted by permission of Orchard Books, New York.

Selection from *Under the Royal Palms,* by Alma Flor Ada. Copyright © 1998 by Alma Flor Ada. Reprinted with the permission of Atheneum Books for Young Readers, an imprint of Simon & Schuster Children's Publishing Division. Cover photograph copyright © 1998 by Alma Flor Ada. Photograph used with permission of the Author and Bookstop Literary Agency. All rights reserved.

Selection from *The View from Saturday,* by E.L. Konigsburg. Text copyright © 1996 E.L. Konigsburg. Jacket illustration copyright © 1996 E.L. Konigsburg. Reprinted by permission of Atheneum Books for Young Readers, an imprint of Simon & Schuster Children's Publishing Division.

Selection from *Where the Red Fern Grows,* by Wilson Rawls. Copyright © 1961 by Sophie S. Rawls, Trustee, or successor Trustee(s) of the Rawls Trust, dated July 31, 1991. Copyright © 1961 by the Curtis Publishing Company. Reprinted by permission of Dell Publishing, a division of Random House, Inc.

"Wolfgang Amadeus Mozart" from *Lives of the Musicians: Good Times, Bad Times (and What the Neighbors Thought),* by Kathleen Krull. Copyright © 1993 by Kathleen Krull. Reprinted by permission of Harcourt, Inc.

Selection from *Yolonda's Genius,* by Carol Fenner. Copyright © 1996 by Carol Fenner. Reprinted with the permission of Margaret K. McElderry Books, an imprint of Simon & Schuster Children's Publishing Division.

Focus Selections

"Arachne the Spinner" from *Greek Myths,* by Geraldine McCaughrean, illustrated by Emma Chichester Clark. Copyright © 1992 by Geraldine McCaughrean. Illustrations copyright © 1992 by Emma Chichester Clark. Reprinted by permission of Margaret K. McElderry Books, an imprint of Simon & Schuster Children's Publishing Division.

"A Better Mousetrap," by Colleen Neuman. Copyright © 1993 by Colleen Neuman. Reprinted by permission of Baker's Plays, Quincy, MA.

"Child Rest," by Phil George from *Whispering Wind,* edited by Terry Allen. Copyright © 1972 by The Institute of American Indian Arts. Reprinted by permission of Doubleday, a division of Random House, Inc.

Excerpt from *"A Commencement Speech"* by Katherine Ortega. Copyright © by Katherine Ortega. Reprinted by permission of the author.

Selection from *The Diary of Anne Frank,* by Frances Goodrich and Albert Hackett. Copyright © 1954, 1956 as an unpublished work. Copyright © 1956 by Albert Hackett, Frances Goodrich Hackett, and Otto Frank. Reprinted by permission of Random House Inc.

"Family Photo" from *Relatively Speaking,* by Ralph Fletcher. Text copyright © 1999 by Ralph Fletcher. Reprinted by permission of Orchard Books, New York.

"Family Style" from *Good Luck Gold and Other Poems,* by Janet S. Wong. Copyright © 1994 by Janet S. Wong. Reprinted with permission of Margaret K. McElderry Books, an imprint of Simon & Schuster Children's Publishing Division.

Focus on Speeches opening page: Illustration is from *The Gettysburg Address,* illustrated by Michael McCurdy. Illustration copyright © 1995 by Michael McCurdy. Reprinted by permission of Houghton Mifflin Company. All rights reserved.

"Good Hotdogs" from *My Wicked Wicked Ways.* Copyright © 1987 by Sandra Cisneros. Published by Third Woman Press and in hardcover by Alfred A. Knopf. Reprinted by permission of Third Woman Press and Susan Bergholz Literary Services, New York. All rights reserved.

"Guitar Solo" from *The Bronze Cauldron,* by Geraldine McCaughrean, illustrated by Bee Willey. Text copyright © 1997 by Geraldine McCaughrean. Illustrations copyright © 1997 by Bee Willey. Reprinted with the permission of Margaret K. McElderry Books, an imprint of Simon & Schuster Children's Publishing Division.

"How Music Was Fetched Out of Heaven" from *The Golden Hoard,* by Geraldine McCaughrean, illustrated by Bee Willey. Text copyright © 1995 by Geraldine McCaughrean. Illustrations copyright © 1995 by Bee Willey. Reprinted with the permission of Margaret K. McElderry Books, an imprint of Simon & Schuster Children's Publishing Division.

Excerpt from the speech *"I Have a Dream"* by Martin Luther King, Jr. Copyright © 1963 by Martin Luther King, Jr. Copyright © renewed 1991 by Coretta Scott King. Reprinted by permission of the Heirs to the Estate of Martin Luther King, Jr. c/o Writers House Inc., as agent for the proprietor.

"Losing Livie" from *Out of the Dust,* by Karen Hesse. Published by Scholastic Press, a division of Scholastic Inc. Copyright © 1997 by Karen Hesse. Jacket illustration copyright © 1997 by Scholastic Inc. Reprinted by permission of Scholastic Inc. Jacket photograph courtesy of the Library of Congress Prints and Photographs division, Farm Security Administration Collection.

"My Own Man" from *My Man Blue,* by Nikki Grimes. Copyright © 1999 by Nikki Grimes. Reprinted by permission of Dial Books for Young Readers, a division of Penguin Putnam, Inc.

Excerpt from the speech *"On Accepting the Newbery Medal"* by Jerry Spinelli. Copyright © 1991 by Jerry Spinelli. Reprinted by permission of the American Library Association.

"Oranges" from *New and Selected Poems,* by Gary Soto. Copyright © 1995 by Gary Soto. Published by Chronicle Books, San Francisco. Reprinted by permission of the publisher.

"The Pasture" from *The Poetry of Robert Frost,* edited by Edward Connery Lathem. Copyright 1944 by Robert Frost. Copyright 1916, © 1969 by Henry Holt and Company, LLC. Reprinted by permission of Henry Holt and Company, LLC.

Selection from *"The People, Yes"* from *Rainbows Are Made: Poems by Carl Sandburg.* Copyright © 1982 by The Carl Sandburg Family Trust. Reprinted by permission of Harcourt Inc.

"Poem" from *Collected Poems,* by Langston Hughes. Copyright © 1994 by the Estate of Langston Hughes. Reprinted by permission of Alfred Knopf Inc.

"Poetry," by Eleanor Farjeon from *Poems for Children.* Copyright 1938 by Eleanor Farjeon. Copyright © renewed 1966 by Gervase Farjeon. Reprinted by permission of Harold Ober Associates Incorporated.

"A Story of Courage, Bravery, Strength and Heroism. . ." by Shao Lee. Copyright © 1995 by Shao Lee. Reprinted by permission of The Asian Pages.

"Sundays" from *Brickyard Summer,* by Paul B. Janeczko (Orchard Books). Copyright © 1989 by Paul B. Janeczko. Reprinted by permission of the author.

Links and Theme Openers

"Alone Against the Sea" from the April 1997 issue of *National Geographic World.* Copyright © 1997 by the National Geographic Society. Reprinted by permission of the publisher.

Selection from *Ancient Romans at a Glance,* by Dr. Sarah McNeill. Copyright © 1998 by Macdonald Young Books. Reprinted by permission of NTC/Contemporary Publishing Group, Inc.

"Barnstorming Bessie Coleman," by Sylvia Whitman from *Cobblestone* February 1997 issue: "Tuskegee Airmen." Copyright © 1997 by Cobblestone Publishing Company. All rights reserved. Reprinted by permission of the publisher.

"Battling Everest" from the January 1999 issue of *National Geographic World.* Copyright © 1999 by the National Geographic Society. Reprinted by permission of the publisher.

"Brazilian Moon Tale," by Jane Yolen was first published in *What Rhymes with Moon?* published by Philomel Books. Copyright © 1993 by Jane Yolen. Reprinted by permission of Curtis Brown, Ltd.

"Build and Launch a Paper Rocket" was adapted from NASA's *Rockets: Physical Science Teacher's Guide with Activities.*

"Courage in the News" from an article entitled "Boy Wonder" published in the October 4, 1995 issue of the *St. Louis Post-Dispatch.* Copyright © by the *St. Louis Post-Dispatch.* Reprinted by permission of the publisher.

"Daily Life in Ancient Greece" from *Ancient Greece,* by Robert Nicholson. Text copyright © 1994 by Two-Can Publishing Ltd. Reprinted by permission of Chelsea House Publishers.

"Different Strokes," by Samantha Bonar from *American Girl,* May/June 1999 issue. Copyright © 1999 by Pleasant Company. Artwork © Alexandra Nechita. Reprinted by permission of Alexandra Nechita and Pleasant Company.

"Doctor Dinosaur," by Carolyn Duckworth. Copyright © 1997 by Carolyn Duckworth. Reprinted by permission of the author.

"Half Moon," by Federico Garcia Lorca © Herederos de Federico Garcia Lorca from *Obras Completas* (Galaxia Gutenberg, 1996 edition). Translation by W.S. Merwin copyright © Herederos de Federico Garcia Lorca and W.S. Merwin. All rights reserved. For information regarding rights and permissions, contact lorca@artslaw.co.uk or William Peter Kosmas, Esq., 8 Franklin Square, London W14 9UU, England. Translation reprinted by permission of New Directions Publishing Corp.

"Help Wanted: Groups Seek Kid Volunteers to Change the World. No Experience Necessary" by Anna Prokos, from the December 1997 issue of 3-2-1 *Contact* magazine. Copyright © 1997 by Children's Television Workshop. Reprinted by permission of Children's Television Workshop.

"Home-Grown Butterflies" from the May 1998 issue of *Ranger Rick* magazine with the permission of the National Wildlife Federation. Copyright © 1998 by the National Wildlife Federation.

"How to Be a Good Sport" from *Current Health 1®,* Vol. 22, No. 4, December 1998. Copyright © 1998 by Weekly Reader Corporation. All rights reserved. Reprinted by permission of the publisher.

"Little Brother, Big Idea," by Ethan Herberman, from *Current Science* magazine, December 1998. Copyright © 1998 by the Weekly Reader Corporation. Reprinted by permission of the publisher.

"Moon" from *Sky Songs,* by Myra Cohn Livingston (Holiday House, New York). Copyright © 1984 by Myra Cohn Livingston. Reprinted by permission of Marian Reiner.

"A Poem for Langston Hughes" from *The Selected Poems of Nikki Giovanni,* by Nikki Giovanni. Copyright © 1996 by Nikki Giovanni. Reprinted by permission of HarperCollins Publishers.

"Poetic Power," by Ariel Eason, Julia Peters-Axtell and Rebecca Owen. Copyright © 1996 by New Moon Publishing. Reprinted with permission from *New Moon®: The Magazine for Girls and Their Dreams,* New Moon Publishing, Duluth, MN.

"Puppy Love" adapted from *American Girl,* Vol. 3, No. 2. Copyright © 1995 by Pleasant Company. Reprinted by permission of Pleasant Company.

"Raising Royal Treasures" from the November 13, 1998 issue of *Time for Kids.* Copyright © 1998 by Time Inc. Reprinted by permission of the publisher.

"A Real Jazzy Kid!" from the March 1994 issue of *U.S. Kids.* Copyright © 1994 by Children's Better Health Institute, Benjamin Franklin Literary & Medical Society, Inc., Indianapolis, IN. Reprinted by permission.

"Sharks Under Ice" from the February 1999 issue of *Geographic World.* Copyright © 1999 by the National Geographic Society. Reprinted by permission of the publisher.

"Summer Full Moon," by James Kirkup. Copyright © 1992 by James Kirkup. Reprinted by permission of the author.

"Sylvia Earle" from *"Exploring the Deep"* in the Winter 1999 issue of *Time for Kids.* Copyright © 1999 by Time Inc. Reprinted by permission of the publisher.

"Winter Moon" from *Collected Poems,* by Langston Hughes. Copyright © 1994 by the Estate of Langston Hughes. Reprinted by permission of Alfred A. Knopf, a division of Random House, Inc.

"Youth" from *Collected Poems,* by Langston Hughes. Copyright © 1994 by the Estate of Langston Hughes. Reprinted by permission of Alfred A. Knopf, a division of Random House Inc.

Special thanks to the following teachers whose students' compositions appear as Student Writing Models:

Writing Models

Cindy Chestwood, Florida; Diana Davis, North Carolina; Kathy Driscoll, Massachusetts; Linda Evers, Florida; Heidi Harrison, Michigan; Eileen Hoffman, Massachusetts; Julia Kraftsow, Florida; Bonnie Lewison, Florida; Kanetha McCord, Michigan

Credits

ndex

dictionary, *383H*
encyclopedia, *383H, 407AA*
magazines, *382*
thesaurus, *407M*
study strategies
  adjusting rate of reading, **380**
  notes, taking. *See* Notes, taking.
  outlining, **387D**
  skimming and scanning, *407O*
  summarizing information graphically, *427*
See also Graphic information, interpreting.

Rereading
cooperatively, *371, 397, 417*
for comprehension, *401, 421, 358A, 358B*
independently, *371, 397, 417*
orally, *365, 395, 407, 413, 443*
to support answer, *407, 424*
with feeling and expression, *365, 395, 407,*
  413, 443

Research activities, *354J, 358A, 358B, 382,*
383, 387A–387C, 387Q, 387R, 407, 407BB, 429I,
429J, 447H

Responding to literature, options for
discussion, *359B, 376, 383O, 383P, 383Q, 383R,*
  402, 407O, 407P, 407Q, 407R, 422, 424,
  427O, 427P, 427Q, 427R, 446, 447, 447O,
  447P, 447Q, 447R, R3, R5, R7
Internet, *379, 403, 425, 447*
literature discussion, *371, 377, 397, 401, 417,*
  423, R3, R5, R7
personal response, *379, 403, 425, 447*
writing, *378, 402, 424, 446*

Reteaching, R8, R10, R12, R14, R16, R18,
R20–R25

Retelling
oral history, *447N*
story, *435, 445*

Revising. *See* Reading-Writing Workshop, steps
of Writing skills revising.

Science activities. *See* Links, content area.

Selections in Anthology
fiction
  The Lord of the Nile, by Jacqueline Morley,
    illustrated by Michael Jaroszko, *M10–M14*
myth
  "Arachne the Spinner," by Geraldine
    McCaughrean, *432–436*
  "Guitar Solo," *437–440*
  "How Music Was Fetched out of Heaven,"
    441–445
nonfiction
  Great Pyramid, The, by Elizabeth Mann, illus-
    trated by Laura Lo Turco, *M17–M22*

Great Wall, The, by Elizabeth Mann, illustrat-
  ed by Alan Witschonke, *390–401*
Lost Temple of the Aztecs, by Shelley Tanaka,
  illustrated by Greg Ruhl, *362–377*
Royal Kingdoms of Ghana, Mali, and
  Songhay, The, by Fredrick and Patricia
  McKissack, illustrated by Rob Wood,
  410–425
social studies article
  "Daily Life in Ancient Greece" by Robert
    Nicholson, *426–427*
  "Raising Royal Treasures" from *Time for Kids*
    magazine, *380–383*
technology article
  "Building Ancient Rome" by Dr. Sarah
    McNeill, *404–407*
See also Leveled Readers; Leveled Theme
  Paperbacks; Teacher Read Alouds.

Self-assessment
reading, *379, 403, 425*
writing project, *387G*

Self-correcting reading strategy. *See*
Strategies, reading, monitor/clarify.

Semantic cues. *See* Decoding skills, context
clues; Vocabulary skills.

Sequence of events. *See* Comprehension skills.

Shared learning. *See* Cooperative learning
activities.

Skills links
adjust your rate of reading, how to, **380**
diagram, how to read, **426**
timeline, how to read a, **404**

Skimming and scanning, *407N, 407O, 407BB.*
See also Adjusting reading rate.

Social studies activities. *See* Cross-curricular
activities.

Sound-spelling patterns. *See* Phonics;
Spelling.

Sounding out words. *See* Decoding: blending.

Speaking
creative activities, *383N, 447N*
describing, *359A, 359B, 397, 426*
discussion, *354I, 359B, 360A, 376, 377, 382,*
  397, 400, 401, 407O, 417, 423
dramatics. *See* Creative dramatics.
explanation, *417*
express ideas, *402*
guidelines
  for giving a speech, *383N*
  for persuading, *383N*
  for speaking clearly, *383N*
literature discussion. *See* Responding to
  Literature, options for, literature discussion.
oral presentation, *M7*

oral reports, *429I*
paraphrase ideas, *405*
personal opinions, *378, 402, 424*
purpose for
  analyzing literature. *See* Literature, analyzin
  contributing information, *359B, 360A, 376,*
    377, 382, 397, 400, 401, 407O, 407Z, 40
    417, 423, 429I, 383N
  persuading, *383N*
  to use new vocabulary or language, *360A,*
    388, 408
read own writing aloud, *383K, 383L, 387G,*
  407L, 427L, M6, 447L
retelling. *See* Retelling.
role play. *See* Creative dramatics.
sharing, *377, 383D, 388, 397, 401, 403, 417,*
  423, 425, 429I, 429J
summary. *See* Summarizing, oral summaries.
writing conferences. *See* Reading-Writing
  Workshop, conferencing.
See also Creative dramatics; Reading modes;
  Rereading.

Speech, parts of
adjectives
  articles, **383I**, *383M,* **M40, R20**
  comparing with, **407I–407J,** *407M, 442,*
    M40, R22
  definition of, **383I**, *383M, M40, R20*
  demonstrative, **383I**, *383M, M40, R20*
  forms of *good* and *bad,* **447J, M41, R23**
  predicate, **447I–447J,** *M41, R24*
  proper, **383J**, *383M, M40, R21*
  types, identifying, *383M*
adverbs
  comparing with adverbs, **427J**, *M41, R24–*
  definition of, **427I, 447I–447J,** *M41,*
    R24–R25
  that modify verbs and adjectives, **447I,** *M*
    R24
See also Grammar and usage.

Spelling
assessment, *383E, 383F, 407E, 407F, 427E,*
  427F, 447E, 447F
consonant changes, **447E–447F**
frequently misspelled words, **387F**
games, *383F, 407F, 407N, 427F, 447F, 447N*
integrating grammar and spelling, *383I–383J,*
  407I–407J, 427I–427J, 447I–447J
prefixes *un-, re-, de-, in-,* **447E**
proofreading, *383F, 387E, 407F, 427F, 447F*
/sh/ sound spelled *sh, ti, ci, ss,* **383E–383F,**
  M38
suffixes
  -ion or *-ation,* **407E–407F, 447E, M38**
syllables
  unstressed, **427E–427F,** *M39*
See also Decoding skills.

Word analysis. *See* Structural analysis; Vocabulary, building.

Word roots. *See* Structural analysis.

Writer's craft
analogies, **443**
comparison, *396*
descriptive language, *443*
discussion shift, *464*
figurative language, *387L, 396, 443*
imagery, *442*
sentence fragments, *433*
similes, **443**

Writer's log. *See* Journal.

Writing activities and types
advertising poster, *424*
cause and effect statement, *399*
commercial, *M7*
comparison and contrast paragraph,
  427K–427L
creative. *See* Writing modes.
descriptions, *358A, 402, M6, 429J, 432*
evaluation, *363*
explanation, **383K–383L**
help-wanted ad, *354J, 447E*
independent. *See* Independent writing.
job description for archaeologist, *358B*
journal entry from ancient world, *354I*
magic words, *429J*
myth, *429I, 429J, 446,* **447K–447L**
paragraph of information, **407K–407L,**
  407M–407N

predictions, *363, 371*
research report, **383S–387H**
schedule, *M7*
script, *M7*
rhyming verses, *387F*
story, *387R, 407BB*
summaries. *See* Summarizing.
supply list for archaeologist, *354J*
See also Reading-Writing Workshop, Writer's
  craft.

Writing conferences. *See* Reading-Writing
Workshop.

Writing modes
classificatory, **427K–427L**
creative, *387F, 387R, 407BB,* **447K–447L**
descriptive, *402, 432*
evaluative, *363*
expressive, *387F. See also* Journal.
informative, **384–387G, 407K–407L**
persuasive, *424*

Writing skills
drafting skills
  clarifying details, using, *383K, 427K*
  examples, steps, parts, including, *383K, 427K*
  introductions and conclusions, writing, *384*
  outline, using, *384,* **387D**
  topic sentence and supporting sentences,
    383K
  topic, stating a clear, *427K*
  visuals and graphics, including, *384, 387B*
formats. *See* Writing, activities.
prewriting skills
  audience and purpose, *383K, 387A, 387B*
  brainstorm ideas, *387A, 427K, 447K*

choosing a topic, *384,* **387A,** *407M*
Internet, searching for ideas, *387A*
locating and evaluating information, **387B**
organizing and planning, *383K, 387,* **387B,**
  407K, 427K, 447K
proofreading skills
  checking for errors, *383K, 407J, 427L, 447K*
  correct forms of adjectives, using the, **407L**
publishing skills
  Author's Chair, *383L, 407L, 427L, 447L*
  class book, *387G, 447L*
  classroom reading center, *354I*
  e-mailing to others, *387A*
  multimedia presentation, *387G*
  reading to the class, *383K, 387G*
  oral reports, *383K, 387G*
  school newspaper, *387G*
  website, *387A, 387G*
revising skills
  adjective or adverb?, **427I–427J**
  adjectives, using, *384,* **387E,** *407L*
  combining sentences with adjectives, **427L**
  dialogue, adding, **447L**
  elaborating with adjectives, **407L**
  eliminating unnecessary words, **383K**
See also Reading-Writing Workshop; Writer's
  craft.

Writing traits
conventions, *383T, 387E, 387H*
ideas, *383K, 387H*
organization, *376, 383T, 387H, 421*
presentation, *387G, 387H*
sentence fluency, *387H, 427K*
voice, *387H, 447K*
choice, *387H, 407K*